WAR COMES TO GARMSER

War Comes to Garmser

Thirty Years of Conflict on the Afghan Frontier

CARTER MALKASIAN

OXFORD
UNIVERSITY PRESS

Oxford University Press

Oxford University Press is a department of the University of Oxford. It furthers the University's
objective of excellence in research, scholarship, and education by publishing worldwide.

Oxford   New York
Auckland   Cape Town   Dar es Salaam   Hong Kong   Karachi
Kuala Lumpur   Madrid   Melbourne   Mexico City   Nairobi
New Delhi   Shanghai   Taipei   Toronto

With offices in
Argentina   Austria   Brazil   Chile   Czech Republic   France   Greece
Guatemala   Hungary   Italy   Japan   Poland   Portugal   Singapore
South Korea   Switzerland   Thailand   Turkey   Ukraine   Vietnam

Oxford is a registered trade mark of Oxford University Press in the UK and certain other countries.

Published in the United States of America by
Oxford University Press
198 Madison Avenue, New York, NY 10016

Published in the United Kingdom in 2013 by C. Hurst & Co. (Publishers) Ltd.

Library of Congress Cataloging-in-Publication Data

Malkasian, Carter, 1975–
War comes to Garmser : thirty years of conflict on the Afghan frontier / Carter Malkasian.
pages cm
Includes bibliographical references and index.
ISBN 978-0-19-997375-0 (alk. paper).
1. Malkasian, Carter, 1975– 2. Helmand (Afghanistan)—History, Military. 3. Afghan War,
2001—Campaigns—Afghanistan—Helmand. 4. Afghan War, 2001—Personal narratives,
American. 5. Postwar reconstruction—Afghanistan—Helmand. 6. Helmand (Afghanistan)—
Politics and government. 7. Helmand (Afghanistan)—Ethnic relations. 8. Taliban—History.
9. Afghanistan—History—Soviet occupation, 1979–1989. 10. Helmand River Valley
(Afghanistan)—Social life and customs. I. Title.

DS371.412.M333 2013
958.104′71092—dc23
[B]
2012045788

9   8   7   6   5   4   3   2   1

Printed in the United States of America on acid-free paper

CONTENTS

LIST OF MAPS

FOREWORD

In 1972, Jeffrey Race published *War Comes to Long An*, a first-person analysis of the war in Vietnam. It was a stunningly original work on war, observed from the inside by an American who was deeply embedded in the language, culture, and politics of the province. Race was a former Army officer who lived in Long An for four years conducting research that became his doctoral dissertation. The book he published is cited as a classic in the 2006 US Army/Marine Corps *Counterinsurgency Field Manual*; for forty years it has had no equal in the depth of understanding it provided of an internal struggle for the soul of a very small place.

Carter Malkasian has followed in his footsteps. Malkasian came to Afghanistan's Garmser District in 2009 as a political officer for the U.S. State Department. Like Race, Malkasian had previous experience of war; his doctoral dissertation on Korea and Vietnam was closely followed by years of service as a counterinsurgency adviser to the Marine Corps in Iraq and Afghanistan. He spent nearly two years in Garmser during the "surge" of US civilians to Afghanistan, teaching himself Pashto and getting to know local leaders from the provincial level down to village elders. But wars have at least two sides, and like Race, Malkasian also became well acquainted with leaders of the insurgency that threatened his province, enabling an intimate understanding of the dynamics of the local conflict.

The most important difference between the two books is that Race sought to understand the war in Long An as an academic exercise, albeit one in which he was immersed. In Garmser, Malkasian's search for knowledge was of immediate practical importance as he worked to cobble together political progress out of the military sacrifices of the US Marines who reinforced and ultimately replaced British troops in Helmand Province. Malkasian was an independent variable in the social science experiment that tripled US effort in Afghanistan in 2009.

It is fitting that he ended up in Garmser. The name means "hot place" in Persian; its location some sixty miles from the Pakistani border and proximity to the birthplace of the Taliban made it a very hot place indeed for the Marines who fought there during Malkasian's tenure. The district has a long, splintered history as the shatter zone of empires, and it has known constant conflict and change for the past seven decades, beginning with the American-led Helmand and Arghendab River Valley Project in the 1950s and the resulting population influx. Local power structures were turned upside down by the Soviet invasion in 1979 and the decade-long effort to repel the invaders followed by a bitter civil war, and then came a semblance of brutal order as the Taliban ascended to power in the late 1990s.

The Taliban's decision to provide shelter to al-Qaeda ensured that the regime would fall after the attacks of 11 September. But the Taliban found refuge in Pakistan and slowly regrouped as America prematurely turned its attention to Iraq. That Mesopotamian war consumed all of the oxygen even as the Taliban re-infiltrated their homeland; unable to focus on two wars at once, America barely noticed until it was almost too late.

Senator Obama campaigned on Afghanistan as "the good war"; President Obama quickly doubled down on the effort there during his first year in office. By the time US Marines started to arrive in numbers, the Taliban had regained control of Garmser and much else, and the Marines had to fight hard for every canal, field, and home they tore away from the insurgents.

Malkasian tells a story that is well known to students of counterinsurgency: increasing numbers of troops spread out like oil spots to protect the local population, gradually transferring responsibility to locally raised and trained forces who hold terrain that foreign forces have cleared of insurgents. Only when that security is in place can a government be built that enables economic progress and builds defenses against the return of the cancer of insurgency.

Along the way, brave local leaders as well as innocent civilians inevitably find themselves the targets of insurgent violence. There are reverses and riots, murders and misunderstandings. But the progress is undeniable and slowly builds upward, even as the American commitment to Afghanistan begins to wane.

Malkasian left Garmser in the summer of 2011 after nearly two years on the ground, with the outcome of the larger war very much in doubt. Who rules Garmser in the years to come will depend on decisions made in Washington and Islamabad as well as in Kabul. War on rebellion is always messy and slow, but Malkasian's experience demonstrates that with patience, an understanding of history and local-level politics, and courage, it can succeed. Whether the tenuous peace and prosperity of Garmser are worth the price is not a question that this book, good as it is, can answer.

What it can do is provide a ground-level feel for the longest of all of America's wars. It is certain to be called a classic of the military art. It is also, undeniably, a work suffused with love for a people who have fought for so long and suffered so much. They are fortunate to have had the chance to work with him, and we are immensely fortunate to have this book.

John Nagl is a retired Army officer who now teaches at the U.S. Naval Academy. Like Carter Malkasian, he studied the history of war at Oxford University under the supervision of Professor Robert O'Neill.

ACKNOWLEDGMENTS

Many people helped me on this book. First and foremost, I am indebted to Robert Murray and CNA, the think-tank for the US Navy and Marine Corps (also known as the Center for Naval Analyses). After seven years there, I took a leave of absence in 2009 to go with the Department of State to Garmser district, Helmand province, Afghanistan. When I returned in the summer of 2011, CNA gave me a place and the time to write. I am grateful for their patience and generosity. There is no better place to learn and make a difference.

For the writing of the book, Eliot Cohen, David Kilcullen, and John Nagl all lent me their advice. Their words emboldened me to follow in the footsteps of Jeffrey Race's *War Comes to Long An*, a book I have long admired. John Nagl deserves to be known not only for his counterinsurgency work but also for the countless hours he spends mentoring young officers, students, professors, and diplomats. I also thank Bing West, Thomas Barfield, David Edwards, Robert Powell, Daniel Marston, Hew Strachan, Greg Jaffe, and Tami and Stephen Biddle for helpful suggestions along the way. J Kael Weston and Rajiv Chandrasekaran, the author of the hugely meaningful *Little America*, deserve special thanks, both for hours of debate on Afghanistan and for supporting my efforts.

Several colleagues from CNA were invaluable: Mike Markowitz drew a number of the maps contained, Jerry Meyerle and Catherine Norman gave solid criticism, and Patricio-Asfura Heim provided all the best photos, including the one on the cover.

Robert O'Neill, my doctoral supervisor, professor of All Souls College, Oxford, and veteran of Vietnam, made painstaking comments on the manuscript—the third that he has seen me through. He forced his students to learn about these kinds of wars during more peaceful times when their study was too often deemed unnecessary. I would have lacked the wisdom to study them on my own. Whatever successes his students have had over this past decade of small wars begin with his teachings.

Hurst and Oxford University Press also have my gratitude. Michael Dwyer at Hurst has been a tireless and true guide. David McBride at Oxford University Press drove me to think harder and press the analysis. The book is better for it. I thank Sebastian Ballard for his map-work and for enduring my countless tiny tactical changes.

Looking farther afield, I benefited tremendously from my civilian colleagues in Afghanistan. The Lashkar Gah PRT was the best and most professional in Afghanistan. It is a badge of honor to have been part of it and to have worked with US diplomats such as Marlin Hardinger and Joe Burke. In Garmser itself, Peter Chilvers, British stability advisor, was an outstanding role model. We all learned from him. Similarly, Garmser will not soon forget Gail Long, our iron-willed USAID development officer, respected by Marine and tribal warlord alike. And without Rafiullah Safi, my Afghan adviser, my Pashto never would have matured. When we are gone, he will still be in Afghanistan, trying to do what is best for his people.

Then there are the Marines. Major General Larry Nicholson, Colonel Dave Furness, and Colonel Randy Newman have helped me for almost a decade now. I owe equally as much to four battalion commanders in Garmser: Christian Cabaniss, John McDonough, Ben Watson, and Matt Reid. But the greatest debt of all is to the sergeants, lance corporals, and privates who watched my back in patrol after patrol in the fields, villages and bazaars of Garmser.

Finally, after a decade of long small wars in far-off places, I thank my wife, Aya.

PREFACE

SMALL PLACES

'As we drew level, a drum suddenly began to beat…we looked at one another and our lips formed the same words, "The *Chiga Dol*!"—the call to arms…we saw a khaki-clad figure in a topi running with the mob and recognized it as the political officer.

His achievement was remarkable. He had persuaded the Fakir Kit *chiga*, the village pursuit party, or at any rate some of it, to turn out to help us. What eloquence, what promises, what threats he had used, I do not know, but there they were, looking none too friendly…The political officer shepherded them into a rough line along a small *nullah* and took his stand behind them, ready to nip in the bud any idea of premature retirement.'

William Slim, *Unofficial History*[1]

Garmser is a small place: one district within one of Afghanistan's thirty-four provinces. Mostly desert, its roughly 150,000 people inhabit a fertile strip along the Helmand River no more than 10 kilometers wide and 70 kilometers long. Known as the 'Gateway to Helmand,' Garmser lies 100 kilometers from Pakistan, a source of trade, smuggling, and violence. The people are almost all Pashtun, known as the most warlike and tribal of the Afghans. Islam is followed piously. Five prayers per day and taking the fast are real obligations. For over thirty years, Garmser has been the subject of wars and short-lived regimes, part of larger conflicts that have engulfed Afghanistan as a whole: first the jihad and the ensuing civil war, then the Taliban, next the weak Karzai government, again the Taliban, and finally the British and American intervention. From 2006 to 2010, the district was almost entirely under Taliban control: the scene of some of the worst fighting in Afghanistan, more intense and divisive than anything before, including the jihad. Garmser is a story about Afghanistan, a story of how a country fell apart so badly that it took massive British and American intervention to put things back together again—and even then the outcome was often in doubt.

I spent nearly two years in Garmser, from 2009 to 2011, as the political officer for the US Department of State. I have found no better job. Bucketing about in Ford Ranger pickups with police, tribal militiamen, and turbaned officials was an education. My job was to mobilize the people to stand up against the Taliban. I mentored the district governor, negotiated with tribal elders, learned about Islam from mullahs, and helped build a police force. Slowly my Pashto improved enough for the Afghans to stop laughing at me. Four other highly professional civilians were on our team. We worked alongside a thousand-strong US Marine battalion; every six months a new one rolled in, to be replaced by an equally impressive one six months later.

But this book is not about my experiences. I have settled for a longer view: a history of war in Garmser from 1979 to 2012. I had the opportunity to talk with hundreds of Afghans, including government officials, tribal leaders, religious leaders, and over forty Taliban. I gathered enough primary source material to tell the Afghan side of more than thirty years of war and short-lived regimes. This book looks at why conflict lasted for such a long period, particularly focusing on how the Taliban movement formed in Garmser; how, after being routed in 2001, they returned stronger than ever in 2006; and how Afghans, British, and Americans fought against them between 2006 and 2012. In other words, why did things go so wrong for so long, and did they ever go right?

Garmser is admittedly a rather small subject for a history book. It can offer only a partial view of the whole Afghanistan experience. Yet America's war in Afghanistan will never be understood without study of the small places—the provinces, districts, and villages. Afghanistan was a rural insurgency. The war was fought away from the cities, in hundreds of villages, valleys, and plots of farmland. The area was vast and every locale unique. Those small places were the front line. Just as we study the Western Front to understand the First World War and Normandy and the Eastern Front to understand the Second, we must study the provinces and districts—the Taliban's front line—to understand the war in Afghanistan. Only there can we truly get at the questions that lay at its heart: why people supported the Taliban, why the government was unable to defeat them on its own, whether American and Allied intervention had any success. And these questions cannot be understood without a long view. The study must span decades; for conflict spanned decades. Memoirs of one- or two-year deployments are mere snapshots.

This book owes a great deal to Jeffrey Race's *War Comes to Long An*, published in 1972, a history and analysis of one province in South Vietnam over two decades.[2] Race lived in South Vietnam for four years. Fluent in Vietnamese, he interviewed hundreds of villagers, government officials, and insurgents. The book he produced offered ground truth for the historical debates that have since surrounded Vietnam. I hope this book can do the same. Garmser, of course, is only one part of Afghanistan. Understanding Garmser alone will not explain the war as a whole. Other studies are needed for that. Garmser is just a start.

America and Afghanistan

It is said that American foreign policy has a liberal and idealistic bent. In Henry Kissinger's words: 'No other society has asserted that the principles of ethical conduct apply to international conduct in the same way that they do to the individual…no country has so tormented itself over the gap between its moral values, which are by definition absolute, and the imperfection inherent in the concrete situations to which they must be applied.'[3] Historians have long detailed the tension in American foreign policy between intervening in far-off conflicts in order to make the world better and staying out in order to avoid the moral messiness that wars—small ones as much as worldwide ones—inevitably entail.[4] Hence the public debate that accompanied interventions in Iraq, Bosnia, Somalia, and, of course, Vietnam. Interventions in the civil wars of developing countries have seemed especially questionable because the threat to the United States is often so unclear, while the wars themselves tend to be prolonged and dirty. Vietnam, in particular, deepened America's inherent skepticism toward the wisdom and morality of small wars in developing countries. This tension, and the idealism surrounding it, was revisited in Afghanistan.

Afghanistan started out as the good war, the war fought for the right reasons, the war blessed with stunning initial successes, the war where America had a chance to right the wrongs of the brutal and oppressive Taliban regime. In the eyes of the American people, al-Qaeda's 11 September 2001 attack on the United States endowed intervention with both strategic necessity and moral legitimacy. Furthermore, the attack suggested that the United States should not stay out of broken countries such as Afghanistan. Problems festered in such places that could come to haunt the United States. If Vietnam had served as a warning to stay out of broken countries, 11 September did the opposite. In Afghanistan, the United States set out to build a good, well-governed, just, and orderly state. The consensus was that doing so would be the best way to prevent al-Qaeda or other terrorists from ever returning. Hopes were high. It was decided that Afghanistan would be a centralized democracy, with elections, a small professional army, and a Western legal system. Militias of various warlords were disarmed. Elections for president and then parliament were held by 2005.

When violence re-appeared in 2005 and 2006, the dominant thought—with more than a little justification—was that not enough had been done to build a good, progressive state. Sarah Chayes, author of the widely-read *The Punishment of Virtue*, wrote:

'The answer is not to lower the bar but to raise it…Additional troops are desperately needed, and they should be deployed to protect the population… Development assistance, well targeted and monitored, is also crucial. But only with a concurrent full-court press on governance can the most limited US goals in the region be accomplished.'[5]

The new counterinsurgency manual, which guided America's strategy in Afghanistan after 2008, further enshrined these ideals: 'The primary objective of any COIN [counterinsurgency] operation is to foster development of effective governance by a legitimate government.'[6] Effective governance was defined as a government in which leaders are supported by the majority of the population, corruption is low, rule of law has been established, and economic and social development is progressing. Sarah Sewall, director of the Carr Center for Human Rights, wrote in the preface that 'A touch of idealism… materialized in the manual.'[7]

When, after ten years of fighting, these goals remained out of reach, America's enthusiasm for its Afghan mission faded. Despair set in. The tension between ideals and the imperfection of reality was clear. Afghanistan had become prolonged and morally messy, exactly the kind of conflict Americans preferred to avoid. Good governance did not materialize as expected. Violence persisted. The whole intervention looked like a great misadventure. By mid 2011, 100,000 American and nearly 10,000 British troops were in the country. Since the beginning of the intervention, almost 17,000 had been killed or wounded (14,700 American, 2,125 British).[8] Over $500 billion had been spent and the United States was now facing its worst recession since the Great Depression. Polls found that as many as 70 percent of Americans wanted to get out.[9] *Time* dubbed Afghanistan 'The Unwinnable War,' writing, 'America's best strategists and military minds and nation builders and engineers were set to work on one of the largest country-building efforts since the Marshall Plan. And it simply hasn't worked.'[10] America's own troops often seemed unable to get along with the Afghans, let alone understand them. When they misbehaved or, in a few cases, purposefully hurt Afghan civilians, it was said that the war was corrupting them, making them immoral. Between rebellious tribal regions, a corrupt government, stories of greedy lazy Afghans, and a hostile Pakistan, Afghanistan appeared terminally ungovernable. Ten years of fighting and trying begged whether the United States should have just stayed out in the first place; whether there was anything that could have been done to succeed.

Afghanistan now stands in the ranks of Vietnam, Somalia, Gallipoli, and the First World War overall as a futile military endeavor, or at least a remarkably costly and unprofitable one; an experience that demonstrated the limits of American power and should have been avoided. That judgment is unlikely to change even if the Taliban are completely defeated over the next two years. The war probably never will be considered a success. It has gone on so long that people will continue to ask if a better outcome was ever possible. Reminiscent of Vietnam, scholars, generals, journalists, and politicians will be debating Afghanistan for years to come.

Can Afghanistan be governed?

Afghanistan has long been known as an unruly place. The two British invasions of the nineteenth century followed by the more recent Russian defeat earned Afghanistan the much over-used honorific 'graveyard of empires,' a warning to would-be interventionists. Professor David

Edwards, the well-known anthropologist of Afghanistan, noted in the 1990s how 'journalists and scholars of various orientations and persuasions began to wonder aloud if, after all, the British hadn't gotten it right in the first place. Afghanistan was once and would remain a singularly wild and anarchic place that could only be managed (if at all) by men of ruthless violence and ambition.'[11] The passage could just as easily describe opinion among American journalists, scholars, and policymakers at the end of 2010. That year, Professor Thomas Barfield wrote in his magisterial history of Afghanistan: 'The belief that Afghanistan and its people are inherently ungovernable has become an unfortunate conventional wisdom that drives policy decisions.'[12]

In academic terms, 'ungovernable' means that conflict in Afghanistan was over-determined: so many factors were pushing the country toward violence that any other outcome was impossible—no matter what the United States tried to do. Historically, Afghanistan had appeared ungovernable because of rebellious tribes, mountainous terrain, and a fierce hatred of foreign intervention. At the end of 2010, Afghanistan was considered ungovernable for these together with a new set of seemingly insurmountable challenges. The government was known as corrupt and fraudulent; publicly criticized by top American leaders; ranked by international organizations as the second most corrupt in the world.[13] The implication was that the Taliban could not be defeated unless the government was reformed, which appeared nearly impossible. One *Foreign Affairs* article read: 'The quality of governance emanating from Karzai's deeply corrupt government will not significantly improve, and without a comprehensive reform of the Afghan government, US success is virtually impossible.'[14] On top of that was Pakistan. The Pakistani government's refusal to clear out Taliban safe havens from their country seemed to promise that the war would go on indefinitely. Scholars and intelligence analysts asserted that peace in Afghanistan would be difficult, if not impossible, as long as those safe havens existed.[15] Finally, the Afghan people themselves were deemed insufferable. A Gallup poll in 2011 found that merely 14 percent of Americans had a favorable opinion of Afghanistan as a country. Only Iran and North Korea were more disliked.[16] Many Americans believed that the Afghans were fickle and unwilling to stand up for their country. Bing West, a respected combat writer, reported numerous stories in which: 'Pashtun elders accepted government services like schools and roads, but didn't urge their young men to join the government's army. The tribes survived by behaving, as Petraeus put it, as "professional chameleons."[17]

The point of this study of one district is to help answer whether the United States and its Allies were bound to be defeated in Afghanistan. This is the grand strategic question that historians will ask as they look back on Afghanistan and policy-makers will ask as they look to future interventions. Should the United States have heeded the warnings of history and stayed out? Or could the United States and its Allies have made a long-lasting difference in spite of all the challenges, without all the years of stalemate and loss? However popular it is to blame the Karzai government, Pakistan, and the Afghan people themselves for America's problems, there is another explanation: America's own decisions may have been at fault. In that case, the war effort was not doomed. A better strategy would have led to a better outcome.[18] This possibility should be just as important for American (and British and other Allied) governments as the possibility that Afghanistan is ungovernable. Major strategic defeats might have been prevented, the deployment of tens of thousands of Western troops might have been avoided, billions of dollars during a global recession might have been saved, and hundreds if not thousands of lives might have been spared. Even late in the war, successes might have been better preserved so that the sacrifices of the previous decade would not pass in vain. The gravity of such alternative outcomes makes it unwise simply to dismiss Afghanistan as ungovernable and success as impossible.

In answering whether the United States and its Allies could have succeeded in Afghanistan, I look broadly upon why conflict persisted in Garmser after 1979, while focusing on why the Taliban lasted so long after 1994 and to what extent they were ever defeated. Garmser is a good vantage point. The Taliban movement in southern Afghanistan shaped the course of the war and America's involvement in it. The United States sent 100,000 troops to Afghanistan (the Afghan 'surge') because of events that involved Garmser. Between 2005 and 2008, the Taliban recaptured most of southern Afghanistan, including most of Kandahar and Helmand, the Pashtun heartland. It was perhaps the worst defeat that the United States and Great Britain faced in over a decade of war in Iraq and Afghanistan. The Afghan government had clearly lost control. Kandahar, the second largest city in the country, the former Taliban capital, and the city of the Pashtuns, was under attack.

Its fall would threaten Kabul itself. In the opinion of many American policy-makers, Afghanistan was on the brink of collapse and al-Qaeda might soon return to their old safe havens. More than anything else, the situation in the south led to the 'surge' of American reinforcements to Afghanistan in 2009. The south then became the main battleground in the war, where success was ultimately defined and debated.

Garmser was an integral part of all this: the rise of the Taliban, their return from 2005 to 2008, and finally the surge of American reinforcements from 2009 to 2011. A history of Garmser gets at why the Taliban had support in Afghanistan, how the strategic defeat in the south came about, and whether the American and British commitment failed or succeeded where it was meant to have the most effect. The answers inform how America should view its time in Afghanistan—a futile endeavor doomed to failure, or a lost chance to have made a difference.

It must be noted at the outset that the United States itself actually caused much of the conflict in Garmser. Between 1995 and 2001, the Taliban governed Garmser, as well as the rest of southern Afghanistan, fairly effectively. If the United States had not intervened in Afghanistan in 2001 and the Taliban had remained in power, it is highly unlikely that war would have resumed at all in Garmser. Although provocative, and discussed at greater length in the chapter on the first Taliban regime, this point is rather unhelpful for understanding why violence lasted so long after intervention when the United States sought to ensure that a non-Taliban government could survive. These are the matters of greater concern to the United States, Great Britain, and other Allies who fought in Afghanistan. How the Taliban returned after 2001, formed a second regime, and dragged the international community and Afghanistan into a renewed, devastating bout of warfare—not just in Garmser but throughout the country—must be one of the most important questions of the war.

This book is divided into twelve chapters. The first chapter introduces Garmser, its peoples, and its history before the jihad, particularly the digging of the massive US-funded canal system from the mid-1950s to the early 1970s, which set the stage for future civil conflict. The second and third chapters go through the jihad and the ensuing tribal civil war. The fourth covers the rise of the Taliban in 1994 and their first regime. The actions the Taliban took from 1994 to 2001 are critical for understanding their resilience later on. The fifth chapter is the all-important discussion of how the Karzai government fell apart in Garmser and how the Taliban came back in 2006. The sixth details the hard years of fighting between the British and the second Taliban regime, culminating in the intervention of the US Marines in 2008. The seventh, eighth, ninth, and tenth chapters serve as one section on the course and outcome of the surge of US forces into Garmser: how the Marines cleared and held Garmser, how the tribes re-united behind the government, and how the Taliban tried to counter-attack. The eleventh chapter looks at Garmser as US forces began to draw down and the government took over, considering to what extent conflict had ended. The last chapter is the conclusion.

Most of the research comes from talks with Afghans who witnessed first-hand the events described. Some also comes from primary written sources, histories of Afghanistan, and my own observations. The accuracy of what Afghans told me can be questioned. All were not objective, and exaggerating a story—or leaving out a few bits—is often expected in the telling. Stories are deeply connected to the honor of the teller. I tried to correct for this by talking to as many Afghans as possible, cross-checking information, and footnoting. In a few cases, I did not reveal sources because they did not want to be known. Throughout, I purposefully stuck with a narrative rather than openly analyzing the information of each source and the narrator's motivations and their implications. I realize this lowers the academic quality of the book but I could not avoid it. I believe the flow of a narrative is the best way to convey what happened. Please understand that in spite of my best efforts a little may be exaggerated and a little may be missing.

As much as possible, this book tries to present the war that the Afghans fought, rather than the war that the Americans and the British fought. Many American and British names, battles, and operations are dealt with cursorily in order to free up space for the Afghans. That is not to disregard the role that Americans and British played. Whatever the ultimate fate of Garmser, US Marines and British soldiers were necessary for any successes that occurred between 2006 and 2012. But their story has been documented elsewhere. This story is about the Afghans. The roots of conflict and much of its course lie in their history as much as ours. I apologize in advance for the cacophony of unpronounceable Pashto words and Afghan names. I have tried to simplify things as much as possible, excluding various Afghans and various places entirely. Those who were there may wonder what happened to the amenable Mohammed Zahir of Lakari or the utterly frustrating Mohammed Anwar Khan of Loya Darveshan; or what I did with many of the villages that Marines and British soldiers patrolled day in and day out; why I annexed the square-blocked community of Durzai to the vast expanse of Safar and ceded Jugroom, Dezakriya, Shamalan, Kopak, and Kharako to Hazar Joft. I wanted to spare the reader all those names. I have also mercilessly simplified Garmser's labyrinthine feuds; each a book unto itself. Any Marine who has talked with the elders of Burghagai may take me to task over that. I hope the result is a book that can be better understood. For any whom I have offended, American, British, or Afghan, I am sorry.

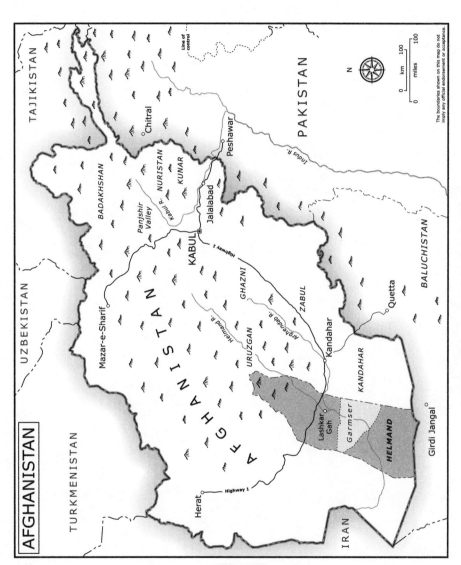

Map 3: Afghanistan (Sebastian Ballard).

1

GRAND PLANS

Political Officer: 'You cannot use violence to solve your problems. You must take the problems to the government.'

Mahboob Khan: 'I accept your speech. We will take the dispute to the government.'

Political Officer: 'And you will accept their decision?'

Mahboob Khan: 'Yes, if the decision is right, we will accept it. If it is not, we will not.'

Political Officer: 'We cannot permit any violence.'

Mahboob Khan: 'Violence cannot be done by tribal leaders. It is not violence if we are doing what is right for the tribe.'[1]

In Persian, Garmser means hot place. The summers break 120 degrees Fahrenheit while the winters barely fall below zero, and then only for a few days. Yet temperature is not the defining feature of Garmser. The Helmand River and its irrigation system define Garmser. The district is huge: over 100 kilometers wide and over 100 kilometers long. Most is empty desert. The vast majority of the population (92,000 in 1978, 150,000 today) live in the 70 km long, 10 km wide irrigated strip along the eastern side of the river. Here the land is rich and green, a shallow fertile valley cut through the desert by the Helmand River. A mere handful of people—largely nomads—live outside it.

Historically, Garmser has been on the edge of empires, changing hands over and over again. The Arabs conquered it in the mid 600s; the

Ghaznavids in the 900s; the Mongols in the 1200s; the Tartars in the 1300s; the Moghuls in the 1500s.[2] The Ghaznavids are the best-remembered. The remains of the mud forts they built to guard their southern frontier stand a ruined watch over the landscape today. In the 1600s, Garmser was part of the Iranian Safavid Empire. According to locals, it was called 'Tor Agha' and was farmed by Iranians. The Pashtun founder of the Afghan state, Ahmed Shah Durrani, conquered the region in 1747 and pushed out the Iranians. He re-named it 'Garmser' and sent fellow Pashtuns to live on the naturally irrigated land near the river. The newcomers settled in tight villages of towered mud-walled compounds: miniature fortified cities surrounded by farmland and desert. In each, a maze of dirt paths cut around keep-like homes, simple somber mosques, and enclosed gardens. The main Pashtun communities, from north to south, were known as Hazar Joft, Darveshan, Laki, and Safar.

Two Pashtun tribes received the vast majority of the land in Garmser: the Noorzai and the Alizai. Both were part of the same grouping of tribes as Ahmed Shah—the Durrani confederation. It would rule

Image 1: A mud-walled compound in Darveshan. The view is to the east. The pine trees of the main canal are visible just below the horizon. (Photo by Patricio Asfura-Heim)

Afghanistan for over 200 years. The Noorzai were bigger than the Alizai, made up of several clans, representing about 60 percent of the population. The first Noorzai clan arrived in Darveshan in the mid-eighteenth century. Ahmed Shah wanted them to block Baluch expansion from the south. To this day, the Noorzai of Darveshan view themselves as the rightful rulers of Garmser. Shortly thereafter other smaller Noorzai clans settled in Safar and southern Hazar Joft. The last major Noorzai clan, the Omarzai, came to Hazar Joft between 1820 and 1830.[3]

The Alizai arrived in Garmser in the late eighteenth century and settled in Laki. A British expedition in 1872 described them as 'rich in corn and cattle.'[4] They were fewer than the Noorzai—making up about 30 percent of the population—but far more unified. They had to be to have their voice heard. The villagers fell in behind the tribal leaders, who were often known for their wisdom and benevolence—at least toward their own tribe. Alizai were easy to spot. They always wore a clean, flowing, lightly-colored collared shirt; young men clean-shaven with a pillbox-shaped prayer cap; older men neatly bearded with a turban. The well-groomed appearance, together with long, Roman-nosed faces, gave an aura of nobility. By comparison, the Noorzai were less uniform, turbaned or bearded but each wearing different colors, different shirt styles, and different turban patterns. Clothes spoke to the tribe. The Alizai viewed themselves as one tribe and one nation. Their first loyalty was to the tribe, not to the government, not to Garmser.

Besides the Alizai and Noorzai, a small community of Barakzai (Durrani Pashtuns) settled on the western side of the river in Bartaka. Additionally, groups of Baluch camped on the outskirts of the eastern desert in makeshift huts. Baluch were not Pashtuns. They came from south of Garmser or from Pakistan. Poor and landless, most were nomads, moving through the desert, coming to Garmser temporarily before heading off again. The Pashtuns looked down upon them.

In the nineteenth and early twentieth centuries, Garmser was known to be fertile and prosperous.[5] The 1872 British expedition noted: 'The valley everywhere bears the marks of former prosperity and population. Its soil is extremely fertile, and the command of water is unlimited.' People chiefly grew wheat, supplemented by grapes, pomegranates, and watermelons. Hardly anyone grew poppy. Of today's 70 km-long canal zone, perhaps half was irrigated, watered by simple lateral canals dug straight into the Helmand. The rest of the land was dry, parched, and

3

cheap—one sheep could fetch a jerib (the Afghan unit of land measurement, equal to half an acre and a fifth of a hectare).[6]

The Helmand and Arghendab River Valley Project changed all this. Beginning in 1946, during the time of King Zahir Shah, this massive modernization program dammed the Helmand River far to the north at Kajaki and dug new irrigation systems along both it and the Arghendab River in Kandahar. From 1946 until the project ended in the 1970s, $130 million was expended, $70 million contributed by the United States Agency for International Development (USAID).[7] The US government saw the program as a Cold War tool to contain Soviet influence by modernizing Afghanistan in a Western mode. Other large-scale infrastructure accompanied the dam and canals: roads, bridges, schools, and a brand new provincial capital built along rectangular Western lines at Lashkar Gah. Through the 1950s and 1960s Helmand prospered under the grand plan.[8]

The Garmser we know today is the result of that massive project. Construction of a new canal system in Garmser began in the mid-1950s and was completed in the early 1970s.[9] The main canal, which feeds the system with fresh water, begins at the intake at the northern tip of the district, and runs over 70 kilometers south to Benadar. It is about 5 meters deep and 10 meters across. Every kilometer or so a sluice gate controls water flow. On both banks run graveled roads, which together serve as the district's main thoroughfare. Smaller lateral canals divert fresh water to the fields. Deep drainage canals parallel the main canal 3–8 kilometers to the east and funnel salty water out of the fields back into the Helmand. Canal after canal crisscross each other. From the air, or on a map, the whole complex looks like a giant snake, with its head in the north and tail trailing off at Benadar in the south.

The canal system divides Garmser into eleven communities, each a collection of 10–30 villages. In the north, at the head of the snake, is Hazar Joft. One of Garmser's oldest communities, more people live in Hazar Joft than anywhere else in the district. The name means 'land enough to employ a "thousand yoke" of oxen or ploughs.'[10] The Helmand River Valley Project turned Hazar Joft into the capital of Garmser. In the late 1960s, USAID built a new district center there, with a bazaar, government building, and bridge over the river. The latter is the southernmost bridge over the Helmand in Afghanistan. Flanking Hazar Joft to the east is the community of Majitek, the dry edge of the fertile zone.

About 10 kilometers south of the district center, Hazar Joft ends and Darveshan begins, heralded by tall pine trees that USAID planted here along the main canal. Darveshan is the oldest community in Garmser, where the first Noorzai settled. It has been fertile for centuries. The old district center was in Amir Agha, a sprawling village on top of a low sandy plateau in northern Darveshan. Darveshan itself means 'close to Allah,' presumably because of the shrine at Amir Agha, the most sacred spot in the district. The shrine is the resting place of a pre-Islamic pilgrim from Israel. Pashtuns honor him because he believed in one God.[11] Darveshan is divided into two parts: Loya ('Big') Darveshan in the north and Kuchinay ('Small') Darveshan to the south.

Past Kuchinay Darveshan lie Koshtay, Bartaka, and Mian Poshtay— Garmser's middle communities. Koshtay is little more than a mass of small villages and mulberry trees. Bartaka is the lone community across the river, sitting under the gray bluffs of the western desert, connected by a ferry crossing to Koshtay. Both Koshtay and Bartaka revolve around Mian Poshtay: an idyllic expanse of green fields partitioned by tree-lined meandering waterways, overlooked by the sheer red cliffs of the eastern desert. At its center, a long eastern drainage canal intersects the main canal, forming a commercial crossroads where a small bazaar is located and people congregate.

South of Mian Poshtay, Garmser grows steadily drier. The trees thin, the skyline opens, the dust thickens; first in Lakari and then in long, narrow Laki, where palm trees start to dot the landscape. Laki is another of Garmser's oldest communities. It is the last place the soil is truly fertile. In southern Laki, 50 kilometers south of the intake with the Helmand River, the main canal breaks into three smaller canals that look like streams. Those small canals run into Safar, a large community, 15 kilometers in length, 5 kilometers in width. Safar is much drier than Laki or Lakari. In the east, salt rises to the tops of the fields. Trees are few. Wide distances separate villages. Three small hills, remnants of once great Ghaznavid forts built to guard against invaders from the west and south, watch over the dusty fields and desert beyond.[12] Safar is so distant from Hazar Joft that the people there often think of it as their own district. At its end, the last drainage canals enter the Helmand while leftover water from the three streams trickles into Benadar, Garmser's southernmost community. Endowed with the barest strip of irrigated land, Benadar is practically desert.

A golden era

The canal project made Helmand province, long agriculturally productive, the breadbasket of Afghanistan—at least temporarily. One of Afghanistan's largest provinces, Helmand had a population of about a million people in the 1970s (nearly 1.5 million live there today, the fourth most populous province, behind Kabul, Kandahar, and Herat). Politically, Helmand was a stronghold of the Durrani Pashtuns, who fell within the orbit of Kandahar, the great southern Pashtun capital. From the perspective of Kabul, Helmand was important for agriculture but second politically to Kandahar.

Helmand has thirteen districts but is easier understood by dividing it into north, center (which could also be called the east), west, and south (see map of Helmand province on inside front cover). Northern Helmand, particularly the districts of Musa Qala and Kajaki, is the homeland and seat of power of the Alizai, where most of their tribe resides. Central Helmand—Nawa and the rich farmland surrounding the cities of Lashkar Gah and Gereshk—is dominated by the Barakzai, who have tended to compete with the Alizai for power. The communities of western Helmand—Marjah and Nadi Ali—were created by the canal system; water was diverted into the desert and tens of thousands of immigrants were introduced to farm the land. Southern Helmand is Garmser and southward. Helmand has two cities: Gereshk (the old capital) and Lashkar Gah (the new one). The majority of the population lives in the rural districts.

The people of Garmser have fond memories of King Zahir Shah's long reign. The great canal project brought jobs, a new district center, a new bazaar, and the promise of thousands of hectares of irrigable land. American aid workers and Peace Corps volunteers came through Garmser, taught classes, supervised the infrastructure projects, and offered medical care. The government set up eleven schools and staffed them with educated teachers. Education was available up to the twelfth grade. An agricultural high school opened in the district center in 1962 where 200 young men and women at any one time could get a higher caliber of secondary education, one of two in all Afghanistan. Its campus was the size of eight football fields. In Hazar Joft and Lashkar Gah, new jobs were available for people to become shop-owners, teachers, and officials. For farmers, the government provided tractors and cotton seed. Farmers grew wheat in the winter and cotton in the summer. Cotton was lucrative. It was sold to the government, which processed it in plants around Lashkar Gah and then exported it. As wealth grew, tractors and cars joined camels and donkeys on the district's dirt roads. Net farm income per person in Garmser rose tenfold from $126 per year in 1963 to $1,280 in 1973, the highest of any of Helmand's rural districts.[13] And Garmser was peaceful. There was no fighting with Pakistan and very little between the tribes.

Zahir Shah's government in Garmser was a district governor, justice officials, and the police. The district governor had seniority and was responsible for coordinating government activities and keeping the tribes behind the government. Five officials helped him with administrative duties. He reported to the provincial governor in Lashkar Gah. The people did not get to choose their district governor, or their provincial governor for that matter. Afghanistan's political system did not work that way. Officials in Kabul appointed the district governor, usually someone from outside the district, a necessary precaution against tribal feuding. The people went to the district governor with problems and disputes that could not be resolved within their communities and to receive assistance from the government. Under his auspices, the tribal leaders met together in a council (called a shura or jirga) to address district-wide issues. Although it only performed an advisory role, the council was the closest thing in Garmser to a representative body. For justice, there were three judges, a court, a prosecutor, and a huqooq (an official who could mediate civil disputes). Only thirty-three police were needed for the whole district. They rarely carried weapons and could travel alone anywhere without being in danger.[14]

By Western standards, the government was weak. It did not have the guns or money to rule over the people and the tribes with absolute authority. Rather, it was the most powerful actor within a system of tribal and religious leaders who also wielded substantial power. Like the government, the tribal and religious leaders could resolve disputes, tax, and field armed men—powers that in other countries were the preserve of the government. On legal matters, for instance, tribal and religious leaders were allowed to make decisions for their communities, to include punishing criminals. Plaintiffs could choose whether they wanted to go to a tribal leader, religious leader, or the government. The tribal leader was often the first choice. The judges in the district center usually came into play when traditional forms of justice could not reach a decision accepted by all sides.

Tribes are not easy to understand. The word conjures Lawrence-like images of waves of Arabian horsemen, united behind a white-bearded patriarch. Pashtun tribes are known to be far more divided. They were not centralized blocks, let alone owners of many horses. Generally, every village had an elder who was accepted as its leader. Villages tended to be dominated by one tribe but contain laborers, shop-owners, and mullahs from a few others. An elder's standard duties were to resolve disputes within his village, win goods and services from the government, protect the community, and find as many jobs for his villagers as possible. His decisions were followed as long as he had the power to enforce them—whether through money, guns, or political connections. It was expected that those decisions would be made in consultation with a council of the other heads of household (another shura). Failure to do so denoted poor leadership. The method of elder selection varied.[15] The ruling family may have enjoyed enough power to enforce their choice; all the village families may have come together and chose the elder; or two or three of the most powerful men in the village may have done so. The elder may have been the son of the last elder; or he may have been the most qualified man for the job.

Particularly powerful village elders gained influence over their entire community—Kuchinay Darveshan, Laki, or Benadar, for example. Such leaders often were known by the title of 'khan' or 'qawmi misher' (tribal leader). I will refer to them as tribal leaders in order to distinguish these more powerful players from the average village elder. Noorzai and Alizai tribal leaders (khans), such as Said Omar of Hazar Joft or Roh Khan of Kuchinay Darveshan, owned great tracts of land and had large retinues of village elders who obeyed their command. Each tribal leader selected a 'malik' to represent him and take his issues to the district government, if he did not go himself.[16] Every tribe had several tribal leaders. Over time, different families may have held influence as power waxed and waned. No single tribal leader was appointed leader of the entire tribe, even if he had more power than the rest. Decisions for the tribe as a whole were expected to be made in a shura with all the tribal leaders, if not with all the village elders. The Alizai tribal leaders were particularly impressive in their ability to hold the tribe together. The Noorzai were less so, divided between powerful families in Hazar Joft, Kuchinay

Darveshan, Safar, and Benadar. At times they loosely coordinated to make a decision for the whole tribe, but as often as not acted independently. The power of a tribal leader tended to end within the tribe, if not within his cluster of villages. Few tribal leaders succeeded in having influence beyond their tribe, let alone reaching across the people of Garmser and uniting them behind him. Tribal divisions were too strong.

Deeply rooted in the tribal system was Pashtunwali, the code of the Pashtuns. Much has been written about Pashtunwali and its customs, sometimes more romantic than true. Pashtuns did not necessarily follow it as law. But it did guide many elders and tribal leaders. Honor mattered to them, defined in terms of martial prowess, land, protecting one's family, giving to the community, hospitality, and being subservient to no other individual. The last point helps explain why shuras (or jirgas) were so important for decision-making. They placed leaders on equal public footing, even if everyone knew who the real leaders were. Pashtunwali is probably best known for the custom that a Pashtun must exact vengeance ('badal') against his enemies. The emphasis on revenge and honor meant that slights and insults, not to mention actual violence, could easily lead to long-running feuds. Especially for young men, a feud was a way of proving oneself. The greater the enemy, the greater the honor. Pashtuns often felt honor-bound to continue a feud until they received a sign of apology or outsiders intervened to mediate. A Pashtun had to accept the apology of any enemy who came to his home. A Pashtun would only apologize in the gravest of circumstances, however, and usually in an indirect manner to lessen the disgrace. The custom of revenge is one reason why dispute resolution through courts, tribal leaders, and religious leaders played such a large role in Afghan society.[17]

The government depended on the tribes. Tribal leaders retained armed guards who helped the police detain criminals.[18] Without their cooperation, the district's thirty-three police probably would have been too few to maintain order. Consequently, the district governor and provincial governor needed to keep the tribes behind the government. They were perpetually balancing against the tribes, artfully using carrots and sticks to keep tribal leaders in line: granting them authority over the affairs of their territory, offering them goods and services, and sometimes taxing them. The government lacked the military might simply to enforce its will over them. The tribes themselves viewed the government as another powerful actor—somewhat like another very powerful

Table 1: Tribal Leaders of Garmser, c. 1975.

Old Tribes

Name	Tribe	Region	Remarks
Said Omar	Noorzai	Hazar Joft	His son, Ayub Omar, later became deputy district governor
Mohammed Anwar	Noorzai	Hazar Joft	
Khodirom	Noorzai	Loya Darveshan	
Roh Khan	Noorzai	Kuchinay Darveshan	His son, Tooriali, later became police chief
Mohammed Khan	Noorzai	Loya Darveshan (Amir Agha)	Member of Zahir Shah's parliament
Mohammed Omar	Alizai	Lakari	His son, Mohammed Nadir, later became tribal leader
Anayatullah	Alizai	Laki	His son, Shah Wali Khan, later became tribal leader
Mir Hamza	Barakzai	Bartaka	His son, Abdullah Jan, later became district governor
Dost Mohammed	Noorzai	Safar	His son, Salay Mohammed, later became tribal leader
Zahir Khan	Noorzai	Benadar	

Immigrant tribes (naqilen)

Name	Tribe	Region	Remarks
Baz Mohammed	Kharoti	Majitek	
Abdul Hakim	Taraki	Majitek	Later became a Taliban governor
Wakil Manan	Sayid	Mian Poshtay	Worked with the communists
Hazrat	Andar	Safar	

tribe—rather than as an entity that deserved their allegiance. The government could be a source of patronage or punishment. From the tribal perspective, aligning against the government was not treacherous if it was necessary. Whatever was in the interest of the tribe was right—Pashtun realpolitik. Since the tribes themselves were divided and the government had substantial resources behind it (including the entire Helmand River Valley Project), during the time of King Zahir Shah, balance was maintained.[19]

The other important group within society with whom the government shared power was the ulema: the religious leaders. Islam played a powerful role in Garmser. Even amid the progressivism of Zahir Shah, Pashtuns scrupulously prayed five times per day, dutifully fasted during Ramadan, and let no woman go outdoors with her face uncovered. Every village had at least one mullah and at least one mosque: a simple mud affair with a low perimeter wall, arched veranda, plain exterior, and long room for praying. The mullah was the village religious leader: always bearded, wearing a white or black turban with a short chest-length tail instead of the elder's dual-colored turban and wrapping waist-length tail. Education might have amounted to a few years in a religious school (known as a madrasa), though often not. A mullah's role was chiefly to lead prayers, offer primary lessons to village children, and occasionally resolve local disputes. A village paid a mullah through donations, known as 'zerkat,' which was one of the five pillars of Islam. Zerkat was usually 10 percent of the harvest. Certain religious leaders were known as 'maulawi,' or religious scholars. They had years of formal education, in addition to twelve years of primary and secondary education.[20] Garmser's leading scholar, Maulawi Mohammed Agha, had studied religion for twelve years in Afghanistan and then had attended a madrasa in India for his graduate degree. Many religious scholars ran their own madrasas in Garmser, where they taught both children and young men seeking to become mullahs. The fifty-year-old Maulawi Baz Mohammed, another famous scholar, taught many of the mullahs most respected in Garmser today. Because of their education, religious scholars were held in high regard as the authorities on Islam. The government went to scholars for advice on religious and legal matters.

The religious system differed from the tribal system. It was not defined by territory or tribal hierarchy. Religious leaders' influence cut across tribes and regions. Islam was the one belief that all people in Garmser shared. There was a mullah in every village, independent from the elders and the khans. Religious leaders usually worked in a village far from their home, with a tribe that was not their own. A mullah might stay in the village for many years, if well supported by an elder, or he might move on after a year or two to a new village. Word of mouth told them which villages had an empty mosque or needed a mullah. Scholars moved around less, since tribal leaders tended to want to keep them in their communities as a sign of prestige. When a new mullah arrived in a village, the village elder and the villagers decided whether or not to accept him. Very rarely did they decide not to. Obligated to respect Islam, it was a disgrace for an elder to push an incoming mullah out of his village. Likewise, an elder was not supposed to tell the mullah what to say or otherwise control him. Religious leaders, scholars in particular, were seen as just, learned, and unbiased. For this reason, tribal leaders themselves sometimes brought disputes to a scholar for arbitration.

Religious leaders had no formal governing structure but met with each other regularly to discuss issues and Islam. Ties between them stretched across tribal boundaries. Ties could be based on family—many mullahs had brothers and fathers who were also mullahs—or a common teacher or common view of Islam. Ties could even stretch across districts and provinces. Consequently, religious leaders could spread their influence in a way that tribal leaders could not. They had a unique ability to rally the people behind a cause. In fact, given their sheer numbers, they rivaled the government in its ability to reach out to the people.

During Zahir Shah's reign, Garmser's religious leadership was advanced, prosperous, and honored by the government. Friday prayers, when the whole district gathered at the district center mosque to pray, took place weekly in the district center, led by a high-ranking scholar. It was an important symbol of oneness between the people, the government, and Islam. In the past, religious leaders in Afghanistan had called for jihad against foreign invaders (such as the British) or openly opposed the government, fulfilling what they saw as their proper role as leaders of the Islamic community, subservient to no secular body.[21] In Garmser, before 1978, the religious leaders were not so vocal. Despite their prestige, religious leaders did not get involved in politics or preach for or against the government. Pakistan, political parties, or the government did not control the religious leaders or what they said. Income came from the donations given by villagers and the philanthropy of tribal leaders. In the village mosques, mullahs taught reading, writing, the Koran, the hadith, and how to lead a good Islamic life rather than jihad or new forms of Islamic government. The scholars who trained young men to become mullahs taught them how to speak, read, and write

Arabic and about shari'a (Islamic law). Derived from the Koran and the sayings and deeds of the Prophet Mohammed (hadith), Islamic law deals with both criminal and civil issues, including punishments, marriage, divorce, and people's basic rights. The government recognized it as one source of law that an official judge could use, alongside secular laws. The scholars taught about Islamic law so that their students would understand how to offer moral advice and how to deal with any disputes brought to their door. They did not endorse the brutal punishments that the Taliban would later espouse. Nor did they call for Islamic law to replace all other laws. The religious leaders were apolitical.[22]

The social experiment

Through the early 1970s, balance existed between the government, Alizai and Noorzai tribal leaders, and religious leaders. The great modernizing experiment—the construction of the canal system—changed that. The Helmand River Valley Project was not merely about digging canals. It was also about redistributing the land and bringing in settlers from throughout Afghanistan. After all, the government had not dug the canals for the benefit of the tribal leaders and their vast landholdings. The idea was partly to spread the wealth and partly to immobilize nomads who created political problems going back and forth to Pakistan.

Before digging had begun, the tribal leaders had given land to the government for the canals. This had not been a problem. Newly-built canals would benefit them and waterways had traditionally been under government jurisdiction. In the 1960s, Zahir Shah took more land away, particularly poorly irrigated land. The government acquired thousands of hectares, perhaps half the canal zone. Said Omar of Hazar Joft gave up 80 of 180 hectares. Haji Roh Khan of Kuchinay Darveshan gave up 1,200 of his immense 1,700-hectare holdings. The tribal leaders were not happy but accepted the decision. The best land remained in their hands.

In the early 1970s, the government handed out plots of this newly-irrigated, newly-sequestered land to thousands of immigrants, known as 'naqilen.' They started arriving in 1973 and became the official owners of that land. Each family received two hectares.[23] They came from provinces throughout Afghanistan—Ghazni, Kunar, Paktia, and Farah are some of the more prominent examples. Some Pashtun tribes, such as the Andar, Kharoti, Shinwari, and Kakar, occupied set blocks of land, forming their own tribal enclaves. Others, such as the Ahmedzai, Safi, and Popalzai, mixed in with the Alizai and Noorzai or other immigrants and never formed their own enclaves. Pashtuns were not the only immigrants. Hazaras, Tajiks, and Uzbeks from northern Afghanistan also came to Garmser and formed Persian-speaking enclaves far removed from their brethren to the north. The immigrant tribes often had a leader who led them to Garmser, and went by the title of 'wakil,' such as Wakil Baz Mohammed of the Kharoti. A wakil essentially filled the same role as a khan within the Alizai or Noorzai. They were the tribal leaders for immigrant enclaves.

The process of distributing land continued after Zahir Shah's cousin Mohammed Daoud overthrew him in 1973. In 1973, roughly 67,000 people, largely Alizai and Noorzai, lived in Garmser. By 1975, the figure had jumped to 92,000. Over 15,000 were immigrants who had been granted land.[24] Another 10,000 had been permitted to move to the district but had not been granted their own land. These included hundreds of Alizai families from northern Helmand, who had lost their homes in the flooding caused by the construction of the dam in Kajaki, and hundreds of nomadic Taraki families, who moved into Majitek and eastern Loya Darveshan. They rented government land. The remainder of the 10,000 came to Garmser to work other people's land.[25]

The canal system was a huge social experiment. Garmser had gone from great tribal homogeneity—Alizai, Noorzai, and a handful of Barakzai and Baluch—to great heterogeneity—scores of tribes, often mixed together. Whole newly irrigated regions—Koshtay, Mian Poshtay, Majitek—were populated entirely by immigrants. The old tribal leaders—the khans—now had to share political power. The new immigrant tribal leaders took part in shuras and meetings in the district center on district-wide issues, introducing a potential for feuding with the old landed elite. The numerous Kharoti, Taraki, and Andar were from the Ghilzai tribal confederation, traditional rivals of the Durrani, the confederation to which all of Garmser's old khans belonged. Coarse and tanned from caravanning through the desert or toiling in dry soil, with fraying turbans and dyed beards, they came from a different class from the khans and their noble lineages. Under Daoud, friction was avoided because the old khans retained political dominance. They still owned a large amount of land and enjoyed better political ties to the government than the immigrants. Consequently, they tended to get their way.

The same immigration of naqilen that Garmser experienced occurred throughout Helmand. Immigrant communities mixed in among the landed tribes. Marjah and Nadi Ali—communities created by the canal project—were almost entirely populated by immigrants, as was Lashkar Gah. Other older communities, such as Gereshk and Nawa, acquired large immigrant populations too. The land issues Garmser faced were mirrored in all these places.

Daoud fell from power in 1978. At that time, in Garmser, roughly 25,000 hectares were under the private ownership of either an old land-owner or a new immigrant. But 6–8,000 hectares of government land were unassigned. Most of the eastern edge of the canal zone, along the desert, from Majitek to Safar, belonged to the government. Patches of land by the river also belonged to the government. Some was slated to go to more immigrants. Most was to stay in government hands for future leasing, sale, or government use. That unoccupied land would become the source of much friction in coming years.

The Helmand River Valley Project was the first of many changes to hit Garmser. In the course of two decades, the amount of irrigable land had doubled, the population had increased by a third, and the old Noor-zai–Alizai order had been melded with the immigrant mass of Tajiks, Hazaras, Uzbeks, and Ghilzai Pashtuns. Thus far, the changes had not led to conflict. Mass immigration and loss of land had been met by compromise and cooperation. In the future, however, the mix of increasingly dissatisfied Noorzai and Alizai tribal leaders, a large number of immigrants, and thousands of hectares of free, unoccupied, government land would help break the district apart.

2

THE JIHAD

Obah pe dang ne beleegee.
'A stick does not divide flowing water.'
Pashto proverb

On 27 April 1978, a military-led coup overthrew and killed Mohammed Daoud. A communist government under Noor Mohammed Taraki took over, heavily supported by the Soviet Union. Taraki carried out a communist agenda involving land redistribution, secular education, marriage reform, and widespread repression.[1] The agenda sparked popular unrest, which resulted in Soviet intervention and, in turn, the jihad—the opening round in thirty years of conflict. Most of Garmser joined the jihad. Main actors in Garmser's longer story step on stage here. The war went on for ten years. The people of Garmser remember it as a heroic resistance to an infidel power. But it was also the sad end to decades of nation-building. Progress would not easily be restarted. The Kabul-run government lost control of Garmser, taking away the weight that had pressed the tribal leaders, religious leaders, and immigrants to get along. In so doing, the jihad created the environment in which change would accelerate and the Taliban would eventually take power.

Communist government

Deputy police chief Mohammed Agha was the first policeman I met in Garmser when I arrived in 2009. All the policemen called him 'Baba,' meaning grandfather, because of his fifty-odd years, grey beard, and thirty years in the police. A Noorzai from Darveshan with a high school education, he often came to see me with a pointed finger and advice on how to improve the police, reach out to religious leaders, or enhance the status of women. He wanted to see Garmser progress. These same ideals are what had compelled him to join the police when the communists had taken over in 1978: 'The Khalqis [communists] had a good program, like your work is today. They wanted to help people and modernize society.'[2]

To this day, the people of Garmser call all communists 'Khalqis,' the faction of the People's Democratic Party of Afghanistan that Taraki led and to which the district's communists belonged. For the sake of the reader, I will simply call them communists. Garmser did not have many: a handful of police (influenced by their direct association with the government), a handful of educated young men, especially from Darveshan, and a good number of poor farmers. Like Baba, they found the communists' progressive ideology appealing. Wakil Manan of Mian Poshtay, who alone of Garmser's tribal leaders worked with the communists and who would play a major role in the district's future, echoed Baba's view: 'We liked the [communist] government because they supported education and built schools.'[3] Indeed, the communist regime had successes, such as the construction of the district center hospital, a clean modern building that functions to this day. Poor farmers, living on government land or farming a khan's land, were the communists' largest supporters. In the words of one, 'The khans were very oppressive. Taraki punished them.'[4] Still, most of Garmser's leaders, deeply rooted in tribal and religious society, opposed the communists. Lashkar Gah, with its educated middle class and detribalizing society, was Helmand's communist stronghold. Garmser was a stronghold of conservatism. As Baba admitted, 'The Khalqis [communists] never had much support here.'[5]

Upon taking power, the Taraki government sent a new district governor to Garmser and expanded the police force from 33 to roughly 100 men.[6] It then introduced reforms meant to improve the lot of the average Afghan and weaken the power of the tribal and religious leaders. The reforms centered on education, marriage, and land. Seeking to end illiteracy and indoctrinate the people, the education reforms established a new secular curriculum focused on reading, writing, and understanding communism. Textbooks from Russia glorified a modern lifestyle. Islam was shelved. Mullahs were no longer allowed to teach. The marriage reforms set a cap on dowry, an important tribal custom. From the communists' perspective, dowry was cruel because it was part of a process of trading women for the tribe's benefit, sometimes against their will and often before they turned eighteen, as if they were livestock or a piece of land. The land reforms, the most important of the reforms, redistributed the holdings of the landowners in a manner far more radical than anything previously attempted. It was decreed that any landowner could have no more than 36 jeribs (a little over 7 hectares). The rest was taken away, much of it given to poorer farmers or new immigrants brought into the district.[7] Tribal leaders who had owned hundreds of hectares were left with only seven.

The Taraki reforms sowed the seeds of the jihad. They pushed Garmser's tribal and religious leaders too far. Land redistribution outraged the tribal leaders, already upset at having lost land during King Zahir Shah's government. Nor did the cap on dowry please them. The law made it difficult for the tribes to use marriage as a means of settling disputes and building family alliances. Religious leaders were no less angry. For them, the government's adherence to communism, a foreign, un-Islamic ideology, was blasphemy. And just about everyone disliked the government's alignment with the Soviet Union. Mohammed Anwar Khan, a tribal leader from Darveshan, summed up the feeling of Garmser's traditional leadership toward the communists: 'The communists divided our land and told us that it did not belong to us. They were infidels.'[8]

One would have thought that at least the poor farmers would have rallied behind the communists, and at first that was the case. But, over time, Islam had a powerful countervailing effect. Mullahs, with their tremendous influence, told the poor to oppose the government. Indeed, Maulawi Abdul Hakim, religious scholar and leader ('wakil') of the largely poor and landless Taraki tribe organized his people against Taraki himself, their fellow tribesman, on the basis of his un-Islamic policies. Soon the poor farmers deserted the communists. Ironically, rather than lift up the marginalized elements of Garmser society, the communist reforms served only to unite the people of Garmser against them.

To carry out their reforms, the communists resorted to repression. Many of the weapons belonging to the tribal leaders were taken away. Tribal and religious leaders were selectively imprisoned and even killed. Three mullahs were hung on top of a hill that overlooks the canal intake to show the power of the new government over religion. Influential tribal leaders such as Said Omar were imprisoned in Lashkar Gah.[9] Rumors spread that other prisoners were being tortured and buried alive, though there is no evidence that this happened to anyone from Garmser.[10]

Tribal and religious leaders began organizing themselves to resist. At first, it was not a centralized movement. It was an underground low-level resistance organized village by village. Young men held meetings at night, cached arms, and took pot shots at communist police. Meanwhile, people started leaving Garmser for Pakistan, especially the tribal and religious leaders. There they began planning for open warfare and organizing larger, more capable cadres of fighting men.

Outbreak of the jihad

Taraki lasted 18 months as head of the communist government. In September 1979, Hafizullah Amin replaced him. Three months later, on 27 December 1979, with unrest rising throughout the country, the Soviet Union invaded Afghanistan. Amin was assassinated. Babrak Karmal was installed as the new leader of Afghanistan. Whereas, under Taraki, resistance in Garmser had been underground, it now came out into the open. For Garmser, Soviet invasion was intolerable.[11] The religious leaders issued fatwas (Islamic edicts) declaring jihad.[12] The tribal leaders took up the call, together as one, and mobilized their cadres. These moves were undoubtedly influenced by events in Kunar, Paktia, Nuristan, and Panjshir, which were already in open revolt.

In Pakistan, the tribal leaders met together and decided to stand up 200 fighters and liberate Garmser from the communists. The fighters were organized into cadres of 20–50 men, each under a separate commander, invariably a tribal leader, his brother, or son. The cadres were likewise tribally based, made up of the family members and tribesmen of each commander. The fighters became known as mujahidin, Arabic for holy warrior.

Shah Wali Khan led the Alizai mujahidin from Laki. His father, Anayatullah, had been Garmser's second largest landowner, known for his just wisdom. Thirty years old, impeccably courteous, over six feet tall and athletic, Shah Wali Khan carried nobility in his every word and move. He was the eldest of five brothers and expected to be one of the tribe's great leaders. His soft, steady voice and manners testified to his heritage; his upright build and determined green eyes warned that he would never let that heritage down. The Alizai elders of Laki, long close allies, naturally followed his lead and were ready to take up arms. In Shah Wali Khan's words: 'It was because of the Russians that we decided to fight. The Russians abused the mullahs and the elders. The communist government oppressed us too. They buried people alive or poured boiling water on them. People were fleeing.'[13]

The great Noorzai families also took their tribesmen to war. The widely respected Said Omar led the Noorzai from Hazar Joft. Said Omar was both a tribal leader and a student of Islam. The people of Garmser often called him 'maulawi' even though he never claimed to be a religious scholar. His imprisonment by the communists for fourteen months added to his reputation. Ironically, he had been involved in government before the communists and very much supported the development of a well-run Afghan state. His whole family would become known for the wisdom he imparted to them. Baqi Khan led the Noorzai from Darveshan. He was the brother of Roh Khan, Garmser's largest landowner (until the communists took over) and leader of that first Pashtun clan that had come to Garmser. The family lived in a sprawling village in Kuchinay Darveshan. The other influential commander was Abdul Hakim from Majitek, the aforementioned leader of the immigrant Taraki.

The tribal leaders would be aided in their attack on Garmser by Mohammed Nasim Akhundzada, an ambitious Alizai leader from Musa Qala, in northern Helmand. The plan was for Nasim to march south and reinforce the Garmser mujahidin for a final assault on the district center. In contrast to Shah Wali Khan, Nasim was not tribal nobility. His family came from a religious background, signified by the title 'Akhundzada.' The family was building up power through their religious influence, poppy cultivation, and their ties with the mujahidin party, *Harakat Inkilab Islami*. They could field hundreds of men. Nasim would become the most powerful mujahidin commander in Helmand, eager to run the whole province.

Roughly one hundred Afghan police held Garmser. Only Soviet advisors were with them: no infantry, no tanks, no artillery. Given the mass

Image 2: Said Omar, mujahidin commander and tribal leader of the Noorzai in Hazar Joft, years after the jihad had ended. (Photo by Patricio Asfura-Heim)

desertions plaguing the army elsewhere in Afghanistan, it is fair to assume that morale was pretty low. The bulk of them were with the communist headquarters in the district center. Those to the south were strung out along the main canal in posts in Laki, Mian Poshtay, Kuchinay Darveshan, Amir Agha, and Hazar Joft. Roughly 10 kilometers separated each garrison—an untenable disposition.

The 200 mujahidin marched north from Pakistan and surrounded each post one by one, cutting off their supply lines and harassing them with rifle fire. At every post, after a few days, the communists fled. The largest battle took place in Loya Darveshan, where Nasim linked up with the mujahidin and surrounded forty communist police.[14] The communists tried to hold out on a small hill but were overrun. All died at the hands of Nasim Akhundzada.[15] In short order, the mujahidin reached the district center. After three days, it fell.[16] Nasim and his men then departed, leaving Garmser under the control of Shah Wali Khan, Said Omar, and Baqi Khan.

The jihad was off to an auspicious start. Success did not last long. The Soviet Union had 80,000 men (seven divisions) in Afghanistan (the total would eventually reach roughly 100,000, 40,000 fewer than the 140,000 that the United States and its Allies would later send). After capturing Kabul, the Soviets advanced into the rest of the country. Of the forces that went to Helmand, 4,000 Soviet and Afghan soldiers branched off to retake Garmser. Garmser mujahidin defended the district center for two days, and then retreated south.

The Soviets set up a base at the district center and left 250 Afghan police there, backed up by fifteen Afghan army soldiers with two tanks.[17] The Soviet infantry and their tanks withdrew to Lashkar Gah. To reinforce and re-supply the garrison at the Garmser district center, the Soviets built posts along the road from the district center to Lashkar Gah. The Afghan soldiers and police had modern Soviet weaponry, including AK-47 rifles and rocket-propelled grenades (RPGs). For fire support, an artillery battery was emplaced in the desert west of Loya Darveshan and fighter-bombers could fly in from Kandahar air force base.

By this point, the jihad had spread across Afghanistan; Garmser was just one small front within a much larger war. Afghans fought the Soviets and the communist government from Herat to Kunar to Kandahar. In most areas, what had started as a traditional tribal revolt against communism became a well-organized insurgency. Islamic parties, such as *Jamiat Islami* and *Hezb Islami*, led the effort. The United States, Pakistan, and Saudi Arabia, seeking to bog down the Soviet Union, funneled aid to the mujahidin. For their part, the Soviets set up outposts throughout the country and launched widespread search and destroy missions.

Early years of the jihad

Whereas elsewhere the mujahidin operated in true guerrilla fashion—hitting and running, hiding among the people—in many ways the

Garmser jihad was not much of an insurgency; it was more like a pro-longed siege of the district center broken by periodic sorties when Soviet columns flew down from Lashkar Gah. The district center was eminently defensible, destined to become the battlefront for long stretches over the next thirty years. On the west, it is flanked by the Helmand River; on the east, by the main canal. Neither spot is fordable. A small hill watches the bridge over the Helmand—here the river is deep and narrow—and a fortified police post guards the canal bridge. The north offers no better approach. The canal curves westward for 5 kilometers until it meets the Helmand, forming a slim triangle of land north of the bazaar that can easily be controlled. With the north, west, and eastern approaches all covered, only the southern approach is open, but here the river and the canal channel attackers into a 2-kilometer space, facing the mud-bricked shops and compounds that line the main bazaar road—ready-made bunkers, a fortified line overlooking the open fields and scattered compounds to the south. Communists laid anti-personnel mines in ditches, paths, and gardens which their posts could not see. Only the most resolute attacker, behind a heavy artillery barrage, could hope to cross that ground. Since the communists had enough forces to man posts in the north, east, south, and west, and were also able to supply them, ring them with mines, and support them with artillery, capturing the district center had become a very costly proposition. For the most part, the mujahidin took stand-off positions 200–400 meters away. Firefights broke out daily but the mujahidin forswore direct assault.

Realizing that the Soviet-backed communist forces were not going to be defeated any time soon, the mujahidin organized themselves for a long war. They had no overarching commander. Shah Wali Khan continued to play a leading role, with another young Alizai tribal leader, Ghulam Rassoul, as his tactical commander. Ghulam Rassoul was in his early twenties, short but well-built, well-known for his battlefield bravery. His cheerful smile masked an all-out Pashtun resolve to uphold tribal as well as his own honor. He had a calm disregard for danger that made him a formidable frontline leader. Said Omar (Noorzai tribal leader from Hazar Joft), Baqi Khan (Noorzai tribal leader from Kuchinay Darveshan), and Abdul Hakim (Taraki tribal leader from Majitek) retained significant influence within the mujahidin as well. Operational decisions were set at a 'military' (nizami) council between the commanders.[18] All told, as many as 500 mujahidin fought in Garmser, divided

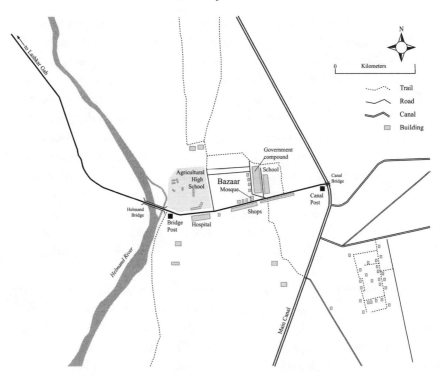

Map 4: Garmser district center (Mike Markowitz).

into cadres along tribal lines. The military council designed a schedule for deployments to the front. Every cadre sent a squad of about ten to man part of the line around the district center for five days, after which the fighters returned to their homes or to Pakistan for leave.[19]

The mujahidin lived off the local economy. Farmers and elders gave the local mujahidin food, shelter, and a small tax. The mujahidin took a percentage of their wheat harvest as tax (which they sometimes used to make their own bread). Powerful khans could pay, feed, and shelter their men themselves. Shah Wali Khan, for example, used profits from his two flour mills as salary for his fifty men.[20]

The tribal leaders were responsible for arming their men. During the first three years of the jihad, mujahidin chiefly carried First World War-era Lee Enfield bolt-action rifles. Fully-automatic AK-47s slowly replaced these old workhorses. Most cadres also had rocket-propelled grenade launchers (RPGs). The better off had *dshka* heavy machine guns, mines, mortars, and a pickup truck or two.[21] Modern weapons had to be acquired through one of the Islamic parties in Pakistan. The tribal leaders did not have enough money to pay for them on their own. 'At first,' Shah Wali Khan said, 'I was not aligned with any of the parties. I fed, housed, and paid my men on my own. But, eventually, we needed better weapons. Then I went to Mullah Mohammed Shah, from *Hezb Islami*. I registered with the party and he gave us weapons.'[22] *Hezb Islami* was one of the seven mujahidin parties headquartered in Pakistan that received supplies, weapons, and money from the United States, Saudi Arabia, and other countries, mostly via Pakistan, to fight the Soviets in Afghanistan. *Hezb Islami*, *Jamiat Islami*, and *Hezb Khalis* were the three major parties in Garmser (*Harakat Inkilab Islami* was powerful elsewhere in Helmand). Eventually, each tribal leader formed a relationship with one of the parties.

Ammunition and weapons were smuggled in trucks from Quetta through Kandahar into Helmand. The Soviets tried to interdict the flow of supplies. Attack helicopters patrolled the desert and shot at any vehicle they saw. Consequently, the mujahidin switched to camels and traveled only at night. The journey was five nights long, but the arms and ammunition almost always arrived.[23]

Medical care was not easy for the mujahidin. Most purchased rudimentary first aid supplies for themselves in Pakistan. Better commanders employed some kind of health worker or medic. For example, a fully educated former nurse capable of applying wound-dressings and administering intra-venous fluids helped the Barakzai mujahidin around Koshtay. Similarly, the International Committee of the Red Crescent (Red Cross) trained two of Baqi Khan's men to be medics. In the last year of the jihad, mujahidin commanders even set up a clinic in Safar with two rotating nurses. Still, medical care left much to be desired. Seriously wounded had to be sent in the bed of a pickup to Girdi Jangal, braving the eight off-road dust-choked hours, not a promising prospect. No doubt the lack of medical care helped deter the mujahidin from launching direct assaults on the district center.[24]

The Soviets were not heavily involved in Garmser. There was only one Soviet brigade (with four battalions) for Helmand and Farah provinces. Its units rarely had time to visit Garmser.[25] Day to day, Soviet bombs and shells were seen, not their soldiers. Large convoys rolled through the desert and fired randomly into the canal zone, not daring to enter them-

Table 2: Garmser mujahidin commanders.

Name	Social position	Party	Home	Number of men	Tribe
Mohammed Nadir Khan	Tribal leader	*Hezb Islami*	Lakari, Garmser	50	Alizai
Shah Wali Khan	Tribal leader	*Hezb Islami*	Laki, Garmser	50	Alizai
Yahya Khan	Tribal leader	*Hezb Islami*	Soorkodooz, Nawa	200	Noorzai
Baqi Khan	Brother of tribal leader	*Mili Malang*	Kuchinay Darveshan, Garmser	50	Noorzai
Said Omar	Tribal leader	*Ihtihad Islami*	Hazar Joft, Garmser	50–60	Noorzai
Ghulam Rassoul	Tribal leader	*Hezb Islami*	Laki, Garmser	30	Alizai
Khodirom	Tribal leader	*Hezb Islami*	Loya Darveshan, Garmser	20	Noorzai
Abdul Qayum	Village elder	*Hezb Khalis*	Hazar Joft, Garmser	100	Alizai
Abdul Hakim	Scholar/tribal leader	*N/A*	Majitek, Garmser	30–50	Taraki
Aurang Khan	Brother of tribal leader	*Hezb Islami*	Safar, Garmser	50	Noorzai
Abdullah Jan	Son of tribal leader	*Jamiat Islami*	Bartaka, Garmser	30–50	Barakzai

27

selves. From time to time, the Red Air Force bombed suspected head-quarters, fighting positions, or supply lines. Baqi Khan's headquarters in Kuchinay Darveshan tended to be the lucky target: sometimes struck by air, sometimes by artillery.[26] Soviet air strikes were inaccurate and did not discriminate between civilian and military targets. They would bomb a farmer's tractor as soon as a truck full of armed men. A few years into the war, any bombing tended to cause large numbers of civilians to flee temporarily southward.[27] The United Nations estimates that in the course of the war Soviet and communist firepower destroyed 30 percent of the homes in Garmser.[28] The district governor later told me: 'Every family lost three or four men to the Soviets.'[29]

About once a year the Soviets swept through Garmser. Usually, 500–1,000 Soviet and Afghan troops with 50–100 tanks, trucks, and armored personnel carriers pushed south. The mujahidin always fell back before them. As the column became extended along Garmser's canals, counter-attacks and ambushes lit off. The mujahidin knew the ground and they knew that Soviet close air support was too inaccurate to hit a close-range, well-concealed ambush, at least not before the attackers could escape.[30] In the later years of the war, mujahidin planted anti-vehicle mines on the western side of the river to obstruct Soviet flanking movements and force Soviet tanks and armored personnel carriers to come down the long narrow canal roads, vulnerable to ambushes.[31] In the face of such tactics and unable to hold what they cleared, the Soviets generally turned back within a few days, never pushing south of Kuchinay Darveshan.[32]

The Soviet attempt to take Amir Agha in 1982 was the most famous sweep. Amir Agha, with its shrine and expansive villages, was a symbol for the resistance and a regular meeting place. In 1982, the Soviets massed forces in the district center, including tanks and armored personnel carriers, to clear out Amir Agha. Information got to the mujahidin. Their commanders feared that the Soviets planned to capture Amir Agha for good. I doubt this is true. According to Baba, who as a policeman worked alongside the Soviets, 'The Russians never could have operated like that. They did not have enough men.'[33] Regardless, roughly 100 mujahidin concentrated in Amir Agha to stop the Soviets, under the command of Aurang Khan, from Safar, and Nasim Akhundzada, the Alizai warlord from Musa Qala. Nasim rushed to Garmser for the fight. Shah Wali Khan and Ghulam Rassoul with the Garmser Alizai from Laki were there too.

The mujahidin and the Soviets met 4 kilometers north of Amir Agha. The mujahidin fought for a day and, outnumbered, fell back another 2 kilometers, where they fought again the next day. Finally, they fell back to Amir Agha itself. Amir Agha and its shrine lie on a long rolling sand dune. Though only 15 meters high, it is a dominating feature over the flat canal zone. The dune runs 2 kilometers west to east, with a gradual incline to the south and a steep incline to the north where it has an actual face, partly concealed by dusty green desert pine trees (*shin ghazi*). A small canal runs parallel to the dune 100 meters to the north. Between the dune and the canal is a boggy marsh 1–2 meters deep, a natural moat. The numerous mud-walled compounds that make up Amir Agha village straddle the length of the dune itself, a line of bunkers and observation posts; all in all, a good place to make a stand.

On the morning of the third day, the Soviets arrayed their armor north of Amir Agha. They had at least ten armored personnel carriers and perhaps a few tanks. In preparation for the assault, the Red Air Force bombed the dune. The people of Garmser still speak of that bombing's intensity. They say exactly 52 bombs fell around the shrine and the village. As bombs exploded around them, villagers ran into the shrine and prayed for salvation. One bomb hit the shrine itself but deflected harmlessly into the sand. The people took it as an act of Allah. What followed reinforced their piety.

Once the bombers had finished their work, the Soviet armor stepped off, crossing the canal in the open. They made wonderful targets. The mujahidin crouched hidden behind the mud walls and peered through the loopholes of the mud houses, holding their fire. When the line of armor waded into the boggy marsh moating the dune, the mujahidin opened up with AK-47s and RPGs. The Soviets returned fire with their own small arms and the cannons on their vehicles. Along the whole front, mujahidin and Soviet armor were engaged. It was hard for the Soviets to spot, let alone kill, the mujahidin fighting from the compounds strong-pointing the dune. Those mud walls, sometimes as much as a meter thick, are known to stop tank rounds: layer after layer of mud slapped together giving the same effect as the earthworks and hesco barriers that modern armies use for fortifications. Still, mujahidin started to fall. Aurang Khan, one of the two mujahidin commanders, was shot in the chest (he barely survived evacuation to Pakistan). Yet, in the end, the strength of the position told. One armored personnel carrier, under a hail of RPG fire, got stuck in the marsh. Another came to help. It got stuck too. Caught in the open, the infantry in the stranded vehicles ran away. Perhaps fearing that more armored vehicles would soon be stuck, the Soviet commanders called off the attack, ordering in air strikes to cover their withdrawal.

Tactically, the battle meant little. Future Soviet sweeps would not stop at Amir Agha. Indeed, the Soviets returned a few days after the battle to find that the mujahidin had dispersed—minus four fighters whom they captured and executed. Nevertheless, for the mujahidin it was a great victory. Today, the rusted hulks of the two armored personnel carriers still lie stranded in the waters just north of the shrine. The locals leave them there: a symbol of Allah's salvation.[34]

Social changes

Garmser remembers the jihad as a time of great achievement. The tribes, religious community, and immigrants stood together against the communist government and their Soviet backers, or at least as together as they had ever stood before or would ever stand again. It was also a time of social, political, and economic change. Tens of thousands fled to Pakistan, poppy cultivation started, religious leaders became politicized, and the tribal leaders reasserted their authority as the government structures built over the past century crumbled.

Most of the population—roughly 67,000 of the total of 92,000—went to Pakistan, fearing the ravages of war. The 25,000 remaining were the young men, tribal leaders, and village elders supporting the war effort, plus a number of immigrants and poor farmers unable to leave.[35] The tribal leaders sent their women, children, and old men to Pakistan, leaving just the members of their family who would fight. The vast majority of shopowners, teachers, former government officials, and other professionals left for Pakistan as well. New villages filled with Garmser refugees sprang up across the Pakistani border in Girdi Jangal, Chagay, and Quetta, little Garmser colonies that would persist for the next thirty years, where people could hide from—or fight against—whatever was happening in Garmser.

Agricultural production dropped considerably during the jihad but did not end altogether. Crops were still harvested. Families and mujahidin alike still had enough to eat. In Laki, for instance, 40 percent of the arable land was farmed. Mostly wheat was sown. In addition to the 25,000 people who stayed in Garmser between 1983 and 1987, another 13,000 from other war-torn districts came for refuge. They worked the land, largely under the purview of the tribal leaders.[36]

It was at this time that poppy was first planted in Garmser. Since the fall of Daoud, cotton had been slowly disappearing from Garmser. By the jihad, little was left. Partly to support the war effort, farmers and the tribal leaders turned to poppy. Nasim, who smuggled Helmand's poppy out to Iran and Pakistan, advocated and encouraged the practice; it was the basis of his power. Nevertheless, this was just the beginning of poppy in Garmser. It did not really take off during the jihad. Too little labor was available for the time-consuming harvesting process (every poppy bulb must be scored by hand, and then a few days later the gummy black residue must be scraped into a jug, also by hand).

While elsewhere in Afghanistan mujahidin commanders took over the jihad and tribal leaders lost power, in Garmser jihad reinforced the power of the tribes. The Soviets had left nearly the entire district in the hands of the tribal leaders. To resolve local problems, they set up a tribal council that met regularly in Amir Agha. All the tribal leaders attended. The tribal leaders also took over education, setting up five schools in Garmser, with 20 teachers and roughly 500 students. In Laki, Shah Wali Khan paid 4 teachers to teach 120 students. In Darveshan, the Noorzai tribal leaders ran two schools with a total of 240 students, paying for the 10 teachers, notebooks, and textbooks.[37]

Most important of all, from their new position of authority, the tribal leaders retook everything lost under the communists, and more. They reclaimed the land that Taraki had taken from them and given to poor farmers and immigrants. Whereas under Taraki the average size of a farm was only 9 hectares, by the end of the jihad the average had risen to 20 hectares: an indicator of the tribal leaders' success in reversing Taraki's land policies and taking back their old holdings.[38] Certain tribal leaders went even further, claiming unassigned government land for themselves or seizing the private land of immigrants. Mohammed Nadir of Lakari, for example, took the land of Hazaras and then sold it to Alizai or other immigrants. Using force to push the poor off land was acceptable to most of the tribal leaders, but it bred resentment in those who lost their land. Those who did not lose their land began to fear that they would be next. The consequences of this tribal land grab would manifest themselves in the coming decade.

The religious leaders supported the jihad and the tribal leaders. Yet unlike elsewhere, in Kandahar or in the north-east for example, they rarely commanded fighters.[39] Most of the religious scholars and the mullahs who had survived Taraki's purges fled to Pakistan once the fighting began and stayed there throughout the jihad.[40] Of Garmser's top mujahidin commanders, only Abdul Hakim was a religious leader. He had extensive religious training but was also the Taraki tribal leader, so he did not really break the Garmser mold.

Whether in Afghanistan or Pakistan, the religious leaders were the voice of the resistance. Jihad politicized them. They were no longer simply teachers. They issued fatwas proclaiming the war against the communists a jihad. Those in Pakistan became recruiting agents, encouraging young men in the refugee camps to join the mujahidin and fight.[41] The few who remained in Garmser continued their traditional duties but also rallied and counseled the mujahidin on the battlefield. The aged Maulawi Baz Mohammed, the scholar who taught many of Garmser's future mullahs, was one.[42] Maulawi Mohammed Hanif from Koshtay was another. Having been educated in Kabul and Kandahar, he served as the judge of all the mujahidin in Garmser, settling disputes between them, while still carrying on his teaching.[43]

New leaders

Over time, new mujahidin leaders emerged. Shah Wali Khan, Baqi Khan, and Said Omar continued to play a leading role, but they were joined by three newcomers: Yahya Khan, Mohammed Nadir, and Abdullah Jan.

Yahya Khan was a Noorzai warlord from Nawa, the district north of Garmser. *Hezb Islami* backed him. He was the most powerful mujahidin commander in Nawa. Gradually he gained influence over the Noorzai in Garmser. Baqi Khan and other Noorzai commanders depended upon him for weapons and money. By 1984, all the Noorzai tribal leaders except Said Omar were in his camp.

Mohammed Nadir was the young tribal leader of Lakari, roughly twenty-five years old. Before jihad, he had taught at the agricultural college. He came from a landed family known for their learning. His brother was a religious scholar and his older cousin, the soft-spoken Abdul Samad, was respected for his wisdom and polished knowledge of

Pashto. Mohammed Nadir had sat out the first years of fighting in Lakari. During that time, his uncle had commanded the mujahidin from Lakari. The cadre was made up of young Alizai, especially the sons and brothers of village elders. The death of Mohammed Nadir's uncle in a communist ambush north of the district center in 1981 caused him to take up jihad.[44] The Lakari cadre came under his leadership. Shah Wali Khan and Ghulam Rassoul—able Alizai commanders in their own right—naturally aligned with their fellow tribesman. Connections to Alizai warlord Nasim Akhundzada in the north and the Garmser Alizai's own tribal solidarity soon made Mohammed Nadir a major political contender in Garmser.

The last of the three new leaders was Abdullah Jan, the son of Mir Hamza, a tribal leader of the Barakzai clan on the western side of the river in Bartaka. The clan had come to Garmser in the 1840s, at the time of the first Anglo-Afghan War, when Barakzai from Kandahar had temporarily taken over Garmser.[45] The Barakzai are the smallest of Garmser's three old land-owning tribes. Yet thanks to their political connections (other than two short-lived exceptions, every Afghan ruler from 1826 to 1978 was Barakzai) and their sense of responsibility to fight for Afghanistan, the Barakzai were disproportionately active in the jihad. Two of Abdullah Jan's three elder brothers were killed in the same communist ambush as Mohammed Nadir's uncle, north of the district center in 1981.[46] Abdullah Jan was in Kandahar at the time, sent there by his family to fight. At twenty-five years old, thin and not terribly tall, with a short black beard, not much had been expected of him. He had hardly studied in school and could barely read or write. Within the family, his learned cousin Mir Atem was known as the intelligent one, and his eldest brother Abdul Ahmed was expected to take over leadership of the tribe. During a few years of bad crops in Bartaka, the family had cast the adolescent Abdullah Jan to Benadar to help tend rented land (here he started a life-long friendship with the Omarzai sub-tribe of the Noorzai). When the jihad broke out, his two other elder brothers took charge of the Barakzai cadre of mujahidin. Abdullah Jan went off to Kandahar. When those two elder brothers were killed in the same ambush as Mohammed Nadir's uncle, he returned to Garmser to lead the cadre. For years, when asked about his time in the jihad, he replied, 'The Soviets executed my two brothers in Khari. I was in Kandahar. I came back to Garmser to fight them.'

Abdullah Jan quickly gained a reputation for himself. He was active and worked harder than the other commanders, always planning, organizing, or skirmishing at the front.[47] He knew how to create and execute a sound operation. Just like any Western officer, he held detailed planning meetings with his lieutenants. Before a multi-cadre operation, he made sure to sit with the other commanders in order to review everyone's role. His cadre showed outstanding unit cohesion and *esprit de corps*, partly because he set an example. He led from the front and was courageous in battle.[48] He did not set himself apart from his men or take privileges for himself. He ate every meal seated with them on the floor. They all shared hardships together. Furthermore, his men and other commanders respected him for his morality. He could be cruel but he did not steal from his men and he tried to protect innocent people from being abused (the guilty were less privileged). He paid special attention to Islam, listening closely to the advice of Abdul Hakim and Mohammed Hanif, the judge of the mujahidin. The latter eventually worked closely with Abdullah Jan and taught out of his mosque.[49] In the words of one

Image 3: Abdullah Jan at a shura at the district center, many years after the Soviets had left Afghanistan. (Photo by Peter Chilvers)

of his fighters, 'Abdullah Jan was a different mujahidin commander. The other commanders were thieves. He was a good Muslim.'[50]

Because of the small number of Barakzai in Garmser, Abdullah Jan had to recruit men from outside his own tribe. His Barakzai relatives were the core, such as his cousins Mir Atem and Ahmed Shah, but the bulk were immigrants living in Koshtay and Mian Poshtay. Many were from poorer Pashtun tribes, such as the black turbaned Mohammed Nabi, a Kakar tribesman (known in the days of the British as a notoriously lawless nomadic tribe) who joined at seventeen years of age.[51] Others were Baluch from the desert by Koshtay. Abdullah Jan reached out to them, paying attention to their grievances. Still others were Noorzai, won over by Abdullah Jan's charisma. Although from different tribes, loyalty fell to their little band. 'We are our own family,' Ahmed Shah later told me. Of all the Garmser commanders, only Abdullah Jan had broken through tribal lines and formed a diverse cadre of mujahidin.

Abdullah Jan demonstrated political acumen as well. He got the backing of the mujahidin party *Jamiat Islami*, which allowed him to arm his thirty men with good modern weapons and, moreover, gave him a measure of independence from *Hezb Islami* and *Harakat Inkilab Islami*, the parties that dominated Helmand. That meant that he was not subordinate to the Alizai, Yahya, or Nasim to the north. To gain further influence, he acquired land in Koshtay, across from Bartaka, on the populated eastern side of the river.

As time went on, the mujahidin split into two camps. One was the Alizai, increasingly led by Mohammed Nadir, though Shah Wali Khan and Ghulam Rassoul did most of the fighting. The other was Noorzai, led by Yahya Khan. Abdullah Jan tried to stay neutral but in the course of campaigning became fast friends with Shah Wali Khan, Mohammed Nadir, and Ghulam Rassoul and drew closer to their camp. For the time being, the two camps cooperated, taking part in the military council and fighting together at the front in Hazar Joft. But Yahya and Mohammed Nadir were ambitious men. Cooperation would not last forever.

Latter years of the jihad

After the Amir Agha battle, fighting in Garmser succumbed to a steady rhythm. Every day mujahidin and communists skirmished around the district center, mujahidin cadres rotating in and out, sometimes led by

Shah Wali Khan, sometimes Abdul Hakim, sometimes Abdullah Jan, and so forth. Artillery bombardments and air strikes droned on. About once a year Soviet armor swept south from Lashkar Gah and then turned back. Many firefights broke out and many Afghans died but stalemate dragged on. Garmser never saw the influx of US Stinger shoulder-fired surface-to-air missiles that marked the latter half of the war elsewhere in Afghanistan. One Stinger came to Garmser. The mujahidin shot it at a helicopter. They missed.

In March 1985, Mikhail Gorbachev became the leader of the Soviet Union. Determined to get out of Afghanistan, he gave the military a year to win the war. Soviet generals launched major offensives throughout Afghanistan that year. In Helmand, the Soviets brought in reinforcements from Herat and Kandahar and struck at mujahidin safe havens. The idea was to inflict such damage on the mujahidin that they could no longer operate effectively. The heaviest fighting was against Nasim Akhundzada in the north.[52]

In Garmser, the Soviets mounted their deepest sweep of the war. According to Afghans, 100 (probably 50 or so) armored fighting vehicles and T-72 tanks punched 20 kilometers south down the main canal to Kuchinay Darveshan. The goal was to knock out the headquarters of Baqi Khan, Noorzai mujahidin commander of Kuchinay Darveshan. Soviet tactics had improved since Amir Agha. Infantry led the advance on foot in order to keep the mujahidin away from the tanks and armored vehicles. The tanks supported the infantry with their big guns. The mujahidin, greatly outnumbered and surprised, retreated before the Soviets while Baqi Khan organized a defense near his sprawling village (the place where the first Noorzai had settled in Garmser in the mid-1700s). Abdullah Jan rushed north from Koshtay to help him. Together, they managed to mass fifty men. They made their stand around Baqi Khan's village. The fighting lasted two days. The infantry screen prevented the tanks from getting into trouble and made the battle tougher than Amir Agha for the mujahidin, who were forced to endure hours of tank main gunfire. The mujahidin tried to use their RPGs to deter the tanks from leaving the main canal road. As much as these efforts, it was probably the canal system with its deep ditches and narrow paths that saved the mujahidin. The Soviet infantry could not advance far without losing the support of the tanks, which could not drive off the main road without getting stuck. The Soviets never pressed their attack. After two days and at least five mujahidin casualties, the Soviets withdrew, having failed to do much damage.[53]

Such was the story throughout Helmand and Afghanistan. The 1985 Soviet offensives failed to defeat the resistance. Consequently, Gorbachev took steps to strengthen the Afghan central government and reach a political settlement in preparation for a Soviet withdrawal. In May 1986, Gorbachev removed Babrak Karmal and replaced him with Dr Mohammed Najibullah. Following Soviet advice, Najibullah made numerous reforms. He reaffirmed the role of Islam in Afghanistan, paid off insurgents to stop fighting (not in Garmser), gave the army and police good weapons, ratified a new constitution, held parliamentary elections, and set up tribal militias. Today, even though most stayed loyal to the mujahidin, people in Garmser often say that Najibullah's reforms were 'strong' and look upon his time as a lost chance for peace.

Ironically, most of Najibullah's reforms never touched Garmser. The government had no influence outside the district center. The exceptions were the police and militia programs. The police received better weapons—mortars, RPGs, and armored vehicles. The militia program paid elders throughout Afghanistan to raise men to defend their villages against the mujahidin. In Helmand, large militias were set up in Nawa and Lashkar Gah. Wakil Manan, the only one of Garmser's tribal leaders to work with the communists, led a 300-strong militia in Lashkar Gah. In his mid-thirties, Wakil Manan was energetic, intelligent, and committed to the government. King Zahir Shah had given his father land in Mian Poshtay. The family was Sayid, a small tribe that claimed Arab descent. Some people in Garmser doubted whether the family was actually Sayid. I myself wondered if it was not a ruse to hide a more common descent from Garmser's status-conscious landed elite. Whatever the case, the family was uniquely adept at organizing the immigrants of Mian Poshtay, where every family was from a different tribe. Wakil Manan's brother, also a communist, had been killed by the mujahidin. Perhaps for that reason, Wakil Manan accepted a daring mission to set up a militia within Garmser itself, attempting what no Soviet sweep had yet achieved—to hold ground south of the district center.

In early 1988, Wakil Manan circled through the desert and infiltrated into Mian Poshtay, his home. There he had the support of his villagers and scores of poor farmers who had received land from Taraki. He quickly raised a militia. They set up a post, patrolled about, and took over the small bazaar. Strategically, the mujahidin were now cut in two. Mian Poshtay is the crossroads of Garmser. It splits Abdullah Jan and the northern Noorzai from the Alizai and the southern Noorzai. The militia survived twenty days, the time required for Abdullah Jan and Mohammed Nadir to ready their separate forces and converge upon Mian Poshtay. The fighting was rough. Mohammed Nadir lost thirty-three Alizai. In the end, outnumbered and almost surrounded, Wakil Manan and his men withdrew to Lashkar Gah.[54] That was the end of Najibullah's reforms in Garmser.

The Soviet withdrawal from Afghanistan began in 1988. It did not end until 15 February 1989, when the Soviets pulled their last forces over the Amu Darya River and back into the Soviet Union. The Soviet brigade left Helmand in May 1988.[55] In Garmser, the Afghan garrison stayed in the district center. Farther north, the communist militias held onto Lashkar Gah. With the Soviet withdrawal, the Afghan garrison's defenses in the district center weakened. At least 250 police, with mortars and armored vehicles, still manned the perimeter, but the robust shelling and air strikes of the last eight years were no longer possible. The artillery battery in the western desert and the fighter-bombers out of Kandahar were gone. It was now difficult for the garrison to drive back mujahidin forays.[56] Day by day, the mujahidin moved their positions closer and closer to the district center. The communists could do nothing about it. Wakil Manan and a detachment of his militia reinforced the garrison. They were not enough. The communist garrison slowly withdrew into the confines of the bazaar, abandoning forward posts along the main canal and across the Helmand, which had been vital to its protection. Mujahidin in Nawa overran posts on the road to Lashkar Gah, reducing the flow of supplies to the garrison. The defense of the district center was becoming untenable.

In August 1988, the mujahidin assaulted the district center. Yahya, Abdullah Jan, Mohammed Nadir, Shah Wali Khan, and Abdul Hakim planned the attack. As always, there was no one leader, just the military council. Roughly 500 fighters took part, well-equipped with rockets and mortars. The commanders encircled the district center but left the main road to the north unblocked so that the communists could easily escape. Before their ground attack, they fired rockets and mortars at the district center. They must have been terribly inaccurate. I have met no one in Garmser who knows how to lay a mortar. Under the random barrage, the mujahidin crept forward, skirmishing with defenders. Wakil Manan and the communists did not fight for long. All but surrounded, they knew they could not hold out. They got into their armored vehicles, left the district center, and retreated to Lashkar Gah along the road the mujahidin had so conveniently left open.[57]

In Garmser, the jihad was over. The whole district was back in the hands of its people. The Garmser mujahidin did not pursue the communists or join their compatriots fighting around Lashkar Gah. Garmser was their concern. Fighting to the north would be worked out by the other Helmand mujahidin commanders. The communists had lost in Garmser for two reasons. First, they simply never had the forces to expand beyond the district center. Unable to hold ground, the sweeps, artillery barrages, and bombings could inflict casualties on the mujahidin but not shake their resolve. Second, the people of Garmser—the old landed tribes, the immigrants, and the religious community, many living in Pakistan—had been united. The land reforms, secular laws, tribal and religious persecution, and above all the Soviet intervention had seen to that. Under these two conditions, the communists could neither take ground militarily nor find many people to work with. Najibullah's reforms, a pragmatic attempt at a political settlement, gained no traction in Garmser because the mujahidin tribal leaders were already in control of most of the district and had no reason to come to terms.

The jihad was a major event in Garmser's history. Today it retains a mystique of an untainted time when Muslims fought together, in contrast to what has transpired since. The reality of the jihad was less idyllic, as old mujahidin and communists alike confide. There are no exact figures for how many people died. Of the 1975 population of 92,000, given all the battles and bombs and bombardments, it is hard to see how the number could have been less than 1,000; and if we believe Afghan stories, as many as 10,000 is possible. Plus, there were social and economic costs. The population largely fled, agricultural production fell by half, and government-delivered goods and services disappeared. Beyond the immediate tragedy, the jihad had long-term implications for Garmser. The prosperity and delicate balance of Zahir Shah's reign had been upset. Disturbing new trends emerged: the politicization of religious leaders, the abusive behavior of tribal leaders, and the cultivation of poppy. New political leadership was perhaps the most important change. The old government that had kept the tribes, religious community, and immigrants in line dissolved. Tribal leaders took its place. Their leadership worked differently from that of a central government. It depended on cooperation between the various tribal leaders to be effective. Against the Soviet invader, cooperation held. Without that common enemy, it quickly fell apart.

3

CIVIL WAR

Koj bar manzel ta na rasegee.
'A crooked load does not reach its destination.'

Pashto proverb[1]

Allies often win wars only to lose the peace, fighting over the spoils, failing to have prepared for a settlement, not so much with the defeated enemy, but between themselves. Such was the case in Garmser. The whole environment encouraged disorder. Communist reforms and the jihad had destroyed the old system whereby the government had balanced the tribes. Within Garmser, there was no legitimately appointed district governor with the power of army and police behind him to manage tribal politics. Above Garmser, there was no provincial governor, only beleaguered communist militias and competing mujahidin warlords anxious to bring the Garmser Alizai and Noorzai into their respective camps. The stage was hardly set for cooperation. Without any district or provincial authority to restrain them, Garmser's tribal leaders pursued their own interests and took few steps to ensure that peace would follow communist defeat. Civil war ensued.

Long before the district center fell in August 1988, the Garmser mujahidin had seen the end of the jihad approaching. As the Soviets withdrew, their longstanding cohesion cracked. Mohammed Nadir, leader of the Garmser Alizai, and Yahya Khan, leader of the Noorzai,

41

started jockeying for power. Both belonged to *Hezb Islami* and wanted to be the party's head representative in Helmand. Yahya took over Nawa (the district north of Garmser, his home) and then turned an eye to Garmser. Capturing Garmser would put him in position to compete for leadership of all Helmand with the ever more powerful Nasim Akhundzada, warlord of the northern Alizai. Abdullah Jan, by then known as a skilled commander, tried to stay out of the growing Alizai–Noorzai competition but Yahya politicked against him too for being Barakzai, not Noorzai.

As long as the communists—the common enemy—were in Garmser, political competition did not break into open fighting. Yet no sooner had the district center been captured than Yahya declared himself ruler of Garmser and turned the hospital into his capitol. At first, Mohammed Nadir, Abdullah Jan, and Shah Wali Khan (the main tribal leader from Laki) let it be and withdrew to the south.[2] They hoped violence might be averted. Nevertheless, four days after the district center fell, fighting broke out.[3] Yahya's men, without any protest on his part, killed a few of the men of Abdul Hakim (the tribal and religious leader of the Taraki tribe that lived in Majitek and eastern Loya Darveshan). Then, Yahya attacked a group of Alizai mujahidin still staying near Hazar Joft. At that point, Abdul Hakim, Mohammed Nadir, Shah Wali Khan, and Abdullah Jan held a shura and allied against Yahya.[4]

Most of the Noorzai leaders stuck with Yahya. Baqi Khan from Kuchinay Darveshan was his main supporter. As a member of the leading family from that first Noorzai clan to have settled in Garmser, he was deeply protective of Noorzai leadership of Garmser. He carried most of the other tribal leaders from Darveshan with him. Salay Mohammed, the most powerful tribal leader in Safar, allied with Yahya as well. For these Noorzai tribal leaders, the Alizai connection with Nasim Akhundzada was a threat. They saw Nasim as a tyrant out for absolute power over Helmand and Yahya as the best way to keep him out of Garmser. In all, Yahya fielded 300–400 men against the 150 fielded by the Alizai and their allies.

A frontline formed in Koshtay, the southern extent of Garmser's northern Noorzai population. Here, the Noorzai butted up against Abdullah Jan's territory. Both sides dug makeshift fighting holes for cover and used nearby compounds as bunkers.[5] Yahya's forces tried several times but could not break through Abdullah Jan's line.[6]

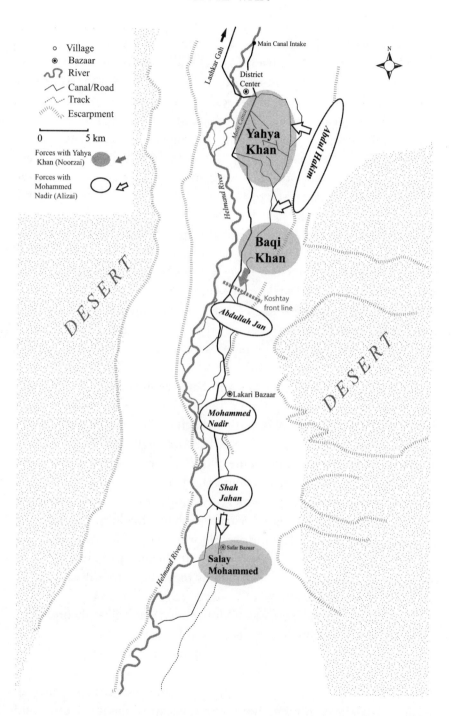

Map 5: Garmser's civil war (Mike Markowitz)

In spite of his numbers, Yahya's strategic position was not terribly good (see map on previous page). In the north, Abdul Hakim was attacking his eastern flank from Majitek and eastern Loya Darveshan, weakening his control of northern Garmser. In the south, Safar was completely disconnected from the rest of his forces and unsupportable. He could not get to his ally Salay Mohammed. In general, mustering widespread popular support, even in Noorzai lands (Hazar Joft, Darveshan, Safar, and Benadar), was a problem for Yahya. He did not have complete Noorzai support. The respected Said Omar and the Omarzai sub-tribe of the Noorzai stayed neutral, taking parts of Hazar Joft and Benadar with them. The fact that Yahya was an outsider clearly out to build his own power weighed against him. He won himself few new friends by heavily taxing vehicles coming over the Helmand bridge.[7]

The Alizai, meanwhile, had fewer fighters but a better strategic position. Other than Abdul Hakim in Majitek, all their forces lay between Koshtay and the southern end of Laki, facing Baqi Khan to the north and Salay Mohammed to the south. They took advantage of their interior lines (a phrase they would never use) to take out Salay Mohammed and capture Safar.

Safar has two major Noorzai clans. Salay Mohammed was from the dominant one. His ageing father, living in Pakistan, was another of Garmser's great tribal leaders and patriarch of the clan. His uncle was Aurang Khan, who had been wounded at Amir Agha. The family owned hundreds of hectares of land. In the 1960s, they had worked closely with USAID to set up the canal system. The US Embassy had even given them letters of appreciation, which the family would proudly produce for US Marines decades later. Safar was their kingdom, much to the chagrin of Safar's other, minority Noorzai clan.[8] The minority clan owned less land and had less influence but felt they had an equal right to run Safar. The two clans had fought together in the jihad, but the civil war loosened those bonds.

The operation to take out Salay Mohammed was brilliantly organized by Shah Jahan, a bright young Alizai from Laki. Shah Jahan was a tribal leader from another old Alizai family, long close with the families of Ghulam Rassoul and Shah Wali Khan (the other two Alizai tribal leaders from Laki). Several years younger than Ghulam Rassoul and Shah Wali Khan, he had been in his early teens at the start of the jihad and could not join the fighting. He spent most of the jihad in Pakistan, but at the end of the 1980s came to Garmser and took over a cadre. He had been well educated in Pakistan and had sharp political insight. Highly ambitious, his political talents would take him far.

In early 1989, Shah Jahan turned the minority Noorzai clan in Safar against Salay Mohammed and his clan. Together, the Alizai and the minority clan attacked Salay Mohammed. Fighting was vicious. In one street battle, Salay Mohammed's relatives stabbed leading members of the other clan. As the Alizai came on, Salay Mohammed's men took up positions atop two small hills in the middle of Safar—the remains of old Ghaznavid forts. But eventually, with the Alizai in front, and the minority Noorzai in the villages behind, the situation became untenable. Salay Mohammed fled to Pakistan. His men surrendered. The Alizai took over Safar. The fraternal blood-letting would not be easily forgotten. It left a permanent division in the Safar Noorzai, which would haunt us twenty years later.

Despite Shah Jahan's success in Safar, Mohammed Nadir could not defeat Yahya in the north. He did not have enough men and according to many was not aggressive enough. The fighting dragged on haphazardly for a year. Truces broke up the open bouts of fighting and allowed for periods of uneasy calm.[9] Fighting in eastern Hazar Joft and Majitek between Abdul Hakim's Taraki immigrants and the Noorzai landed elite was particularly nasty. The two sides tried to seize each other's land, pushing off squatters and rightful landowners alike, leading to years of bad blood. In the end, it was the intervention of Nasim Akhundzada that turned the tide. In September 1989, Nasim marched through the western desert at the head of 600 Alizai from Musa Qala. The Garmser Alizai linked up with him at staging grounds in Koshtay, Mian Poshtay, and Lakari. At this point, Abdullah Jan pulled out of the civil war. Nasim's fighters were mistreating the people. Abdullah Jan cared neither for their behavior nor their leader's plans to lord over Helmand. Nasim and Mohammed Nadir attacked Yahya's men in Koshtay. The ensuing battle lasted twenty-one days. The Alizai won; fifty to sixty Noorzai and thirty Alizai had died. Yahya himself fled to Lashkar Gah—the provincial capital still held by communist militias—and started working with the Najibullah government.

Garmser's civil war probably cost 150 lives on both sides.[10] A year of violence and uncertainty had been piled on top of the jihad. Fortunately, the Alizai were magnanimous in victory. They did not exact vengeance.

Rather, they used tribal traditions to try to find peace. Under those traditions, seizing Noorzai land or making them subservient to the Alizai would have been a grave insult, grounds to carry on the feud. The Alizai took no land. The Noorzai tribal leaders continued to rule over their tribal areas, including Salay Mohammed who was allowed to return to Safar. Additionally, Noorzai status as Garmser's majority tribe was honored. The Noorzai were not kept out of district political decisions or denied representative seating in shuras and councils.

Nor did the Alizai demand leadership of the district. A shura of all Garmser's tribal leaders was convened over several weeks in the late autumn of 1989 to determine how the district would be governed.[11] This was the traditional and inclusive way of dealing with such a problem, the way that Ahmed Shah Durrani had been chosen as Afghanistan's first ruler in 1747. The tribal leaders decided that Garmser needed a district governor. They could have opted for each tribal leader simply to run his own territory independently, but that would have left the district vulnerable to outside intervention, which no one wanted. A district governor could work to keep the tribal leaders together for the defense of the district. Even the Alizai agreed that Nasim, or a successor warlord, should not be allowed to interfere in Garmser freely. Instead of seizing the mantle for themselves, the Alizai backed Abdullah Jan, whom they trusted to represent their interests. Ghulam Rassoul and Shah Wali Khan were especially close with him. Certain Noorzai tribal leaders, particularly the respected Said Omar, backed Abdullah Jan as well because he was Barakzai—traditional rivals of the northern Alizai—and had not aligned with Nasim in the final battle of the civil war. After some deliberation, the majority of the tribal leaders agreed that he would be fair.[12] So Abdullah Jan was elected district governor. Said Omar became the deputy district governor, further placating the Noorzai. By reverting to long-standing tribal traditions that naturally brought the Noorzai back into the fold, a workable settlement to the civil war had been pieced together.

Yahya and Nasim themselves exited the stage shortly thereafter. When President Najibullah fell in 1992, Yahya fled to Pakistan, where he was killed while praying. He outlived Nasim, who had been assassinated in March 1990 in Pakistan. Nasim's brother Mohammed Rassoul Akhundzada took his place as leader of the powerful northern Alizai. Neither Yahya nor Nasim had survived long enough to see any reward for all the violence they had caused.

CIVIL WAR

The governorship of Abdullah Jan

Upon becoming district governor in late 1989, Abdullah Jan faced no small challenge. There was much work to be done. Homes were bombed out, fields were fallow, schools were empty, clinics were shuttered. Thousands of refugees were in Pakistan and the canal system had fallen into disrepair. Every sluice gate on the main canal plus the main intake at the northern end of the district was busted. After July each year, the system dried up south of Lakari. The damage was partly thanks to Soviet bombs, partly thanks to lack of maintenance, and partly thanks to ten years without canal-clearing. A colossal flood in 1991 that would wash away the Hazar Joft bridge would not ease Abdullah Jan's burden.[13] On top of all this, Abdullah Jan had to hold together peace between the tribes at a time when civil war was raging elsewhere in Afghanistan.

Abdullah Jan started out in a weak position. He ruled at the pleasure of the tribal leaders rather than the laws of a higher government, which did not exist. The tribal leaders had not elected him in order to submit to his dictates. They wanted a moderator, not a commander-in-chief. Abdullah Jan did not have much of a staff, let alone a budget. Without a national government, there was no mechanism to appoint, let alone pay, a judge, a prosecutor, a police chief, or other standard elements of a working Afghan district. Fortunately, he did have Said Omar for advice. Abdullah Jan ruled by consensus, establishing a standing tribal council that included all the main tribal leaders. He used it to make important decisions and to help resolve disputes.

During 1990, Abdullah Jan reinforced his political position by marrying Shah Wali Khan's sister. The marriage solidified the alliance between the Alizai and Abdullah Jan. For the Alizai, it reassured them that Abdullah Jan would protect their interests. For Abdullah Jan, it legitimized his stature by connecting him, a young man from the small Barakzai tribe, to Garmser's tribal nobility (Shah Wali Khan led one of the largest landowning families in the district). Such an endorsement was no small achievement.

Recognizing the challenges of his position, Abdullah Jan delegated authority down to the tribal leaders, allowing them to govern their territory. I doubt they would have accepted his rule if he had not. Most tribal leaders still had their own guns. With only forty men of his own, Abdullah Jan could neither disarm them nor defend the district without them. The downside was that the district turned into a set of armed fiefdoms. Said Omar and Mohammed Anwar (another Noorzai khan) ran Hazar Joft; Abdul Hakim ran Majitek; Khodirom (Noorzai) ran Loya Darveshan; Baqi Khan's brother Roh Khan ran Kuchinay Darveshan; Mohammed Nadir ran Lakari; Salay Mohammed ran Safar; and Shah Wali Khan, Ghulam Rassoul, and Shah Jahan ran Laki. Abdullah Jan himself ran Koshtay, Bartaka, and Mian Poshtay. Each levied their own taxes. Anyone passing through their territory along the main roads had to pay their men. Poppy cultivation in the fiefdoms increased rapidly since poppy turned a much higher profit than wheat. From time to time the tribal leaders even seized land, forcing their decisions on people by the barrel of a gun. Immigrants who had been granted private land by Zahir Shah or Daoud were relatively safe; the tribal leaders usually respected their status as legitimate landowners. Others were not so lucky. Land seizure was not widespread but its effects were. Immigrants who had received land from Taraki or who had been leasing land during the time of Daoud feared that the tribal leaders would kick them out of their homes.

Abdullah Jan himself was not above reproach. He allowed the taxation and poppy cultivation to go on. The fact that he was trying to build up the power of the district government and pay for its expenses does not entirely excuse him. Not only did he permit the tribal leaders to seize government land, but he himself forcibly pushed out squatters in Koshtay, Bartaka, and Mian Poshtay. Abdullah Jan's ability to reach out to Garmser's immigrants, demonstrated by his formation of a diverse mujahidin cadre, was juxtaposed against a deep-seated intolerance of squatters. From his point of view, those who had been officially given land or once rented it were part of the Garmser community, regardless of their tribe. The same went for the poor Baluch living out in the desert. But those who squatted on land for free were outsiders, poachers not to be trusted. Abdullah Jan also had a penchant for harsh punishment. The innocent were left alone but the guilty, whether a rapist or simply a wayward guard, were sure to feel his wrath.

The irony was that the oppression of the tribal leaders had no immediate backlash. The district stayed peaceful. There was no peasants' revolt. Life was harsh but better than it had been during the jihad. Nor did the tribes go back to fighting each other. The different tribal leaders minded their own business. No one had much interest in upsetting the post-civil war balance. It was a hard peace, but peace nonetheless.

The wider civil war

If Garmser had found a peace of sorts, the province had not. From 1988 to 1993, civil war wracked Helmand as various communist and mujahidin warlords competed for power with each other. In 1989, when the Noorzai and Alizai civil war had ended in Garmser, Najibullah's government had not yet fallen. For over two years, well-armed communist militiamen (including Wakil Manan) held on in Gereshk and Lashkar Gah, Helmand's two major cities, commanded by Allah Noor, a communist strongman who happened to be Barakzai.[14] The rest of Helmand was divided between mujahidin warlords, with Rassoul Akhundzada in the north, brother of the deceased Nasim Akhundzada, holding the most power. The front line swayed to and fro around Lashkar Gah and Gereshk. The Najibullah government finally fell in April 1992. Burnahideen Rabbani, leader of *Jamiat Islami*, soon became the president of Afghanistan. For Garmser, little changed. Helmand, let alone the country as a whole, was hardly under Rabbani's control. Fighting in the north with *Hezb Islami* for control of Kabul, Rabbani could not enforce order in Helmand.

Shortly after President Najibullah fell, Abdullah Jan, still ostensibly at war with the remaining communists, reached out to Allah Noor, taking advantage of their common Barakzai ties to negotiate a ceasefire. It was part of a larger ploy by Abdullah Jan to keep Rassoul Akhundzada under control and build up his own power. He hoped that by lessening pressure on Lashkar Gah he could prevent Rassoul from becoming provincial governor without getting too involved in the war against him. Abdullah Jan also managed to bolster his own position in the process. As part of the deal, Allah Noor turned over hundreds of communist weapons to Abdullah Jan. At the same time as Abdullah Jan was negotiating with Allah Noor, President Rabbani endorsed Allah Noor and his allies as the government (in name only) of Helmand. Since Abdullah Jan was a member of Rabbani's party, *Jamiat Islami*, I have long suspected that he helped broker this deal.[15]

Allah Noor's guns gave Abdullah Jan military weight hitherto lacking, which he used to arm nearly 700 locally recruited tribal militia, known as 'arbekai.' Afghans in Garmser used the term 'arbekai' to describe locally recruited tribal militia who sometimes served as unofficial police.[16] For the sake of simplicity, I will refer to them as tribal militia rather than arbekai. They were made up of former mujahidin and others who had been too young to fight in the jihad. Abdullah Jan gathered Ghilzai, Noorzai, Baluch, and even a number of former communists around his banner. He placed most of them under lieutenants from his own cadre. During 1992, these lieutenants took over posts in Hazar Joft, Majitek, Amir Agha, and Benadar while also maintaining hold of Koshtay, Bartaka, and Mian Poshtay (where Abdullah Jan had always posted men). The Alizai ran their own tribal militia (their old mujahidin cadres) in their lands, as did the Noorzai in Kuchinay Darveshan and Safar. Because the tribal militias received no salary from the government, Abdullah Jan held a shura with all the elders and asked them how to purchase food. All agreed to a tax on wheat and poppy, even signing papers authorizing Abdullah Jan to implement it.

The 700 tribal militia both made Abdullah Jan the foremost power among the tribes and deterred outside warlords from attacking Garmser. The civil war finally ended in 1993 with the intervention of Ismael Khan, the great warlord of the north-western province of Herat, who together with Rassoul Akhundzada defeated Allah Noor and the former communists. Rassoul became the new provincial governor. For the most part, Abdullah Jan had managed to stay out of the conflict (he had sent merely twenty men—a pittance—as reinforcements to Allah Noor). After Allah Noor's defeat, Abdullah Jan wisely pledged allegiance to Rassoul and apologized for his support of Allah Noor, thus sparing himself the vengeance of the powerful Akhundzada family.[17] Rassoul and Abdullah Jan came to work together amicably. Formal apologies have a powerful effect in Pashtun society. Abdullah Jan's diplomacy had kept Garmser safe and independent.

On balance, between 1989 and 1994, the situation in Garmser had improved. Between his efforts to keep consensus among the tribes, his formation of his tribal militia, and his diplomacy in the province-wide civil war, Abdullah Jan had given Garmser some breathing space. Whatever the oppression of his tenure, no one ever rose up; no one ever turned to outside powers for help. As violence subsided, life returned to normal. Refugees slowly made their way back from Pakistan. From 1989 to 1994, 62 percent of the population returned to Garmser, compared to the jihad when only 27 percent of the population had lived there.[18] By 1991, over 80 percent of the irrigable land was being farmed. Poppy cultivation, even though nothing was done to control it, stayed fairly low.[19] The main crops were corn and wheat, but some grapes and cotton were cultivated as well. Once Rassoul Akhundzada took power in 1993, Lashkar Gah began buying cotton from farmers again and exporting it. Makeshift repairs to the Hazar Joft bridge helped such trade.

In terms of Garmser's longer history, the civil war and its aftermath show the pains of adapting to a government-less state. While life slowly improved, society drifted apart. Tribal leaders established their own territories and stepped up their mistreatment of the district's immigrants, deepening the existing rift between the two groups. The tribal leaders themselves were hardly one. The tribal system that took the government's place was inherently unstable. The tribal leaders had no hierarchy. Thus they were prone to competing and even fighting with one another, like great powers on the world stage. The civil war that followed the jihad is little different from the competition between the Soviet Union and the United States that followed the Second World War: one-time allies turned against each other once the common enemy disappeared. At the same time, tribal traditions, like a well-crafted treaty, could bring peace. But doing so took complicated maneuvering—akin to the diplomatic orchestra of the Congress of Vienna. There was no guarantee that tribal leaders would always work together, a truth that would soon be demonstrated once more. Abdullah Jan's peace would be short-lived. A new threat was forming to the east that independent-minded tribal leaders alone could not defeat.

4

THE TALIBAN REGIME

Ala bla ba grdun mullah.
'Now the responsibility is on the mullah's shoulders.'
Pashto proverb[1]

The Taliban movement did not start in Helmand, let alone Garmser. It started in Kandahar, Helmand's larger, more influential, neighbor. War-lords had divided the province into their own competing spheres of influence and had gone about oppressing the people. Their atrocities outraged a group of madrasa-trained former mujahidin. Calling them-selves 'Taliban'—meaning students of Islam—in 1994 they decided to restore order and implement shari'a (Islamic law) throughout Afghan-istan. Abdul Salam Zaeef, the future Taliban ambassador to Pakistan, who was present when the movement was created, wrote in his memoir: 'The shari'a would be our guiding law and would be implemented by us. We would prosecute vice and foster virtue, and would stop those who were bleeding the land.'[2] They chose the one-eyed Mullah Mohammed Omar, who was running a madrasa in Kandahar, to be their leader. Like many Taliban, he had ties to Uruzgan province and his tribe, the Hotak, was from the Ghilzai tribal confederation, traditional rivals of the Durrani ruling class.[3] Successful skirmishes with mujahidin warlords won Mullah Omar notoriety and Pakistani funding. Thanks to a combination of boldness, morality, diplomacy, and Pakistani support, in November 1994 the Taliban captured Kandahar city, the heart of southern Afghanistan. Thousands of young madrasa-trained Afghans flocked out of Pakistan to their colors. These new Taliban foot soldiers had largely grown up in Pakistan as refugees. They had little fighting experience, but they gave the movement great weight in numbers.[4] Kandahar was firmly in the Taliban's grip and the movement was looking outward for its next targets.

In December 1994, roughly 500 Taliban marched on Helmand. Governor Rassoul Akhundzada had died of cancer. His brother, Abdul Ghafar Akhundzada, was now governor of Helmand province. Helmand should have been able to resist. Between the Akhundzadas and the other warlords, at least 3,000 experienced former mujahidin were available, enough to stop the Taliban at the strategic crossroads at Gereshk. A popular story in the West is that the oppressed of Afghanistan rose up against the warlords and in support of the Taliban. That story rings true in Kandahar but not in Helmand. There was no indigenous Taliban movement to sap the warlords' strength. Few sympathetic disturbances broke out. People in Garmser were aware of the changes afoot in neighboring Kandahar, and a few commended it, but no internal challenge emerged to Abdullah Jan or the tribal leaders. Defending Helmand was simply a matter of the warlords and tribal leaders uniting against the Taliban. Alas, Governor Abdul Ghafar decided not to fight. He believed his family, with its religious roots, could work with the Taliban. That decision essentially opened the door. Mullah Omar led his men into Lashkar Gah. The other remaining warlords, unsure whether to fight or comply, met with him. They knew that without the Akhundzadas any opposition to the Taliban would be hard-pressed. Mullah Omar demanded that the warlords turn over their weapons. Abdullah Jan, who was present, refused to make a decision and went back to Garmser to confer with the tribal leaders. Helmand's other major warlords—Amir Dad Mohammed from Sangin in northern Helmand and Abdur Rahman Jan from Marjah in western Helmand—fled from the province with their men and their guns. Abdullah Jan and Garmser were quite alone.[5]

Once back in Garmser, Abdullah Jan called together a shura of all Garmser's tribal leaders and asked them what they wanted to do. Half wanted to fight, including Mohammed Nadir and Shah Wali Khan, leaders of the Alizai. Two wanted to join the Taliban and promote their cause: Tooriali, the capable son of Roh Khan (the great Noorzai landowner of

Kuchinay Darveshan), and Abdul Hakim (leader of the Taraki immigrants of Majitek and eastern Loya Darveshan), who, being a religious scholar and a Ghilzai, knew Mullah Omar and appreciated his Islamic program. The remainder had no love for the Taliban but were tired of fighting and did not want to carry on alone. In the opinion of a few, the Kabul government was broken, the Helmand governor worked for himself, and the district received nothing from either.[6] Without the clear support of the tribal leaders, Abdullah Jan decided he was in no position to fight and that he had to turn the district over to the Taliban.[7]

After the shura, the Taliban advance party—just ten men—arrived in Garmser, led by a Taliban leader named Akhundzada Lala (no relation to the Akhundzada family of the Alizai). Abdullah Jan, Mohammed Nadir, Salay Mohammed, and Shah Wali Khan met them at the district center and conveyed their decision. Lala ordered them to bring all the tribal leaders to the district center to surrender their weapons. The four promised to do so and then—as Abdullah Jan and Shah Wali Khan proudly told me fifteen years later—promptly left Garmser with their weapons. They took refuge in Girdi Jangal, just across the border in Pakistan.

To the north, Abdul Ghafar Akhundzada realized that he had made a strategic error. He was not able to reach a compromise with the Taliban. Rather than surrender, he led the northern Alizai to war. Abdur Rahman Jan of Marjah and Abdullah Jan joined him. Abdullah Jan and his fighters together with Ghulam Rassoul and a cadre of Alizai assaulted the border town of Baram Chah, a growing hub for smuggling and poppy. With a force of 300, he captured the town, held by only a few Taliban pickets. Meanwhile, Abdul Ghafar won several battles around Musa Qala. Abdul Ghafar, Abdur Rahman Jan, and Abdullah Jan were giving the Taliban their toughest fight yet, but Abdul Ghafar's procrastination cost them. The chance to unite all of Helmand's forces together in a strategic position at Gereshk had been lost. Now, fighting in the north, Abdul Ghafar was separate from Abdur Rahman Jan fighting in the west around Marjah, and Abdullah Jan fighting in the south. The Taliban picked them off one by one. They concentrated superior numbers against Abdul Ghafar in the north, forcing him to retreat to Herat in January 1995. Abdur Rahman Jan then withdrew to Iran. About a month later, 400–500 Taliban launched a well-orchestrated surprise attack against Baram Chah and pushed out Abdullah Jan. Abdullah Jan lost seventy-two men in the fighting. He and his fighters went to Herat to fight the

Taliban with Ismael Khan. Later in the year, they accompanied Ismael Khan on his offensive that briefly captured Gereshk but was ultimately defeated. After Herat fell in September 1995, Abdullah Jan and his men joined Ahmed Shah Massoud far to the north in Panjshir.[8]

Thus the Taliban captured Garmser and all Helmand. Their success had little to do with the oppression of the warlords and tribal leaders or the appeal of Islamic law. In Garmser, the Taliban had received minimal assistance from the poor and downtrodden. The Taliban had succeeded because the tribal leaders and warlords had failed to ally together. With neither a common enemy nor the unifying ideology of jihad, the territorial and divided nature of the tribal system, upon which even warlords such as the Akhundzadas depended for power, was ill-suited to establishing order. The fractures endemic to the tribal system are easy to see in Garmser's fiefdoms and the split over whether to go on alone against the Taliban. The same can be seen in Helmand as a whole. Warlords and tribal leaders were too concerned with their own interests to unite together. It had taken almost five years for the Akhundzadas to defeat Allah Noor and the former communists, partly because other mujahidin factions, such as Abdullah Jan, went their own way. Then, when the Taliban arrived, the Akhundzadas themselves went their own way. If the warlords had banded together when Mullah Omar had first entered Helmand in 1994, if Abdul Ghafar had not miscalculated the chances of compromise, then the Taliban would have been hard-pressed to capture the province. Abdullah Jan later said: 'If the great tribal leaders and warlords had stood together at Gereshk, we easily could have defeated the Taliban and defended Helmand.'[9] Lack of unity and political cohesion had ushered the Taliban into power.

Taliban government

The Taliban held uncontested sway over Garmser for nearly seven years, from the beginning of 1995 until the end of 2001. Out of fear or outright support, every home flew the white Taliban flag. Mohammed Nabi, Abdullah Jan's fierce lieutenant who stayed in Garmser through the Taliban regime, explained: 'It is the law of Afghanistan that when someone takes over by force, the people do not stand against him.'[10] Harsh interpretation of Islamic law, oppression of women, executions, and stonings have draped the Taliban in infamy in the West. Their reputation in Garmser is not so malevolent. The assessment of Richard Scott,

56

an American engineer working with Mercy Corps (a humanitarian non-government organization) at the time, is telling:

'The Taliban in Helmand are not trained administrators nor [sic] technical people but they are intelligent, honest, serious and work hard to see that the role of government is accomplished as they see it. They are open to suggestions that will help their administration and the people. They appear to be strict in their administration but they are also subject to political pressures from the local populations that support them. They did not appear to be at all xenophobic in our many discussions on the many issues covered but they had a clear understanding that MCI [Mercy Corps International] was there to help.'[11]

If far from what Afghans consider good government, Taliban rule in Garmser was bearable, marked by few of the atrocities witnessed elsewhere. What is impressive is how the Taliban went from being a government imposed on Garmser from the outside to a local movement. Upon arrival, they had only a handful of supporters. Upon departure, nearly seven years later, they left behind a dedicated movement. Today hundreds, if not thousands, still support them. The Taliban regime was a turning point for Garmser. The changes they made re-ordered society and would fuel later conflict. Those changes define much of Garmser today.

When they took over Garmser, the Taliban were just a few mullahs and scholars from Ghilzai and other poorer tribes, backed up by cadres of armed men. A few were Garmser refugees. Many were from Pakistan, Kandahar, and elsewhere in Helmand. Garmser's religious leaders had not spontaneously mobilized behind them and only one tribe—the Taraki—immediately sided with them. The four key Taliban leaders were Akhundzada Lala, Maulawi Abdul Hakim, Mullah Abdul Majan, and Mullah Naim Barech.

Akhundzada Lala was the district governor, responsible for all military and civil affairs. Mullah Omar appointed him personally. He was from Marjah and ruled until late 1997.[12] He was responsible not only for Garmser but Musa Qala, Khaneshin, and Dishu districts too; in other words, all the way south from Hazar Joft to the border with Pakistan and all the way west to the border with Nimroz. Why he was given Musa Qala far to the north is unknown, an oddity of Taliban administration. Lala set up his headquarters in an orphanage by the Hazar Joft hospital. He gained a reputation for letting his men harass civilians and for meting out harsh punishments.

Maulawi Abdul Hakim, the mujahidin commander, Taraki tribal leader, and religious scholar from Majitek, became District Governor

Lala's deputy, responsible for civilian affairs. He was in his late forties at this time. Lala trusted him. Upon the Taliban arrival in the district, Abdul Hakim put all his armed men at their service. Partly for this reason and partly because he was from Garmser, Lala listened to his advice on how to run the district. Abdul Hakim worked out of the old government building. One of a handful of Garmser leaders to give immediate support to the Taliban and to hold a position in their government, he was considered less abusive than Lala. Another mullah served as his assistant—Mullah Abdul Majan. Perhaps twenty years old, Abdul Majan had been studying under Abdul Hakim. He was also from the immigrant Taraki tribe and lived in Majitek. He soon earned a reputation as a thoughtful leader. He respected the elders and forswore the harsh punishments of other Taliban leaders. Years later, when Taliban fighters captured an elder from Hazar Joft and intended to execute him for his lack of support, Abdul Majan interceded and forced them to release the elder.[13] A force of forty fighters protected Abdul Hakim and Abdul Majan. The two worked for two years in Garmser before being promoted and sent to Uruzgan: Abdul Hakim as the governor; Abdul Majan as his deputy.

Mullah Naim Barech was the most famous Taliban leader in Garmser. He would gain a great deal of power and eventually become Taliban governor of Helmand. Naim was not really Barech. People called him that out of respect. The Barech are a mysterious Pashtun tribe that had lived in the old Ghaznavid fortresses around Lashkar Gah 500 years ago and had won great victories in India.[14] Naim was actually from the Tarin tribe, a poorer tribe related to the Kakar. His family had come to Garmser from Pakistan at the turn of the century. Naim's father, a mullah, had worked in Laki until the jihad, when the family fled to Pakistan. Naim studied in a madrasa there. He was in his late twenties in 1994 when he returned to Afghanistan to join the Taliban in Kandahar. Mullah Omar befriended him. A cadre of thirty men formed under his command. It later grew to 200. Accompanying the Taliban offensive into Helmand in 1994, upon Garmser's surrender Naim set up a military command center in Laki for a short while before being sent to Kandahar as Mullah Omar's minister of aviation. He left at least fifty fighters in Laki to protect his home there and prevent the Alizai from causing problems. Greatly trusted, Mullah Omar eventually sent Naim north to command units at the front.[15] He was wounded once fighting there. From time to time he came back to Garmser, where his rising star gave him tremendous influence. In the words of the keeper of the Amir Agha shrine, 'Naim was a good man. He was not oppressive. He tried to help the country.'[16]

The Taliban arrived in Garmser with a degree of moral authority because their leadership was made up of mullahs and scholars. Religious leaders had always been respected as teachers and sources of knowledge. They had not played a large role in politics, other than calling people to arms during the jihad. Many people believed religious leaders were a reasonable alternative to the harsh rule of the tribal leaders; they appeared to be fair arbiters and unconcerned with personal power. This helped the Taliban avoid friction with the local population as they set themselves up.[17]

The Taliban government was structured differently from that of Zahir Shah or Abdullah Jan. They did not rely on the tribes, as King Zahir Shah had done and in whose footsteps Abdullah Jan, with far fewer resources, had followed. Mullah Omar held near-absolute power. He set up a centralized hierarchy so that there would be no independent leaders with separate sources of power and no question of who was in charge in any province or district. Gone were the tribal fiefdoms, replaced by a religious command structure. In Garmser, the district governor, Lala, was in charge. Unlike tribal leaders, he did not have to make decisions by consensus. All officials answered to him, he to Lashkar Gah, and thence to Mullah Omar in Kandahar, the Taliban capital (after Kabul fell in 1996 and became the official capital, the key Taliban leaders remained in Kandahar). No autonomous Taliban leaders existed. Even someone as powerful as Mullah Naim answered strictly to Mullah Omar, who gave him responsibilities that lay outisde Garmser. Naim was not competing for power in Garmser with Lala, Abdul Hakim, or anyone else. There was no such thing as a Taliban warlord.

Maulawi Mohuddin Baluch was a high-ranking religious scholar who later served on the religious council for all Afghanistan. His family was originally from Garmser but had moved to Kabul before the reign of King Zahir Shah. His brother was a Taliban. When asked why government leaders so often fought with each other while the Taliban did not, he replied: 'Government leaders fight with each other because there are so many factions and parties. The Taliban are very organized. There is one party. They are not divided into sections. The Taliban are unified. They have one leader.'[18]

Mullah Omar chose his ministers, provincial governors, and district governors himself and could remove them at will. They were appointed first on the basis of ties to the movement and second on the basis of merit. No one could buy their office. The same was true of lower-level cadre leaders and judges. Dedication to Islam and religious and tribal (Ghilzai) connections to the Taliban leadership mattered. Mullahs who had gone to madrasa with senior Taliban leaders or fought with them in the jihad—mullahs who could be trusted to be loyal—were likely to be chosen.[19] Because of their beliefs or tribal ties, many educated people were kept out of leadership positions. As time passed and the experiences of the movement widened, merit, especially administrative and combat performance, played a greater role in leadership selection. Poor performers were weeded out. Better ones, who could be trusted to be loyal, were promoted.

In terms of quality of individual leadership, the Taliban system was slightly worse than the tribal system. Under the tribal system, tribal leaders, as well as mujahidin cadre leaders, had been chosen on the basis of stature and merit: usually the most capable political or military leader from the leading family. Because of the education and experience of these families, having routinely led large numbers of people and filled government jobs, the tribal system had tended to select from a set of higher quality leaders than the Taliban system. In contrast, the mullahs and fighters loyal to the Taliban were often poor, uneducated, and unfamiliar with handling large-scale organizations and administration. It is hard to argue that, one for one, Naim, Lala, or even Abdul Hakim were better than Abdullah Jan, Said Omar, Ghulam Rassoul, or Shah Jahan. The emphasis on loyalty, however, helped the Taliban instill discipline and centralize their structure, which turned out to be more important than the quality of individual leaders.

The Islamic nature of the regime reinforced centralization. Islam stresses oneness and unity. In many ways, it is the natural antithesis of tribalism, with all its divisions. Indeed, it has often been a means of overcoming tribal divisions in both Arab and Pashtun societies. By placing Islam over tribalism, the Taliban were effectively placing oneness over division. Equally important was that low-level commanders did not want to disobey their superiors. In their minds, doing so might have been un-Islamic or even sinful. Mullah Dadullah Lang, revered as the best frontline commander in the wars in the north, had been known to lay down his arms on Mullah Omar's order. Such examples of the moral authority of Mullah Omar and other-ranking Taliban religious leaders had a strong effect on the average cadre leader and fighter.[20] The upshot of all this was that the Taliban were far more united than the tribal leaders or old government had ever been. Between hierarchical structure, the emphasis on loyalty, Islam, and the respect that low-level Taliban held for their leaders, the Taliban were less prone to fighting with each other and were thus better able to enforce their will over the people.

The Taliban district government was sparsely staffed. But between Lala as district governor, Abdul Hakim as deputy, and Abdul Majan as assistant deputy, it was no worse off than Abdullah Jan's had been. There was no clear delineation of duties other than that Lala looked after security matters and was in charge. All three resolved disputes, managed land ownership, oversaw taxes, and encouraged poppy cultivation. They were further augmented by a religious court that tried criminals and also resolved disputes. Maulawi Mohammed Shah from Koshtay sat as the judge on the court. He had several assistants. A cruel man, in the words of Khodirom, a Noorzai tribal leader, 'he made decisions quickly and killed people without due process.'[21]

For security, three entities fell under Lala. A thirty-man force, akin to normal police, kept order and enforced the stringent laws. Another smaller force collected certain taxes. A third, especially despised, force conscripted men to go fight against the mujahidin warlords still defending the north (later known as the Northern Alliance).[22] Besides these entities, the robust personal retinues of Abdul Hakim, Abdul Majan, Naim and a handful of other mullahs—totaling at least 200 men in all—made sure Garmser stayed docile.

It is nearly impossible to find an Afghan in Garmser who does not believe that the Taliban curtailed crime and violence. Doing so gave them credibility. One teacher, a former communist official, said: 'Before the Taliban, the situation was not good. Everyone had weapons on themselves. There were many thieves. People accepted the Taliban because they provided security…There was no more thievery.'[23] According to Baz Mohammed, a tribal leader of the immigrant Kharoti tribe: 'Taliban rule was brutal but the people were safe. The government has never been able to do the same.'[24] Justice was indeed harsh. Under Zahir Shah, Islamic law had been respected. The government recognized it as one source of law. Religious scholars could turn to it to resolve local disputes without government interference. Judges could use it at their discretion. Under the Taliban, there was only Islamic law. And a harsh interpretation it was. Lala was ruthless. Beards were mandatory, music was forbidden, punishments for crime were severe, and strict obedience to the tenets of Islam was enforced. Those found guilty of small crimes had their faces blackened, were put on the back of a donkey, and were pulled through the bazaar. For worse crimes, they lost their hands or were executed.[25] In short order, the tough penalties of Islamic law—a hand for thievery and a head for murder—deterred crime. Dr Salam, an Alizai elder greatly impressed by the Taliban's effectiveness, told me: 'Executions and cutting off hands frightened people from being criminals.'[26]

The Taliban regime was quite strict in its treatment of women— though I never saw evidence of stonings or the horrors of elsewhere in Afghanistan. Women were instructed to leave the home rarely and when they did to be fully covered. They were to play no role in open society. To be honest, women in Garmser had been treated poorly in the first place and would continue to be after the Taliban left. Under Pashtun tradition, not just Taliban edict, women were to be covered and stay in the village. This is probably why I heard few complaints about how the Taliban had treated women. In all our patrols and daily meetings, the only place we regularly saw women was the clinic, clustered outside its front gate, covered from head to toe, waiting for care. Otherwise, women were seen in glimpses—draped and huddled in the back seat of a car, behind closed doors at the government center when a particularly grievous injustice demanded attention or rushing unexpectedly out of a home enraged when a husband was being detained. Locals recognized that the Taliban were tough on women; they forbade them from moving about their own villages freely and curtailed education, two freedoms Pashtun men had countenanced. Overall, however, Taliban oppression was just a gradation in the general Pashtun oppression of women.

With the dissolution of the tribal fiefdoms, District Governor Lala got rid of all the checkpoints on the roads that had taxed passers-by, at least until his superiors in Kandahar discovered they needed greater revenues, particularly for the war in the north. When that happened (in late 1995), Lala taxed the villages directly, delegating authority to every village mullah to collect taxes for him in addition to the zerkat (donations from the community) they were collecting for themselves. Soon Taliban taxes outstripped anything Abdullah Jan and the tribal leaders had taken.

To raise further revenue, Lala promoted poppy cultivation.[27] Production skyrocketed and poppy rapidly displaced wheat as Garmser's primary crop. It was shipped out to Pakistan for processing via Baram Chah, which itself exploded with new shops and homes, becoming the thoroughfare of the Helmand poppy trade. Of course, poppy, and its substantial profits hardly upset the people of Garmser. Indeed, those profits probably offset anger over taxes and the tiring war in the north.

Taliban reforms

More effectively than anyone since King Zahir Shah and Daoud, the Taliban rearranged Garmser's social structure. They marginalized the tribes and uplifted the mullahs and the poor farmers; all to build popular support. Between the mid-1950s and the mid-1970s, Zahir Shah and Daoud had built the canals and introduced the naqilen immigrants, weakening the hegemony of the tribal leaders. But after that, in spite of the communists' best efforts, the tribal leaders had ruled over society. The religious leaders, immigrants, and poor had, for the most part, stayed behind them, although the civil war and its aftermath had undoubtedly weakened those bonds. The Taliban broke the bonds in two. The changes were drastic and lasting.

In order to enforce their will over the people, the Taliban disempowered the tribal elite. The tribes had already been weakened by the flight of many tribal leaders and their men to Pakistan. Besides Abdullah Jan and the Alizai, Said Omar and Salay Mohammed had also left for Pakistan. District Governor Lala disarmed the remaining tribal leaders, except Abdul Hakim, and, as noted above, revoked their authority over their territory, their fiefdoms. Those who could not be trusted were sent to jail in Kandahar, including former communist Wakil Manan and former mujahidin cadre leader Khodirom. The Taliban could not catch Shah Wali Khan so Lala imprisoned his brother instead. Conditions in prison were harsh: eighty-two people died there. No Garmser elders were ever executed but, to make the point, Lala and judge Maulawi Mohammed Shah hanged a number of former mujahidin fighters.[28] Lala kept a rump tribal council, which helped resolve tribal problems. Every few months it convened, largely composed of immigrant tribal leaders and lesser village elders. A very informal body, the council had no budget and little authority.

The Taliban lifted the religious leaders into the place of the tribal leaders—a policy they enacted throughout Afghanistan. Most of Garmser's mullahs had departed Garmser either before or at the start of the jihad. A few had returned under Abdullah Jan. As a means of spreading their own influence, the Taliban imported new mullahs from outside Garmser, particularly from Uruzgan and Quetta.[29] These mullahs were young and tended to have been educated in madrasas in Pakistan. Their interpretation of Islam differed from that of the old scholars of Zahir Shah's time.[30] The old religious scholars had been heavily influenced by the Deobandi school of Islamic thought that was taught in India, where many had trained. At that time, it was a fairly open-minded school of thought. It did not explicitly endorse killing or prohibition of music and secular schools. Over the course of the jihad and later during the war against the United States, it became radicalized. The new younger mullahs out of Pakistan trained in this less open-minded version that justified jihad and harsh laws.[31] Education in Pakistan was cursory, further encouraging a one-sided view of Islam. During the jihad, the mujahidin parties, such as *Hezb Islami*, had provided education up to the twelfth grade in refugee camps. When the jihad ended, so did these schools. Several camps managed to organize education to the sixth grade on their own, but teenagers had to go elsewhere for schooling beyond that. Pakistani high schools were tough to enter and Garmser's own schools were far away so they often went to Pakistani madrasas, which were free. Many graduated as mullahs.[32] The new young mullahs became heavily involved in politics (something else the old scholars had eschewed) and called for jihad against Massoud and Rabbani in the north.[33] Countenancing jihad against fellow Muslims was a huge shift from the teachings of the past. In the coming years, these mullahs would readily label anyone working with non-Muslims as infidels and endorse killing them.

Garmser's own religious leaders finally returned in large numbers from Pakistan between 1995 and 1997, encouraged by the security and religious reforms enacted by the Taliban. Their nature had changed. Most of the old scholars had died or were now too old to lead. Younger mullahs dominated. A few had been well educated in Pakistan. Many had not. Rather than religious knowledge, many won influence by carrying a gun. In time, Garmser mullahs came to play a large role in the Taliban movement, greater than that of the Pakistani imports. Numerous young mullahs became cadre commanders, a few fighting for Mullah Naim in the north. It was hard for any, whether old or young, whether educated or uneducated, to be unswayed by the Taliban.

Islam blossomed under the Taliban. Adherence to its fundamental tenets had never been and would never again be so strong. The Taliban instituted and enforced Islamic law, forced the people to pay zerkat (alms), and opened madrasas for thousands of children. Friday prayers in the district center were packed; mobs thronged outside the mosque to pray. During Ramadan, no one broke the fast. The mullahs themselves were endowed with great authority. I have already mentioned that certain mullahs had armed men, that village mullahs were responsible for collecting taxes, and that a religious court was established. This was not all. A religious council of thirty or so mullahs was set up to discuss pertinent political issues. Furthermore, the mullahs were empowered to run the villages of Garmser—the Taliban version of administrative infrastructure. In addition to collecting taxes, they monitored all activities and enforced obedience with the regime's decisions. Transgressions were reported to the district government. Every mullah was expected to resolve disputes in his village, in effect becoming the village judge, supplanting the elders' traditional role in dispute resolution. Lala and Abdul Hakim delegated many problems to either the religious court or the mullahs themselves for resolution. Mullahs were even permitted to ask for a small payment in return for services. The remaining elders were not forbidden from resolving disputes but the mullahs effectively crowded them out.[34] Finally, the mullahs were given greater influence over education. All schools became madrasas. So did the old agricultural college, where twelve mullahs taught 500 students. A total of twenty-five madrasas were opened. Large ones were built in Laki, Lakari, and Majitek. The curriculum focused on basic reading, basic writing, and above all Islam. Secondary-level education did not exist. Most of the teachers were mullahs, although a few old secular teachers were permitted to stay and teach math. In all, 10,000 students attended the madrasas. Girls were forbidden from going to school.

All this suited Garmser's religious leaders, both new and old. The majority of Garmser's old mullahs told the people to support the Taliban. They derided the governments of Rassoul Akhundzada and Abdullah Jan for taxing and oppressing the people. Their arguments helped win the Taliban greater support.[35] Dissenting opinions were rare.

The majority in favor of the Taliban encouraged those with different opinions to keep those opinions to themselves. No longer simply leading prayers or giving religious lessons, the mullahs now served as political leaders for all society. Maulawi Abdullah Jan, one of the district's most educated religious leaders today, told me: 'The Taliban government was better than Karzai's. It was better for Islam. It was better for human rights. It was better for the people.'[36]

In the mullahs, the Taliban established one important base of popular support. In the immigrants, particularly the poor and landless, they established another. District Governor Lala and Deputy District Governor Abdul Hakim did so by first reaching out to the blocks of Ghilzai and poorer immigrant tribes living on the edges of the canal zone: the Taraki, Kharoti, and Kakar in the east, and the Andar in the south. Abdul Hakim was himself Taraki, of course, and most of the other Taliban leaders were also from Ghilzai tribes. Those who had sat out the jihad in Pakistan returned to Garmser to work with the Taliban. The landed tribal leaders had not been kind to these immigrant tribes, either because they saw them as Ghilzai (traditional political opponents) or as squatters illegally poaching land that had once been theirs. Common Ghilzai identity or memories of abuse at the hands of the landed tribal leaders inclined immigrant leaders to help the Taliban. According to one elder, a former official who had no love for the government, 'People decided to join the Taliban because there had been no security and no help from the mujahidin. There had been only robbery and insecurity.'[37] Lala and Abdul Hakim plumbed immigrant dissatisfaction. They gave them permission to keep their government land and respected their elders. With a few exceptions, namely the non-Pashtun Hazaras, Tajiks, and Uzbeks, the Taliban garnered the support of the immigrants.

The Taliban further broadened their support by bringing in a new wave of poor and landless immigrants. The immigrants came from Uruzgan and other areas strongly supportive of the Taliban. Many had tribal connections to Taliban leadership. As deputy district governor for civilian affairs, Abdul Hakim oversaw much of this process, giving away government land to incoming immigrants. To a lesser extent, he also gave away tribal leaders' private lands. He took special vengeance on his Noorzai foes of the civil war. That blood-letting had not been forgotten. A few lost more than half their holdings. Many of the immigrants that Abdul Hakim brought in were his own Taraki tribesmen. They moved into Majitek and eastern Darveshan, along the eastern edge of the canal zone. Over 200 new homes were constructed. Large numbers of families from various Ghilzai tribes also came from Deh-a-Rud district in Uruzgan and settled in Lakari and Mian Poshtay. A total area of 80 hectares was given away in Mian Poshtay. In Laki, scores of Naim's own Tarin tribe moved into the villages surrounding his home.[38] The process continued after Abdul Hakim left for Uruzgan in 1997. Qari Mohammed Nabi, Garmser's last Taliban district governor (Akhundzada Lala moved on in 1997), was still giving away private and government lands to immigrants in 2000 and 2001.

Thus the Taliban changed Garmser and built themselves a support base among the mullahs and the immigrants; partly by their own construction—the mass import of mullahs from Pakistan and poor farmers from Uruzgan and elsewhere; partly by giving Garmser's existing mullahs and poor farmers a stake in the Taliban regime. The effect was the same: loyal support. These new bonds would prove tough to break, as would re-uniting Garmser society. Taliban success, after all, had only come by dividing the religious leaders and the immigrants from the landed tribes.

Latter years of Taliban rule

The Taliban established a degree of order in Helmand that the tribal leaders and warlords had never been able to achieve. As their rule progressed, the luster rubbed off. Although the religious leaders and the immigrants were still better off than they had been in the past, the war in the north, low economic growth, and the harshness of Taliban rule wore on the general population, forming a new kind of oppression.

Throughout the Taliban regime, long after Kabul fell in 1996, war persisted in the north against Ahmed Shah Massoud and other northern mujahidin commanders. The Taliban always needed men to fill the ranks on the front-line. In 1995, District Governor Lala brought in all the elders and ordered them to give up men to go north and fight. Many did and many did not, but no one really wanted to send anyone. The people of Garmser wanted to be left alone. The Taliban were forced to conscript by the barrel of a gun, setting up the aforementioned recruitment police. They went to villages to pick up selected men and punish elders who did not have their appointed allotment ready to go. Roh Khan's whole village in Kuchinay Darveshan was imprisoned for refusing to submit to conscription, including his son, Tooriali, the same who months earlier had spoken out in favor of the Taliban. Year after year, Taliban police demanded new crops of young men to be sent off untrained and ill-equipped to the faraway northern front. Morale was rotten. Countless Garmser recruits deserted on the road northward and fled to Pakistan. No other policy cost the Taliban so much popular support.

While they won over parts of society, the Taliban never enjoyed overwhelming popular support. Teachers, doctors, and other officials, let alone former communists, were not exactly enamored. Unsurprisingly, the Taliban had few backers in Noorzai and Alizai lands. Those tribes there were too cohesive, too strong, too tribal. As a one-time government official who had no love for the mujahidin pointed out to me, 'The Taliban won little influence in Laki because the tribe there is so strong.'[39] According to Baba, the former communist policeman who lived through the Taliban years in Loya Darveshan, Taliban mistreatment did not help: 'The Taliban had no respect for the elders. Over time all the elders grew tired of them.'[40]

The latter years of Taliban rule saw a few half-hearted attempts at economic reconstruction. A clinic was built in Laki. In 1998, the Taliban allowed Mercy Corps to fully repair the Hazar Joft bridge across the Helmand. In 1999 and 2000, Saudi entrepreneurs tried to set up a mine, with an airstrip, in the far desert south of the district to extract a precious gem known as zemaroot (it was never completed). In general, however, economic development was lackluster. Baba told me: 'The Taliban did little to help the people. They did nothing to build Garmser. Nothing like the Americans have done.'[41] The mullahs running the government in Lashkar Gah did not know how to get goods to outside markets, repair damaged infrastructure, or keep the canal system running. Farmers became more and more dependent on poppy profits, which themselves ended in 2000 when the Taliban banned its cultivation, deciding it un-Islamic.[42] Unsurprisingly, punishment was so severe that no one dared grow it. Government goods and services also left much to be desired. Healthcare was scarce; the main clinic in the district center never re-opened. Education was little better; no intermediate or high school education followed up the basic reading, writing, and math offered by madrasas.[43] Meanwhile, the people heard that Arabs were gaining influence within Afghanistan and did not care for it.

By 2000, Afghanistan had been continuously at war for over twenty years. Governments had come and gone without the prosperity of bygone years. For a decade, Garmser had escaped the worst of it. Governing with a firm hand, the Taliban regime had brought order, both inside and outside Garmser, something the communists had lost and Abdullah Jan had barely balanced. They had created a dedicated movement. But, like the tribal leaders, they had failed to win over all society. Order came at the cost of marginalizing the old landed tribes. Economic backwardness and the never-ending war to the north exhausted many others. On the eve of 2001, the Taliban found themselves in the same position as the tribal leaders seven years before. Most people were too tired to pick up arms and fight rather than simply accept a new government.[44]

The impact of the Taliban regime

Taliban reforms were a major turning point for Garmser. The religious leaders and immigrants had never before been raised over the tribal leaders and given charge over the villages. They now looked to the Taliban as their benefactors. They would not easily revert to supporting a secular government, let alone tribal leaders. These changes would play a defining role in future conflict in Garmser. They remain defining to this day.

In spite of its many shortcomings, Taliban government was effective. Violence within Garmser was held down and law and order prevailed. For those today who claim that Afghanistan is ungovernable, Taliban rule offers a striking counter-example. This finding clashes with the standard narrative of Taliban rule, which paints them as brutally oppressive, narrow-minded, and backward when it came to the nuts and bolts of running a state. The Taliban were indeed many of these things, oppressive foremost among them. But they had a penchant for discipline. Unlike the tribal leaders, they seldom fought with each other and instead accepted a hierarchy. Discipline gave them the power to reorder society successfully and keep it mobilized for seven years of war in the north. It allowed them to enforce harsh punishments and prevent opponents, such as the tribal leaders, from pushing them out of power. If their regime had survived, peace probably would have persisted, if of an impoverished sort for the people of Garmser. Put simply, the Taliban could govern the 'ungovernable' land.

This begs whether the United States should have invaded Afghanistan in the first place; perhaps if the United States had put more effort into negotiating with the Taliban and convincing them to give up Osama bin Laden and al-Qaeda, intervention could have been avoided and a decade of conflict along with it. The United States never would have become bogged down in Afghanistan and the Afghan people might have been spared another decade of war. It is beyond the scope of this book to assess whether the US decision to topple the Taliban was wise. From Garmser, I was in no position to judge whether Mullah Omar and the other Taliban leaders would have accepted a deal to give up Osama bin Laden in return for remaining in power. My opinion is that, although attractive in retrospect, such a deal may not have been feasible at the time. For one, the Taliban would have been loath to curry the dishonor of surrendering a guest. Moreover, their commanders had helped defeat the Soviets and had pressed the Northern Alliance into the northern corners of Afghanistan. For them, defeating the United States was a reasonable proposition. Under these conditions, as well as the calls of the American people for action after 11 September, it is difficult to see how an agreement would have been possible. Today, a benevolent Taliban regime, bereft of al-Qaeda and accepted by the international community, sounds quite appealing. In 2001, neither side wanted to get there. Hence the United States and its Allies sent forces into Afghanistan, and Garmser was once again set upon a new course.

5

VICTORY INTO DEFEAT

Tse che kree, hagha ba rebee.
'What is sowed will be reaped.'
Pashto proverb

In October 2001, the United States invaded Afghanistan and, together with the Northern Alliance, overthrew the Taliban. Victory and the birth of a new government under Hamid Karzai brought forth hope that peace and prosperity would come to Afghanistan at last. America and the Northern Alliance appeared all-powerful; the Taliban broken and defeated. The world's great powers devoted billions of dollars to Afghanistan and the patient and moderate Hamid Karzai strove to bring Afghanistan's disparate factions together, his Loya Jirga a symbol of reconciliation. The fact that his tribe was Popalzai, the same as Afghanistan's founder, Ahmed Shah Durrani, bestowed upon him legitimacy unknown to any Afghan ruler since Daoud. Afghanistan's future shone bright.

What happened in Garmser over the next five years was a tragedy. The opportunity of 2001 could not overcome old feuds and the power-hungry khans. Garmser's own divisions undermined progress. Meanwhile the Taliban licked their wounds in Pakistan safe havens. So close to the Pakistan border, Garmser proved ill-prepared to meet their attack. Its people needed to be united rather than divided. These bitter years explain why unprecedented violence would soon ravage Garmser and why the United States and Britain would eventually send hundreds of men to this slim band of farmland in the southern reaches of Afghanistan.

A second try

In November 2001, while high-ranking Taliban leaders were fleeing Lashkar Gah and Kandahar for Pakistan, Garmser's Taliban commanders sat in the district center. It was not yet clear to them that retreat was called for. Far from the center of the fighting, not a single bomb had fallen on Garmser (that did not stop Mullah Naim, the senior Taliban, from firing wildly at bombers way overhead).[1] Mullah Abdul Majan and several others were there with Naim. All would later fight the Afghan government tooth and nail. For now, they waited to see what would unfold.

Meanwhile, in Pakistan, Garmser's great khans trickled together, watched, and planned. As the situation developed, they sent messages to their people not to help the Taliban and not to fight the Americans. When Kandahar city fell in December, they decided it was time to return. They formed a delegation to negotiate the Taliban surrender in Garmser. The delegation consisted of Said Omar, Shah Wali Khan, Ghulam Rassoul, Shah Jahan, Mohammed Nadir, and Abdullah Jan. In December 2001, they made their way from Pakistan back to Garmser.

Naim and the other Taliban leaders met the delegation in the district center. The tribal leaders told them to leave, lest American bombs turn Garmser into a graveyard. Naim agreed, perhaps because he knew there would be no hiding in Garmser if the tribal leaders were united against him. He promised to turn over all the Taliban weapons to the delegation and then leave for Pakistan. In his words, the weapons could be used to keep Garmser safe, seeing as no government yet existed. All seemed in order until at the last minute Naim changed his mind. Instead of handing the weapons to the delegation as a whole, he gave them to Shah Jahan, Shah Wali Khan, Ghulam Rassoul, and Mohammed Nadir—the Alizai tribal leaders from near his home in Laki—for safekeeping. Then he fled to Pakistan, along with most of the other Taliban leaders.[2] Only the fair and respected Abdul Majan, former Taliban deputy governor of Uruzgan, stayed. He turned over his weapons and vehicles to Abdullah Jan and then went to his home in Majitek.[3] The removal of the Taliban had been bloodless but the seeds of discontent lay in Naim's surrendered weapons.

With the Taliban gone, the tribal leaders of Garmser, led by Said Omar, organized a shura to elect a new district governor. As one of Garmser's oldest land-owning tribal leaders, a former mujahidin commander, and well-read in Islam, Said Omar was widely respected. Days before the shura, Abdullah Jan knocked at Said Omar's door in Hazar Joft. Said Omar had been his deputy district governor and before that his ally in the jihad. Abdullah Jan had spent the last seven years fighting the Taliban, first with Ismael Khan in Herat and then with Ahmed Shah Massoud in Kabul and Panjshir. His cadre of fifty men and five tan Toyota Land Cruisers (a number that dwindled over time) had seen many battles. In 1998, as the Taliban pressed northward, he returned to Pakistan, traveling from Kunduz to Badakhshan in the far north-west, through the mountains to Chitral, and southward to Baluchistan, only to be gunned down in the bazaar of Girdi Jangal, the town near the Helmand border where his family and the Alizai tribal leaders had taken refuge.[4] Taliban assassins killed his two guards, shot Abdullah Jan in the leg, but failed to finish him off. Shah Wali Khan—brother-in-law and long-time Alizai friend—sped him to a hospital in Karachi. He survived. Now sitting in Said Omar's guest room, Abdullah Jan told his old ally that he wanted to become district governor once more. Years of his life had been spent fighting for Afghanistan, both against the Soviets and then the Taliban, he said. His men had died and he himself had been wounded. What he wanted now was Said Omar's support. The Alizai already backed him. The respect that Said Omar held, plus his control of the Omarzai clan of the Noorzai, would make his candidacy unbeatable. Said Omar, kingmaker of Garmser, agreed. Abdullah Jan's integrity, aggressiveness, and unswerving dedication to Afghanistan had always impressed him.

A few days later, Said Omar convened the shura. All Garmser's tribal leaders attended: Mohammed Anwar from southern Hazar Joft, Khodirom from Loya Darveshan, Baz Mohammed from Majitek, Roh Khan from Kuchinay Darveshan, Wakil Manan from Mian Poshtay, Mohammed Nadir from Lakari, Salay Mohammed from Safar, Zahir Khan from Benadar, and Shah Jahan, Ghulam Rassoul, and Shah Wali Khan from Laki. Behind the scenes, Said Omar had rallied the Noorzai behind Abdullah Jan. At the outset of the meeting, he put the old and

Image 4: Abdullah Jan sitting pensively at a shura. (Photo by Patricio Asfura-Heim, 2010)

revered Zahir Khan of Benadar at the front of the room and asked him who should be district governor. Benadar was where Abdullah Jan had spent years of his childhood, forming fast friendships with the Noorzai there. Zahir Khan replied, 'Abdullah Jan.' The one person opposed to Abdullah Jan—Roh Khan, leader of the oldest Noorzai family in Garmser—offered no objections. The political backing of Said Omar and the Alizai was too much.[5] There is a certain point in Pashtun politics when openly opposing a winning contender, especially over the endorsement of a revered elder, is just plain bad manners. Hence Abdullah Jan was unanimously re-elected.

After nearly seven years in opposition, Abdullah Jan was once again district governor. Now about forty-five years old, the traits that had first made him a capable mujahidin commander—energy, initiative, setting an example, team-building—remained with him after all the fighting in the north. He could still march 10 kilometers at a quick step without getting winded (in spite of the Girdi Jangal shooting that had left a permanent knot in his left femur). His fighters were still a tight-knit family; he still took his meals on the ground with them, sitting and listening as they talked, sometimes instructing them on how he wanted them to behave. Innocent people were not to be harmed and his checkpoints were not to tax passers-by (he had other systems for taxation). He imposed a discipline upon his men that he never could upon the tribal leaders, later telling me: 'If you do not keep an eye on fighting men, they will hurt the people.' His political skills were sharp too. Years of experience had taught him how to craft an efficient government and how to protect the district. He was Garmser's benevolent warlord.

The Kabul government was not yet in a position to give Abdullah Jan much assistance. It was just getting on its feet. Kabul confirmed Abdullah Jan's appointment. Under the new Afghan government, Karzai technically chose all provincial and district governors. In this case, he went along with what the local leaders wanted. Otherwise, however, the fledgling government could not help Abdullah Jan in the way of money, arms, or men. Abdullah Jan was on his own.

It was essentially a tribal government that Abdullah Jan set up. After all, the tribal leaders had negotiated the departure of the Taliban and re-elected him. A product of the tribes himself, governing through them came naturally to him. Within their own regions, Abdullah Jan gave each tribal leader a great deal of autonomy. Abdullah Jan oversaw security, collected taxes, and delivered goods and services, but he allowed the tribal leaders to resolve disputes as they wished, levy their own taxes as they wished, and grow poppy as they wished. Each tribal leader, or sometimes group of tribal leaders, again held his own fiefdom. Granting the tribal leaders these privileges was necessary to keep them together behind the government and behind his district governorship, a balancing act that Abdullah Jan had to perform. It was not the best arrangement and demanded no small amount of diplomatic skill, but the national government, which was still forming, afforded him little assistance. He needed the tribal leaders. Without them, Garmser could not be controlled.

Initially, at least, the diplomatic success that had started with his own election continued to greet Abdullah Jan. This was nowhere clearer than in how he rallied the tribal leaders behind his security plan. There were few official forces in Garmser: no Afghan army, no American or British forces, and only forty official police.[6] The United States would eventually start training a new Afghan army, named the Afghan National Army (ANA). The plans for the army would not be finalized until summer 2002. It would be a professional force of 70,000 volunteers, slowly built over several years in order to ensure high quality. Troops could not be expected to arrive in Garmser for years, if at all. The United States, Great Britain, and their allies had few of their own forces in the country. Of those, most were on the border in eastern Afghanistan. Southern Afghanistan received barely any attention. From 2001 to 2006, one or two battalions were stationed in Kandahar. They rarely visited Garmser. Nor were any advisors or special forces assigned to Garmser. It was left to Abdullah Jan to find a way to protect his district. True, the Taliban were defeated, but Naim and Mullah Omar still lived, unreconciled and untouched in Pakistan, organizing their return. Garmser had to be able to defend itself.

To do so, Abdullah Jan re-established his old tribal militia system. Each community fielded roughly thirty fighters, who functioned essentially as police. There were 300 in all. Twenty-five checkpoints dotted the district. The militias were recruited specifically from their local community, where they would serve. Old mujahidin commanders or tribal leaders themselves were given charge of each force: Mohammed Nabi in Majitek, Mohammed Nadir in Lakari, Ghulam Rassoul in Laki. To pay for food, wages, and ammunition, wheat and poppy were once again taxed, once again with the blessing of the tribal leaders: 25 kilograms of wheat per hectare (a hectare yields 700 to 1,500 kilograms in Helmand).[7] According to Abdullah Jan, the tribal militia was a proven system: 'The best men from every tribe joined the arbekai [tribal militias]. These men tried to help the people. They came from good families and would not steal from their own people. The people admired them and were willing to donate money for their salaries.'[8]

For three years, the tribal militias prevented Taliban fighters from returning to Garmser. When five Taliban tried to infiltrate into Mian Poshtay in 2004, they could not get more than one AK-47 through Abdullah Jan's defensive belt. It took only one policeman to go down to Mian Poshtay and flush them out.[9] Perhaps the best endorsement of the tribal militia comes from Khodirom, former mujahidin commander and a tribal leader from Loya Darveshan, who was not friends with Abdullah Jan: 'Haji Abdullah Jan's tribal militia system was very good. Yes, he had to tax people to maintain it but there was security and the different arbekai (militias) never fought with one another.'[10]

Safar, the dusty Noorzai expanse near the southern end of the district, did not fall under Abdullah Jan's tribal militias. Salay Mohammed—the powerful tribal leader from Safar—commanded an Afghan Border Police brigade that defended the entire Helmand border. His 400 men, replete with heavy machine guns and pickup trucks, ensured that Safar and, to a lesser extent, the border were secure. Mainly recruited from Garmser and barely trained, they were no better than the militia in terms of professionalism. Their chief allegiance was to Salay Mohammed. Fortunately Salay Mohammed and Abdullah Jan were friends so the border police fed into Garmser's security system. They would later be put to the test against the Taliban re-organizing across the border. As it was, for three years, the tribal militia and border police would keep the Taliban out of Garmser.

Besides security, in the realms of justice, representation, and delivery of goods and services, Abdullah Jan set up a district government that matched what the Taliban had offered. By the end of 2002, Karzai's government, backed by the international community, was able to help a little in this regard. Administrative, development, health, and justice officials were sent down to districts, although police and army were still a long way off. For all the merits of the Taliban rule of law, Karzai's government in Garmser enforced a system that was at least as fair and accessible. Garmser had an official judge (a well-educated religious scholar), a huqooq (an Afghan official, somewhat akin to a paralegal, who can mediate civil disputes), and a prosecutor.[11] The judge ruled by shari'a, just like the Taliban. Although his punishments were far less harsh, which meant that more criminals were out and about, his decisions were viewed as just. Ali Shah Khan, a lesser village elder who did not get along with Abdullah Jan, admitted: 'Justice during the time of both the Taliban and Abdullah Jan was good. There is one Shari'a.'[12]

Following tradition, Abdullah Jan established a tribal council, composed of representatives from every area of the district, thirty-six in all. The tribal leaders themselves or their son, brother, or uncle served on the council, essentially filling in the role of the old maliks. Meeting weekly, the council chiefly resolved disputes that could not be handled in the villages and debated how the tribes should address larger security and political issues. It became Abdullah Jan's consultative body. Its existence helped him keep support of the tribes and keep them working together for the good of Garmser as a whole. Dr Salam, a future Taliban supporter, years later still spoke highly of the council: 'Abdullah Jan's council was good because it was a real council made up of real tribal leaders. Every community sent their biggest problems to it for resolution.'[13]

Goods and services were delivered through international and national Afghan development programs. Abdullah Jan's security was good enough for them to work in Garmser. The district government itself did not have a budget for development. Its taxes—technically illegal—went to the tribal militia. Afghan development funds were funneled from Kabul through the various ministries, which then executed the projects in the district. Representatives from eight ministries, including education, reconstruction and development, agriculture, and health, came to the district to help bring goods and services to the people.

The bulk of the government's development work came from the National Solidarity Program, the crown jewel of development in Afghanistan. Designed by international development expert Ashraf Ghani, the program set up 'community development councils'—the village council under a new name—in villages throughout Afghanistan. Each community development council received grants to start projects of their choosing. The idea was that the grants would teach villages to work together to better their lives while connecting them to the new government. Between 2003 and 2006, the National Solidarity Program set up seventy-two community development councils in villages from Shamalan to Laki. The program did not exactly fulfill its high hopes—the councils chiefly implemented an unsustainable plan to bring electric power to the villages—but it definitely brought communities together and showed that the government was trying to do something.[14]

Between 2001 and 2005, the international community's work fell to the United Nations, non-governmental organizations (NGOs), and the United States Agency for International Development (USAID). The provincial reconstruction team, which would later guide development in Helmand, had not yet been established. The United Nations drilled wells throughout the district. USAID constructed a clinic in Bartaka and Ministry of Agriculture buildings in the district center bazaar, as well as a practical and modern compound for the district governor.[15]

Real ground was made in education. USAID built four beautiful and modern white schools, including a girls' school in Laki. In total, Garmser had fifteen schools, staffed by thirty-five teachers. All were trained; very few were mullahs. Altogether 1,500 students attended, less than during the Taliban regime but better educated.[16] Thousands of other students went to local madrasas for schooling.

All in all Abdullah Jan had attained some noteworthy successes, particularly in security. But there were shortcomings. One was poppy. When the Taliban departed, poppy cultivation resumed: Garmser's cash crop, everyone took part. The tribal leaders grew it, taxed it, smuggled it, and sold it. Flush with profits, tribal leaders built bazaars in Lakari and Safar to export it. Opium was run into Pakistan and Iran, often through Baram Chah, Helmand's great bazaar on the Pakistani border. Abdullah Jan did little to stop poppy's growth within his district.

Poppy was hardly the biggest problem (in fact, it probably raised general prosperity). The tribes had been kept together, but society writ large was not united under their sway. Nor was Abdullah Jan's tribal government structured to unite it; there were too many fiefdoms; it was too decentralized. Abdullah Jan could pressure the tribal leaders to work with the government but, in order to win their support, he had forfeited his right to tell them how to treat the people within their own lands. As a result, two important sections of society—the mullahs and the immigrants—remained disaffected from both the tribal leaders and the government.

While the tribal leaders gained power, the religious leaders lost the pre-eminence they had enjoyed under the Taliban. Those who had come from Pakistan in the 1990s largely fled back there with Naim. Those who had immigrated from Uruzgan stayed, as did those who had been living in Garmser all along. They lost their positions as judges, recruiters, teachers, and tax collectors. Still, after years of Taliban empowerment, they retained plenty of influence, greater than they had enjoyed under King Zahir Shah or during the jihad. For nearly seven years, from 1994 to 2001, the people had brought their problems to them, submitted to their taxes, and obeyed their rulings. Such influence died hard. Among the religious leaders themselves, support for the Taliban lived on, which made it all the more important that the government, the tribal leaders, and the religious leaders come together, something that Abdullah Jan recognized.

Abdul Majan, the most important Taliban to stay in Garmser, tried to work with the government. Admiring his wisdom and kindness, Abdullah Jan helped him, even giving him a car. He knew that reconciling with Taliban and religious leaders like him would only make the government stronger. With that in mind, he formed a religious council that met every fifteen days. Its thirty members resolved disputes and offered the government advice on religious matters. The council was a notable inroad into the religious community. Maulawi Mohammedullah, a future Taliban judge, later said: 'Haji Abdullah Jan respected the mullahs. Many mullahs went and spoke with him.'[17]

But other tribal leaders took their pound of flesh from the religious leaders, whom they viewed as untrustworthy. From time to time, their men cursed, imprisoned, and beat religious leaders who had been with the Taliban or appeared suspicious. The practice was not universal but it happened frequently enough to keep the hearts of plenty of religious leaders with the Taliban. Many of the remaining scholars fled back to Pakistan. Indeed, in 2004, after two years, harassed by police day after day, Abdul Majan left.[18] The departure of this cooperative and influential Taliban leader was a real loss. Abdullah Jan had ordered the police to stop but their chief was Tooriali, the son of Roh Khan, the tribal leader of Kuchinay Darveshan. Abdullah Jan could not confront him militarily without upsetting his powerful Noorzai clan. The best hope for reconciling with the religious community had been lost.

It was not only the religious leaders that the tribal leaders upset. In scattered communities along the river and the whole eastern desert edge from Majitek to Benadar, the class of poor farmers living on government land was still around: all those farmers who had received land from Taraki in 1978; all those immigrants from Uruzgan and elsewhere to whom the Taliban had granted land between 1994 and 2001. The Taliban had been their benefactors. The change of regime endangered their livelihood. The Karzai government did not recognize their claim to the land. The old land documents issued by the communists, as well as any papers from the Taliban, were null and void. The law afforded the landless no rights. At the same time, the tribal leaders chafed at the thousands now squatting on unassigned government-owned land that had once been theirs. To the tribal leaders, the poor farmers and recent immigrants were but thieves and terrorists. The landless immigrants themselves disliked the government for dismissing what they had gained from Taraki, the Taliban, or by their own hand.

Condoning this policy was one of America's greatest mis-steps in Afghanistan. Land had been causing conflict in Garmser since the canals had been completed in the early 1970s. Of the land in Garmser 20 percent is government and every bit of it was rented out or, more likely, squatted upon. The same, to a greater or lesser extent, is true throughout most of Helmand and much of Kandahar. This problem is hardly novel. Land has often driven people to rebel. Land reform has been part of the defeat of many insurgencies. The Afghan government had no land reform policy that might have allowed the landless immigrants to actually own the land they farmed and perhaps undercut the support for the Taliban that still existed in these communities. Abdullah Jan and the tribal leaders were free to do what they pleased.

The tribal leaders and the government turned a deaf ear to the grievances of the landless immigrants. Where they deemed fit, the tribal leaders took land back for themselves. This was not merely the private land stolen by the Taliban but government land too. In Laki, the Alizai tribal leaders Ghulam Rassoul and Shah Wali Khan laid claim to government land and pushed off squatters by force. Most of the occupants fled and started working with the Taliban in Pakistan. Abdullah Jan acquiesced to these actions.[19] After all, he was known to have remarked at the time: 'I will throw all the immigrants who came under the Taliban into the river.' Abdullah Jan often tried to protect the innocent, but, in his mind, immigrant squatters were not innocent, a view shared by the government itself. Benevolence only went so far. The perspective of the poor, according to one school teacher who was close to them, was that: 'The district governor does not listen to the people. He only listens to the elders. He should listen to the poor people instead.'[20] Years later, Abdullah Jan admitted that he and the tribal leaders had been mistaken: 'The tribal leaders have to know that it is not like it was before. We cannot do what we did before. It was wrong.'

The upshot of these rifts in society was that the Taliban never lost their base of support among the religious community and the immigrants, not to mention the support of the villages of their major leaders, such as Naim's in Laki and Abdul Hakim's in Majitek.[21] Yet sympathy for the Taliban was not enough to allow the Taliban to return in any kind of force. Between 2001 and 2005, the tribal militia, the offspring of tribal unity, prevented insurgent cadres from actually forming. Taliban leaders could not move freely in the district, weapons could not be imported, and mullahs could not preach jihad. With or without sympathetic religious leaders and immigrants, as long as the tribal militia, border police, and tribal unity stood, the Taliban could not return to Garmser. Only when politics and power broke down these instruments of order did Garmser fall apart.

It all started with Naim's guns. The Alizai had accepted his weapons in 2001 and never turned them over to the tribal shura or to the government. At the time, Abdullah Jan had criticized them for this. As far as he was concerned, the weapons were meant to protect all Garmser, not just the Alizai. The disagreement did not lead to problems at first, but over time it festered. The Alizai still had four main leaders: Shah Jahan, Mohammed Nadir, Ghulam Rassoul, and Shah Wali Khan. Shah Jahan, mastermind of the 1989 Alizai conquest of Safar, the Richelieu of Garmser, was building a political career and chafed at Abdullah Jan's authority. Mohammed Nadir did too. He was proud of his role at the forefront of the Alizai during the jihad and civil war. His family was educated and wealthy and politically connected. The other two Alizai tribal leaders—Ghulam Rassoul and Shah Wali Khan—were less antagonistic but still unhappy. Ghulam Rassoul, frontline Alizai commander and determined fighter, had been friends with Abdullah Jan since fighting side by side in the jihad. Shah Wali Khan, head of the most established Alizai family and one of the first mujahidin commanders, was Abdullah Jan's brother-in-law. He had rushed Abdullah Jan to the hospital after the shooting in Girdi Jangal. Nevertheless, they too started to question why their great tribe had given the district governor's chair to Abdullah Jan, a man from, in one elder's words, 'a single family.'[22] Indeed, the Barakzai tribe in Garmser was little bigger than the families of Abdullah Jan and his three first cousins in Bartaka. Thousands of families made up the Alizai.

Over time, frustration grew. Abdullah Jan and the Alizai were in fundamentally different political positions. From a small family, Abdullah Jan's only choice was to run Garmser via a united tribal front. He lacked the numbers behind him to demand submission by force of will or force of arms. His power was a function of his ability to win allies. The Alizai, on the other hand, did not need Abdullah Jan. They conceivably had the people, money, wider tribal connections, and guns to run Garmser, or at least to manage things with the Noorzai, on their own. It was all about power; all about who would lead Garmser. The rest of the Alizai may have had no personal fight with Abdullah Jan, but they fell in line behind the leadership. Remarkably cohesive, the Alizai tribe is a nation unto itself.

The dispute came to a head in early 2004. Every year, the national government held a poppy eradication campaign. Since the provincial governor and countless tribal leaders smuggled poppy, the campaign was a bit half-hearted in Helmand—meant really for publicity and to please the international community. Handfuls of tractors plowed under a few score hectares in every district. In 2002 and 2003, the campaign in Garmser covered from Hazar Joft to Mian Poshtay. In 2004, Abdullah Jan ordered that it go all the way to Benadar, the southern end of the district. One-hundred twenty hectares were eradicated in Laki and Lakari. Mohammed Nadir and Shah Jahan were outraged, believing that they had been targeted purposefully. They publicly decried Abdullah Jan.

Mohammed Nadir and Shah Jahan took their criticism to provincial governor Sher Mohammed Akhundzada, fellow Alizai, nephew of their wartime ally, Nasim Akhundzada, and son of the short-lived governor, Rassoul Akhundzada. The young and ambitious Sher Mohammed held great power. His family had led the jihad against the Soviets and fathered the poppy trade in Helmand. His sister was married to Hamid Karzai. In 2002, Abdullah Jan and Sher Mohammed had enjoyed a good relationship. Poppy had since come between them. Sher Mohammed's poppy business cut across Helmand.[23] Abdullah Jan considered Garmser his territory. More than once he had turned around Sher Mohammed's opium-laden pickups trying to get to Pakistan via Garmser. Such acts, of course, infuriated Sher Mohammed. It was easy for Mohammed Nadir and Shah Jahan to turn him completely against Abdullah Jan. Technically, the power to install or remove district governors lay with President Karzai and the Ministry of Interior in Kabul. In reality, a powerful provincial governor could act on his own. For a time, Abdullah Jan's old Noorzai friend Said Omar, who had become a member of the provincial council and had participated in both of Karzai's Loya Jirgas, was able to convince Sher Mohammed to leave Abdullah Jan alone. It was not until Said Omar (by then in his late sixties) retired from the provincial council that the axe fell. In December 2004, Sher Mohammed removed Abdullah Jan. The official reason was poppy cultivation, the business Sher Mohammed himself was deeply involved in.

Garmser unravels

Since 2001, the Taliban had been waiting to return to Garmser. The leaders, such as Naim who had fled there in 2001, had neither given up nor abandoned their beliefs. Naim, for one, believed deeply in the Taliban cause. He later told Shah Jahan: 'I was Taliban. I am Taliban. I will be Taliban.'[24] In Pakistan, Mullah Omar was re-forming the Taliban movement. Extensive training and organizational activities were ongoing. In 2003, he created the Quetta shura (located in Quetta, the capital of the Pakistani province of Baluchistan) to coordinate the activities of multiple Taliban sub-groups. The principal operational commander for southern Afghanistan was the one-legged Dadullah Lang, a Kakar tribesmen (a non-Durrani tribe) and 25-year veteran of Afghan wars.[25] He had commanded Taliban forces fighting Ahmed Shah Massoud in the 1990s. The name 'Lang' was given to him after he had lost his leg in the jihad. It means lame. The same name was given to the Tartar conqueror Timur Lang (or Tamerlane), who had ravaged Iran and Afghanistan in the late 1300s. The comparison magnified Dadullah's infamy. Mullah Abdul Salam Zaeef, former Taliban ambassador to Pakistan, wrote of him: 'The one-legged commander was always ready to lead each military operation himself, standing among his men on the front line and dashing into the offensive as the first person over the ridge. His style of command was so strict that no one dared to escape or failed to perform their duty.'[26] Dadullah Lang commanded the Taliban in Helmand, Kandahar, Uruzgan, and Zabul. Garmser itself fell under Naim.

Abdullah Jan's removal set the stage for the Taliban return. With the appointment of a new district governor, Abdullah Jan stood down his tribal militia. He called in his post commanders and told them: 'I can no longer take responsibility for your men. I cannot defend you [from retribution by Sher Mohammed Akhundzada] if something goes wrong.'[27] With that, he dismissed his fighters and took back his weapons, which went with him to Lashkar Gah. A small cadre of his veterans went too as his personal bodyguard. The Alizai militia posts under Mohammed Nadir and Ghulam Rassoul remained, as did Salay Mohammed's border police. All the rest—everything from Hazar Joft to Mian Poshtay, 30 kilometers of ground—stood down.[28] The old defensive belt was gone, a casualty of the broken tribal alliance.

The new district leadership was weak. The first district governor lasted three months, from December 2004 to March 2005. The second stayed nearly a year, from March 2005 to February 2006, but was equally ineffective.[29] Neither could recreate the tribal militia, hold the tribes together, or keep the police in line.

In September 2005, a new police chief arrived: Kabeer Khan, a cruel and abusive Barakzai from Nadi Ali district (west of Lashkar Gah). His patron was the Marjah warlord and Helmand police chief, Abdur Rahman Jan. Kabeer Khan's forty-five police, who were not from Garmser, were far too few to secure the district, rarely getting out beyond Hazar Joft in the north. Their behavior worsened the situation. They stole, taxed, and charged fees just to do their job. Cuts of that money were sent to Abdur Rahman Jan in Lashkar Gah. When the police demanded money to arrest murderers and kidnappers, the people could not but hate them. Lakari elders turned against Kabeer when he wanted to be paid to arrest a kidnapper and then stole goods from the bazaar. On one occasion, his own son shot and beat nearby villagers when Taliban fired a few rounds at him. One of the tribal leaders of the Kharoti tribe, who would later side with the Taliban, remembered: 'Kabeer Khan treated people very poorly. He gave the people a reason to support the Taliban.'[30]

The district governor was too weak to do anything about Kabeer Khan. Under Afghan law, police chiefs and other district officials were not appointed by the district governor. They were appointed in Kabul by the head of their respective ministry; in the case of a police chief, by the Ministry of Interior. The district governor was senior to the police chief, but the district police chief answered to the provincial police chief. The same was technically true of the provincial governor. He did not appoint the provincial police chief, NDS (intelligence) director, or other line ministry directors. If he wanted to make a change, he had to argue with Kabul. Thus, the district governor was senior in name only. He had no real power over the police chief, NDS chief, or line directors. They were supposed to obey his wishes, but, if they did not, the district governor's only recourse was to complain to the provincial governor, who would then have to pressure the provincial police chief or Ministry of Interior, expending his own political capital along the way. Authority is divided in this way in many Islamic countries in order to prevent governors or generals from becoming too powerful and threatening the central government.[31] In this case, the new Garmser district governor lacked the political clout to convince Governor Sher Mohammed Akhundzada to go through the effort of confronting the powerful provincial police chief Abdur Rahman Jan and getting him to remove Kabeer Khan.

Taliban attacks soon jumped. In 2005, the Taliban dispatched new mullahs to Garmser: young and foreign, from Uruzgan, Quetta, and Peshawar, scholars of Taliban ideology. They did not have extensive religious education but they could read and write, which was more than could be said for most of the people of Garmser. Thus they had influence. Together with pro-Taliban mullahs who had never left the district, they preached against the government and encouraged young men to join the Taliban.[32] The government was condemned as thieves for its taxes and infidels for its friendship with the United States. Later, when we were trying to work with the mullahs, one elder ruefully asked me: 'Why do you want to talk to the mullahs? They caused all the problems.'

A few religious leaders believed in the government, but they were too scared to do anything against the sizeable pro-Taliban faction. To clear the path for their mullahs, the Taliban were assassinating many of the knowledgeable and educated religious scholars elsewhere in Afghanistan. The religious leadership of Lashkar Gah and Kandahar was being gutted (the head of the Kandahar religious council was assassinated in May 2005). While no one was killed in Garmser, the scholars and moderate mullahs were terrified. The provincial and national governments took few steps to protect these scholars. As a result, Garmser's pro-government religious leaders would not speak out against the teachings of the Taliban.

Shortly after the mullahs came in mid 2005, small cadres of Taliban fighters began arriving. These cadres did not try to overthrow the government—at least not yet—but organized the young men whom the mullahs had recruited and started low-level guerrilla attacks: intimidating local leaders, laying IEDs, and mounting hit and run attacks. The new small cadres worked out of the villages of landless immigrants and influential pro-Taliban mullahs, especially in Majitek, Mian Poshtay, and Lakari.

Along the eastern edge of the canal zone, the peoples in Majitek and farther south had supported the Taliban in the 1990s and the Taliban had treated them well. This was the home of the poor Ghilzai tribes—the Kharoti and Taraki—often abused by their richer Durrani cousins residing along the main canal.[33] Majitek's fields were less productive and quickly thinned into the desert. The tribes had originally been nomads and many still lived right on the desert's edge. For years, Mohammed Nabi, working out of his militia (arbekai) post at the strategic crossroads known as 'Munday corner,' had locked down Majitek. Munday was his nickname, meaning short yet strong. Having fought for Abdullah Jan as a teenager in the jihad and with the fearsome looks of a Taliban—black turban, black beard, dark skin, tattooed hands—he was the kind of Pashtun who could grip the rebellious people of Majitek: feared for his war-making, accepted for being from the Kakar tribe, tied to the other poor tribes (Kharoti, Taraki, Andar, Tarin) and to the Taliban. But now his fighters were gone, their weapons with Abdullah Jan. Without Mohammed Nabi to protect the eastern flank, Taliban started filtering in. 'It was during this time,' one Kharoti elder told me, 'that the Taliban started coming to our homes at night.'[34]

Farther south, in Mian Poshtay, the tree-lined midpoint of Garmser, immigrants from Uruzgan who had arrived under Taliban rule provided another base of support. One of those immigrants was Mullah Ismael. His family had come from Uruzgan during the first Taliban regime, acquiring land less than a kilometer west of Wakil Manan's village. Wakil Manan, who had worked with the communists during the jihad and later had been imprisoned by the Taliban, was still the main tribal leader in Mian Poshtay. In his twenties, with a crippled shoulder and a pale sickly face, Mullah Ismael was a hateful young man. We would come to know him and his atrocities well. He is the only Taliban commander I know who was truly murderous, in line with the Western stereotype. When Abdullah Jan's nearby militia post stood down, Mullah Ismael started turning people away from Wakil Manan and recruiting them to support the Taliban. He preached to them, held meetings with them, and offered them money to join his cadre. Wakil Manan himself did not have enough supporters to fend off Mullah Ismael, largely because he had failed to use his own money and land to win the loyalty of the people. He had been more concerned with amassing personal wealth. When the Taliban started to re-emerge he did not seize the initiative by holding his own meetings or using his own poppy money to buy local support. Mullah Ismael's men eventually started harassing Wakil Manan, coming at night and threatening to kill him. More and more, Wakil Manan took refuge in his fortress-like home.

Mian Poshtay was soon rife with Taliban. At night, Mullah Ismael's men moved about freely. They soon set up a shadow government. One resident reported: 'The Taliban are still authoritative in our area, they outnumbered [sic] the officials during the night here…You would [sic] be punished according to Shari'a if you listened to music or shaved your beard.'[35] To expand his influence, Mullah Ismael started giving away government land and Wakil Manan's private land. He promised to give away more land once the Taliban took power. Those who had received land during the Taliban's first regime were told they would be allowed to keep it.[36] By the end of 2005, sensing the shift in power, local village elders started working with the Taliban.

Majitek and Mian Poshtay were not alone. A more surprising and damaging development was at hand in Lakari, immediately south of Mian Poshtay, in Alizai territory. Dr Abdul Salam was an Alizai village elder, landowner, and pharmacist in Lakari. His village was next to the village of Mohammed Nadir (one of the four main Alizai tribal leaders). Dr Salam had been a communist and had fled to Pakistan during the jihad. He returned afterwards and then stayed in Garmser through the first Taliban regime. As a communist, he had believed deeply in reducing the power of the tribal leaders. Later, the security the Taliban brought and their redistribution of power impressed him. He became friends with Naim, whose family home was nearby in Laki. When the Taliban departed, he accepted government rule. But his connections to the Taliban remained. In early 2005, Dr Salam started helping Naim. Dr Salam collected taxes and financed his mullah, who taught young men how to become Taliban fighters.[37]

By the autumn of 2005, Lakari had become the leading center of underground Taliban activity. Commanders met there; fighters staged there; mullahs preached there. Dr Salam held secret meetings with Taliban at night and helped organize their network in the district. He even donated land to their commanders and their mullahs, which then turned hefty poppy profits. In return, the Taliban reinforced Dr Salam's stature by paying his villagers good money for their support. He reveled in his newfound fame as the Taliban philanthropist.

Mohammed Nadir, who as a great Alizai tribal leader should have been able to put a stop to the cancer on his doorstep, did nothing. He failed to hold together his militia cadre. Living beside Dr Salam, they were exposed to all kinds of Taliban teachings. Those unconvinced by Taliban ideology were intimidated by Taliban guns. By the summer of 2005, Mohammed Nadir's militia had turned. Mohammed Nadir stood aside and spent his days planting, reaping, and selling his poppy.[38] Shah Wali Khan, playing a traditional role as head of the leading Alizai family, had to go to Lakari from Laki to tell Dr Salam to stop helping the Taliban. Dr Salam, of course, would not listen. Rather than march into Lakari and crush Dr Salam, possibly instigating a tribal civil war, Shah Wali Khan let the problem be. It was a sign of how weak the government had become that the Taliban were able to edge their way into Lakari and win influence within the powerful Alizai tribe. Shah Wali Khan and Shah Jahan could not possibly have missed how the balance of power was shifting; their tribe in the middle.

With active cadres operating in Majitek, Mian Poshtay, and Lakari, the government was losing Garmser. At the end of 2005, the Taliban did not yet control these areas outright—the tribal leaders, the district governor, and what police remained were still in charge—but they could move about freely. Poppy fields were taxed. Community development council projects were run off. Teachers were threatened. Schools were burnt down. Defenseless elders got the idea: fewer and fewer spoke openly in favor of the government at the very time when such action was most needed. Before the end of the year, small hit and run attacks broke out in Hazar Joft, the densest concentration of population and the location of the district center in the north. In early December 2005, the Taliban hit the district center itself in a carefully planned commando-style raid; fifteen fighters from Pakistan were brought in to work with fifteen other fighters from Garmser. Informants gathered intelligence on the district center's defenses. The Taliban struck on a night when the district governor and most of the police were out at a dinner. The police guards were overwhelmed and the governor's compound fell into Taliban hands. Hours passed before the police could gather enough men to recapture the compound. Nine police officers died in the fighting. Six others were wounded. Four police trucks were damaged. The Taliban suffered at least ten killed themselves. After the raid, the Pakistani fighters withdrew to Pakistan. The attack was a blow to the government's credibility. Under Abdullah Jan, the tribal militia had prevented armed Taliban from entering the district. Thanks to tribal infighting, those militia were now gone. One hundred Taliban could never have massed for an attack if hundreds of tribal militiamen had still been in place.[39]

Garmser's downward march

In 2005, although Abdullah Jan's tribal militia were gone, one thing still standing in the way of a Taliban assault on Garmser was Salay

Mohammed's 400 border police, headquartered in Safar. The Taliban could not attack Garmser without overcoming them. Safar was on the southern end of the district. Dirt tracks from Kandahar, Iran, and the Pakistan border met there. It was where any Taliban attack on Garmser would strike first. Plus, the border police controlled Baram Chah, Helmand's great bazaar on the Pakistani border and poppy smuggling hub. The Taliban needed to capture it if they wanted to launch a full-scale offensive against southern Helmand. In late 2004, Dadullah Lang (Taliban commander for southern Afghanistan) and Naim (commander for southern Helmand) had started attacking the border police around Baram Chah from Pakistan. Before long, the town turned into a war zone. Border police vehicle patrols were shot at, mined, and ambushed. In the words of one of the border police company commanders, 'We were fighting every day. We lost many men.'[40] Long lines of communication back to Safar made it difficult to supply the police posted over 150 kilometers to the south. Still, the border police carried on and helped shield Garmser from the gathering Taliban peril.[41] Baram Chah lingered on, beleaguered and besieged.

Unfortunately, the same kind of tribal infighting that had sunk Abdullah Jan in 2004 wrecked the border police in 2005. Salay Mohammed had long been at odds with Governor Sher Mohammed Akhundzada. Their families had clashed when Salay Mohammed had fought against the Alizai and Nasim Akhundzada during the tribal civil war that had followed the jihad in Garmser. The Garmser Alizai, allied to Nasim, had forced Salay Mohammed to abandon his home and flee to Pakistan. Later, after Karzai had taken over, Salay Mohammed and the Akhundzada family clashed again, this time over control of poppy smuggling in southern Helmand.[42] Governor Sher Mohammed Akhundzada wanted control of the smuggling hub at Baram Chah. In 2005, he made Shah Jahan district governor of Khaneshin, which included Baram Chah. But that did not give him control of the town. Salay Mohammed still had police posts there. The United Nations had begun an idealistic militia disarmament program in Helmand. In spring 2005, Sher Mohammed took advantage of the program, directing them to disarm Salay Mohammed's border police, on the basis that they were untrained tribal levies (never mind the fact that Sher Mohammed had plenty of untrained militiamen of his own). The brigade was dissolved and Salay Mohammed had to surrender all his heavy machine guns and RPGs (he retained the

AK-47s).[43] The police themselves went home. Furious over the abuse, Salay Mohammed lost all faith in the government. He no longer opposed the Taliban and even allowed Qari Abdullah, a young madrasa-trained mullah, to preach in favor of the Taliban from a shrine 500 meters from his front door. He soon left Garmser for the comfort of Kabul, leaving his younger brother Sultan Mohammed in charge of Safar.

Governor Sher Mohammed now had Baram Chah but it was still under attack. In the summer of 2005, he sent sixty border police reinforcements from Lashkar Gah to push back the Taliban encroaching upon the town. Ghulam Rassoul, the Garmser Alizai's frontline commander, and ten of his men went with them. Ghulam Rassoul was renowned for his bravery during the jihad. He and his men set in on a hill between the town and Pakistan. The Taliban outnumbered and outgunned the whole force. Using the surrounding hills, they got in and around the border police and started shooting at them. Ghulam Rassoul thought one hundred were surrounding his position alone. Taliban heavy machine guns shot to pieces the pickup trucks of both Ghulam Rassoul and the border police commander. After fifteen days, the border police and Ghulam Rassoul had to pull out, crammed into the pickups that had not yet been destroyed. Eleven men had been killed, including two of Ghulam Rassoul's.[44]

After that, Governor Sher Mohammed attempted to form an alliance with local Baluch leaders and turned the defense of Baram Chah over to their militia. The Baluch leaders betrayed him and negotiated with the Taliban. Before long, Taliban were walking into Baram Chah. No attack had been necessary. In October, Sher Mohammed made one last attempt to recapture Baram Chah. The attempt failed and left the official district governor and eighteen of his men dead. Baram Chah was lost. Garmser, long bereft of Abdullah Jan's old tribal militia, was wide open.

In late 2005, southern Afghanistan as a whole, especially Helmand and Kandahar, were experiencing increased intimidation and hit and run attacks. The south's peril had caught the attention of the leaders of the United States and the North Atlantic Treaty Organization (NATO). Intelligence was indicating a Taliban resurgence. The Afghan army was not yet large enough to handle the problem on its own. Training and organization were proceeding at a glacial pace. Of the 70,000 troops planned, between 2002 and 2006, only 36,000 had been created. On 8 December 2005, NATO foreign ministers finalized a plan to send

British, Canadian, Dutch, and Australian forces to southern Afghanistan. The idea was to plant a more robust footprint in the south—the Pashtun heartland. The Canadians took Kandahar, the British took Helmand, and the Dutch and Australians took Uruzgan. Their governments and military leaders did not realize how badly the situation had deteriorated.[45]

In December 2005, Sher Mohammed Akhundzada was removed from provincial governorship under British insistence, after opium had been found in his offices. Mohammed Daoud, an engineer respected by the West, replaced him. In February 2006, Daoud reinstated Abdullah Jan as Garmser district governor. Abdullah Jan had been wounded again in the interim; a roadside bomb in Kandahar had mildly damaged his hearing.

Abdullah Jan returned to a dire situation. Masses of battle-hardened Taliban loomed over the horizon in Baram Chah. Another shadow was cast on Garmser from the north. At the beginning of February, Dadullah Lang (Taliban commander for southern Afghanistan) kicked off his offensive against three of Helmand's northern districts—Sangin, Nowzad, and Musa Qala. The fighting there would absorb the 1,200 British and 1,700 Afghan National Army soldiers then reinforcing Helmand, leaving the south undefended. Garmser's own defenses were down. The forty-odd police were confined to Hazar Joft. The only tribal militia were Abdullah Jan's thirty veteran mujahidin and Ghulam Rassoul's thirty men down in Laki. Neither could hold off any kind of sustained Taliban attack out of Pakistan. The tribal leadership felt unprotected and was wavering. As Shah Wali Khan put it: 'The government of Garmser had become weak. They offered us no protection against the Taliban.'[46]

Wasting no time in attempting to right the sinking ship, Abdullah Jan tried to rebuild his old tribal militia, but the support was no longer there. Whereas in 2002 good young men had flocked to his colors, in 2006 the good ones were too scared. They knew the Taliban were back, watching them. They knew the border was open. Mohammed Nabi, for example, Abdullah Jan's fearsome lieutenant who had commanded thirty men in 2004, now lived alone in Majitek. He stuck with Abdullah Jan but could bring none of his old militia with him: 'The Taliban had returned to Majitek and all Kharoti. There had been no post to stop them. My men were scared.'[47] A handful of militia were raised in Koshtay and Mian Poshtay. They were raw and their loyalty suspect.[48]

Abdullah Jan also spoke to the religious leaders and asked them to support the government. He told them the Taliban would be coming and that everyone needed to be united. They did not listen. Abdullah Jan even called Naim himself. He asked him to stop fighting and work with the government, arguing that violence would only bring more destruction. Naim, of course, was not interested in bargaining with Helmand's defenseless government.[49]

Meanwhile, police chief Kabeer Khan did nothing to correct his own abusive behavior. Abdullah Jan tried to stop him but Kabeer Khan's connections to Abdur Rahman Jan made it impossible to exert enough pressure to bring him into line. Kabeer Khan disregarded everything Abdullah Jan had to say.[50] Abdur Rahman Jan, the powerful warlord and provincial police chief, had appointed him and paid him. He owed nothing to Abdullah Jan. Governor Daoud could not help much. He was too busy dealing with attacks in the north to have the time to pressure Abdur Rahman Jan to get rid of Kabeer Khan. This would not have happened under the Taliban regime. Taliban military forces had answered to the district governors. Their commanders could be fired by him. There were not separate chains of command to outside warlords.

If only the tribal leaders had still been united, there might have been a chance. They still had influence and might have recruited enough fighters to make a stand. But they were not and had not been since 2004. Salay Mohammed of Safar had given up. The Noorzai family of Roh Khan in Kuchinay Darveshan refused to take sides and focused on their businesses in Lashkar Gah. Wakil Manan hid in his home in Mian Poshtay. And, amid the crumbling authority of Karzai's government, Mohammed Nadir, Shah Jahan, Shah Wali Khan, and Ghulam Rassoul, the Alizai powerhouse of the jihad, all scorned renewed friendship with Abdullah Jan.

It would seem that a new alliance between Abdullah Jan and the Alizai would have been easy to form with the Taliban so close. Unfortunately, Shah Jahan and Mohammed Nadir, who had worked to remove Abdullah Jan in 2004, still craved power. What was to be gained by staying with the government? The odds of defeating the Taliban were low. They did not want to fall under Abdullah Jan, who was likely to be defeated along with the rest of the government anyway. Sher Mohammed Akhundzada, their government benefactor, was no longer provincial governor; Shah Jahan, now district governor of Khaneshin, south-east of Garmser, had no patron in Lashkar Gah to propel his political career.[51] On top of that, after his fall from power, Sher Mohammed had given his followers permission to approach the Taliban. The door was open. There was little reason for the Alizai to stick it out with the government.[52] The Taliban offered political opportunity. The government offered nothing but war and submission to Abdullah Jan.

In early 2006, a delegation of Alizai elders, including Mohammed Nadir, went to Quetta and met with Naim, ostensibly to protest the cruelty of Kabeer Khan, who had recently taxed the people of Lakari, but really to open relations with the Taliban. They said they would support Naim and return his old weapons if he came to Garmser.

Abdullah Jan saw what was happening. He sent a delegation of elders to Laki to try to broker a peace. Unfortunately, the delegation could not convince the Alizai khans to reconcile. Abdullah Jan then went to Laki himself and confronted Mohammed Nadir, Shah Jahan, and Shah Wali Khan. He and Mohammed Nadir had been close friends. Shah Wali Khan was his brother in law. He asked them not to help the Taliban. 'We fought in the same *sangar*,' he pleaded, 'why are you now fighting me?' Mohammed Nadir replied: 'Anyone working with the government is an infidel.'[53]

In the end, the power of the tribe mattered more than the personal friendship and history they shared with Abdullah Jan. Ghulam Rassoul later told me: 'Everyone in the tribe became consumed with power, consumed with the district governor's chair. The competition was over power. Nothing else. It did not matter that we had fought alongside Abdullah Jan in the jihad. It did not matter that Abdullah Jan was married to Shah Wali Khan's sister. We had gone mad in pursuit of power.'[54]

The fall of Garmser

June 2006. At last the storm broke upon Garmser: 500 Taliban marched northward out of Pakistan, part of Dadullah Lang's larger Helmand-wide offensive that had been ongoing since February. There was little left to meet the shock of the Taliban onslaught. Years of corruption and infighting had taken their toll. The old tribal alliances of the jihad had fallen apart and the new government had withered away. The peace of America and Karzai had come to an early end.

Naim led the Taliban invasion into Garmser. Abdul Hadi Agha, the former mayor of the district center bazaar under the Taliban, and Abdul

Majan, back with the Taliban after his failed attempt to reconcile with the Karzai government, came as his lieutenants. Augmented by a few Punjabis and Arabs, the fighters were mostly Pashtun and Baluch originally from Garmser, uniformed in black turbans, armed with AK-47s, PK medium machine guns, RPGs, mortars, and 107 mm rockets. The weapons had been acquired by the Taliban leadership while re-organizing the movement in Pakistan. Many of the fighters had been formed into trained squads there.[55] British officers who would later confront them concluded that their understanding of light infantry tactics could only denote regimented training.

The wave first rolled over Khaneshin, the dry desert district south-east of Garmser, where Shah Jahan was district governor. Whether because he was outnumbered or he had already decided to turn, Shah Jahan surrendered the district to Naim and fled to Laki. The Taliban then surrounded the thirty-man police force, which was still trying to defend the district. They fought for four nights before withdrawing themselves. All but five were wounded.[56]

Abdullah Jan obtained warning of the Taliban offensive and went to Safar with his thirty men to organize the defenses. He was unable to stay. His truck struck an IED laid in plain sight of the bazaar. Fortunately, he was untouched. Nevertheless, he had to fall back north. When Naim and his army arrived in Safar, a small contingent of former border policemen put up a fight until they were overwhelmed. Sultan Mohammed, Salay Mohammed's younger brother, surrendered and turned over the remaining light weapons of the old border police. The Taliban took over the bazaar. Sultan Mohammed became one of Naim's assistants.

And then Naim with 200 of his men came to Laki. Here was the reckoning. Would the Alizai really betray Afghanistan? Abdullah Jan waited pensively in Hazar Joft. He knew that if the old Alizai mujahidin fought, the Taliban could be slowed and he might be able to rally reinforcements from Lashkar Gah. Laki is long and narrow with the river guarding one flank and a desert ridge the other, a natural chokepoint. Alas, it was but a hope. Shah Jahan and Mohammed Nadir had made up their minds. Shah Wali Khan and Ghulam Rassoul—the real fighters of the Alizai—did not demur. They were not going to break ranks.[57] When the Taliban arrived in Laki, Shah Jahan sat down with Mullah Naim and negotiated Taliban entry into the Alizai lands. I do not know the exact terms. But hours later, on the desert ridgeline overlooking Laki, Shah

Jahan, Shah Wali Khan, Ghulam Rassoul, and Mohammed Nadir returned all of Naim's old weapons, truckloads of AK-47 assault rifles, machine guns, and RPGs, which they had been keeping safe since 2001.

The Taliban paused for a week or so and staged in Safar, Laki, and Lakari. Mullahs throughout Garmser—not just those who had arrived the previous year from Pakistan—called for jihad against the government and Abdullah Jan. Recruits were rallied and mustered. Immigrants quickly joined the Taliban ranks. The tribal leaders and their families stood back and did not get involved. They talked to the Taliban, fed them, housed them, armed them, but spilled no blood for them. Mullah Naim armed scores of recruits with his newly returned weapons. The main staging ground was Dr Salam's village in Lakari; fifty Taliban from Pakistan came there. Other groups of Arab and Pashtun fighters soon arrived as well and reinforced Naim's burgeoning army.

In late June, Naim was back on the move. He swept north quickly. Few police remained to challenge him. In Mian Poshtay, the tribal militia commander and his six men joined the Taliban. Wakil Manan fled. In Koshtay, the newly-recruited militia ran, taking their weapons with them. Young and inexperienced, they had no fight in them. The Noorzai of Kuchinay Darveshan either sided with the Taliban or fled. The contagion spread rapidly. Regions started turning on their own, ahead of the Taliban advance. Majitek openly declared for the Taliban, well before Naim's cadres arrived. One night, Mohammed Nabi, then with Abdullah Jan in the district center, decided to go to his home, 7 kilometers to the east. Abdullah Jan warned him it was too dangerous. In true Pashtun style, Mohammed Nabi shrugged him off: 'It is my home. I know everyone. I have my gun. I will have no problems.' AK-47 slung over his shoulder, he rode home on his motorcycle. The white flags of the Taliban greeted him the next morning, flying from every roof. He hurried out and carried the ill-tidings to Abdullah Jan: 'Woleswal, all Kharoti is with the Taliban!'[58] Indeed, the whole eastern flank of Garmser had gone over. Hazar Joft, the most populated area of Garmser and the last bastion of the government, was little better. Communities there rose up against Kabeer Khan's police. Posts put up a few hours of resistance at most before fleeing, along with Kabeer Khan himself. No tears were shed when Taliban assassinated him in Lashkar Gah a few days later.

In early July, Naim's lieutenant, Abdul Hadi, whose home was in Hazar Joft, led the Taliban offensive against the district center. Abdullah

Jan tried to hold them back with twenty-five of his men just north of Amir Agha, but they were outgunned and outnumbered. The Taliban had seven PK machine guns. Once the Taliban had turned his flanks, he withdrew. Another delaying action was fought in Hazar Joft before Abdullah Jan retreated into the district center.[59]

By this time it was mid July. Abdullah Jan had thirty of his own men defending the district center. Sixty police reinforcements arrived from the provincial headquarters in Lashkar Gah, but their morale was poor; forty deserted almost immediately, which caused their commander to lose his nerve and flee as well, leaving Abdullah Jan with thirty men again. Abdullah Jan called Governor Daoud: 'I am alone. Everyone has fled. I cannot defend the district center with only thirty men.'[60] Daoud had no answer. Only when Abdullah Jan temporarily withdrew from the district center and the Taliban temporarily captured it (burning an Afghan flag) did twenty new police reinforcements arrive, escorted in by a Canadian battalion temporarily rushed over from Kandahar. The Canadians could not stay. Fighting had engulfed much of Kandahar province, where they were located, and they had to get back. The British were similarly stretched thin, fighting off heavy Taliban attacks in Helmand's northern districts.

Back in the district center, Abdullah Jan made his stand. While in Lashkar Gah, he had managed to reinforce his own cadre to forty men—reaching out to old friends—and convinced the provincial police chief to leave the twenty police reinforcements in Garmser. There were now enough defenders to man the ramparts. In an odd reversal of roles, Abdullah Jan—the old mujahidin commander—looked out upon the communist vista of twenty years before, defending the key points of the district center: the canal crossing north of the bazaar, the hill overlooking the bridge over the Helmand, the post overlooking the eastern canal bridge, and the mud-brick shops along the bazaar road. North, west, east, and south were all covered. The command post was the governor's compound. Abdullah Jan's own men knew how to fight. They were well-armed with AK-47s, RPGs, and PK medium machine guns, and did not want for ammunition.

Abdul Hadi had his 350 Taliban surround the district center, as the mujahidin had for all those years of the jihad. Arabs were in their ranks (Abdullah Jan's veterans thought little of their fighting skills).[61] Skirmishes took place nightly as the defenders sallied southward to keep the Taliban at bay. Eventually, however, numbers told and casualties mounted. After three weeks, in early August, the Taliban stormed the eastern post holding the crossing over the canal and the bridge over the Helmand. Soon the fighting was around the governor's compound itself. Taliban fired from buildings 10 meters from the district center and shelled the defenders with 82 mm mortars and 107 mm rockets.[62]

For twenty-five days, through the entire month of August, the Taliban could not finish off the defenders. They were few and strung out but fought on. When thirty Taliban massed against the district mosque, for instance, only Ahmed Shah with a Kalashnikov and Mohammed Sakhi with a PK medium machine gun were there to stop them. Ahmed Shah was Abdullah Jan's cousin, a veteran of the jihad. Mohammed Sakhi was a young Baluch and future community council member. The Taliban were creeping forward along a mud-walled alleyway, 50 meters away, when Sakhi took careful aim and dropped three with his first burst. Unnerved, the Taliban ran. Around the perimeter, firefights raged day and night. Mir Hamza (the NDS chief) and Abdullah Jan stood at the forefront of the fighting. As ammunition ran out, they handed out their own magazines to their men. When six weeks had passed, Abdul Hadi called Abdullah Jan over the ICOM radio and requested his surrender. Abdullah Jan refused.

At this point, nine of the defenders had been killed and many more had been wounded. Only fifteen were still standing.[63] Sakhi was covered in blood from carrying a colleague into shelter. On 7 September, three days after food had run out and when the police were down to one magazine apiece, Abdullah Jan decided the time had come. That night, he led his men through the enemy lines, using the ground they knew so well to sneak between the Taliban pickets, across the Helmand River, and north to Lashkar Gah. He left Abdul Majan's old weapons with Mohammed Nabi, who surrendered himself and those weapons to Abdul Majan. Abdul Majan—the fair and respected Taliban leader—had handed those weapons to Abdullah Jan in 2001 and had tried to reconcile with the government. The times had seemed bright. His hopes had been disappointed and now he was back with the Taliban—a good man lost. Garmser had fallen.

Lost opportunity

So the opportunity for lasting peace was lost, destroyed from within. True, Naim and his 500 had marched out of Pakistan well-armed and well-trained. True, no British, American, or Afghan soldiers had been there to meet them. Garmser was alone. But why could Garmser not stop them? During the jihad, Garmser had held off hundreds of communists and their tanks, artillery, and bombs for nine years. How did 500 Taliban with pickups and machine guns compare to that? The problem was that Garmser was no longer one. Jihad, civil war, and then the Taliban had split society asunder. After 2001, there was no reconciliation: no reconciliation with the landless, no reconciliation with the mullahs, no reconciliation with the Taliban. Above all, the tribal leaders formed no long-standing alliance to keep out the Taliban. Abdullah Jan tried, but in a tribally based system he did not have the weight to enforce his will. Rivalries flared and unity cracked. The 300 tribal militia and 400 border police that might have been able to handle Naim's 500 were lost to tribal infighting. Lashkar Gah enforced no unity. Governor Sher Mohammed himself was caught up in pursuit of personal power. Fighting with each other, the tribal leaders, police chiefs, and governors opened the door for the Taliban to return, sinking the prosperity of four years of peace, letting in five years of the worst war yet seen.

The tragedy was that it could have been avoided. The Taliban's return was not inevitable. Between the end of 2001 and the summer of 2006, there were plenty of opportunities for intervention on the part of the Afghan government or Britain or the United States. A popular argument has been that the invasion of Iraq in 2003 prevented the United States from sending enough forces to Afghanistan to keep out the Taliban.[64] But this explanation is not satisfactory for Garmser. Taliban strength was never so great as to require hundreds of foreign troops. Things could have been done as late as the summer of 2006 that might have reversed the tide. If Abdullah Jan had been reinforced by 20–30 advisors who could call in air strikes, for instance, the district might not have fallen. The British were operating in Helmand at the time and could have sent something south, shown by the fact that a few days after the district center's fall they actually dispatched a detachment to retake it. Why could that detachment not have come earlier? A few military advisors might have given the police and Abdullah Jan's men the tactical edge to stem the Taliban tide. If Naim had suffered early setbacks, in Safar in June, for example, he might have been unable to rally much of the district behind him. Thinking more broadly, in the face of Dadullah Lang's offensive throughout the south, if forces were in short supply, why did the United States and Great Britain not give President Karzai enough money to raise a Durrani tribal army or a Northern Alliance militia to stop the Taliban in their tracks? Historically, Afghan rulers had put down revolts in that fashion. Such an initiative could have made a difference.

Looking farther back, more possibilities come into focus. Political infighting is what weakened Garmser. In lieu of a strong central government, what was needed was a little outside pressure to hold everyone together. Again, there were plenty of possibilities. Catastrophe might have been averted had Karzai pressured Governor Sher Mohammed Akhundzada to make better decisions before his removal in December 2005. Or the United States could have accelerated its provincial reconstruction team program and, as early as 2002, placed civilian advisors from the US Department of State with Sher Mohammed and Abdullah Jan to help mitigate infighting. Nimble political officers could have prevented the 400 border police and 300 tribal militia from dissolving. A wise advisor with Sher Mohammed might have convinced him to leave Abdullah Jan in place. An advisor in Garmser itself might have settled the Alizai rift, perhaps using a few projects to buy them off. And the United States and Britain could have pressured the Afghan government to institute a land reform policy in Helmand, reaching out to landless immigrants. Any of these actions could have been enough to tip the balance.

One last, larger action could have made a difference. The United States should have built a capable Afghan army and police force by 2006. A fundamental problem was the weakness of the central government, under which the tribal system was unstable. Given that this was clear at the time, the Afghan army and police were far too few in Helmand. In all Afghanistan, the army numbered a scant 36,000 in 2006. More troops were desperately needed. The United States had four years before 2006 to build an army—ample time in other countries. The failure to do so must be one of America's greatest failures in Afghanistan. After 2006, that task could still be accomplished but only in the midst of a raging insurgency. From 2001 to 2006, it could have been done in relative peace. Seven hundred Afghan soldiers positioned in Garmser in 2005 might well have prevented the Taliban from ever returning, at a fraction of the cost of the 1,000 US troops that would eventually deploy to the district.[65]

The years from 2001 to 2006 represented not only an opportunity for the Afghans to have peace; those years also represented an opportunity for the United States and Great Britain to make a difference in Garmser with a few dozen men, a better alternative to the tens of thousands of men that would follow. Once the Taliban took the district center, it was too late. Too many Afghans had aligned with them and been emboldened by their success. Instead of confronting a few hundred Taliban, there were now thousands. Opportunity had slipped away.

With the fall of Garmser to the Taliban in 2006, longer-term reasons for the district's instability since 1978 become clear. The landed tribes, immigrants, and religious leaders had drifted apart following the demise of King Zahir Shah in 1973. The jihad, spelling the end of government control, let rifts between these groups grow. The first Taliban regime broke them open by winning over the immigrants and the religious leaders. By 2001, the tribes, immigrants, and religious leaders could no longer be easily brought back together. The divided environment allowed the Taliban to maintain popular support. On top of this, time and again after the jihad, tribal leaders proved unable to cooperate with one another. The tribal leaders and Abdullah Jan, while powerful as individuals, were too divided and too prone to competition to control the district. They resembled eighteenth-century European states vying for power. No government formed that could unite them. Indeed, led by tribal leaders itself, the government was party to, rather than above, tribal politics. This debilitating trend was apparent in the civil war that immediately followed the jihad, in the self-interest that prevented the tribal leaders from uniting as one against the Taliban in 1994, and finally from 2004 to 2006 as this chapter has described. Conflicts started and the Taliban twice gained control because tribal leaders did not cooperate. The existence of Pakistan exacerbated the problem, giving the Taliban sanctuary to recover and mass the forces necessary for their 2006 offensive. So did the canal project begun in the 1950s. The immigrants and the land issues that it introduced were a permanent source of strife for the district, exploited by the Taliban. A grand plan gone awry, agricultural prosperity had been short-lived; but social discord long-lasting.

Yet none of this made Garmser ungovernable. Between 1994 and 2001, the Taliban with their set hierarchy proved otherwise. The Karzai government and United States might have replicated their success between 2001 and 2006, but US and Allied strategy proved wanting—a final reason for Garmser's instability. It did far too little to prepare to stop a Taliban resurgence, both in terms of building a capable Afghan military and taking the political steps necessary to unite Afghans against outside threats. For all these reasons, the Taliban were able to return in 2006 and drag the United States, Great Britain, and their Allies into renewed war. For anyone who asks why the United States and Great Britain fought so long in Afghanistan for so little gain, the ground between 1978 and 2006 is rich with answers, most tragically in the lost opportunity of 2001 to 2006.

6

THE SECOND TALIBAN REGIME

Islam ter toray landay die.
'Islam is under the shadow of the sword.'
Pashto proverb[1]

With the fall of the district center in September 2006, the second Taliban regime was born. The people of Garmser never looked at the Karzai government the same again. Its influence had proven transitory; the Taliban's long-lasting. In the people's minds, there was one power in Kabul, another in Quetta; the latter stronger than the former. To confront the Taliban in Helmand, a new force had arrived—the British. Karzai and the West were not about to surrender Garmser. From September 2006 until June 2009, companies of storied British regiments filed through Garmser: Royal Marines that had yomped from San Carlos Bay to Port Stanley in the Falklands, Argyll and Sutherland Highlanders that had gone kilted over the top at the Somme, Grenadier Guards that had routed Napoleon's Imperial Guard at Waterloo, Gurkha Rifles that had stormed Gallipoli's highest ridges. The British arrival heralded a long season of unforgiving war, equal to the worst the jihad had offered.

British intervention

The situation in Garmser, and Helmand as a whole, could no longer be salvaged without Western help. The Taliban were too strong and the government was too weak. British forces had started arriving in Helmand in February 2006. Unfortunately, there was only a single battalion, reinforced by a variety of augments, for a grand total of about 1,200 men, hardly enough to protect the whole province. The Helmand-wide offensive of Dadullah Lang, the infamous Taliban commander of southern Afghanistan, forced the British to break apart and disperse the battalion. Detachments were penny-packeted out to districts in northern Helmand: Nowzad, Musa Qala, Kajaki (overlooking the strategic Kajaki Dam), and Sangin. The British committed a platoon or, in the case of Sangin a company, to each. The platoons took position in district centers or fortified posts—later known as 'platoon houses.' Alone and unafraid, the platoon houses became targets for the Taliban. Some of the worst fighting of the war followed.

When the Garmser district center fell, the British scratched together a handful of advisors to go south. On 11 September 2006, those seventeen advisors, hundred Afghan army soldiers, and seventy police assaulted the Garmser district center. It took six days of fighting, artillery barrages and 54 air strikes to clear out the 400 or so Taliban—an impressive feat of arms for the fledgling Afghan army and police. The cost was sixteen friendly casualties, including the Afghan army commander, who died leading a frontal assault on a Taliban position.[2]

The British set up a base on the grounds of the old agricultural college and named it Forward Operating Base (FOB) Delhi. A company from 45 Royal Marine Commando occupied it. With eighty men, the British could only defend the district center, itself nothing more than rows of empty bazaar stalls and an empty government building. The defense was along the same lines as Abdullah Jan's a month earlier and the communists' before him. The British strongpointed the bridge and the main canal crossing and manned the southern line of shops. Of the Afghan government, only a handful of police stayed in Garmser. It was the jihad all over again. The government controlled the district center; the insurgents everywhere else.

The new Taliban jihad

With everything but the district center in their hands, the Taliban organized their military forces and set up a government. Mullah Naim, having led the initial offensive into southern Helmand, handed over control of Garmser to his lieutenant, Abdul Hadi Agha. Originally a mullah from Hazar Joft, Abdul Hadi had joined the Taliban soon after their arrival in 1994. First, he had served as the mayor of the Garmser district center bazaar and later as deputy governor of Faryab province in the north. In 2001, the Northern Alliance warlord General Dostum captured him and turned him over to the United States. He spent a few years in Guantanamo Bay prison before being released and rejoining the Taliban. With Mullah Omar's permission, Naim made him one of his deputies and appointed him district governor of Garmser. The appointment was based on the fact that he had been with the Taliban a long time and could be trusted. An elder who had been with the Taliban said of him: 'Abdul Hadi was a harsh man. He did not have much knowledge.'[3] In spite of that, he was effective. Education does not make capable Afghan leaders. He would do much to mobilize Garmser against the British and the government. Naim himself attended to higher province-wide matters, working out of Laki, where he was from and his wider family still lived. Poppy taxation kept him especially busy. Sometimes he stayed in Abdullah Jan's old compound in Koshtay—taking on the trappings of the old regime's power.

Beneath Abdul Hadi fell a large number of cadre commanders, such as Qari Abdullah, Mullah Ismael, Mullah Azizullah, and Mullah Abdullah (see Table 3). They were in charge of cadres of ten to forty fighters. Most were young lower-class Baluch or Ghilzai men from Garmser itself. Many called themselves mullahs, and more than a few had some degree of religious education. I have heard that anywhere from 500 to 1,000 Taliban fighters were stationed in the district. Conscription was not re-instituted. This was one of the many ways that the second Taliban regime improved upon the first. Getting rid of conscription went a long way toward slipping the discontent that had afflicted the first regime's latter years. Abdul Hadi went village by village and recruited men.[4] He sat with them in their homes and asked them face to face to join him. The majority of the recruits, like the cadre commanders, came from Garmser's poor immigrant class—Taraki, Baluch, Kakar, and Kharoti.[5] In the words of Mohammed Nabi, now one of Abdul Majan's lieutenants, 'In Majitek, everyone was fighting.'[6] Many Afghans have also told me (so many that I must give the story some credence) that Arabs, Uzbeks, Pakistani Pashtuns (Waziris), and Punjabis were in the Taliban ranks, as were Afghan Pashtuns out of Kandahar and Musa Qala. The

Taliban cadre that was based in Mian Poshtay, for example, evidently had twenty-five men who were from Mian Poshtay (originally immigrants from Uruzgan) and twenty men from Pakistan.[7] Similarly, in March 2008, one Taliban mullah informed Western media that 40 percent of the insurgents fighting in Garmser were outsiders.[8] Garmser was becoming one of the main battlefields in Afghanistan. Outsiders came in order to fight the British. Taliban commanders told the rank and file that they would capture Lashkar Gah and once again attack Kabul.[9] Morale was high.

With infidels in Lashkar Gah and the district center, something of the spirit of the jihad returned. That the British looked like the communists of twenty years before, bottled up in the district center, hardly helped. Nor did their imperial past. The brother of Mohammed Nadir told me: 'The English killed many civilians and upset the people. Everyone fought the English.'[10]

In 2011, I visited an abandoned USAID-built school in Bartaka, a sturdy white symbol of lost progress. The Taliban had taken it over and used it for shelter, covering its walls with graffiti. The commanders who had camped there had scribbled their names in the classrooms— Dadullah Lang, Mullah Borjan, Mullah Azizullah. Most telling, however, were the reasons these guests gave for fighting. 'Karzai says that he is a Muslim. He is not. He is working for the infidel.' Or, 'I am mujahidin. I will stay until I drive the foreigners out of the country.' And finally, 'I do not want my life. I want freedom for Afghanistan. Kill the infidel.'[11]

This is far from the only evidence I encountered of the importance of the idea of jihad for young Taliban. Upon recruitment, it was known that new fighters put their hand on the Koran and promised to fight the infidel until their death.[12] A captured insurgent once told me: 'I did not want to blow up Afghans. I just wanted to blow up Americans.' His words sounded harsh but the willingness to defend one's country against foreigners might also be called patriotic. I certainly doubted the boy would have felt this way without foreigners in his country. Nor did I think he harbored terrorist thoughts of going after Americans in America itself. I was also involved in meetings with Taliban who had decided to surrender. Most had joined the movement between 2006 and 2008. Some were educated. Some were not. One, fairly uneducated, said that he had joined the Taliban in order to fight the infidel. Another, more educated, attested to the same thing: 'We were young. We decided to

Table 3: Taliban commanders in Garmser, 2006–11.

Name	Duty	Social status	Home	Tribe
Mullah Naim Barech	Helmand governor	Mullah	Laki, Garmser	Tarin
Abdul Hadi Agha	Garmser district governor	Mullah	Hazar Joft, Garmser	Sayid
Obaid Rahman	Garmser district governor	Unknown	Kandahar	Noorzai
Mullah Misher	Garmser district governor	Farmer	Loya Darveshan, Garmser	Alizai
Sayid Wali	Garmser district governor	Unknown	Amir Agha, Garmser	Noorzai
Mullah Azizullah	Cadre leader	Mullah	Safar, Garmser	Baluch
Mullah Ismael	Cadre leader	Mullah	Mian Poshtay, Garmser	Tokhi
Mullah Habibullah	Mullah/facilitator	Mullah	Hazar Joft, Garmser	Noorzai
Mullah Mujahed	Cadre leader	Unknown	Loya Darveshan, Garmser	Itsakzai
Mullah Abdullah	Cadre leader	Unknown	Kuchinay Darveshan, Garmser	Noorzai
Qari Abdullah	Cadre leader	Mullah	Safar, Garmser	Baluch
Mohammed Nabi	Cadre leader	Elder	Majitek, Garmser	Kakar
Mullah Qadrat	Frontline commander	Unknown	Unknown	Baluch
Mullah Jumaludin	Cadre leader	Unknown	Mian Poshtay, Garmser	Noorzai
Mullah Abdul Majan	Advisor	Mullah	Majitek, Garmser	Taraki

fight. We wanted to take up jihad and fight the infidel.' One more remembered: 'Abdul Hadi Agha came to my home. He told me that foreigners were in Afghanistan. They were going to conquer our home. I was convinced.' Dr Salam, the Alizai landowner who had helped the Taliban return to power, reported that many insurgents believed that the United States ran the Afghan government, a deep affront to a Pashtun.[13] Of course, young Taliban fighters took up arms for all kinds of reasons—to make money, to see the thrill of combat, even to spite their parents. Plenty had grievances with the government or tribal leaders. Nevertheless, the importance of jihad and fighting infidel invaders cannot be discounted.

Back to the front

Like the mujahidin before them, the Taliban ringed the district center. Just 200 meters from the British posts, they dug fighting positions—small trenches, fighting holes, makeshift bunkers, often based on irrigation ditches and mud-walled grape vineyards. Thatched roofs were placed on many in order to hide them from aircraft. Strung together, the positions formed an in-depth defensive line, reminiscent of what might be found in a conventional war. Twenty or fifty meters behind one position would be another position. Others would be 50 meters to the right or left. Capturing one position would only invite fire from the surrounding ones. The British dubbed the positions the 'FLET' (forward line of enemy troops). The Taliban always manned a few of the forward positions, observing or harassing the British. The others were occupied during firefights. There were as many as 300 fighters assigned to the frontline at a time, either posted in a forward position or staged in reserve farther back. The Taliban fighters rarely assaulted British positions. Rather, they stood back 200 or 300 meters and shot AK-47s, PK medium machine guns, and RPGs at them. Two or three *dshkas* were sighted in on the British. These large tripod-mounted heavy machine guns can range over 1,000 meters, their rounds piercing through cars, sandbags, and HESCO barriers.[14] Mortar rounds and rockets were lobbed at the defenders as well, with varying degrees of inaccuracy. Similar to the old mujahidin system, cadres fought for a few weeks around the district center and then rotated out for rest in their home areas (whether Darveshan, Koshtay, Mian Poshtay, Lakari, Laki, or Safar).[15] Cadres in the frontline fell under a single tactical commander. The first was Mullah Qadrat, made famous by his efforts to organize the front-line. His headquarters was inside a large compound in Jugroom, a village roughly 5 kilometers down the main canal road from the district center, near Loya Darveshan.

For nearly twenty months, British infantry and Afghan police slugged it out with the Taliban fighters across the Garmser no-man's-land.[16] Every day stand-off firefights broke out. Heavy fighting caused the population in Hazar Joft to flee to Pakistan, Lashkar Gah, or camps in the desert.[17] With few civilians in or around the district center, the British commanders lifted standard restrictions on engaging targets. Those restrictions usually required that a target be 'positively identified' as hostile before any triggers could be pulled. In Garmser, British soldiers could shoot at whatever they pleased. Anyone moving south of the district center was considered hostile. Air strikes pounded the FLET. Bomb fragments still litter Hazar Joft's fields and villages today. One Taliban later said: 'There was very hard fighting when the British were here. We shot our weapons every day. Many airplanes bombed us.'[18] From time to time, the British forayed south against Jugroom or east against Majitek. Such forays encountered stiff resistance and often had to turn back. Even if resistance was overcome, forces were too scarce to hold anything permanently, other than the empty yet beleaguered district center. The balance of forces favored the Taliban.

This was never clearer than when the Royal Marines assaulted Jugroom in early January 2007. A large compound there was the location of Mullah Qadrat's frontline headquarters. The compound stood alongside the river. The British dubbed it a 'fort' for its outer wall and watch towers. It was really just a well-fortified Pashtun village. The British decided to seize the compound in order to draw Taliban fighters into a battle in the open, where they could easily be killed. Once the killing was done, the British would withdraw—a classic set-piece plan of attrition. The operation was preceded by a set of carefully planned air strikes against Abdullah Jan's old compound in Koshtay, about 12 kilometers farther south, where District Governor Abdul Hadi staged fighters before sending them onward to Qadrat on the frontline. Hitting it was expected to disrupt the defense of Jugroom. On 11 January, a B-1 bomber dropped four 2,000-pound and six 500-pound bombs on the compound. British Apache attack helicopters cleaned up what was left. When they were done, nothing remained of Abdullah Jan's compound except a few sections of wall, burnt tree trunks, and the generator room.

Locals say twenty-five Taliban were killed (along with fourteen Taliban prisoners) and forty were wounded.

Jugroom itself was hit four days later on 15 January. Roughly 100 Royal Marines swept west through the desert in order to assault the compound from across the river. The preparatory air and artillery barrage included twenty 2,000-pound bombs from another B-1 bomber, the largest expenditure of ordnance at any one time in Garmser's history that I am aware of. Unfortunately, the Royal Marines waited an hour to cross the river, plenty of time for the Taliban to recover. Mullah Qadrat rushed in reinforcements from Majitek, Darveshan, and Laki. When the Royal Marines finally got across the river, there was no easy killing to be had. Heavy resistance resulted in an eight-hour firefight. A-10 and B-1 air strikes could not dislodge the Taliban from the compound. The Royal Marines could not move forward and fell back across the river. Under a hail of fire, helicopters flew in to rescue one of the fallen Royal Marines. In all, the British took five casualties.[19] The Taliban suffered too. Locals still mention the battle today: twenty-six insurgents were killed, including Qadrat. If bitter for the British, from the viewpoint of a Taliban cadre leader: 'that battle was a defeat for the Taliban.'[20] For a few weeks Taliban attacks around the district center slackened.

Company after company held the district center from autumn 2006 to spring 2008, a shield for Lashkar Gah. For much of this time, the Taliban believed they were winning in Helmand. In October 2006, in northern Helmand, the British and the government had signed a truce with the elders of Musa Qala. The district center was turned over to the elders, which, in reality, left it in the hands of the Taliban. In early 2007, Dr Salam led a delegation to Lashkar Gah to negotiate a similar British withdrawal from Garmser. Fortunately, Provincial Governor Asadullah Wafa refused (his predecessor, Governor Daoud, had been removed). The government had learned from Musa Qala and would not abandon its foothold in Garmser. Over time, Afghans reinforced the British: twenty police and 300 or so border police; too ill-trained to enable the British to take the offensive but numerous enough to make life easier for the British soldiers manning the frontline.[21]

A Taliban district

While the battles around the district center raged on, the rest of Garmser fell firmly under the Taliban. District Governor Abdul Hadi set up his capital in Amir Agha and reintroduced Taliban law and order.[22] He spent a good deal of time running the war but also handled civil matters—appointing judges, collecting taxes, and overseeing land redistribution. Garmser had become a Taliban district, one of many in Helmand.

This second Taliban regime was better than the first: more inclusive, more prosperous, less oppressive. Naim (who was running the southern Helmand war effort out of Laki) and Abdul Hadi recognized that oppressing the tribes in the late 1990s had been a mistake. This time, they tried to win over as much of Garmser's society as possible. The religious leaders and the landless immigrants supported them already—and the Taliban continued to try to address their grievances. Additionally, the Taliban worked to win over the landed tribes. They avoided imprisoning or executing tribal leaders. For this and other strategic reasons previously discussed, the second regime initially enjoyed wide support from tribal elites. The entire Alizai tribe, tribal leaders and all, were behind them. The leading families kept out of the direct fighting but gave money, poppy, shelter, food, and, of course, weapons. The Noorzai tribal leaders were less united. Several fled. Others passively submitted. Certain Noorzai village elders gave the Taliban intelligence and weapons.

The Barakzai, Abdullah Jan's tribe, were the exception. Abdullah Jan had not only fought against the Taliban in 2006; he had gone out of his way to fight them from Baram Chah to Herat to Panjshir in the 1990s. He and his tribe were their inveterate opponents. Now, the Taliban punished them. Dr Salam invited Abdullah Jan's cousin, the educated Mir Atem, to come back to Garmser from Lashkar Gah, guaranteeing his safety. Abdullah Jan and Ahmed Shah (Mir Atem's brother) begged him not to go. Mir Atem believed he could trust Dr Salam. Even though Salam might have helped the Taliban come to power in Garmser, he was still a Pashtun and a guarantee of safety meant something. When Mir Atem arrived at his home, Naim and Mullah Ismael were waiting to greet him. They executed him on the spot. Naim was generally known as a merciful leader, open to reconciliation. But just like Abdullah Jan's patience with squatters, Naim's mercy had its limits.

The Taliban kept the hierarchy and unity that had marked their first regime. There was clear and centralized command and control. Abdullah Jan had dealt with police chiefs who did not listen to him and tribal leaders who tried to remove him. No such infighting cursed the Taliban.

Their chain of command was much more sensible. The cadre leaders and mullahs fell under the district governor, Abdul Hadi. In turn, Abdul Hadi obeyed Mullah Naim; who obeyed Dadullah Lang; who obeyed Mullah Omar. Alizai tribal leader Shah Jahan was living in Laki at the time. His politically astute mind noted this hierarchy and how it was strengthened by the close friendships that commanders had developed in the madrasas and during the years fighting together:

'The Taliban leaders did not fight with themselves like the government because their system was healthy. The leaders had close relationships. They did not question each other because they were close friends. They never disobeyed Naim. They always gave money to him. They never argued over money or cars or other things. They obeyed everything Naim said. Everything was one.'[23]

Even as losses mounted after day after day of fighting with the British, cadre leaders steadfastly obeyed their superiors. Whatever plays for power and arguments occurred behind the scenes, there were no major defections, incidents of Taliban fighting with each other, or cases of good Taliban commanders being removed because of a feud.

For justice, Naim and Abdul Hadi created a new two-tiered system. It was an improvement over the old religious court of the first regime. As before, the village mullahs were empowered to settle disputes in their own villages. Above them, the Taliban appointed twelve new senior judges to roam the district and resolve disputes between the people. They handled cases that the mullahs could not resolve on their own. The judges also met together regularly in a council in Amir Agha. Like the cadre leaders, they reported to Abdul Hadi, another facet of Taliban hierarchy. Punishment remained harsh. Guilty persons were imprisoned or sentenced to death. The Taliban made this clear on 2 September 2006, before they had even captured the district center, by hanging a murderer in the middle of Safar bazaar.[24] As much as possible, the judges and mullahs tried not to offend elders and tried to include them in decisions that pertained to their villages. Outside their villages, however, elders were given little responsibility for resolving disputes. Taliban justice seems to have been well received. One fighter told me: 'The work of the judges had a good benefit. They made decisions that solved problems.'[25]

One judge was Maulawi Mohammedullah, a Taraki originally from Loya Darveshan. The Taraki tribe was one of the poorest in Garmser, living on the driest land by the desert and having originally been nomads. The Taraki had long supported the Taliban because of their respect for Islam and the help they gave to the landless. Maulawi Mohammedullah had studied for nine years in Pakistan before coming back to Garmser. In 2006, he was about thirty years old and working as a scholar in Darveshan. He joined the Taliban, in his words, because: 'The people had many problems at that time. I believed the Taliban regime could bring them peace. The local villagers asked me to become a judge with the Taliban. I knew that the Taliban fighters could not do this work. So I asked Abdul Hadi Agha if I could become a judge.'[26] Mohammedullah's responsibility was to handle crimes, land disputes, water disputes, and family disputes in Mian Poshtay. The people were obliged to accept his judgment. If they did not, he could call in fighters to enforce his decision.[27] That said, I never heard any complaints about Maulawi Mohammedullah's judgments. I suspect people heeded his decisions because they were fair rather than because they feared him.

The most famous judge was Maulawi Abdul Razik, from Darveshan. Roughly thirty-eight years old and an Islamic scholar, he ran a madrasa, was the district director of education, and served as the religious leader for all Garmser. Ghulam Rassoul respected him tremendously as a merciful man who did not exact cruel punishments: 'He was a very knowledgeable man and never ruled to execute someone.'[28] Abdul Majan, the former Uruzgan deputy governor who had tried to reconcile with the government during the Karzai regime's first years, was in Garmser again too. He had handled civil matters in the past and had helped resolve disputes. Under the second Taliban regime, he did not serve as a judge but advised District Governor Abdul Hadi on justice. He had long been respected as fair and just.

Regarding law enforcement, with so many fighters in the district, there was no need for a police force. Counter-intelligence was a different matter. The first Taliban regime in Garmser had not been under attack, so ferreting out spies and informants had not been a priority. The second regime, on the other hand, faced constant threat of air strikes and special forces (commando) raids aiming to kill or capture Taliban leaders. They had to protect themselves. People giving information to the government or the British had to be removed. Abdul Hadi created a layered system to weed out spies and the disloyal. At the bottom, village mullahs were charged with keeping the people in line. Many mullahs had arms and a small number of men. They watched the people and kept lists of who was doing good work for the government. At night, they checked in on the people in their homes. To augment the mullahs, Abdul Hadi ran a network of intelligence agents who secretly searched for spies. And on top of that, he formed a 'commission' that devised plans to hunt down spies and served punishments for those captured.[29] Punishment was usually execution. On 8 April 2007, for example, the Taliban beheaded Afghan journalist Ajmal Naqshbandi in Garmser, for supposedly gathering information on their activities.

Economically, Garmser was booming. Poppy cultivation took off. The old ban was never re-imposed. Rather, the Taliban actively encouraged cultivation. Taliban officials themselves managed the shipping and the all-important taxation of the crop. Poppy taxation was the Taliban's main source of revenue (they also taxed land and kept Abdullah Jan's old tax on wheat). Farmers dedicated thousands of hectares to poppy.[30] They collected the wet opium goo from the bulbs, took it to a bazaar, where it was sold to smugglers, who transported it to Pakistan or Iran for processing into heroin. The Taliban levied two taxes against the poppy. In the villages, mullahs took a percentage of farmers' poppy crop and passed it up to District Governor Abdul Hadi. Mullah Ismael—the cadre leader with the crippled shoulder who had pushed Wakil Manan out of Mian Poshtay—was a particularly efficient tax collector. In the bazaars, official tax collectors took a cash percentage from smugglers in return for permission to pick up wet opium in Garmser. Abdul Hadi passed all the taxes to Naim in Laki. As the Taliban commander for southern Helmand, Naim gathered the taxes from the districts of Khaneshin, Dishu, Nawa, and Marjah, as well as Garmser.[31] Thus the war effort was financed.

The bazaars were the hubs for the poppy trade and grew accordingly. In Amir Agha, Abdul Hadi built a brand new bazaar, known as the 'Taliban bazaar.' Most of the old shop-owners from Hazar Joft relocated there. It became the center of district economic activity, fed by poppy production. The Lakari and Safar bazaars drastically expanded: Lakari under the patronage of Mohammed Nadir, former mujahidin commander and Alizai tribal leader; Safar under the patronage of Sultan Mohammed, tribal leader of the dominant Noorzai clan there (Salay Mohammed's brother). These bazaars had been set up during Abdullah Jan's last tenure. Poppy profits opened up more and more shops in each. Wet opium, weapons, and ammunition were sold. As the entry point into Garmser, with roads coming from Pakistan, Kandahar, and Iran,

Safar bazaar grew especially large. It became a thriving marketplace and thoroughfare for the poppy trade: goods from Pakistan and Iran imported in, wet opium exported out. It even had two clinics, where real doctors treated injured Taliban (pharmacists offered lesser treatment at the other two bazaars). Abdul Hadi's tax collectors in each bazaar taxed wheat and bazaar shop revenues in addition to poppy. Overall, it was an impressive bout of economic activity. Never before had three bazaars been bustling in Garmser.

The second Taliban regime had done much to run a better government, but it was far from perfect. Goods and services were weak and, though less oppressive than the first regime, punishments were still harsh. Most people I met appreciated the law and order that the Taliban brought but their shortcomings wore on them, just as police abuse and tribal leader heavy-handedness had worn on them during Abdullah Jan's tenures. One fighter told me, with more than a little hyperbole: 'The Taliban gave no help to the people. Infrastructure fell apart. Roads were broken. Bridges were broken. The people had to give help to the Taliban. They had to pay taxes and to fight.'[32] The Taliban were not this bad but the sentiment underlines their shortcomings in delivering goods and services.

This was most notable in education. Under the first regime, the government schools had been kept open, religious leaders largely replacing secular teachers. Under the second regime, the government schools were shut, including the brand new ones in Koshtay, Bartaka, and Amir Agha. Mullah Omar had issued a Taliban 'code of conduct' in 2006 that ordered secular schools to be closed or burned. It allowed only mullahs and religious scholars to be teachers. The reason was that secular schools and teachers strengthened the 'system of the infidels' and were 'destroying Islam.'[33] In Safar, the school was leveled and the land used for poppy. In Laki, Naim turned the elementary school into a madrasa. His men occasionally held prisoners in its classrooms. The story was that the prisoners were tortured there. The nearby middle school was demolished.[34] In two or three places, large madrasas took the place of the secular schools. In most places, children simply attended their local mosque where their mullah taught basic reading, writing, math, and religion. Overall, education during the second Taliban regime fell short of what had been done during the first.

Land was the Taliban's biggest headache. Upon retaking power, Naim regranted immigrants the land that they had received during the first regime. This pleased the poor tribes living near the desert in the east who had been on government land since the 1970s, such as the Taraki. It also pleased the newer immigrants from places such as Uruzgan who had come during the communist regime or the first Taliban regime and mixed in within the canal zone. All were relieved to be fully recognized citizens again. Under the Karzai regime and the tribal leaders, their land deeds had been invalidated. They had been forced to live under the threat of eviction. The Taliban also resumed their program of redistributing land. District Governor Abdul Hadi brought in new Ghilzai immigrants and gave them government land. Private land was sometimes seized as well.

But in Garmser it always proved hard to please one group without upsetting another. Land became a point of friction with the tribal leaders. In a few cases, Taliban leaders acted in a manner reminiscent of the heavy-handed tribal leaders. Qari Abdullah (the cadre leader working out of the shrine in Safar) took Noorzai land in Loya Darveshan by force and gave it to poor farmers. In Laki, Naim took some of Shah Wali Khan's land and annexed it to his village. Meanwhile, hundreds of Taraki who had fled under Abdullah Jan returned, reclaiming the land originally given them by the Taliban. Abdul Hadi allowed the Taraki to dam the long eastern canal and divert water to their fields by the desert, something the canal system had not been designed to do. The dam stopped up the water farther north and flooded fields around Amir Agha, infuriating the Noorzai.

The Taliban could never square the circle between the interests of the tribal leaders and the needs of the poor landless immigrants, the Taliban's primary support base. From what I learned, Naim, Abdul Hadi Agha, and Abdul Majan were aware of the problem and were trying to find solutions. They held shuras with religious and tribal leaders. They had the judges come down with rulings. But the fundamental divide remained. By early 2008, Taliban leaders and tribal leaders were growing apart. Near Amir Agha, the Taliban imprisoned several Noorzai elders for not fully supporting them, causing the people of the village to rise up and free their elders. Taliban reinforcements locked down the village, but it was clear that support among the landed tribes was wavering.[35] What was happening in Laki would be far more damaging. Shah Wali Khan, Ghulam Rassoul, and Shah Jahan—three of the great Alizai tribal leaders—began quarreling with Mullah Naim's tribesmen over land. Naim had grown up in Laki and his tribesmen farmed land right next to Shah Wali Khan's village. The quarrel led to fighting. In early 2008, Shah Wali Khan, Ghulam Rassoul, and Shah Jahan, the core of the Taliban's tribal support base, left for Pakistan (see Chapter 9). Because of land, the unity between the tribal leaders and the Taliban had weakened.

The second Taliban regime once again showed that the Taliban could govern Garmser effectively. Their hierarchy precluded the infighting that had crippled the Karzai government between 2001 and 2006. In many ways, outside the fighting around the district center, the second regime was even more prosperous than the first. This and their land redistribution and religious policies ensured the continued support of the immigrants and the religious leaders. In general, the fact that the Taliban had come back to power a second time and ruled effectively convinced many in Garmser that they were as legitimate as the Karzai government. But the second Taliban regime was not perfect. In spite of the Taliban's best efforts, the religious leaders, immigrants, and tribal leaders, whom Taliban policies had helped split apart in the first place, could not be brought together. The rifts in Garmser's society remained. In the end, the Taliban simply suppressed discontented tribal leaders. What mattered here was their disciplined political structure. It meant that they could overpower them in a way that had never been possible for Abdullah Jan or the Karzai government writ large.

Attrition

As the Taliban dealt with the challenges of governing, month after month the fighting along the front line raged on. Taliban casualties mounted. The British estimated that at least 500 Taliban were killed or injured between the end of 2006 and the spring of 2008. Besides attrition at the front line, air strikes and special forces (commando) raids killed Taliban leaders. In 2007 and 2008, in Kandahar and Helmand, such targeted attacks killed or captured over twenty-five Taliban district governors, cadre leaders, and other important figures.[36] The British were always trying to find Taliban leaders and masses of fighters behind the frontline. When they found them, aircraft bombed or special forces raided their location. These actions never broke the Taliban but did inflict losses on their leadership. In 2007, Abdul Hadi himself was killed in a raid. Obaid Rahman, a Noorzai from Kandahar, replaced him as Taliban district governor of Garmser.

117

The real coup occurred in May 2007. The infamous Dadullah Lang, Taliban commander for southern Afghanistan, held a meeting in Darveshan that month with his commanders to discuss future strategy. Naim was there too. Somehow the British learned of the meeting and sent in SBS (Special Boat Service) commandos. Flying in on helicopters, the commandos burst into the compound where the meeting was taking place, instigating a confused firefight. The SBS killed Dadullah and hit Naim in the leg and stomach. Several other commanders were injured as well. Ghulam Rassoul rushed Naim to Pakistan for treatment. Naim recovered but never returned to Garmser for more than a quick visit.

Such losses wore on the Taliban. At the end of 2007, British forces reported that the frequency of attacks on the district center had dropped. In early 2008, the Gurkhas pressed out of the district center and captured one dirt knoll 500 meters west of the river and another 500 meters east of the canal. The Taliban suffered roughly forty casualties in futile attempts to retake the hills. These counter-attacks aside, Taliban attacks were no longer as bold or as large as they had been in 2006. They had learned that it was better to maintain pressure than take casualties in hazardous attacks. Firefights were shorter and at longer distances.[37] Mir Hamza, the NDS Chief (NDS is the Afghan intelligence service) who had fought alongside Abdullah Jan in the district center in 2006, returned to live there and help the British. His arrival improved the British ability to capture Taliban.

The combat losses also caused elders—already distant because of the Taliban land policies—to fear for their own well-being. Nothing frightened them more than the death of Mohammed Nadir, the most prominent of the four great Alizai tribal leaders. He had been one of Garmser's most famous mujahidin commanders and had led the Alizai during the civil war with the Noorzai. To build the power of the tribe and his own family, he had sided with the Taliban in 2006, leaving behind his friendship with Abdullah Jan. After the government had fallen, he had stayed in his village in Lakari and built up its bazaar. When Shah Wali Khan, Ghulam Rassoul, and Shah Jahan (the other three Alizai tribal leaders) fled to Pakistan, he remained behind. He was not fighting alongside the Taliban personally but the British had caught wind of his relationship with them and bombed his home. The mujahidin commander died sitting in his home on 24 January 2008. The Taliban had never given him the power he craved. Mohammed Nadir's family and

Dr Salam fled to Pakistan. Other elders, mainly Noorzai, made their way to Lashkar Gah.

In 2006, the Taliban had appeared unstoppable. By 2008, stalemate was evident. The Taliban could not take the district center. The 300 or so British and Afghans could not break out southward, even after the death of Abdul Hadi and the wounding of Naim. The Taliban cadres weathered the attrition at the frontline, losses from targeted air strikes and raids, and the flight of tribal leaders. Fallen leaders were replaced. Support from the immigrants and religious leaders did not waver. Young men still volunteered to fight. There is no reason to think the Taliban would not have ruled effectively and held on at the frontline for many more years, if not indefinitely. A much larger commitment on the part of the British and the Americans was needed to reverse what the Taliban had accomplished.

The Marines come to Garmser

If there is a decisive battle of the thirty years of war in Garmser, it is the assault of the 24th Marine Expeditionary Unit on Hazar Joft and Amir Agha. Other battles—Amir Agha in 1982 or the capture of the district center in 1988—affected the course of Garmser but none had the resounding impact of the Marine assault of May 2008.

At the beginning of 2008, the administration of President George W. Bush realized that Afghanistan was faltering. The situation in the south was particularly bad. In Helmand, the British had been reinforced from 3,000 to 8,500 men but were still essentially on the defensive. In Kandahar, insurgents were edging closer and closer to Kandahar City. In both provinces, the Taliban had seized control of entire districts. Garmser was known throughout Afghanistan as a Taliban safe haven and entry point for fighters from Pakistan moving into Helmand and Kandahar. The Bush administration planned to reinforce Afghanistan but could not do so until Iraq calmed down. To staunch the bleeding, the 24th Marine Expeditionary Force, the theatre reserve for the Middle East and South Asia, was sent to Afghanistan. General Daniel McNeill, the commander of all coalition forces in Afghanistan, instructed the Marines to occupy the old Saudi-constructed air strip in the far southern desert and interdict Taliban coming north from Pakistan. To get there, the Marines would first clear out eastern Hazar Joft and Majitek in coordination with the British.

119

The 24th Marine Expeditionary Unit arrived in Afghanistan in March 2008. It consisted of a 1,200-man reinforced Marine infantry battalion (1st Battalion, 6th Marine Regiment), an artillery battery, and an air element of 6 AV-8B fighters, 8 AH-1W attack helicopters, and support helicopters, together with logistics and headquarters personnel. I observed the first ten days of the 24th Marine Expeditionary Force's battle for Hazar Joft and Amir Agha from their headquarters at Kandahar Air Force base: too far away to know what was really happening on the ground; just close enough for a memory of how America's intervention in Garmser began.

The US Marine Corps is known as a small but aggressive fighting force, endowed with remarkable *esprit de corps*. It has a reputation for fighting in America's toughest battles—Belleau Wood, Iwo Jima, Chosin Reservoir, Khe Sanh—and attracts young men and women who want that experience. Lieutenants and captains, corporals and sergeants are trained to show initiative and take risk. They would have been a formidable opponent under any circumstances. The Taliban had the particular bad luck of facing 1st Battalion, 6th Marine Regiment (1/6). The battalion had seen heavy fighting in the city of Ramadi in Iraq in 2006 and 2007 and was said to have turned the tide there through relentless patrolling, outposting, and cooperating with the Iraqi police and army. Most of those Marines, including the intelligence officer, operations officer, two of the four company commanders, and the sniper platoon commander, remained with the unit for Garmser. A crack battalion.[38]

By the end of April, 1/6 had staged in the desert, near the district center. The northern part of Garmser (Hazar Joft, Majitek, and Amir Agha) was dubbed 'the Snakeshead' for the shape of the northern section of the canal system. The Marines faced at least 600 Taliban in Hazar Joft and Amir Agha. They were mostly Pashtuns from Garmser but, as had been the case since 2006, Pakistani Pashtuns, Baluch, and Arabs were present as well. Aware of the pending Marine attack, the Quetta shura— the Taliban ruling council set up by Mullah Omar—decided to stand and fight. District Governor Obaid Rahman was in charge, answering to Naim in Quetta. The tactical commander at the frontline was a man called 'Pakol' who was not from Garmser. His deputies were Haji Selani, Mullah Misher, and Mullah Abdullah. The Taliban's defenses consisted of the in-depth network of trenches, bunkers, and fighting holes surrounding the district center, backed up by strongpoints at Jugroom and

Amir Agha. There were few improvised explosive devices (IEDs) at this time; insurgents preferred to rely on AK-47s, PK medium machine guns, RPGs, rockets, 82 mm mortars, and *dshka* heavy machine guns.

Colonel Peter Petronzio, commander of the 24th Marine Expeditionary Unit, decided to attack from the east rather than out of the district center, upon which the Taliban defenses were oriented and from which Pakol, I later learned, expected an attack. Colonel Petronzio planned to send his men into Majitek in order to outflank the Taliban positions, catch them off guard, and then cut them off by taking Amir Agha.[39] On the night of 28 April, the Marines launched their assault. Of 1/6's three infantry companies, one (C/1/6) advanced on the ground toward the northernmost corner of Majitek. Two others landed by helicopter (B/1/6 and A/1/6) farther south. The northern of the two patrolled westward and posted the long eastern drainage canal. The other pushed southeast toward Amir Agha.[40]

As the Marines set up patrol bases and pushed out, heavy fighting erupted. Most of the population of Hazar Joft, Amir Agha, and Majitek fled. Some went to camps in the desert. Others ran south. The Quetta shura stuck to its decision. They wanted to hold Hazar Joft and Amir Agha and rushed in reinforcements. The fighters too believed that the Marines could be defeated. Years of fighting a lone outnumbered British company had left them over-confident. One cadre leader told me: 'We were determined to fight. Our leaders ordered us not to retreat. They said foreigners were trying to seize Afghanistan. We accepted their orders. We thought that we must fight. We did not realize how strong the Americans would be.'[41]

The degree of Taliban resistance caused General McNeill to scuttle the plan to occupy the Saudi-constructed airstrip in the middle of the desert and focus the Marines on clearing the Taliban out of Hazar Joft, Majitek, and Amir Agha, with the intent of freeing the district center once and for all. During the first thirty-five days, the Marines engaged in 170 firefights, many several hours in length. The advance toward Amir Agha faced the toughest resistance. At one point, the company was even encircled. The Taliban had a daily schedule. An hour after sunrise, they would fight for one to three hours, rest at noon, and then, in the late afternoon, attack again for an hour or two before sunset. Activity rarely occurred at night.[42] Fighting was fierce. Groups of five to twenty insurgents ambushed and attacked the Marines.[43] They used compounds, ditches,

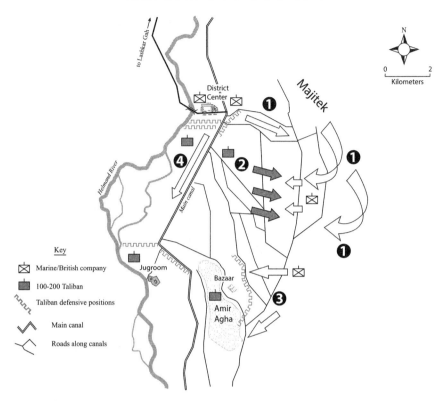

Map 6: Assault of the 24th Marine Expeditionary Unit on Hazar Joft and Amir Agha (Mike Markowitz).

(1) On 28 April 2008, two Marine companies conducted a helicopter assault into Majitek and eastern Hazar Joft, outflanking the main Taliban defenses around the district center. Another company moved east and two days later established a strongpoint in the north in Majitek.
(2) From 29 April to 25 May, the Taliban counter-attacked Marine posts and patrols.
(3) From 15 to 25 May, the southernmost Marine company cleared Amir Agha.
(4) On 29 May 2008, a Marine company and British company assaulted through the main Taliban defenses and attacked Jugroom.

and, where available, fighting positions for cover. Sometimes, they maneuvered into position in pickup trucks and on motorcycles. *Dshka* heavy machine guns at long ranges provided fire support. Volleys of RPGs engaged helicopters. No helicopters were shot down but pilots had to avoid certain areas.

The Marines leveled a tremendous amount of firepower at the Taliban in return. More than an entire battalion, 1,200 men, was focused against an 8 by 10 kilometer area: an unprecedented concentration of forces in southern Afghanistan (the Canadians had one reinforced battalion for the whole of Kandahar province). All day long, artillery and mortars let loose rounds on targets, helicopters fired missiles and rockets, and air-craft dropped bombs. One attack by ten insurgents was met with roughly sixty 60 mm mortar rounds and twenty 155 mm high explosive artillery rounds. Marine infantry followed on the heels of air and artil-lery strikes. Taliban had scant seconds to put their heads up to fire before being overrun. Hundreds of Taliban, including valuable commanders, fell fighting Marine riflemen and their supporting helicopters and air-craft. A special forces raid killed Pakol, the Taliban frontline com-mander, in early May. Marines who were wounded were quickly picked up by the Marine Expeditionary Unit's (MEU's) support helicopters and, in less than an hour, taken to first-class medical care at Bastion (the giant British logistics hub) or Kandahar air base.

Step by step the Marines reached the outskirts of the newly built Amir Agha bazaar. Despite the losses, Naim tried to hold onto Amir Agha and Jugroom. While the Marines had been driving south, Taliban District Governor Obaid Rahman had been fortifying Amir Agha and its bazaar. Because of the shrine and the victory against the Soviets there during the jihad, Amir Agha held symbolic, even holy, importance. Thanks to reinforcements, at least 100 insurgents defended Amir Agha village and the bazaar. The village, on the low rolling sand dune, had always been densely populated and tough to attack due to the steep face and marshes on its northern side. The recent construction of the bazaar to the north fortified it further. The 200 or so mud and concrete shops made for good defensive positions. On top of these natural defenses, Obaid Rahman laced Amir Agha with well concealed trenches, bunkers, and mutually supporting machine gun positions, placed behind canal embankments, in tree lines, and around compounds. Trenches were 1–2 meters deep and roughly 50 meters in length, hidden by brush lain over bamboo poles and wicker mats. Bunkers had roofs reinforced with steel I-beams, packed earth, and sandbags.[44]

Over the last two weeks of May, the Marines carefully cleared out Amir Agha bazaar and village, first surrounding the bazaar and then entering it. Neither was easy. The Taliban cadres sprang carefully laid ambushes and attempted counter-attacks. The fighters were determined. Air and artillery strikes often failed to kill them or cause them to run.

Nearly two years of fighting the British had taught them how to survive by making use of mud compounds, irrigation ditches, and their own fighting positions. According to the Marine fire support officer: 'The enemy would simply wait for the impact of the 500 lb bombs to complete and he would shift to an alternative fighting position and continue the engagement. I observed AH-1 Cobras [attack helicopters] shoot TOW missiles at enemy bunkers and receive return fire within one minute after the impact.'[45] Marines found that Taliban fortifications and mud buildings could withstand a tremendous amount of firepower. Multiple artillery strikes and 500 lb bombs often could not destroy them.[46] In the end, Taliban determination did not matter. If bombs themselves did not root out the Taliban, Marine infantry did. By 25 May, both the bazaar and the village were in Marine hands. A Taliban cadre leader who was at Amir Agha said: 'In Amir Agha, many men were killed. We fled. Airplanes bombed us. The Marines knew how to fight.'[47]

The clearing of Amir Agha opened the way for an assault on Jugroom. The Taliban still held Jugroom as well as their in-depth defensive system running up to the district center. Petronzio's plan was for the Marines in Amir Agha to drive west while the Marines in the north pressed south down the main canal road. The Scottish Argyll and Sutherland Highlander company now in the district center would assault the in-depth defenses between the canal and the river. On the night of 29 May, the Marines and the British attacked. The Marines blew through the weakened Taliban defenses west of Amir Agha. The British and the Marines coming from the north through the dense network of trenches and bunkers south of the district center faced stiffer resistance. Large numbers of bombs and artillery shells were expended to break through it. Nevertheless, the next day the Marines were in position to seize Jugroom.

Roughly forty Taliban defended the compound. A Marine platoon (about fifty men) was assigned to take it. Air strikes, an artillery barrage, and a high explosive line charge (meant to detonate any improvised explosive devices) preceded the Marine assault. The Marines followed in the line charge's wake. Helicopters hovered overhead as they attacked; 7-ton trucks with turret-mounted 50-caliber machine guns fired from behind. Marine infantry cleared room after room in the compound until the Taliban retreated. When they did, Marines in enfilade positions to the north-east cut them down.

The capture of Jugroom and Amir Agha broke the Taliban. Morale collapsed. Mohammed Nabi, Abdullah Jan's former lieutenant, fought with the Taliban during the battle. He recalled: 'The Taliban did not fear the British. They never held anything. The Taliban feared the Marines. The Marines came and stayed and then hunted them down. The Marines knew how to make war.'[48] The Quetta shura believed that the Marines would capture the entire district.[49] Naim ordered Garmser to be evacuated. He sent a fleet of cars from Baram Chah to pick up District Governor Obaid Rahman, Abdul Razik (the head judge), Abdul Majan, and key tactical commanders. There was not enough room for everyone, so many fighters and cadre leaders were left behind. One of the cadre leaders left holding the line south of Amir Agha said: 'Our leaders fled to Pakistan. Then we were weak. So we ran too. They called and ordered us to stay. We ran anyway. They were not here.'[50] It was a rout. Almost all the cadre leaders and fighters fled south, many all the way to Pakistan. In the end, only a handful of judges and fighters stayed north of Lakari.[51] Colonel Petronzio did not pursue because he knew his unit would be departing in three months, in September, and that there would be too few British to hold anything south of Amir Agha.

According to several sources, the Taliban suffered terrible losses in the battle. The Marines estimated that 450–550 Taliban had been killed. Through his sources, Abdullah Jan heard that the number was exactly 498. Even if that estimate is high, other more precise counts confirm heavy Taliban casualties. Marine snipers alone—usually an accurate source of information—recorded over eighty kills.[52] Marines captured another fifty insurgents.[53] Just those numbers—eighty dead and fifty detained—make Naim's stand against the 24th Marine Expeditionary Unit the worst defeat suffered by any force in the recorded history of the district. A veteran and experienced guerrilla force had been ruined. The Marines suffered one killed.

Naim's decision to stand and fight had been a strategic error. He did what no good guerrilla commander should do: fight a set-piece battle with a superior opponent. If he had withdrawn into Darveshan and waited out the Marines, his veteran forces probably could have retaken much of Hazar Joft in the winter from the smaller British forces that replaced the Marines. That might not have ended the contest for Garmser, but it would have left the initiative with the Taliban. As it was, Naim lost scores, if not hundreds, of his best men and many of his best commanders. Together with the losses of two years of fighting the British, the battle left him with few good leaders. Years later, I asked former

Taliban about who had commanded them at the front from 2006 to 2008. With a bit of exaggeration, the answer was often: 'They are all dead.' One Taliban cadre leader exaggerated: 'The judges and mullahs were killed in the fighting. Now there are no great mullahs.' Another Taliban replied: 'There are no more big commanders. They were all killed in the fighting two years ago.'

In Lashkar Gah, the victory in Garmser was welcome news. It was one of the Taliban's first two real setbacks (the recapture of Musa Qala in December 2007 was the other). Heavy fighting in Helmand did not abate. In September, Marjah fell and the Taliban gained a foothold in Nadi Ali, the district bordering Lashkar Gah to the west.[54] Nevertheless, the victory gave the government and the coalition the opportunity to return to the district and start the process of retaking the rest of it. The totality of the defeat forced the Quetta shura to focus less on Garmser. Fighters from outside the district were not redeployed there. Taliban in Garmser were now on the defensive. The days of a besieged district center were over. The Karzai government had a second chance.

7

PUSHING FARTHER SOUTH

De khwar mullah pe azan, hitz tsok rojah na matawee.
'When the poor mullah calls for prayer, no one breaks the fast.'

Pashto proverb[1]

The Taliban defeat in Hazar Joft opened a new chapter in the history of Garmser. Since 1978, five different regimes had ruled. None had survived. The Taliban had come closest. Now, it was the British and American turn to try to bring peace, preferably of a kinder sort than what the Taliban had offered: part of the broader effort to defeat the Taliban in southern Afghanistan.

During the second half of 2008, the United States turned its attention from Iraq to Afghanistan. Forces were now available to put a stop to Taliban offensives in the south that endangered the whole country. American generals, including David Petraeus, believed that a surge of forces and the use of the new counterinsurgency strategy could bring the war in Afghanistan to an end, repeating the successes seen in Iraq. Over the last months of the Bush administration in 2008 and the first months of the Obama administration in 2009, American policy-makers and generals crafted a plan to send reinforcements to Afghanistan. This was the origin of the 'Afghan surge,' the large-scale American and Allied effort to end major violence in Afghanistan and leave behind a government that could run the country effectively after American withdrawal.

Debate over the plan's various aspects would go on for months. It would not be until early 2009 that President Obama would approve the first reinforcements. In Garmser, however, the effort really began in the summer of 2008, once Hazar Joft had been cleared. For the next three and a half years, until President Obama announced the drawdown, the British and Americans strove to set up a strong and just central government in Garmser. Not since the digging of the canal system had such resources, foreign or Afghan, been poured into Garmser.

New plans

In March 2008, Ghulab Mangal became Helmand's provincial governor. An educated former communist, Mangal was active, progressive, and had the political weight to be taken seriously by Helmand's tribal leaders and warlords. Mohammed Arif, a long-standing Afghan advisor to the US Embassy, noted: 'If we had ten governors in Afghanistan like Governor Mangal, Afghanistan would be a safe place.'[2] Mangal worked closely with the British provincial reconstruction team (PRT; twenty-six provinces in Afghanistan had a PRT). In each, civilian, political, and development advisors worked alongside coalition military units to do such things as mentor Afghan officials, help build political institutions, and run projects. They were the coalition's main tool for advancing good governance and economic development in the provinces. Since taking over in 2005, the British had turned the Lashkar Gah PRT into an impressive machine, with a staff of nearly 150 and a budget of millions of British pounds for programs and projects. The leadership included top civil servants, diplomats, and development experts. The head of mission outranked the brigadier running British military operations in the province. Different offices handled specific aspects of counterinsurgency: governance, rule of law, counter-narcotics, and politics, each with a well-prepared program. No other PRT in the country could match the British in skill or resources.[3]

Together with Governor Mangal, in the spring of 2008 the British military headquarters (Task Force Helmand) and the PRT wrote the 'Helmand road map,' a broad program to bring peace to Helmand. It was generally in keeping with the counterinsurgency doctrine that both the United States and Great Britain followed in Iraq and Afghanistan. The overall idea was that the government had to be capable and fair enough to win over the people. To allow this to occur, the British and Afghan security forces would protect the people by holding the ground that had been cleared. Meanwhile, the PRT would help the government to deliver goods and services, counter corruption, start reconstruction, and eradicate poppy. The road map's drafters thought that without such improvements the Taliban would not be defeated; if the people were overly taxed, if the government did not set up clinics or schools, if jobs were scarce, if the only income came from poppy, then the Taliban would still have popular support. Thus, the Helmand road map embodied a large state-building project, both for Garmser and the entire province. The same idea was being followed in Afghanistan as a whole, as the international community tried to fix what had come to be seen as a corrupt and ineffective central government. The task would not be easy. In Garmser, at least at first, it would be limited to Hazar Joft.

When the 24th Marine Expeditionary Unit withdrew from Garmser in September 2008, General McNeill, commander of coalition forces in Afghanistan, decided that the ground they had taken could not be surrendered again. Hazar Joft was agriculturally rich and had the highest concentration of people south of Lashkar Gah (Helmand's provincial capital). A district government could actually govern—versus sit besieged in the district center—as long as the wider region of Hazar Joft was held. Strategically, the region—the head of the snake-like Garmser canal system—was like a plug on the Taliban to the south in the long body of the snake. It did a lot to protect the southern approaches to Lashkar Gah. Consequently, a 500-strong British battalion and a 200-strong Afghan National Army battalion (2nd Battalion, 1st Brigade, 215th Corps) replaced the Marines.[4] NDS chief Mir Hamza (director of Afghan intelligence for Garmser) and his fifteen men, two border police battalions of 150 men each, and a police force of about twenty men stayed in Garmser as well. These forces were to protect Hazar Joft. They were not to push farther south, lest the Taliban seep back into the north. The British occupied a forward line of three patrol bases (the 'PB line') that ran east to west along the northern edge of Darveshan, from Jugroom to Amir Agha. The Afghan army occupied a second, eastern line of patrol bases, running north to south, in Majitek. Of Garmser's 150,000 population, 55,000 lived within this defensive shell.[5]

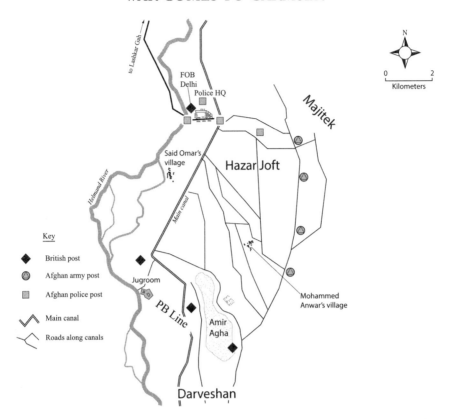

Map 7: British and Afghan outposts, September 2008–June 2009 (Mike Markowitz).

Taliban on the defensive

To the south of Hazar Joft, the Taliban were still in control. In June, Mullah Naim had expected the Marines to retake the entire district and had ordered a general retreat. By August, however, it had become clear that the offensive would go no farther south than the northern edge of Darveshan. Therefore, Naim sent fighters back to Garmser under Obaid Rahman, the Taliban district governor. Local villagers fed and sheltered the fighters. Obaid Rahman set up a new frontline opposite the line of patrol bases in northern Loya Darveshan, with his headquarters in Mian Poshtay. The British and Afghan army would fight the Taliban for nine months in northern Loya Darshevan, though at a lesser intensity than what had passed around the district center. As before, cadres of ten to twenty fighters rotated in and out of the frontline, resting in their home areas to the south in Mian Poshtay, Laki, Safar, or Pakistan refugee communities. Overall leadership rotated as well. Haji Selani eventually replaced Obaid Rahman, Mullah Misher replaced Selani, and so forth. After his brush with death in 2007, Naim himself usually stayed in Pakistan, occasionally visiting Laki to review the situation. In mid-2008, he was promoted from commander for southern Helmand to Taliban governor of the whole province.[6]

The composition of the Taliban had changed. The foreigners, both Arabs and Pakistani Pashtuns, were gone. People of Garmser alone now filled the Taliban ranks. Some lived in Garmser—cadre leaders came to people's homes, especially those of poor immigrants, and asked for men.[7] Others lived in Pakistan and traveled back and forth. Large communities of Garmser refugees were still in Pakistan; their numbers rose and fell with the ebb and flow of Taliban fortunes. Those communities were a recruit pool for the Taliban. The young men in them had the local ties and knowledge to work in Garmser and had grown up under the influence of madrasas that called for jihad. The presence of foreigners who were not Muslim in Afghanistan and inside Garmser itself remained a powerful motivation for young men to fight.

The Taliban governed the southern two-thirds of the district—everything south of Amir Agha. In this area, their governing and justice systems were intact. Their judges still settled disputes and punished the guilty.[8] Laki, Lakari, and Safar continued to be centers of Taliban taxation, organization, and planning. Life was harder for Afghans because the war was closer, but support for the Taliban held, particularly among the religious leaders and the immigrants. People went to the judges and accepted their rulings. The poppy harvest took place in the south in 2009, exported out through Safar and Lakari bazaars, allowing some degree of prosperity to persist. North of Amir Agha, Taliban did not govern but their influence remained strong. The two Taliban regimes had enough supporters to ensure that their fighters could find food and shelter and that Mullah Omar and Mullah Naim would be respected as much as the government, which had only really controlled Garmser from 2001 to 2005. The poorer tribes (Taraki and Kharoti) in Majitek, just to the east of Hazar Joft, along the desert, were especially supportive. Taliban cell leaders could roam Hazar Joft, their tax collectors could visit poppy farmers, and their mullahs could stay in place in the villages, unmolested by elders or tribal leaders.

A third try

Governor Mangal had supported the clearing of Hazar Joft, judging that Garmser, the 'Gateway to Helmand,' was vital to protecting the province.[9] After Hazar Joft had been cleared, he sent Abdullah Jan back as district governor. The PRT assigned two 'stability advisors'—Peter Chilvers and Ian Purves—to work with Abdullah Jan. Armed with British development money and years of experience, their job was to advise Abdullah Jan, start development projects, and execute PRT programs.

As part of the emphasis on building a good government, the United States and its Allies instituted a new system for choosing district and provincial governors. Karzai still had the final say, but all candidates were now required to pass a written examination. The purpose was to ensure that district and provincial governors could read, write, and understand the basic elements of their job. The system never really worked. Powerful political players could trump it, as was the case with Abdullah Jan whose reading and writing skills were always in question. Moreover, hefty bribes of tens of thousands of dollars were known to be required for a post. Such sums could produce a passing test score. So, in spite of America's best efforts, appointments had less to do with merit than political connections and money. This system did not necessarily produce bad leaders. Taliban leaders were generally no better or worse than government leaders. People with whom I later spoke rated Abdullah Jan as the best leader in the district, ahead of Naim. The problem was that the government system left an opening for weak leaders to be chosen. Politicking and money could put men in important positions who lacked the experience or aggression needed to fight the Taliban.

Aged over fifty now, grey dusting his black beard, and losing sight in one clouding eye, Abdullah Jan had been living in Lashkar Gah since 2006, occasionally visiting the empty Garmser district center for a few days at a time. He came back in September 2008 to stay with renewed determination. The shock of the Marine assault, the large numbers of British sent to the district, and the long-awaited arrival of the Afghan army made him think that this time it would be different. He believed that the British and Americans would stay in Garmser for several years, perhaps more than a decade. I think that the work of Mangal and the British in Lashkar Gah had also convinced him that the government was becoming much stronger and wiser. With Mangal and the British behind him, Abdullah Jan saw this as the chance to bring peace and

Image 5: Abdullah Jan (right) and Governor Mangal (seated) confer during a shura at the Garmser government building (Photo by Richard Cavagnol).

progress to Garmser at last—and to some extent make up for the sins of the past. 'The name of Garmser everywhere has been ruined,' he later said; 'I do not want Garmser to lose its name again.'[10] Beyond this, Abdullah Jan was a Pashtun. The Taliban had taken his district, killed his family members, and sat on his land. What had begun as a battle over control of Garmser and Helmand had turned into a deep feud. In the 1990s, he had fought the Taliban from Baram Chah to Herat and Panjshir. Taliban had shot him in the leg in the Girdi Jangal bazaar in 1998 and tried to blow him up in Kandahar in 2005. In 2006, he had gone toe to toe with Naim over the fate of Garmser, standing nearly alone against hundreds of Taliban. After the district had fallen, Mullah Naim and Mullah Ismael executed his cousin, Mir Atem. Naim turned Abdullah Jan's land in Koshtay into a base, sometimes staying there himself. Fighting the Taliban had become part of Abdullah Jan, rarely spoken of, hard to see beneath his calm exterior, but there, driving him to take risks. When no one else was around, his men would whisper to me, 'District governor has a great feud with Mullah Naim. Everyone knows they are at war,' or 'Abdullah Jan and Ahmed Shah [his cousin] will find and kill Mullah Ismael. That is what must happen.' It was a permanent fixture, a feud so deeply ingrained that it had become part of the texture of Garmser.

When Abdullah Jan returned to Garmser in September 2008, hundreds of army soldiers, police, and border police and 500 British soldiers helped underpin his power. Before 2006, little effort had been made to develop the Afghan security forces in Helmand, and none at all in Garmser. British intervention changed that. At the same time, the Taliban successes of 2006–8 had forced coalition leadership in Kabul to expand the recruiting, training, and equipping of Afghan soldiers and police. They recognized that only the police and army would be able to field the numbers necessary to defeat the Taliban throughout Helmand and then keep them out after the Americans and British had departed.

A symbol of the growing power of the Afghan government, the Afghan National Army was the first national military force to come to Garmser since the days of the communist army. The battalion's 200 men fell well below their assigned strength of 900, and they were a long way from being able to survive on their own. Still, they provided valuable numbers and their officer leadership was devoted to Afghanistan. In their green camouflage, armed with American M-16 assault rifles, they were professionals: in good shape, not prone to drug abuse, and fit for a fight. The United States had been carefully building the army since 2002. Afghan soldiers went through six months of training; the officers through an academy. Ethnic groups historically opposed to the Taliban—Tajiks, Uzbeks, and Hazaras—filled its ranks and made it reliable. Garmser's particular battalion included many eastern Pashtuns from around Jalalabad, perhaps 30 percent of its strength. The leadership was strong too, dominated by Major Hezbollah, a grizzled old communist officer who cared deeply for Afghanistan and its people.

A new police chief, Ghuli Khan (a Baluch from Darveshan), came with Abdullah Jan. He took over the old twenty-man police force and reinforced it with his own men from Lashkar Gah for a total of fifty—a disheveled, inactive, if rather cheerful, lot. With only twenty locals, they did not know that much about Garmser. Police throughout Afghanistan have the reputation of being brutal thugs—which was certainly true of many. Ghuli's men were not. They sometimes taxed people entering the

Image 6: Major Hezbollah (foreground), pictured here some time after being promoted to lieutenant colonel.

bazaar, drove around too fast, and got into fist fights with other young men, but they were not systemically taxing, beating, or wrongly imprisoning people. Their problem was their size and aggressiveness. At 50 out of an authorized number of 150, they were drastically understrength and needed to expand if they were to manage Garmser. Ghuli himself was a courageous man but with a small-town outlook and mindful not to get into fights above his weight class with the Taliban. He kept his men focused on securing the bazaar, a task they could easily accomplish and still have time to rest, chat, and drink tea. They did not mind bounding off on the occasional patrol, but rarely exchanged fire with insurgents or took any captives. Abdullah Jan's own forty men were better: all from Garmser and veterans. They were committed to the defense of his offices and person. Three hundred border police worked alongside the police. They were no different from a militia, ill-equipped and ill-trained, with officers bent on raising money for themselves as much as fighting the Taliban.[11]

The last Afghan security organization that needs to be introduced is the National Directorate of Security (NDS). NDS was Afghanistan's intelligence organization, the rough equivalent of the FBI and CIA in one. Its operatives collected intelligence on political, insurgent, and foreign threats and were empowered to capture and interrogate suspects. Many had served in the communist intelligence organization (the KhaD) and had received training from the KGB. They had a penchant for Western clothes and neatly trimmed beards. Mir Hamza had been Garmser NDS chief since fighting alongside Abdullah Jan in 2006. Son of a powerful Alikozai senator from Sangin, he had grown up on family land in Garmser and lost two brothers to the Taliban. One had died fighting alongside Abdullah Jan in Baram Chah in early 1995. After all the fighting Mir Hamza had seen, he sometimes seemed a little shell-shocked; but he was an inveterate enemy of the Taliban and the exuber-ant host of countless lavish dinners for the British and the Marines, whom he deeply admired.

The British took several steps to improve the police and the border police in Helmand. Since 2007, advisory teams had been assigned to both. Starting in 2008, whole district police forces were sent on eight weeks of training at the regional academy in Kandahar. The Garmser force attended mid-2009.[12] Later that year, the British set up a new eight-week training academy in Lashkar Gah. More police could now be trained per year. Other problems remained, including the lack of ser-geants and officers, an inconsistent supply chain, corruption, and low recruitment. The PRT planned to solve these problems by continuing to professionalize the police along Western lines. Sergeant and officer acad-emies were eventually opened. They were meant to cleanse leaders of bad habits and teach them essential skills, such as logistics. All sergeants and officers were supposed to attend. Programs were also designed to teach the police investigative skills, such as fingerprinting, gathering evidence, and preparing case files.[13] Getting personnel through these courses would be a very long process.

Abdullah Jan, the British, and the new Afghan security forces had their work cut out for them. Garmser was in poor shape. Hazar Joft and the district center had been battered by years of fighting. The district center bazaar was empty, pockmarked, and cratered. Farther south, canals had again gone untended. The government could offer little in the way of goods and services. When Abdullah Jan arrived, there were no prosecutors or judges; no directors of health, education, or agriculture; no tribal council; no teachers or schools; no doctors or clinics. Of greatest concern, the people were not rallying to the government. Religious leaders and immigrants had long been in the Taliban camp. Tribal leaders were absent or on the fence; lesser village elders would not commit to the government. The vast majority of the farmers, shopkeepers, and villagers were unsure; they had seen the tide shift too many times before. Even contractors who stood to profit from doing reconstruction projects were unwilling to work in Garmser. So while Abdullah Jan had unprecedented foreign and central government backing, his government in 2008 was in many ways an empty shell. Other regimes that had come to power since 1989 had received the support of some part of society, whether the tribes, the religious leaders, or the immigrants. In 2008, in Garmser, the Karzai government did not. Only the communists had been more unpopular. Whether Abdullah Jan would be viewed as a real Afghan leader or the puppet of infidel foreigners, waiting to be overthrown, was yet to be seen.

Abdullah Jan and Chilvers, his British stability advisor, started with the district center. Chilvers believed that repairing it would help show the people that life was returning to normal. He took the time to find a contractor from Kandahar willing to come down and do simple work in the bazaar, chiefly repairing wells. Slowly, that caused shopkeepers and other contractors to become interested in small projects. Chilvers then upped his efforts. During the autumn, he repaired the governor's compound, the school, the most damaged shops, and the hospital. The crowning achievement was the paving of the bazaar road. It was the first paved road in Garmser. Chilvers lit it with solar-powered street lights. Meanwhile, Abdullah Jan shut down the Amir Agha bazaar, which for two years had been Garmser's main bazaar, and ordered all the shop-owners to re-locate to Hazar Joft. Months later, he leveled the empty stalls. By early 2009, business had returned to the district center. Over 100 shops had opened. People were going to the governor's offices for meetings, 200 patients were visiting the hospital daily, and 200 students were attending the district center school. Soon two other schools were running in nearby villages. Both taught small classes of girls. The clinics and schools were run by the government. The Ministry of Public Health worked through the well-known non-profit non-governmental organization (NGO) BRAC to supply the clinics and pay the staff. The Ministry of Education paid for teachers' wages and textbooks.

Image 7: Police and army on patrol in the Hazar Joft bazaar, before the bazaar was paved (Photo by Peter Chilvers).

The next challenge was getting communities to be represented in the district government. There was no official mechanism to do this. The Afghan government centralized power in Kabul. The people had no say in how officials were appointed or how money was spent. All district officials were technically appointed in Kabul. The people themselves only elected the president, representatives to the Wolesi Jirga (parliament) in Kabul, and representatives to the provincial council in Lashkar Gah. Money was also centralized. District governors had no budget. Funds for programs, goods, and services flowed down from Kabul via the 'line' ministries. These were the ministries that handled goods and services, such as the Ministry of Education, Ministry of Health, and Ministry of Agriculture. In the districts, the line ministries had 'directors' as representatives (though not yet in Garmser) that executed certain programs; but decisions on the nature of those programs were made in Kabul. Consequently, the connection of the people to the government was thin.

The PRT's answer to this problem was community councils, an initiative run by the Independent Directorate for Local Governance (IDLG), the Afghan government agency under President Karzai that appoints all district and provincial governors. The program established councils of 35–45 representatives in select districts and provinces. The British PRT successfully lobbied for the program to come to Helmand. In coordination with the Independent Directorate for Local Governance, Jon Moss and Derek Griffiths—two British governance experts—specially designed the Helmand part of the program, which would be funded and supervised by the PRT.

The role of the community councils resembled that of the old tribal councils—resolving disputes and bringing issues to the government—but with greater weight. They were official standing bodies. Governor Mangal expected them to take part in government events and gave them a role in identifying projects, duties that the old tribal councils had never enjoyed. Eventually, they would even receive a budget. Moss and Griffiths hoped that the community councils would link the people to their government; with an outlet to voice their views and to present their grievances, communities would be less marginalized and therefore less likely to support the Taliban.

Community council elections were set for March 2009. Garmser's council would have thirty-five seats. The March elections were for twenty, representing Amir Agha, Hazar Joft, and Majitek. The remaining fifteen seats were left open, reserved for the regions farther south sometime in the future. It would not technically be an election. Only tribal leaders, elders, religious leaders, teachers, and other notables were allowed to vote.[14] Land ownership was not a requirement.

Abdullah Jan worked hard to convince tribal leaders—both landed and immigrant—to take part. At that time, a minority of the tribal leaders lived in Garmser. Most were in Pakistan, Lashkar Gah, or Kabul. The five or six in Garmser were reluctant to participate. Most thought that the government would soon fall again. The Noorzai from Hazar Joft did not want to expose themselves to Taliban intimidation. The poorer immigrant Taraki and Kharoti from Majitek held faith with the Taliban, their benefactors. Behind the scenes, Abdullah Jan's old ally, Said Omar, backed the process. Said Omar had returned to Garmser shortly after Abdullah Jan. Long since retired from his life as a mujahidin commander and provincial council member, he stayed in his village and avoided government activities, revered by his tribesmen and visitors from Lashkar Gah. His silent presence was a huge endorsement for Abdullah Jan. He soon sent his second son, Ayub Omar, to become

Abdullah Jan's deputy. Abdullah Jan also convinced Mohammed Anwar, another old Noorzai tribal leader from north of Amir Agha, a khan since the days of King Zahir Shah, to support the council. But neither Said Omar nor Mohammed Anwar would stand up and run. Both were well over sixty-five years old and did not want to draw attacks upon themselves. They appointed representatives instead. To further grease the process (and secure his own influence), Abdullah Jan pressganged a few of his old soldiers into running, including Mohammed Nabi, his former militia post commander and recent Taliban cadre leader.

In the end, 120 notables attended the elections, a respectable turnout. With no tribal leaders running, second-tier elders and shopkeepers won seats. The chairman was Dr Habibullah, a talkative pharmacist from Hazar Joft. Other members included Atlas Khan (a straightforward and honest old mujahidin fighter) and Mohammed Nabi. The election was undoubtedly a success. At the same time, it showed that Taliban influence lived on. Abdullah Jan was always disappointed that the big tribal leaders had declined to join the council. He often compared it sadly to his old tribal council, which all the tribal leaders had joined.

The community council met weekly. It resolved disputes, reported on the behavior of the army and police, and picked development projects. Chilvers had the community council select a set of projects that he executed with PRT money. In future years, the PRT issued the council a $100,000 to $200,000 budget. Funneling project money through the community council gave the Afghan government say over the development process and empowered them in the eyes of the people. As one community council member said: 'People have stopped by and warned me that the Taliban have an order out for my head. They told me to be careful at night. They told me this because they like me. They like me because I help them. I am their link with the government.'[15]

Protecting the people, developing police, spurring reconstruction, and building local government are parts of most counterinsurgency campaigns. Helmand had an additional issue: poppy. Since 2005, poppy cultivation had grown dramatically. The PRT and Governor Mangal knew that the Taliban taxed poppy and that those taxes were the movement's major revenue stream. They wanted it cut. The problem was that poppy was also the major source of income for most farmers. Ending poppy cultivation would hurt their livelihoods. The damage might turn them against the government. With the PRT, Mangal crafted a program to overcome the poppy dilemma. In order to avoid overly upsetting the farmers, in the autumn, before planting season, he would give land-owning farmers wheat seed as a substitute for poppy. In the spring, government tractors would plow under poppy in the areas where wheat had been distributed. That way, those land-owning farmers subject to eradication would receive a degree of compensation for their lost income. In order to reduce discontent further, the program would be phased. Seeds would only be handed out and poppy would only be plowed under in secure areas. Violent areas would be left alone. The PRT funded an extensive media campaign to promote the program.

In Garmser, wheat seed distribution focused on Hazar Joft and Majitek, where in 2008 over two-thirds of the fields had been sown with poppy. Darveshan and Amir Agha were ignored. Altogether 3,600 beneficiaries received seeds in the autumn of 2008. When distribution began, Mangal came down for a large shura at the government center. Mangal and Abdullah Jan warned everyone that come spring poppy would be eradicated so they had better plant wheat now. Many people argued loudly, claiming they would be impoverished. The landless immigrants—largely the poor tribes living near the eastern desert in Majitek—were most aggrieved. Those who owned no land were forbidden from receiving seeds, but were still subject to eradication. Landless immigrants held a few small protests and went in large delegations to the district center, all to no avail. Mangal and Abdullah Jan firmly believed that anyone with the audacity to both squat on government land and grow poppy deserved to face eradication. For the landless, the return of the government and the arrival of the Marines and the British marked the end of the prosperity that the Taliban had brought. In the end, most people complied and did not plant poppy. Wheat seeds and the threat of eradication made enough of a difference. So did Islam. As much as they complained, many farmers and elders were quick to admit that poppy was wrong. They seemed to know that it was a passing boon that one day had to go away. That spring, police chief Ghuli and his fleet of tractors drove out daily to plow under fields in Hazar Joft and Majitek. The next year, 5,300 seeds were handed out, again in Hazar Joft and Majitek. Again, Ghuli plowed under fields in the spring. In both years, poppy cultivation in Garmser fell.

The American surge

The British army fought in Garmser from September 2006 to June 2009. Under their watch, government and development initiatives took hold. By the end of 2008, Iraq had settled and the United States had forces free to go to Afghanistan, coinciding with the election of President Barack Obama. In early 2009, President Obama sent 17,000 reinforcements, followed by another 30,000 in 2010, for a total of 100,000 troops in Afghanistan, triple what had been there in 2007. In his December 2009 speech that announced the second tranche of 30,000 reinforcements, Obama promised that these reinforcements would start being recalled to the United States in 2011. This Afghan surge was America's bid to end the war.

As part of the strategy, 10,000 US Marines deployed to Helmand.[16] They went to southern and western Helmand. The British kept the center and parts of the north. Brigadier General Larry Nicholson, the Marine commander in Helmand, sent one of his battalions—2nd Battalion, 8th Marine Regiment (2/8)—to Garmser. It took over in June. The British left. Only Peter Chilvers stayed behind. All told, for nearly three years the British had held the line in Garmser, often with the fewest of men, witnesses to the toughest of fighting.

The surge of American troops was accompanied by a surge of civilians. The US Department of State and USAID deployed hundreds of civilians to work on provincial reconstruction teams and in the districts. In August and September 2009, a USAID development officer and I (as the Department of State political officer) joined Chilvers. Together, we formed the 'district support team' (DST), the first of its kind in Helmand, meant to copy the role of the PRT, albeit on a much smaller, district-level scale. Chilvers led the team. A rule of law advisor and another USAID worker would arrive in the future. The PRT and Nicholson's headquarters received a total of about five American civilians too. The district support team fell under the PRT and followed the PRT road map.

The district support team lived at the battalion headquarters on FOB Delhi. Relations with the Marines were very good. Chilvers shared an office with the battalion commander, Lieutenant Colonel Christian Cabaniss, who readily gave the district support team the lead in political, government, and economic matters. We drew up plans for the district together. Funds were treated as a pool to be applied against a common set of priorities. This cooperation would hold for every battalion that came through Garmser.

As political officer, my duties were to advise the district governor on political matters, talk with tribal and religious leaders, oversee any negotiations with Taliban leaders, and help build the police force. I had no predecessor, but Chilvers knew a great deal and gave me excellent guidance. In addition to Chilvers, I reported to the US political officer at the PRT. After Chilvers left in June 2010, I would take over leadership of the district support team.

The arrival of US civilians and Marines in the summer of 2009 hailed an increase in resources available for reconstruction. Whereas the British had spent roughly $2 million in 2008–9, new US programs massed over $15 million combined for 2009–10. For the Americans and British in Helmand, it was conventional wisdom that giving people jobs would lessen support for the insurgency. The logic was that people need money and they will be less inclined to get it from insurgents if they have a job.

USAID brought two major programs to Garmser. The first was 'AVIPA-Plus.' The acronym stood for Afghanistan Vouchers for Increased Production in Agriculture. It was worth roughly $8 million. Focused on agriculture, in 2009 and 2010, the program handed out 10,000 seed packages, employed over 1,000 people on cash for work projects, and organized twenty-three cooperatives. AVIPA was a major kick to the economy, designed to get people working and keep them too busy to spend their time as Taliban.

The second USAID program was the Afghan Stability Initiative (ASI). It fell under a special branch of USAID named the Office of Transition Initiatives (OTI). Gail Long, our USAID development officer, controlled the program. Long was a determined and no-nonsense professional (and a relentless runner, in spite of the ankle-twisting gravel rocks of FOB Delhi). She had years of experience working in the development field, first in Kosovo and then during Iraq's worst times. Her detailed understanding of development and how to get things done would impress battalion commander after battalion commander. Long never wavered from sharing her thoughts, even if we did not always agree. Our whole approach in Garmser was better off from open and honest discussions. Long focused on high priority projects, often in dangerous areas. Early projects included repairs to roads, schools, and the main intake to the canal system at the northern end of the district. She had the community council identify all her projects as a means of strengthening the institution. The Afghans praised the quality of Long's work, saying again and again: 'She is strong, very strong.'

The Marines also brought a substantial source of funding—the Commanders' Emergency Response Program (CERP). The US Department of Defense created CERP so that military commanders could have a source of money for projects. The money could be used quickly and easily. A company commander had authority to spend up to $5,000 per project and could keep enough funds on hand to run five to ten projects at once. The battalion commander had authority to spend up to $50,000 per project and could draw the money to do so within days. Larger projects took a month or so to arrange, but that was still quicker than any USAID project could be started. CERP was a real asset.

Spreading south

The Marine arrival marked the resumption of offensive operations. Roughly 1,000-strong, twice the size of its British predecessors, 2/8 had the manpower to hold a lot more than Hazar Joft. Brigadier General Nicholson ordered Lieutenant Colonel Cabaniss to clear 15 kilometers south of Amir Agha. Cabaniss planned to send one company (a force of 170) to Kuchinay Darveshan, 10 kilometers south of the front line of patrol bases (the 'PB' line) along the northern edge of Loya Darveshan, and one company to Mian Poshtay, another 5 kilometers south. The last of the battalion's three infantry companies would stay in Loya Darveshan along the line of patrol bases.

Opposite the Marines stood perhaps 200 Taliban: roughly 100 in Darveshan and roughly 100 in Mian Poshtay. Mullah Omari, who had not experienced the heavy fighting in Hazar Joft or Amir Agha, commanded them. As many as 100 fighters stood in reserve in Lakari with another 200–300 in Safar.[17]

On 2 July 2009, Cabaniss attacked. The company slated for Kuchinay Darveshan stepped off on foot from Hazar Joft while the one slated for Mian Poshtay assaulted via helicopter. The former broke through a belt of IEDs (improvised explosive devices built in Pakistan or southern Garmser that functioned similarly to a mine) opposite the line of patrol bases and pushed south, engaging in a series of fifteen firefights with over forty insurgents. After a week, the Marines reached Kuchinay Darveshan and set up their outpost. To the south, the heli-borne assault on Mian Poshtay also met tough resistance. The helicopters landed at Mian Poshtay's small bazaar, where the main canal and the long eastern drainage canal intersect. At the moment when the Marines stepped out of the helicopters, Taliban opened fire from the old school and clinic 100 meters away, on the other side of the eastern drainage canal. The Marines hastily took cover in nearby bazaar shops and behind canal embankments. The next day, they assaulted across the canal and captured the school, the clinic, and the bazaar. An outpost was set up in the old clinic and the school. From there, the Marines pushed out to the south and north in daily firefights.[18]

Given their previous bloodletting in Hazar Joft and Amir Agha, the level of resistance that the Taliban put up is surprising. Again, the Taliban leadership had ordered their men to fight. That decision seems to have been partly the fault of inexperienced commanders at the frontline. Many of the good ones had fallen in the fighting around the district center and Amir Agha from 2006 to 2008. The good leaders who had survived, such as Obaid Rahman, Qari Abdullah, Mullah Misher, Mullah Ismael, and Haji Selani, were not in Garmser at this time. Mullah Ismael, for example, who had made his name seizing control of Mian Poshtay, had been sent to fight elsewhere. Mohammedullah, the Taliban judge for Mian Poshtay, said: 'The Taliban tried to fight in Mian Poshtay. They tried to control the area in order to force the Marines to leave. Their leadership was poor. None of the good commanders from the Amir Agha battle were left. Obaid Rahman had gone back to Pakistan in the spring. The cadres fought because they did not have a leader who knew that it would have been better to fall back.'[19] A Taliban fighter echoed him: 'The Taliban fought because they thought they could defeat the Marines in Mian Poshtay and then take back Amir Agha. But the Marines were strong.'[20] Whether Naim wanted his commanders to fight is unclear. Once they had started, he did little to stop them. Regardless of the strategic wisdom of the decision, Taliban resistance made for tough fighting.

Slowly, the Marines in Kuchinay Darveshan and Mian Poshtay pushed the Taliban cadres half a kilometer back from their outposts. At the edges of these small bubbles, patrols were in constant firefights: 300 meters south of the Mian Poshtay bazaar, every day, Marines fought with Taliban teams 8–20 strong ensconced in compounds and grape

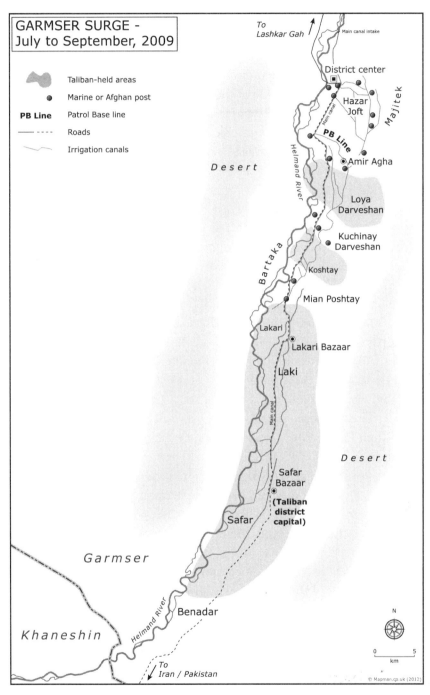

**GARMSER SURGE -
July to September, 2009**

Taliban-held areas
Marine or Afghan post
PB Line Patrol Base line
Roads
Irrigation canals

To
Lashkar Gah
Main canal intake

District center

Hazar
Joft

Majitek

PB Line

Amir Agha

Desert

Helmand River

Loya
Darveshan

Kuchinay
Darveshan

Bartaka

Koshtay

Mian Poshtay

Lakari

Lakari Bazaar

Laki

Main canal

Desert

Safar
Bazaar

**(Taliban
district
capital)**

Safar

Garmser

Helmand River

Benadar

N

Khaneshin

To
Iran / Pakistan

0   5
km

© Mapman.cp.uk (2012)

Map 8: The surge in Garmser (Sebastian Ballard).

vineyards. It was the new frontline. A day without an air or artillery strike was unique. One day in August, Marines called in thirty-five 155 mm artillery rounds. North of the bazaar other Taliban cadres stood between the Mian Poshtay Marines and those in Kuchinay Darveshan. And yet more Taliban separated the Marines in Kuchinay Darveshan from those on the line of patrol bases along the northern edge of Loya Darveshan. Marines there still faced IEDs and small-scale skirmishes. The main canal road could not be opened. The Mian Poshtay and Kuchinay Darveshan outposts had to be resupplied via the eastern desert, an arduous three to four hour slog (unless an armored vehicle got stuck in soft sand, in which case it could take half a day to dig it out). One community council member lamented: 'The people can see the security problems. The Marines went south. But behind the Marines there is no security. Between every post, the enemy places IEDs.'

Even within security bubbles around the Mian Poshtay and Kuchinay Darveshan outposts, Taliban influence persisted. When the fighting cadres left, shadow infrastructure stayed behind. Taliban freely rode about on motorcycles, dropped off night letters, laid IEDs, and threatened people seen with the Marines. Every village had a Taliban tax collector, often the mullah. It was one thing for the Marines to stop ten Taliban from massing near their outposts. Such numbers were easy for patrols, guard towers, and other surveillance systems to spot. It was quite another thing to stop three or four Taliban, often unarmed, from driving around, watching the roads, or visiting an elder at night. Being outsiders, the Marines could not easily identify them as Taliban. A story went around, for instance, that a Marine patrol had talked face-to-face with the famous Taliban religious and political leader, Mullah Abdul Majan, and then walked on. Around the same time, the Marines detained a man named Abdul Ahad on suspicion of being an important cadre leader. He was whisked away to Bagram. Only later did we find out that Abdul Ahad the tobacco dealer had been detained, not Abdul Ahad the Taliban cadre leader. It was not the Marines' fault; they were not from Garmser, could not speak Pashto, and could not possibly know all the local villagers. The roughly 200 men of the Afghan National Army battalion were little better. Divided between Tajiks, Hazaras, and eastern Pashtuns, many could not speak Pashto and those who could did not know the people of Garmser.

Thus Taliban influence survived. Few Afghans worked with the Marines. In Mian Poshtay, the small bazaar right outside the Marine front gate stood derelict. The Taliban had ordered it shut. When Abdullah Jan held shuras there, only a handful of villagers and one or two elders showed up, cutting painfully close to the image of a puppet leader we were trying to avoid. None wanted to take money to start or work on a project, no matter the profit or wage. None even wanted compensation for damage to their property. In September 2009, I had to beg one elder to take $400 to repair holes blasted through his walls during a firefight. Put another way, you could not pay villagers to work for the government. People neither wanted to be seen with the government nor provide all-important intelligence on Taliban identities and locations. Many preferred the Taliban. The Marines were foreign occupiers; a good Muslim was obliged to fight them. Additionally, under the Taliban, there had been a degree of peace. Afghans often told us that before the Marines had arrived their villages had experienced less fighting and people could live out their lives unmolested. Indeed, in Mian Poshtay and Kuchinay Darveshan, south of the frontline in Hazar Joft, there had been no massive firefights and only occasional air strikes and raids. The rest of the people, those who did not prefer the Taliban, were kept in line by continuing Taliban presence. The mullah of Roh Khan's village in Kuchinay Darveshan said: 'There is no security…we cannot work on projects without security. I am scared to help you at all without security.'[21] Mohammed Yunis, the nephew of Roh Khan and highest ranking elder left in the area, told us: 'The Taliban come here from the south and north. We do not know their exact names. They watch us from outside, from the fields and the canal roads…The Taliban pull village children aside and have them tell my uncle that they will kill him if he talks to the Americans. We cannot come and speak with you because we will be killed.'[22] The Taliban beat Yunis a few days after he spoke with us. He fled to Lashkar Gah and did not return for six months.

Heavy fighting continued into November. It was probably inevitable that clearing Amir Agha to Mian Poshtay would take time. Two companies, about 400 men, were covering roughly the same space that the 1,200 Marines of the 24th Marine Expeditionary Unit had covered in Hazar Joft in 2008. Abdullah Jan was convinced that more forces were needed, both for the south and Hazar Joft.[23] The Taliban had suffered heavily too. They might have broken sooner if not for the determination of their leaders to carry on. Former Taliban today do not speak highly of those battles. Naim himself was apparently upset with the performance of his frontline commanders. Nevertheless, in November, he sent reinforcements and the fighting dragged on.

Political stalemate

Challenges in mobilizing the people were not confined to the south. In Hazar Joft too, reluctance lingered. Many, many people still supported the Taliban. That is not to say that the reforms and development of 2008 and early 2009 had won the government no friends. Talking to the government and accepting projects, however, was as far as most were willing to go. Few felt obliged to fight against the Taliban.

Unsurprisingly, the Taliban could look to the religious leaders and poor landless immigrants for support. The religious leaders avoided the government. They did not legitimize it by offering to hold Friday prayers or forming a religious council. Abdullah Jan had a hard time even finding a mullah to open his shuras. The Taliban could rely on many mullahs to preach against the government in their villages. They were also able to keep madrasas running in Laki, Safar, and Hazar Joft. The Hazar Joft madrasa was a few kilometers from Afghan army and police outposts. It housed over 150 young children, taught by four young black-turbaned and black-bearded mullahs. Taliban leaders were known to pay for the madrasa and sometimes take shelter in it.[24] The police and army could do little. As much as Americans and the government spoke of respecting Islam, the Taliban were still the true protectors of the religion. Closing the Hazar Joft madrasa would have enraged the religious leaders, further worsening the government's position.

The provincial government at this time was not reaching out to religious leaders in Garmser. A ministry of the hajj and religious endowment existed in Kabul and a director worked in Lashkar Gah, the provincial capital. The ministry had funds to pay for a few representatives in each district. Additionally, the Ministry of Education could pay for supplies and teachers' wages for madrasas. Although some of these efforts were apparent in Lashkar Gah, they did not extend to the districts, where the influence of religious leaders was strongest. For the religious leaders, it was still the Taliban who respected Islam. The Taliban instituted Islamic law, ensured that Islam was the primary subject taught in schools, gave religious leaders authority, and were not aligned with infidels. Their commanders conferred with religious leaders, asked for their advice, and listened to the teachings. The government did very little to compete with this.

Abdullah Jan and his new deputy governor, Ayub Omar, created their own plan to reach out to the religious leaders. Ayub Omar was the thirty-five-year-old son of Said Omar, the Noorzai tribal leader from Hazar Joft and former provincial council member. Always cheerful, Ayub Omar was easy to get along with. Abdullah Jan chose him out of long friendship with his father and for his education. Said Omar, known for his scholarly knowledge, had made sure his son was versed in both politics and Islam. Ayub Omar was well placed to help Abdullah Jan work with the religious leaders. Refurbishment of the Amir Agha shrine was part of their plan. Chilvers funded the project. Abdullah Jan heavily publicized it. Abdullah Jan also wanted to build a district center madrasa. He believed that religious education should take place in Afghanistan, funded by the government, not across the border in Pakistan where extremists could influence the minds of young Afghans, let alone in Taliban-run madrasas inside Garmser itself. Through these and other efforts, Ayub Omar and Abdullah Jan hoped to convince the mullahs that the government was Islamic, so that Friday prayers in the district center could resume, and so that a religious council, as had stood during Abdullah Jan's previous tenure, could be formed.

To open a dialogue, Abdullah Jan and Ayub Omar held a shura on 6 January 2010 with 100 of Garmser's religious leaders. Abdullah Jan spoke for an hour on the virtues of Islam and cooperation:

'This is our first ulema shura in four years…We hope that you will change your views…We want your supervision and advice. We need to work together. Without your cooperation, we can do nothing…Please help us stop the killing. We are all Muslims…Many things we [the government] do are wrong. You know what those things are…Tell us what we are doing wrong…The Taliban returned because the mullahs and the elders did not cooperate.'[25]

The religious leaders recited their grievances for ten minutes before a black-bearded young man with a disheveled turban declared: 'Now is the time for jihad against the infidels. Why do you not talk about jihad? You will go to hell if you do not take up jihad. The elders should tell the people to take jihad.' The audience rumbled in agreement when he announced: 'Jihad is blessed. We must kill infidels.' Another mullah stood up and added: 'Anyone who works with the Americans is an infidel. After the Americans leave, we can talk. We must take jihad now.'[26]

150

Image 8: Deputy District Governor Ayub Omar and USAID development officer Gail Long in the Mian Poshtay bazaar. (Photo from Gail Long)

Abdullah Jan did not flinch from the debate: 'We are fighting our own people. Traitors fight their own people...This is not jihad like it was against the Russians...You were not even born in the time of our jihad. We did jihad. We fought face to face and treated the Afghan communists honorably.' Midway through his rebuttal, one young mullah in a light blue turban and grey tunic, looking disturbingly sweaty and nervous, tried to seize the podium. Abdullah Jan growled at him and the young mullah hurriedly sat down, perhaps having heard of the old war-

151

rior's quick hand. The most educated and moderate in the audience said nothing to defend the government. Rather, the eldest mullah derided Abdullah Jan: 'A good Muslim prays. A good Muslim kills no innocents. A good Muslim does not love or support infidels. A good Muslim protects Islam from infidels. He will go to heaven if he dies.' The best that it got was when Ayub Omar's old mentor, who had taught him in the mosque as a boy, got up and spoke in favor of cooperation, if not the government: 'ISAF came here to destroy. They destroy our crops [i.e. poppy]. But do not call any Muslim an infidel. Anyone who recites the *kalima* is not an infidel. Everyone, whether working with the government or working with the Taliban, can be a good Muslim.'[27]

Abdullah Jan and Ayub Omar did not abandon their plan to reach out to the religious leaders, even though it would not be easy. On 1 February 2010, Abdullah Jan held a follow-on meeting with Garmser's most prominent Islamic scholar and his entourage. He asked the scholar to work with the government. 'We cannot support the government,' the scholar said. 'It needs to stand up for itself. It is controlled by foreigners. Non-Muslims need to get out of our country. We can only support the government when the foreigners leave.' The mullahs claimed that the war was a jihad against the coalition. Abdullah Jan replied: 'Then why were you fighting when no Americans were here? Why did the Taliban announce jihad against me?' Unmoved, one of the mullahs warned: 'District governor, they will leave you! You will be alone'—a comment that highlighted both how transient our presence looked to those who had endured thirty years of war and how deeply the religious leaders believed in the Taliban.[28]

The religious leaders were one group opposed to the government. The immigrants were another. Land-owning immigrants, particularly the Ghilzai tribes in the east, with their tribal ties to the Taliban, generally refused to get too close to the government. Landless immigrants living on government land aligned with the Taliban outright. They feared the government would take back the land the Taliban had given them. Many hoped the Taliban would return and protect them. The government had no policy to let them lease their land, let alone recognize ownership. Thankfully, no one was evicted. The government and the Noorzai—the traditional landowners of northern Garmser—were hostile to anyone on government land. One Noorzai community council member said:

'The small tribes that live in Garmser will not support the government because they know the government will take back their land…the east is all Taliban. Only a few families are good. They do not support the government because they want to keep their land [which the Taliban had given to them]…All these tribes are not originally from Garmser. The only solution is for them to go back to their old homes.'[29]

The landless—unlike the land-owning immigrants whom the government respected—were all but excluded from community council elections; their communities were represented by Abdullah Jan's partisans, not their own elders. The provincial and district governments did not believe they deserved representation. One day when we were in Amir Agha, Abdullah Jan brought us to the eastern canal and showed me the dams that the Taliban had illegally built to irrigate the government lands given to the Taraki immigrants to the east. 'See that area over there,' he said, waving his hand carelessly over a 5-kilometer wide expanse. 'Those people are all Taliban. You must destroy the dam. It will only take you five minutes.' A month of shuras and talks with both parties followed. Nothing ever happened, largely because we refused to do anything. We did not want to starve the people living there, squatters or not. For a month, two or three times per week, Abdullah Jan asked me if we were going to blow up the dam. I never told him no, but argued with him over the morality of the action. Eventually he stopped and never asked again. He may have thought us naïve for protecting Taliban but he seemed to accept our position.

The opposition of the mullahs and immigrants was to be expected. The Taliban had cared for them. The hesitancy of tribal leaders to work with the government was more troubling. They had backed the government in the past. Yet now Abdullah Jan had the support of just two: Said Omar and Mohammed Anwar. Most of the tribal leaders stayed neutral, largely hiding out in Lashkar Gah. A few in Majitek and Loya Darveshan aligned with the Taliban, giving them shelter, food, and information. The lesser village elders beneath the tribal leaders lacked the power to resist the Taliban on their own, and many did not care to anyway. They may have been willing to come to the district center or even join the community council, but few wanted to provide intelligence, speak out openly, or instruct their villagers to stay away from the Taliban, let alone actually fight them. As Ayub Omar put it, 'The elders think ISAF is weak.'[30] In his opinion, the elders did not believe that the United States would stay long enough to prevent the government from falling once more. Mohammed Nabi, now a community council member, was blunter about our weakness: 'You have 1,000 men. With thirty men, I kept eastern Garmser quiet. I am surprised you cannot defeat the Taliban.'[31]

Intimidation—threats, attempted kidnappings, assassinations, and terror attacks—underlined the Taliban's strength. Mullah Omar and Naim used intimidation to maintain popular support and remove key opponents. Too often, Americans tended to look at intimidation as an instrument of terrorism. From another perspective, it was merely the Taliban equivalent of the American and British campaign to kill or capture Taliban leaders with special forces raids and air strikes. In 2009, Taliban intimidation was a careful thing, neither murderous nor indiscriminate. Mullah Omar issued a code of conduct in August 2009 that explicitly forbade executing prisoners and ordered that 'all mujahidin with all their power must be careful with regard to the lives of the common people.'[32] Mullah Omar and Naim did not want to harm innocent civilians or to incite needless feuds with tribes. Most intimidation came in the form of threats, a visit at night or letter posted on the door. To make a point, someone might be kidnapped for a few weeks or beaten. From time to time, Naim allowed people who worked with the government to be assassinated. Such killings were reserved for spies, government informants, long-standing opponents (such as Abdullah Jan), influential leaders working with the government (such as the head of a religious council), and those who betrayed the Taliban. Because of this restraint, Taliban intimidation did not create a backlash (such as had occurred in 2006 in Anbar province, Iraq, where tribal shaykhs turned against al-Qaeda in Iraq). As the war went on and the stakes rose, the Taliban's admirable restraint would loosen.

Intimidation kept many elders otherwise opposed to the Taliban on the fence. A handful of attacks on presidential election day in August 2009, for example (including a failed attempt to kidnap the tribal leader Mohammed Anwar of Hazar Joft), showed that the Taliban were around, even if the elections themselves were fairly successful (of the 55,000 people living in northern Garmser, 5,100 voted).[33] The Taliban tried to intimidate the community council as well, threatening certain members, such as Atlas Khan: 'Three days ago, two Taliban came to my house at night. They ordered me to stop taking cash for work projects…They came in on two motorcycles, past the army checkpoints…They knew that Americans had visited my home…I was alone…My people are not happy that I am on the community council. They fear they might lose me.'[34] In the summer, two community council members resigned out of fear of the Taliban. The other members questioned whether the council would survive. The assassination of three Nawa community council members in November added to the fear. Abdullah Jan was greatly concerned. 'The Taliban will attack the community council,' he warned, 'The community council is a symbol. They will go after it.'[35]

From our perspective, the best way to defeat Taliban intimidation was to expand the police. The Marines and Afghan army soldiers could not clear out all the Taliban on their own. There were simply too few of them to lock down every village. Nor, being outsiders, could they easily identify insurgents. The police, on the other hand, could recruit locals, who would speak Pashto and know the families, histories, and relationships within the district. With such knowledge, insurgents could be captured, intimidation could be thwarted, and the people could be given a sense of security. To defeat the Taliban, few things appeared more important than police recruitment.

Unfortunately, sympathy for the Taliban and intimidation stunted police recruitment too. By September 2009, there were only 85 police out of an authorized strength of 150. Abdullah Jan and police chief Ghuli tried to get the elders to give up recruits. Abdullah Jan wanted good men from good families—the sons of elders.[36] The two stood before the community council and asked that each member ante up four men, which would have made for seventy-two new recruits. All refused, saying that security was the Marines' responsibility, not theirs. Dr Habibullah, the council chairman, told me: 'The people are farmers. Right now, they are scared. Over time they will be ready to join the police.'[37] Another member was less optimistic: 'Everyone is scared. I do not go to the mosque in the morning or at night. The Taliban are around. They are like thieves, watching us. The people will refuse to join the police. We do not want police defending us. They will attract attacks…no one wants police.'[38] In one of our long talks, Ayub Omar explained: 'The community council is not able to find police. They are afraid of the Taliban. They think police will not be able to defeat the Taliban. The people are afraid to send their sons to become police.'[39] In the end, Ghuli recruited a handful of new police from Lashkar Gah and sent more of Abdullah Jan's men to the academy. It was a vicious circle:

the best means of reducing Taliban influence was to recruit police, but no elders would let police be recruited until Taliban influence (and intimidation) had disappeared.

A year of holding

In the year and two months between September 2008 and November 2009, unprecedented resources and effort had gone into Garmser. Hazar Joft had been held, a government had been re-formed, a community council had been set up, and projects had started. A solid foundation had been laid. Yet society did not stand behind the government. Religious leaders and a good chunk of the immigrants sided with the Taliban. Tribal leaders were on the fence. Abdullah Jan, the Marines, and the civilians would not succeed if this situation continued. Without locals willing to identify insurgents and defend themselves, stopping intimidation and small-scale attacks would be nearly impossible. The government would be an empty shell, bound to fall apart once the Marines withdrew. The simple fact of the matter was that if the government was some day to control Garmser, people had to stand behind it; people had to die for it.

The shallowness of popular support can partly be attributed to time. Two years of Taliban rule between 2006 and 2008 and seven years between 1994 and 2001 could not be erased in the course of a year, especially with the south still in their hands. Logically, as elders and tribal leaders saw the Taliban weaken and the government strengthen, they would get off the fence.

Nevertheless, to some extent, our strategy was missing something. In November 2009, Ayub Omar asked me: 'You spend all this time talking about projects and programs. When are we going to do the important work: the political work?' He had a point. It is no criticism to say that the PRT road map had focused on building the capacity of the government and had not set out how to mobilize the people to stand up and fight. No plan, after all, survives first contact. Ours was a Western plan, endowed with a certain idealism about what we were doing. Understanding of Garmser's fissures and people was thin. The tribes, the immigrants, and religious leaders that made up Garmser society received little attention in official planning. The 1988–9 civil war, the history of Ghilzai immigrations, and even the names of great tribal leaders—Shah Wali

Khan, Tooriali, Wakil Manan—were unknown to us. Issues that mattered—Islam and land—went untouched. We thought representation and economic development alone would convince Afghans to risk their lives for the government. We assumed that people would just stand up out of patriotic love for Afghanistan, a nation that had been broken for three decades. What was missing was a grasp of Afghanistan and an Afghan way of doing things. Fortunately, Abdullah Jan understood these problems and knew how to move forward. His knowledge and diplomacy could make up for our shortcomings.

8

WAKIL MANAN, MIAN POSHTAY, AND THE RIOTS

Ka ghar lor die, kho pe sar e-ay lar da.
'Even if a mountain is high, there is a path to the top.'
Pashto proverb[1]

The last two months of 2009 and the first two months of 2010 witnessed three key events in Garmser. First, the Marines instituted aggressive new tactics. Second, Abdullah Jan laid out a new plan to mobilize the tribal leaders, showing us an Afghan way of war that we could not have implemented on our own. Third, the Taliban launched an unexpected counter-attack. They reminded us that they too had their own Afghan way of war that did not always match our Western mindsets, using words to accomplish what a thousand bullets and RPGs could not. These four months would be marked by great turmoil.

In movement there is blessing

In November 2009, Lieutenant Colonel Cabaniss and 2nd Battalion, 8th Marine Regiment turned Garmser over to a new battalion—2nd Battalion, 2nd Marine Regiment. Lieutenant Colonel John McDonough was the new battalion commander. He was determined to take the fight to the Taliban and break their hold over the south. 'Let me tell you something,' he told me. 'I am going to take all of this. I am going to outpost all of Cowboys [the Marine name for the main canal road] and place posts south of Lakari. I am going to go after the Taliban. We are going to be able to move freely from Lakari to Hazar Joft.' His energy and willpower inspired his Marines.

McDonough had trained his men to operate at a very high tempo, constantly patrolling and 'closing with the enemy' in firefights—assaulting their positions in order not to let them escape—in spite of the risks posed by gunfire and IEDs. The battalion started out with fifteen posts, most of which had been founded out of great hardship by Cabaniss and his men. McDonough decided to take the next step. He established new posts by cutting down the size of their garrisons. The size of patrols was cut down too, from 13–40 to 6–13 men, so that more patrols could go out per day. Smaller outposts and smaller patrols meant that more and more ground could be covered and the large gaps between the companies might be filled. It was a natural progression from the hard-fought bridgeheads that their predecessors had won in Darveshan and Mian Poshtay.

Every company executed this model, along with the Afghan army who operated alongside them. McDonough had hand-picked his company commanders for their aggressiveness. For those captains and their Marines, it was a point of pride not to call in air strikes or artillery during a firefight and to defeat the enemy with rifles and grenades. The security bubbles that had been half a kilometer in radius around the major posts were pushed out to two or three kilometers. In Loya Darveshan, Captain Vincent Noble got his Marines off the line of patrol bases and pushed south. Week after week, he carried out carefully planned clearing operations. After each, he left a post to hold what had been cleared and stop large numbers of Taliban from returning. It was slow but the Taliban were steadily pushed back. In Kuchinay Darveshan, Captain Brandon Gorman was doing the same thing. He set up enough posts on the main canal to link up with Captain Scott Cuomo's company in Mian Poshtay. Cuomo's men, meanwhile, faced heavy fighting in November and December as they outposted Mian Poshtay and pressed south toward Lakari. In one month, they found 64 IEDs. The Taliban cadre leaders in Mian Poshtay, already exhausted from months of hard fighting, realized they could no longer hold the Marines back. Mullah Omari, their commander, had been killed in an air strike in Safar and his replacement was a poor tactician. The remaining leaders decided to pull their fighting cadres out of Mian Poshtay and back to

Lakari.[2] In January, one elder reported: 'Fifteen days ago, there were Taliban around here. They had a patrol post with motorcycles. When the Marines started pushing and patrolling everywhere, they left.'[3]

By the end of the year, the Marines had seized the tactical initiative but the Taliban were not yet defeated. A gap still divided the Marines in Kuchinay Darveshan from those in Loya Darveshan. The Taliban still held Lakari, Laki, and Safar. And in most places throughout Garmser, including Mian Poshtay, Taliban shadow infrastructure remained—the observers, mullahs, intimidators, and hit squads that kept the people under Taliban influence. In mid-2009, the small security bubbles around the posts in Kuchinay Darveshan and Mian Poshtay had not convinced the people to work with the government. Far larger security bubbles had not removed that problem. The fighting cadres may have pulled back but Taliban moving about in twos and threes ensured that the government ruled only in name.

Wakil Manan

Wakil Manan is the strangest looking Pashtun I have ever met. His dark, white-bearded face looked as if it had seen a lifetime of fist fights, with its crooked spongy nose, busted teeth, and swollen eyes. In spite of his sixty-odd years, it was easy to see why Afghans say he was a powerful figure in his youth. At least 6 feet tall and lanky, he towered over me. But what really set Wakil Manan apart were his gold-rimmed sunglasses. He wore them for his cataracts, but together with his turban they made him look like a rich poppy smuggler. Yet he was no smuggler. He was just a proud, stubborn, and rather paranoid old man upon whom Abdullah Jan pinned his hopes for Mian Poshtay.

For months, Abdullah Jan had been working on his own plan to get more people behind him. He knew that the Taliban still held influence and that many people, particularly the tribal leaders and elders, were reluctant to support the government. He knew that police were not being recruited, locals were not providing intelligence, and that, as a result, Taliban were moving about freely. His solution was to bring back powerful tribal leaders living in Lashkar Gah and Pakistan and task them to secure their territory, as he had done in the past. In his view, they had the power to organize the people, counter the influence of the mullahs, recruit police, and keep the Taliban out. The other leaders then

161

living in Garmser—community council members and lesser elders—lacked the power or bravery to take on the Taliban. To protect returning tribal leaders and overcome fears of the Taliban, he envisioned a light version of his old tribal militia (arbekai) system: a few guards for each tribal leader—enough to stop intimidation yet too few to enable warlordism. The abusive behavior of the tribal leaders of the past—how they had used their militias to tax people, seize land, and build up their own fiefdoms—loomed large in Abdullah Jan's mind. He did not want to see that occur again: 'It is good to have tribal militia. All that is needed to stop intimidation is two to three guards. They can and will defend themselves…They will fight to the death. The people can defeat the Taliban…Only the important community council members and important elders need guards: two to three men each.'[4]

It was Abdullah Jan's knowledge and ideas that made the real difference here. The Marines and the civilians on the district support team did not know who had power and might be brave enough to return, let alone how to find them. The most powerful tribal leaders in Garmser were a mystery to us. Abdullah Jan understood these things in ways we never could. The first tribal leader he decided to try to bring back was Wakil Manan.

Wakil Manan had been in Lashkar Gah since Mullah Ismael had driven him out of Mian Poshtay in 2006. He and Abdullah Jan had never been the best of friends. Enemies during the jihad, Wakil Manan had been a communist militia commander out of Lashkar Gah; Abdullah Jan a renowned mujahidin commander. They had fought against each other in Mian Poshtay and at the district center. Abdullah Jan had treated Wakil Manan poorly before they finally reconciled. He had even imprisoned Wakil Manan when he returned to Garmser from Lashkar Gah in 1993 and had not released him until his tribesmen had paid a ransom. Now Abdullah Jan needed someone who had no love for the Taliban. Wakil Manan's communist past, imprisonment under the first Taliban regime, and abuse at the hands of Mullah Ismael ensured that. The same could not be said for other tribal leaders, many of whom had helped the Taliban at one point or another. They would need to be tested before they could be trusted. Wakil Manan could be trusted right away.

In November 2009, Abdullah Jan started talking to us about Wakil Manan. McDonough, Chilvers, and I agreed that he should return. We also agreed that he should have a few fighters. What we really wanted,

Image 9: Wakil Manan (with turban) meets with General Stanley McChrystal in his home in Mian Poshtay. General McChrystal, commander of all coalition forces in Afghanistan, visited Garmser in March 2010. Deputy police chief Baba, a policeman since the communist days, sits next to Wakil Manan. Peter Chilvers, the British stabilization advisor, is next to Baba. (Photo from Scott Cuomo)

however, was for locals to join the police. Setting up a tribal militia, even a very small one, entailed certain risks. They might abuse the locals. Or Wakil Manan might disregard the instructions of the government and create his own fiefdom. Or the Karzai government, wanting a monopoly on the use of force in the country, might eventually turn against the small militia. Debates were ongoing in Kabul at this time between General Stanley McChrystal (then commander of all coalition forces in Afghanistan), Ambassador Karl Eikenberry, and President Karzai over whether to approve a tribal militia program for the whole country. If Karzai rejected the idea and refused to pay wages, militia in places such as Garmser might dissolve or go rogue once the United States withdrew from Afghanistan, putting at risk whatever successes had been attained. For all these reasons, we wanted any militiamen in Garmser eventually to go to the police academy and become real police, working for the police chief. Doing so would give them training, place them under the government, and ensure that they would have a future.

Abdullah Jan accepted our argument. He advised that the best way forward was to send Wakil Manan down to Mian Poshtay, protect him, and then move forward with police recruitment: 'Give Wakil Manan three or four tribal militia. Have them stay with him for a month. Then he can send men to the academy who can return as police for Mian Poshtay.'[5] One night a few weeks later we worked out the details of the plan. Wakil Manan would go down to Mian Poshtay with four guards. Abdullah Jan would provide the weapons. We would pay the wages. We would also give him a few small projects in order to bolster his influence in the area. Wakil Manan's mission would be to recruit police, discourage people from working with the Taliban, help start reconstruction projects, and assist the Marines. Abdullah Jan said: 'This is a good test for Wakil Manan…Wakil Manan will be my representative in Mian Poshtay.'[6] It was the first step in a larger strategy. If Wakil Manan worked out, Abdullah Jan intended to bring other tribal leaders back to Lakari and Laki.

To ensure his plan had provincial blessing, Abdullah Jan introduced Governor Mangal to Wakil Manan. They talked for an hour. Mangal endorsed the plan: 'It is your district. I trust you. Do what you think is necessary.'[7] A few days later, provincial police chief Sherzad called Garmser police chief Ghuli Khan and told him that Wakil Manan would be recruiting police and ordered him to send those men to the academy.[8]

WAKIL MANAN, MIAN POSHTAY, AND THE RIOTS

Wakil Manan was not an easy character to work with. Upon arriving in the district center he said that he had heard many stories about the dangerous state of Mian Poshtay. He was tempted to abort the mission. To carry on, he demanded eight guards, instead of three or four. Abdullah Jan refused, later telling me: 'If Wakil Manan has more than four men, there will be problems. Mian Poshtay has many feuds. His men will take advantage of their power. We do not want to create a militia.'[9] In the end, Abdullah Jan prevailed. The final agreement was that four men would go with Wakil Manan to Mian Poshtay. Two would be militia— Wakil Manan's sons-in-law who were former police. Two would be from Abdullah Jan's academy-trained police—Sardar Mohammed and Mohammed Sakhi (the Baluch who had stunted that Taliban assault on the district center with his PK machine gun back in 2006). In addition, in order to show him we were committed, I would go down with Wakil Manan for a few weeks to introduce him to the Marines and get him set up. We would depart on 12 January.

Abdullah Jan's plan added a new, controversial element to the counterinsurgency effort by empowering the tribal leaders, the elite of Garmser society: the same people who had failed to bring justice twice before and whose perfidy had opened the door for the Taliban in 2006. Tribal strategies had gained popularity, particularly within the US military, after the 'Anbar Awakening' of 2006 in which Sunni tribes in the Iraqi province of Al Anbar rose up against al-Qaeda and defeated them. In spite of the Anbar experience, tribal strategies attracted a lot of criticism in 2009 Afghanistan. Old Afghan hands, particularly Western civilians who had been working in the country for years, opposed the idea of empowering tribal leaders and letting them raise militias. Respected scholars such as Ahmed Rashid and Sarah Chayes criticized it as short-sighted and somewhat imperialist, smacking of the old 'divide and rule' policies of the British; working with the tribes might bring a few security benefits in the short term but over the long term their warlordism and abusive behavior would cause people to despise the government. In Garmser, we were aware of all this but backed Abdullah Jan's strategy because the tribal leaders offered the only path to get the people to stand against the Taliban. By limiting the size of any tribal militias and placing them under government control, we hoped to prevent future warlordism. A few readers may question why we did not try to raise the villagers up on our own or build a more representative group of elders, religious leaders, and immigrants. Anyone who was there at the time knows that this was impossible. Every day, Marines went out and spoke with elders, mullahs, and poor farmers—to no avail. Abdullah Jan and Ghuli had been pressuring the elders and mullahs too. As the previous chapter described, the elders and mullahs were not interested, even those who were receiving goods and services and projects in Hazar Joft. Many favored the Taliban. Others were frightened. Leaders with authority and power were needed to rally the people. That is what the tribal leaders brought to the table.

The riots

With the heightened Marine activity and preparations to send Wakil Manan south to Mian Poshtay, things were progressing smoothly. It was at this time that the Taliban launched their own counter-attack. We tended to think about the Taliban threat purely in terms of violence: an ambush, an IED, or a murder. The Taliban, or rather the Afghans as a whole, thought in terms of violence and politics. They knew how to rally the people, often through propaganda and rumor, to create favorable political outcomes. In counterinsurgency, politics is primary; and it was politics that upset our best-laid plans.

In the small hours of 11 January, a US and Afghan special operations unit raided a home in Loya Darveshan. They had information that an insurgent leader was hiding there. The compound wall was breached with explosives. The home was searched. No one was detained. The Marines received little warning of the raid. This was a fairly common occurrence. Special operations units lived outside Garmser. Every two weeks or so, they would hit a target in Garmser, often without telling us in advance, often without capturing anyone. What differed this time was the reaction.

Thus far, we had escaped major blowback from raids. We had been lucky. When asked what they wanted most, Afghans often told Marines 'security.' But they did not simply mean absence of Taliban. Raids were considered a form of insecurity as criminal as Taliban intimidation and IEDs. Pashtuns despised them. A home is sacred. Pashtun men are obliged to keep out all uninvited guests. Foreigners crashing through doors, stomping about, and peering in on women had the same effect as spitting on a man's honor before his whole village. Raids pushed people toward the Taliban. Abdullah Jan frequently lectured us on the foolishness of night raids, telling us not to conduct them. The counter-argument was that raids captured, wounded, or killed Taliban leaders. Indeed, in 2007, a special operations raid had killed the dreaded Dadullah Lang and wounded Mullah Naim. Just as intimidation of key government leaders jarred on us, so targeted raids jarred on the Taliban. The Marines and I still worried about upsetting local people. Therefore, the Marines trod lightly, rarely raiding a home at night, usually knocking and asking permission to enter first, never ransacking the home or blasting through walls, and sending only Afghans into a home's private spaces. Special forces, which worked out of far-away bases and rarely met Afghans, were not so cautious.

The next day a crowd approached Captain Noble's Marines in Loya Darveshan and claimed that a Koran in the home had been stabbed with a knife. Intelligence later revealed that Taliban leaders had made up the story and planted the Koran in order to upset the people, already agitated by the night raid itself. We did not know that at the time and, without information about the raid, were in a bad position to explain what had really happened. That night, after we had been over the logistical arrangements for getting Wakil Manan to Mian Poshtay, Major Hezbollah, now the Afghan army battalion's acting commander, warned me that we had to respond to the Koran situation or there would be riots. He suggested we hold a shura in Loya Darveshan the next morning. Taking his advice seriously, I spoke with McDonough. We decided that the situation warranted attention but not to rush south immediately. Personally, I did not want to delay going to Mian Poshtay any longer.

The next morning, as I bounced southward in the back of a heavily armored MRAP (mine resistance ambush protected vehicle), the situation escalated. At daybreak, mullahs in Darveshan related to Abdul Razik, the head Taliban judge, called out on their mosque speakers for everyone to go to the district center and protest against the Koran stabbing. One hundred people marched north. Stories of the Koran spread and the Darveshan crowd picked up people from villages along the way until they had swelled to 500.

The Marines learned about the crowd as it marched out of Loya Darveshan. Peter Chilvers, the British stability advisor and senior civilian, went to the district center to talk to Abdullah Jan about the situation. Unperturbed, Abdullah Jan told Chilvers not to worry; he would calm the crowd when it reached the district center. He said there was no

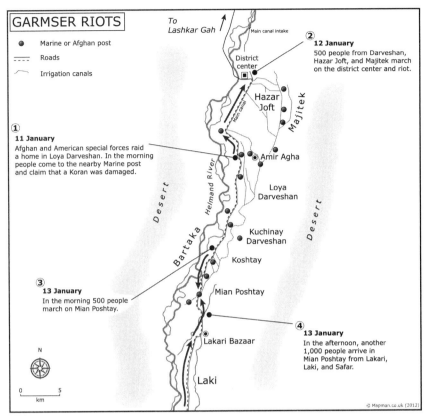

GARMSER RIOTS

● Marine or Afghan post
--- Roads
⌒ Irrigation canals

To Lashkar Gah
Main canal intake

District center

①
11 January
Afghan and American special forces raid a home in Loya Darveshan. In the morning people come to the nearby Marine post and claim that a Koran was damaged.

②
12 January
500 people from Darveshan, Hazar Joft, and Majitek march on the district center and riot.

Hazar Joft

Majitek

Amir Agha

Loya Darveshan

Desert

Helmand River

Desert

Kuchinay Darveshan

Bartaka

Koshtay

③
13 January
In the morning 500 people march on Mian Poshtay.

Mian Poshtay

④
13 January
In the afternoon, another 1,000 people arrive in Mian Poshtay from Lakari, Laki, and Safar.

N

Lakari Bazaar

Laki

0   5
km

© Mapman.co.uk (2012)

Map 9: The Garmser riots (Sebastian Ballard).

need to rush south or barricade the entrances to the district center. Chilvers and McDonough accepted that course of action. A diplomatic approach seemed right. A month before, Abdullah Jan had singlehandedly turned back an angry crowd of 100 at the district center's gates who were protesting their exclusion from wheat seed distribution. Likewise, police chief Ghuli had calmed other wheat seed protesters two weeks before that. That crowd had actually applauded him. We thought the same might happen here.

When the crowd reached the main canal, Ghuli and a cadre of police greeted them. Diplomacy failed. People swarmed around Ghuli and stoned him. Struck twice in the head, he bravely stood his ground but to no avail. As the crowd entered the bazaar, Taliban fighters, who had been hiding in the mosque, got on the loudspeakers and called for an uprising. Two climbed on top of the mosque to shout orders.[10] The crowd pressed to the governor's compound and police station. They lobbed rocks over the 3-meter wall but did not try to breach the gate, behind which the police and a handful of Marines crouched ready to fire. Instead, egged on by Taliban fighters, they torched the school across the street. After that, the Taliban re-directed the crowd to the NDS (National Directorate of Security) compound, 300 meters down the main road. The protesters demanded that all prisoners be freed. Ten to twenty Taliban fighters with AK-47s ducked in and out of the protesters and climbed on top of roofs to shoot at the compound. NDS chief Mir Hamza and his men yelled and shot back. One of Mir Hamza's men was wounded and one of his vehicles was set on fire. Mir Hamza stood over his stricken man waving his pistol in the air and cursing the protesters as shots passed back and forth.

McDonough, anxious to get hold of the situation, launched a column of giant armored MRAPs to the NDS compound, himself in the command vehicle. As they drove down the main road, AK-47 rounds started plinking off the armor-plated hulls. Then civilians jumped on the vehicles and tried to climb in. McDonough realized he would soon have to open fire, lest a rioter pull one of his Marines out of a vehicle. Rather than risk a massacre, McDonough turned back.

At this point, the police sallied out of their headquarters onto the main road. They pulled down the mosque speakers and, seeing the chaos before the NDS compound, lined up and opened fire at 300 meters. The protesters broke apart and ran, allowing the Marines and Afghan forces to lock down the district center. Abdullah Jan then called the local elders together for a shura, berating them for allowing such violence to occur. Six to eight people had died. The Marines had killed one; he had been aiming his rifle at someone. NDS and police shooting probably accounted for the rest.

That night, Chilvers and McDonough sat with Abdullah Jan in his office in the rock-strewn government compound. Exhausted and disappointed, Abdullah Jan whispered sorrowfully that the hard work of eighteen months had disappeared in a day. The riot was a huge surprise. Few of us had expected so many people to behave so violently. It forced us to question how much progress had really been made since the autumn of 2008. The newly built school had been a symbol of the new Afghanistan; its loss was sorely felt. The roof had burnt down, the insides had been consumed, and sections of wall had collapsed. The riot roused attention in Kabul and Lashkar Gah. The day's events were broadcast on television, filled with pictures of the burning school. The fact that the Taliban could mass 500 people for violence in the heart of the district was a huge disgrace for Governor Mangal, who had been touting Garmser as a model of success.

While all this went on, Wakil Manan and I arrived in Mian Poshtay. Captain Cuomo, the Marine commander in Mian Poshtay, and Lieutenant Saifrahman, the commander of the Mian Poshtay Afghan army detachment, gave Wakil Manan a warm welcome, greeting him personally at our rendezvous point in the desert. Having spent weeks spurring his Marines into non-stop patrolling, Cuomo was anxious to have Wakil Manan start organizing the people. Wakil Manan, however, had to wait. Reports about the riots came into Cuomo's command post that afternoon. Since 250 people had also protested (peacefully) 5 kilometers to the north in Kuchinay Darveshan, we expected to see something in Mian Poshtay.

The next morning 500 people marched on the small Mian Poshtay bazaar from the north while another 1,000 marched toward Lakari from the south, well-equipped with motorcycles, flags, trucks, and loudspeakers. At about 9 a.m., the northern group came into sight, chanting 'Allah ah Akbar' and waving long bamboo poles. The front ranks started to charge the bazaar until ten Marines and four Afghan soldiers, sprinting from the outpost, startled them with a warning shot and then blocked their path. Cuomo, Saifrahman, and I broke out a delegation of twenty-five elders and mullahs and brought them to the Afghan army post, 400 meters out of sight of the protesters. In most shuras, the elders lead. This time, the mullahs led, a Taliban judge at the forefront (we did not know his identity at the time). The elders sat in the back, largely quiet. We later learned that the mullahs had rallied the people to rise up.[11] The mullahs were convinced that a Koran had been damaged and that Americans were to blame. They told Saifrahman that he was their brother and that the Marines were doing a bad job. One black-turbaned mullah said: 'We do not need your kind of security. You burn down our homes.'[12] This was a good man, with whom Marines later had earnest conversations. He had taught at the school in Bartaka during Karzai's early days and then lived through the months of heavy fighting around Mian Poshtay. His words bespoke the people's frustration with the government and us. The

Taliban did not blow up homes or raid them at night, let alone damage Korans. We calmly tried to explain the situation, pledging our respect for Islam and promising that no one in Garmser had harmed a Koran.

The fairly polite and respectful conversation seemed to be allaying their concerns until shots rang out from the bazaar. We had made a mistake by removing the crowd's leaders from view of the protesters. Back in the bazaar, without their leadership, young men had pressed forward to the line of police and soldiers, chanting and waving their poles. With no one to control them, they rushed forward and hit the Marines and Afghan soldiers with their poles and large rocks. In the confusion, shots broke out. By the time the mullahs, elders, Cuomo, and I had reached the bazaar, the firing had ceased and six civilians lay wounded on the ground. One Afghan soldier was holding his bruised and bloodied head. Cuomo and the Marines brought the wounded into his headquarters for treatment and then evacuated them by helicopter. Saifrahman tried to bring the protesters under control. Many had fled but others were incensed. They called Saifrahman a traitor and an infidel—a horrible experience for the young twenty-three-year-old army officer. In the end, the mullahs and elders, averse to further bloodshed, told the protesters to go home. They duly dispersed.

The day's challenges were not over. While we had been dealing with the northern crowd, the larger southern crowd (it was more like an army) had passed Cuomo's outpost in Lakari, stoning Marines along the way. The vast majority of them were from Laki, Safar, and Benadar—regions still under Taliban control. We later learned that Taliban commanders in Safar had encouraged the people of these regions to march north and riot. I am sure that many would have gone of their own accord regardless. The Marines in Lakari reported that they were led by angry mullahs and that they intended to go to the district center. There were also reports of weapons and suicide vests among them.

The long winding column arrived late in the afternoon. A line of thirty Marines and Afghan soldiers stood before the post and the crowd, behind strands of barbed wire that Cuomo had laid to prevent any more unwanted rushes. Cuomo, Saifrahman, and I again broke out the leaders, but this time spoke with them within eyesight of the rank and file protesters. When angry young men in the crowd again started to chant and surge back and forth, the leaders stepped out from the shura and told them to cut it out. In the meeting itself, the mullahs, again, led the conversation, another Taliban judge at the forefront. The mullahs demanded that we respect the Koran and stop raids on homes at night. We promised that there would be an investigation into the alleged Koran desecration and that the Afghan army would be involved in any night raids conducted by Marines. After an hour of discussion, the mullahs were satisfied. Or perhaps with nightfall approaching they wanted to pray; or they were simply exhausted from a day's marching. In any case, the mullahs and elders walked out of the meeting and back to the crowd. The great beflagged column then turned around and moved back south. It was a welcome success. Smaller demonstrations took place the next day before they petered out altogether.[13]

During the week following the district center riots, Abdullah Jan, the Afghan army, and the Marines held shuras throughout Garmser to dispel the rumors that a Koran had been desecrated. The day after the district center riots, Governor Mangal's security advisor brought the Afghan officer who had commanded the raid to Garmser. He testified at a special shura at the district center that no Koran had been damaged. That and the shame of the burnt-out school seemed to convince the elders that the riots had been a mistake. A week later, Governor Mangal himself came to speak with the people. The event was coordinated with the ground-breaking for the reconstruction of the school, which Chilvers had already contracted at a cost of $150,000. Over 500 people attended. Meanwhile, smaller shuras were taking place throughout the south to explain the truth. Captain Cuomo, Lieutenant Saifrahman, and I patrolled to villages in Mian Poshtay and Lakari and talked with the people about both the Koran and the civilian casualties. Local leaders told us that the casualties were tragic but unavoidable given the situation. Their concern was the Koran. Almost everyone insisted that we complete an investigation and punish whoever had desecrated it. The elders and even the mullahs seemed to appreciate that we came to their villages out of respect. The Taliban made another attempt at the end of January, placing a torn-up Koran in a hole alongside Marine water bottles and ration wrappers in Lakari, but no one ever became very angry. Behind closed doors, elders and villagers told us that everyone knew it had been staged.

In retrospect, the riots should not have been a surprise. The signs were there in the anger of religious leaders, the disaffection of the landless immigrants, and the neutrality of the tribal leaders and village elders.

WAKIL MANAN, MIAN POSHTAY, AND THE RIOTS

The fact that an ill-executed raid and well-timed propaganda could spark widespread riots only underlines the ambivalence toward the government that still existed in Garmser—a sentiment that Abdullah Jan, the district support team, and the Marines were fully aware of. We just did not realize that it would manifest itself in so explosive a manner.

Getting back on track

With discontent receding, Wakil Manan at last started his work. Captain Cuomo and I were uncertain of success. During the riots, Wakil Manan had not come across as a great leader. Never mind that his sunglasses with turban amused young Marines rather than awed them, he said little about his plans and lived for days in the Afghan army post. At the height of the riots, he hid in the post rather than negotiate with the mullahs. The years of fighting as a communist, followed by mistreatment by the former mujahidin commanders, imprisonment by the first Taliban regime, and intimidation by Mullah Ismael had scarred him, making him distrustful of any Pashtun. Mian Poshtay was filled with Taliban immigrants who had helped Mullah Ismael. Wakil Manan was not going to jump in head first. But he was determined. Now, with riots behind us, he began orchestrating change.

Once the riots had ended, Wakil Manan left the Afghan army post and moved into his fortress-like compound across the canal. During the day, he met with groups of elders, villagers, and mullahs. During the night, he met with us. His work took time. When Cuomo and I went to his home and asked him about recruiting police, getting the people to oppose the Taliban, starting small projects, and setting up a large public shura for Abdullah Jan, he advised, 'Slowly, slowly. We will get there.' It seemed as if he was procrastinating, but we were wrong. Of all Garmser, Mian Poshtay is the most divided, populated by families who had immigrated to Mian Poshtay in ones and twos, not tribal blocks. Every village has several different families, each from a different tribe. Such heterogeneity makes Mian Poshtay difficult to govern. To build consensus, much time has to be spent talking with elders from the different villages. Wakil Manan understood this.

We worried about making sure Wakil Manan was safe. The Taliban targeted him. A week after his arrival, Taliban shot his nephew in the leg in Kuchinay Darveshan. He had been going to the district center to register to be a policeman. A few days later, Wakil Manan himself received a message from Naim, still shadow governor of Helmand, declaring that his name was at the top of the Taliban leader's hit list.[14] As commander of the Marines in Mian Poshtay, Cuomo made Wakil Manan's survival a top priority. We advised Wakil Manan on good security measures ('Do not travel through Darveshan!'), set up communication with Cuomo's headquarters, and even spent the night at his home. Cuomo and I did not want him or his men to feel that they were alone. Many a night we knocked on his giant iron front gate to be greeted by a hesitant voice and then the bleary eyes of Mohammed Sakhi or Sardar Mohammed, who had been bundled next to a small fire, on guard through the freezing night. With only four guards and plenty of work, none of them got much sleep. Suddenly, Wakil Manan's old request for eight guards did not seem so unreasonable.

In order to reinforce his influence within his own community, we gave Wakil Manan a small canal clean-up project. The idea was that locals would be more likely to help him if he helped them. Wakil Manan was ferocious when it came to projects. He would argue for hours to get a higher price or a bigger project, often wanting work he was not qualified to do, such as paving a road or building a school. In the end, negotiations worked out to our liking but only after tiresome two- or four-hour sessions on the floor of his concrete keep. For all his complaining, Wakil Manan knew the difference between right and wrong. On one occasion, he got into a long argument over projects with Master Sergeant Julia Watson, the Marine civil affairs leader at Mian Poshtay.[15] As always, he wanted more money. Watson was rather stern with him, lecturing him on the proper behavior of a community leader. The next day, when Wakil Manan came to Marine post to complete the conversation, he was rather quiet. She asked him what was wrong. With his eyes on the ground, he replied: 'Oh, nothing. You were firm and treated me how we should be treated. We need to be forced to do the right thing.'

To avoid upsetting the other elders by favoring Wakil Manan, we tried to spread the wealth. With Wakil Manan's return, Cuomo's patrolling, and efforts to re-open the bazaar, other elders had at last, if tentatively, expressed interest in reconstruction projects. Gail Long, our development officer, came down to see whether USAID could do a set of projects in Mian Poshtay. She toured the area and identified five projects, including critical repairs of the main canal. The USAID projects would not be underway for a month, but their selection had allowed us to reach out to the whole Mian Poshtay community and mitigate any backlash against Wakil Manan.

The real prize was the bazaar. It sat derelict, right outside Cuomo's front gate. For two months, he had been painfully negotiating its reconstruction. That the Taliban had permitted the negotiations to go on at all was a sign of their growing weakness in and around Mian Poshtay. The negotiations were horribly complex because four elders demanded to run the project together and refused to permit an outside contractor to come in. Cuomo entertained the demand for the sake of the bazaar. He wanted it opened as soon as possible. Writing a contract with four contractors as signatories was a bureaucratic nightmare. In the end it was worth it. In late January, reconstruction started. Again, in order to spread the wealth, we were careful not to make Wakil Manan a beneficiary.

Meanwhile, Wakil Manan had been talking to the elders. Mian Poshtay was his home and he knew nearly every family. He knew who had come as immigrants under the Taliban and who had sons who had turned to the Taliban in 2005. Old friends and family connections, many of whom the Taliban had threatened, passed him valuable information about what was going on in the various villages. He asked families who had sons with the Taliban to get them to lay down their arms.[16] He instructed villagers to stop paying taxes to the Taliban. Many heeded both requests. At the same time, he found police recruits. I would take four back with me when I returned to Hazar Joft at the end of the month. We did not realize it at the time but Wakil Manan's presence was driving back Taliban influence. Word came to Wakil Manan from people attending the mosques that his return had frightened the Taliban. They were dismayed he had tribal militia to protect him and feared he would identify and detain them. Wakil Manan himself told us: 'You do not know who is good and who is bad. I do.'[17] Soon, Taliban stopped traveling through Mian Poshtay or trying to control the elders there. Their observers disappeared. The mullahs went quiet. The hit men headed south. Intimidation, at least for the time being, dropped off. Months later, one community council member, who had many Taliban friends, confided: 'After Wakil Manan came to Zhan Zhir with a few police, the Taliban became scared. They knew Wakil Manan knew them. They stopped walking around the bazaar and fled from the area. The bazaar became safe for everyone.'[18]

On 20 January, Abdullah Jan came to Mian Poshtay for a shura, earlier than he had originally planned, in order to speak about the riots. Wakil Manan gathered 100 people, including all the village elders, many of whom had been in hiding for years. Abdullah Jan had not sat with them since 2006. They told Abdullah Jan that they were willing to work with the government again. A bigger success came when Abdullah Jan returned three weeks later. He set up a standing local council that would meet weekly to discuss problems, prioritize projects, and bring issues to him. The main elders of Mian Poshtay served on it, including Wakil Manan. We let the council pick and prioritize projects that CERP or USAID would fund. The council was meant to reinforce stability in Mian Poshtay. By bringing the community together, the marginalized would be given a chance to speak and receive benefits, which might reduce their need to turn to the Taliban for help.

In early February, the small bazaar re-opened. A month later, nearly seventy shops were doing business and the bazaar was bustling. Nothing showed better how Mian Poshtay had turned. Plenty of mullahs and poor farmers still preferred the Taliban, but most of the village elders were now working with the government.

Success in Mian Poshtay spread to Lakari. Captain Cuomo had assaulted into Lakari bazaar with fifty Marines and twenty Afghan soldiers in December, set up a new outpost, and then fanned outward from it. Fighting had been heavy in December but fell away in January due to Cuomo's intense patrolling. Compared to Mian Poshtay, the Taliban commanders had less stomach for a fight.[19] Alizai village elders started speaking with the Marines. In late February, the Lakari bazaar, far bigger than the one in Mian Poshtay, started to come back to life on its own. Eight weeks before, the Taliban had been patrolling it.[20]

As Marines worked with more and more elders in both Mian Poshtay and Lakari, they were able to gather more and more intelligence. They put together the names, faces, and locations of Taliban fighters. Many Taliban could see what was happening; a good number decided to surrender to the government. Most were lowly fighters or observers but tax collectors and judges surrendered as well. A few said they surrendered because they could see that the government was bringing projects; most because they feared being killed or detained. One had seen his cell leader killed; another had been told by his mother to stop fighting. Overall, it was evident that, encouraged by the elders, many Taliban felt they could no longer move about freely. In the words of one, 'The elders of my village came and met me. They said I must surrender. They said the Marines have too much information. I returned my weapon to the Taliban. I fear the people will soon tell the Marines about me and they will detain me…The young generation wants to come back. They want to leave the Taliban.'[21]

Abdullah Jan graciously accepted every surrender (known as 'reintegration' in official US parlance). Pashtun culture stresses that an honorable khan must mercifully accept the apology of a hated enemy. Islam stresses oneness and unity within a community. Both these ideals ran strong within Abdullah Jan. As far back as the 1988–9 tribal civil war, he had valued magnanimity in victory and reconciliation as a means of uniting people broken apart by conflict and feuds. He was deeply proud of this work, ranking it above governance or reconstruction. He made the Taliban who came forward pledge not to return to violence, sent them to register with the Marines so that they could be vetted and monitored, and then allowed them to return home. By April, twenty Taliban had surrendered, reportedly joined by many more who laid down their arms but never formally surrendered to the government. In all 2009, the number had been four.

Battlefield successes and political setbacks

After the February shura in Mian Poshtay, Lieutenant Colonel McDonough and Abdullah Jan rode back to Hazar Joft together in the same armored MRAP vehicle. The MRAP hit an IED. The blast cracked Abdullah Jan's fibula and severely wrenched McDonough's back. Abdullah Jan was on crutches for weeks. McDonough tried to keep working but ultimately had to be sent back to the United States for treatment. He did not return until April and then only for a few weeks. It was a testament to McDonough's leadership that the battalion pressed on during his absence. His company commanders continued to set up new posts, thinning themselves out more and more. In late February, Captain Noble's Marines in Loya Darveshan made contact with Captain Gorman's Marines in Kuchinay Darveshan. The long-standing geographic gap between the two companies was finally closed. By the end of March, thirty-two Marine posts dotted the district (they had begun with fifteen) and, as promised, the main canal road had been opened from the district center to Lakari (a pickup could go from the district center to Lakari in ninety minutes, an MRAP in three hours). Attacks had fallen from 125 in November to 32 in March. Marine tactics—small patrols and small posts, spread out from Amir Agha to Lakari—had been hugely successful in clearing out Taliban fighting cadres.

The same was true of Abdullah Jan's tribal strategy. Abdullah Jan had pulled us away from our Western ideas of building a progressive government and expecting the people to stand up behind it to a more Afghan way of doing business. His strategy was politically risky but in Mian Poshtay it worked, overcoming the shallow popular support and Taliban shadow infrastructure that had cursed our earlier efforts. Mian Poshtay had laid out a template that would be repeated: first convincing a tribal leader to return; second, allowing him to have a very small militia; third, bringing him to his home; fourth, empowering him with small projects; finally, working with him to organize the people against the Taliban. Tribal leaders were expected to side openly with the government, find recruits for the police, and help build a local council that would make decisions for the community. More cases would follow.

Physical signs of the riots vanished as quickly as they had appeared. Burnt-out cars were towed away. Shops were repaired. The school re-opened on 28 February. Yet if Garmser had forgotten the riots, Lashkar Gah and Kabul had not. Officials from Kabul summoned Garmser elders to Lashkar Gah to answer questions about Abdullah Jan's performance. In Kabul, Sher Mohammed Akhundzada, former governor of Helmand, criticized Mangal and lobbied for Abdullah Jan's removal. He came to Garmser twice in January to gather facts on what had happened, supposedly on behalf of Karzai (that was never verified). The PRT believed he was out to discredit Mangal and reclaim the provincial governorship. Sher Mohammed had never forgiven the British for removing him in 2005. Karzai himself often criticized Mangal and disliked British and American attempts to defend him. Coming under heavy political fire, Mangal summoned Abdullah Jan to Lashkar Gah on 15 March and informed him that the Attorney General of Afghanistan was placing him under investigation for the deaths of the six civilians in the riots. If found guilty, he could be sent to jail. In the meantime, he was forbidden from returning to Garmser. Police chief Ghuli Khan and NDS chief Mir Hamza were also placed under investigation but were allowed to stay in the district. The investigations took months to complete. Without the district governor, governing Garmser suddenly became much tougher. We depended on Abdullah Jan to hold shuras, organize the people to support government initiatives, resolve disputes, talk with elders, win over mullahs, and accept the surrender of Taliban. Losing him seemed to place progress at risk.

Chilvers and I, strongly supported by General Nicholson, lobbied the PRT and the US Embassy to advise Mangal to leave Abdullah Jan in place. The PRT and US Embassy disagreed. The ensuing argument exemplified a growing philosophical debate between civilians and Marines in the districts, who believed that everything possible should be done to defeat the Taliban, and civilians in Lashkar Gah and Kabul, who believed that we should build a democratic government and that meant not interfering in decisions that we happened to dislike. In the end, Chilvers and I conceded; in my case, because it seemed part of my job to adapt to possible changes and roll with the punches. I have never figured out if that was the right decision or not.

The burning of the district center school had been a great victory for the Taliban, topped only by Abdullah Jan's summons to Lashkar Gah. Their longtime foe was now fighting for his job and banned from Garmser. They had succeeded by propaganda and rumor rather than brute force. I could not help but wonder if we should have done something different: if we should have heeded Major Hezbollah's warning and held a shura in Darveshan; or if we should have resorted to a whiff of grapeshot at the bridge over the main canal at the district center. It was horribly ironic that our hesitance to accept draconian measures had resulted in a bitter political setback. Our ideals had met the harsh reality of Afghanistan.

9

THE ALIZAI RETURN

Pe harakat kay, barakat day.
'In movement there is blessing.'
Pashto proverb

One Friday in January 2008, Ghulam Rassoul and Shah Wali Khan went to Lakari bazaar to buy some goods. Ghulam Rassoul was the Alizai tribe's hardened front-line commander, known for his bravery on the battlefield. Shah Wali Khan was the patriarch of what traditionally had been the leading Alizai family. It had been sixteen months since the Alizai tribe had allied with the Taliban. Ghulam Rassoul and Shah Wali Khan were living in their homes in Laki, about 7 kilometers south of Lakari bazaar. Both Laki and Lakari were the domain of the Alizai. On this Friday, Ghulam Rassoul was looking at new shoes when he felt a harsh tug on his sleeve. All of a sudden, five men were upon him, led by Noor Ali, a local Taliban enforcer. They bound his hands, covered his eyes, and stuffed the stocky former mujahidin commander into the passenger seat of his Toyota Corolla—no mean feat. Noor Ali whispered: 'I have killed thirteen men and now I will kill you!'[1] The Corolla, with Ghulam Rassoul in the front, two Taliban in the back, and one at the wheel, sped southward along the main canal. Noor Ali trailed behind.

181

Ghulam Rassoul is a former wrestler. He had trained in Tae Kwan Do in Kabul before the jihad. He did not give up. Noor Ali's boys had not tied his hands well. Ghulam Rassoul wrenched them free and lunged for the steering wheel. Everyone then started beating on each other and the car flew headlong into the 6-meter-deep main canal. As the car sank, the Taliban smashed through the windows with their weapons. After two minutes underwater, Ghulam Rassoul and the Taliban broke their way free to the surface, where they immediately started beating on each other again. The Taliban, weighed down by their ammo vests, did not fare well against the experienced wrestler, who elbowed two of them into submission.

When Ghulam Rassoul hauled himself out of the water, Noor Ali tried to hold him at gunpoint. Ghulam Rassoul was saved by 100 or more Alizai, led by Shah Wali Khan, who had run to the scene from the bazaar. They pushed Noor Ali away and rushed Ghulam Rassoul, wet and turban-less, to safety in the bazaar. Ghulam Rassoul calmly bought a new turban—he was still a khan, after all—and then returned to Laki with Shah Wali Khan.[2]

The attack was the culmination of an eight-month feud. In 2007, the alliance between the Alizai and Mullah Naim, then Taliban commander of southern Helmand, had fallen apart. The issue was land. The land where Naim's family lived in Laki had been given to the government back in the 1970s by Shah Wali Khan's father, as part of the land redistribution that had accompanied the construction of the canal system. The government did nothing with the land. During the jihad, Naim's people seized 62 hectares of it. Shah Wali Khan permitted them to do so and even signed a document confirming their ownership. At the time, the land was overgrown and unproductive. Naim's people steadily improved it. Then, during the first Taliban regime, when Shah Wali Khan was in Pakistan, Naim took some of Shah Wali Khan's private land for his people. Upon his return in 2001, Shah Wali Khan reclaimed that land and then proceeded to try to take back the government land too.

The Alizai alliance with the Taliban in 2006 offered only a short respite to the friction. The Alizai had aligned with the Taliban in order to increase their power, not limit it. Shah Wali Khan, hereditary lord of Laki, was not going to kowtow to Naim and his family of squatters. Trouble resumed after British commandos shot Naim in Darveshan in May 2007. The story is that Ghulam Rassoul drove him to Pakistan with

Image 10: Ghulam Rassoul. (Photo from Scott Cuomo)

tears in his eyes. His grief must have passed quickly because, once back in Garmser, he and Shah Wali Khan promptly set to reclaiming all the land. Shah Wali Khan shut the sluice gates on the main canal leading to those lands in order to force Naim's family out. The Taliban leadership convened a shura of twenty mullahs to resolve the problem. The mullahs ruled that the land had belonged to the government and therefore Shah Wali Khan had no claim.[3] Shah Wali Khan and Ghulam Rassoul did not care for that ruling and friction persisted. Nor were Naim's people their only targets. They went after other people's land as well, many of whom were Taliban supporters. Noor Ali, Ghulam Rassoul's future attacker in

Lakari bazaar, had seized government land by force a few years earlier and was one of the targets of Ghulam Rassoul's revanchism.

By the end of 2007, open fighting between Shah Wali Khan and Ghulam Rassoul and several smaller tribes connected to the Taliban had broken out. Shah Wali Khan's brother was killed in Laki. Two of Ghulam Rassoul's relatives were killed in Baram Chah. With the situation worsening for them, at the end of December, Shah Wali Khan and Ghulam Rassoul made a secret trip to Lashkar Gah to reach out to the provincial government. The secret was poorly kept. Naim, having recovered, issued orders for Ghulam Rassoul to be killed.[4] Three days later, Noor Ali jumped Ghulam Rassoul in Lakari bazaar.

One week after Noor Ali's attack, Shah Wali Khan, Ghulam Rassoul, and Shah Jahan fled to Pakistan with their immediate family members. Shah Jahan was one of the two other powerful Alizai tribal leaders. The last was Mohammed Nadir, who lived in Lakari. Shah Jahan had been politically sharp enough to stay out of land disputes with the Taliban, but his strong ties with Ghulam Rassoul and Shah Wali Khan put his life in danger too. Two weeks after they left, British bombs killed Mohammed Nadir, sitting in his home in Lakari (as mentioned in Chapter 6). The Alizai in Garmser were now leaderless. Shah Wali Khan, Ghulam Rassoul, and Shah Jahan found no peace in Pakistan. They had no means of income. Naim was hunting them. Taliban were everywhere. Before long, a Taliban hit squad shot up Shah Wali Khan's residence in Pakistan. Looking for a way out, the three Alizai khans reached out to an old friend: Abdullah Jan.

Recapturing Laki

In August 2009, Shah Wali Khan phoned Abdullah Jan and asked for his help getting out of Pakistan. Years of infighting and betrayal had wrecked their friendship and had deeply hurt Abdullah Jan. But Abdullah Jan was a wise politician, always amenable to reconciliation. He recognized the opportunity that the return of Garmser's three great Alizai tribal leaders represented. In terms of Pashtun culture, Shah Wali Khan's call implicitly apologized for the pain of the past, an admission of wrong and a plea for forgiveness. A magnanimous Pashtun khan such as Abdullah Jan was expected to accept their apology. I also think some part of him was relieved to have the chance to be together with his old friends again.

After several calls, Abdullah Jan smuggled Shah Jahan, Ghulam Rassoul, and Shah Wali Khan to Lashkar Gah and put them up in a house. They met with Governor Mangal, who forgave them for siding with the Taliban and gave them land to get them on their feet. For months, Mangal and Abdullah Jan kept the three in Lashkar Gah in order to test their loyalty while crafting a plan to send them back to Garmser.[5]

During that time, still furious over the attempt on his life, Ghulam Rassoul led police onto two of Naim's men in Lashkar Gah. In return, Naim put hits out on Ghulam Rassoul, Shah Wali Khan, and Shah Jahan. He nearly succeeded. In early March, Shah Wali Khan went to pray in a mosque in Lashkar Gah. Two Taliban, waiting behind the door, shot him in the leg as he knelt down. Fortunately, they did not finish the job and Shah Wali Khan survived. The attack merely made Ghulam Rassoul and Shah Wali Khan more determined than ever to take back Laki. It also raised their credibility with Mangal and Abdullah Jan. In private, Abdullah Jan told me: 'You can trust Ghulam Rassoul. He has one face.' That meant Ghulam Rassoul would tell me when he was my friend and when he was my enemy. He would not have two faces and work with the Taliban behind my back.

For all of 2009, the Taliban had held onto Laki. About 3 kilometers wide, Laki starts just south of Lakari bazaar, where a new drainage canal begins to parallel the main canal, and ends just beyond where the two canals meet, 10 kilometers to the south. Shah Wali Khan's village lies almost exactly in the middle. In the small hours of 3 January 2010, roughly fifty Marines slipped into the center of Laki under the cover of darkness. Lieutenant Colonel McDonough himself led the Marines on foot over 10 kilometers from Lakari. He had meant merely to raid, but when he got there he decided to leave a platoon from his Weapons Company behind, roughly a kilometer from Shah Wali Khan's village. Alone and unafraid, that platoon would see heavy fighting. But their presence opened the way for Shah Wali Khan, Ghulam Rassoul, and Shah Jahan. Abdullah Jan decided that if the Marines could stay in Laki, so could the tribal leaders.

By early 2010, Abdullah Jan and Mangal were ready to send Ghulam Rassoul and Shah Wali Khan. They had proven themselves, and the situation on the ground was ripe. At the end of January, Mangal told Shah Jahan, Ghulam Rassoul, and Shah Wali Khan that they had spent enough time in Lashkar Gah and that they could no longer rest in its luxuries. He wanted them to go back to Garmser and help the government.[6] A few days later, I returned from Mian Poshtay. Abdullah Jan told me that Shah Wali Khan and Ghulam Rassoul would soon go to Laki and that they would need help.

This was the next phase in Abdullah Jan's larger tribal strategy. Wakil Manan's success in Mian Poshtay had confirmed that the strategy could work. Abdullah Jan's plan for this second phase called for Ghulam Rassoul and Shah Wali Khan to return to Laki, help the Marines, recruit police, and organize the people against the Taliban. Since two tribal leaders were going to Laki, Abdullah Jan believed that a ten-man tribal militia was warranted (Abdullah Jan continued to warn me of the dangers of giving tribal leaders too many men). Ghulam Rassoul would get the weapons himself. We would pay wages. Again, the tribal militia would eventually go to the police academy. Again, projects would be given to boost the two tribal leaders' influence. Again, I would go down to help set things up. Abdullah Jan added: 'They are much bigger than Wakil Manan. You must help them a lot.' Another elder, Haji Raess, hyperbolized: 'You must protect Shah Wali Khan and Ghulam Rassoul. They can do more than 1,000 elders.'[7]

That left Shah Jahan. As the former district governor of Khaneshin, Shah Jahan was a powerful figure. I met with him several times. His political acumen was impressive. I wanted to wait to bring him back, however, because I was not sure how well we could control him. Abdullah Jan advised patience. Therefore, I asked Shah Jahan to wait in Lashkar Gah until he was needed. He acceded to my request.

Mangal summoned Abdullah Jan to Lashkar Gah to answer for the riots in mid March, before Shah Wali Khan and Ghulam Rassoul were in place. This delayed things. Shah Wali Khan and Ghulam Rassoul initially did not want to go to Garmser without him. Abdullah Jan instructed them to proceed regardless. On 22 April, they finally arrived in Garmser. They spent a few days at the district center with Deputy District Governor Ayub Omar, making final preparations before going south. It was a memorable day when their convoy of three Corollas and two motorcycles, packed full of men and guns, rolled down to Laki. Ghulam Rassoul reported to Captain Cuomo (Marine commander for Mian Poshtay and Lakari) in Lakari bazaar and told him: 'I am here to help you remove the Taliban. I am going to go and find them.'

The situation in Laki was much more dangerous than Mian Poshtay had been when Wakil Manan had arrived. Like Mian Poshtay, the

Marine positions in Laki were cut off. Taliban controlled the canal road to the north. Checkpoints periodically searched traffic en route to Lakari bazaar. Insurgents still buried IEDs in the road. Unlike Mian Poshtay, which had roughly 200 Marines and at least twenty Afghan soldiers, Laki was held by only eighty Marines and twenty Afghan soldiers. Around Shah Wali Khan's village, a security bubble was still forming. Taliban were openly running a madrasa, manning checkpoints, and launching attacks. Abdullah Jan had held a shura in early February—500 meters from Shah Wali Khan's village and 300 meters from a Marine post. Insurgents attacked it with AK-47s, RPGs, and medium machine guns (Abdullah Jan kept speaking through the whole thing, unphased). To the south, the situation was worse. Safar bazaar, the Taliban capital of Garmser, was 10 kilometers south of Laki. The Taliban were determined to stop further Marine expansion southward and hotly contested long-range Marine forays. Fighting resembled Mian Poshtay during the previous summer: twenty to thirty insurgents engaged the Marines whenever they moved 2 kilometers south. Captain Matthew Kutilek, the company commander, and Gunnery Sergeant Scott Parry, his operations chief, were both wounded in firefights there.[8]

The danger made what Ghulam Rassoul and Shah Wali Khan did all the more impressive. 'Right now it is war with the Taliban,' declared Shah Wali Khan when I met him in the district center. 'We do not hide ourselves. We fight.'[9] Ghulam Rassoul and Shah Wali Khan—still on crutches—moved into Shah Wali Khan's home in the middle of Laki. The ten-man tribal militia took up post around the home, vigilant day and night. All were family members and retainers. Two had fought in the jihad and another was an actual policeman in Lashkar Gah who took time off to go with the family. The remainder were the nephews of Shah Wali Khan and Ghulam Rassoul, too young to have fought in the jihad. Ghulam Rassoul paid great attention to teaching them how to be soldiers. What they lacked in experience, they made up for in loyalty and energy. These were the good young sons of tribal leaders that Abdullah Jan had so often wanted in the police. For them, being in the militia was a stepping stone to becoming a policeman and then an officer, where they could make a name for themselves and their family.

Ghulam Rassoul immediately set to patrolling the area and dragging in Taliban. He drove back and forth on the main canal road between Shah Wali Khan's home and Lakari bazaar, making heavy use of his

Image 11: Police chief Omar Jan (left) and Shah Wali Khan (right).

motorcycles, disdainful of IEDs. His men also foot-patrolled through Lakari bazaar. A few days after arriving, he saw two Taliban on the main road, pulled them over, detained them, and took them to Captain Cuomo. A week or so after that, a Taliban tax collector walked into Shah Wali Khan's village. The militia grabbed him and turned him over to the Marines too. The Marines in both Lakari and Laki met with Shah Wali Khan and Ghulam Rassoul every few days to coordinate. Marines often went with the militia on patrol. Results were not long in coming. The militia regularly pointed out IEDs and insurgents.

While Ghulam Rassoul patrolled, Shah Wali Khan met with the elders. Scores of them came to the house every morning. His goal was to bring the Alizai back together and back to the government. The Alizai in Garmser have ten different sub-tribes. For two years, since Shah Wali Khan, Ghulam Rassoul, and Shah Jahan had fled to Pakistan and Mohammed Nadir had been killed, they had been leaderless. Some had backed the Taliban. Some had waited for the Taliban to leave. Shah Wali

Khan, step by step, pulled them back together. He told the village elders it was time to stop fighting; Taliban could not be allowed to lay IEDs near villages; young Alizai men needed to put away their guns.[10]

The hardest part was teaching Ghulam Rassoul what evidence was required to send a captured insurgent away to prison. The Lashkar Gah courts had a high standard. They wanted eyewitness statements and physical evidence—weapons, bomb-making material, documents. Anything less and the prosecutors would not take the case to court. Even a confession would not do. Ghulam Rassoul's opinion was that we should take his word that the prisoners were Taliban because he was a khan and Laki was his home. In fairness, there were so many Taliban running around that he hardly had time to conduct a full-fledged criminal investigation. Nor did the Marines. Everyone was simply trying to survive. We went through the evidence process with Ghulam Rassoul over and over again. Slowly he got the hang of it and worked with the Marines to gather eyewitness statements and physical evidence.

As with Wakil Manan, we gave Shah Wali Khan and Ghulam Rassoul a few small projects so that they could help the people and thereby reinforce their influence. At the same time, we wanted to give projects to the community at large. Unlike Mian Poshtay, there was an immediate demand for projects. Culverts, canal clearings, and new sluice gates were requested. Gail Long brought two engineers down to scope out projects. As in Mian Poshtay, they identified a set of small projects to complete. Those small projects were meant to win community support. Of greater concern for long-term development were the school and clinic, clustered together with a half-built mosque and a handful of shops near Shah Wali Khan's village. The school was the madrasa that Naim had built so poorly after he had recaptured Laki in 2006; now it was in a state of collapse. The mosque was half constructed. The clinic was in disrepair but still running. Plans were set by the Marines to rebuild the school (to be run by the government) and refurbish the clinic.

With the return of Shah Wali Khan and Ghulam Rassoul, the situation in Laki was improving. The security bubble slowly expanded past Shah Wali Khan's village and the Marine outpost. Lesser Alizai elders in Lakari openly worked with the Marines and visited the district center. A kilometer south of Shah Wali Khan's village, southern Laki was still under Taliban control; but the Alizai as a whole were coming together, and there was no shortage of support for the government.

WAR COMES TO GARMSER

Controlling tribal militia and tribal leaders

My biggest worry in working with tribal leaders, whether in Laki or Mian Poshtay, was that they might revert to their warlord ways of the past and abuse people. If the tribal leaders taxed the people, took their land, or beat them, the people would turn to the Taliban for help, as Lieutenant Colonel Hezbollah, recently promoted to be the Afghan army battalion commander, often reminded me: 'The Taliban returned to Garmser [in 2006] because men with militias misused their power. The people then moved away from the government. They thought a Taliban government would be better.'[11] The Marines and I were mindful that we needed to watch the tribal leaders and prevent any abuse. We did not want to be implementing a strategy that would lead to oppression. Lieutenant Colonel McDonough (who briefly returned in April) and I were already trying to honor Abdullah Jan's instructions that the total number of tribal militia should be small and that their expansion should be step by step. We also kept the militia under the police and strove to send them to the police academy, as per the original plan. In addition to these two steps, McDonough, Hezbollah, and I ordered that militia (and later the police who came out of the academy) only be used for self-defense, not law enforcement, let alone the resolution of personal disputes. Mixing in law enforcement would create an insurmountable temptation for any tribal leader to bend the law for personal gain. And finally, the Marines and Afghan army soldiers monitored the tribal leaders and their militia, both through working with them side by side and gathering information from locals.

A few problems appeared in Mian Poshtay after Wakil Manan returned and re-asserted himself as the region's main tribal leader. Immigrants from Uruzgan had been given parts of Wakil Manan's land by Mullah Ismael, the Taliban cadre leader who had operated out of Mian Poshtay. A few months after returning to Mian Poshtay, Wakil Manan got into some vocal arguments with these immigrant farmers. He wanted his land back, partly for the profits, partly because he did not want Taliban sympathizers next door. The farmers feared that Wakil Manan would take their newfound land. Wakil Manan feared that the farmers, plowing his private land, would murder him. The danger was that his guards might get involved. Indeed, against Wakil Manan's orders, once or twice his men scuffled with the farmers. We warned him neither to use his militia in civil matters nor to enforce the law; he had

190

to keep them in line or we would disarm them. He complied and on his own accord fired and disarmed disobedient militia. Well-versed in Afghan law and bureaucracy, Wakil Manan took his land cases to the courts in Lashkar Gah and abided by the government's rulings, whether for or against him.

Problems in Laki were worse. The land dispute between Shah Wali Khan and Naim's family had never been resolved. Indeed, it had deepened. When the Marines had arrived in Mian Poshtay in July 2009, Mullah Naim had believed Taliban defeat imminent and had seized more of Shah Wali Khan's land—162 hectares in all—giving it to his people.[12] Naim, of course, the Taliban governor for all Helmand, was in Pakistan. His subordinates carried out this land grab. Now Shah Wali Khan and his family members wanted that land back, as well as at least some of the original government land that had been signed over to Naim's family during the jihad. Before long, Naim's people were going to the Afghan army, Marines, and the district center, loudly complaining that the Alizai were about to attack them. The Alizai had not actually done anything other than stew over their lost land, but the degree of hatred on both sides made it clear that violence could break out. Naim's people, of course, were still with the Taliban, who had done far more for them than the Alizai ever had or ever would. Taliban fighters hid in their homes and laid IEDs in nearby roads. Ghulam Rassoul wanted to detain them, putting us in a tough position. It was hard to tell if he wanted to do so because they were Taliban or because he wanted to punish them over the land issue. We decided to put justice above tactical gains. We told him the militia should stay out of Naim's village. If action needed to be taken, the Marines or the government would have to do it. Furthermore, we reminded Ghulam Rassoul and Shah Wali Khan that the Alizai militia could not be used to settle the land dispute. Both promised to let the issue lie until the Taliban had been defeated, at which point they would take it to the government. Relations between Naim's people in Laki and the Alizai never improved, but the land was never seized and there were no major incidents of violence (although months later one illegally-built foot bridge was burned down; best not to build a bridge onto Shah Wali Khan's land without his permission).

The upshot of the return of the tribal leaders to Mian Poshtay and Laki was that something like the majority of the people in these communities decided to work with the government. The tribal leaders electrified the standing tribal networks and got the landed village elders off the fence. Far less enthusiastic were the landless immigrants. The Taliban protected them and their land claims. The landed tribes did not. The Marines and the government tried to step in and fill this role by preventing tribal leaders themselves from making land decisions. Tribal leaders and immigrants alike were pressured to go to the government to settle their problems. Indeed, the government actually prevented Wakil Manan and the Alizai from taking land that did not actually belong to them. This was a success of sorts. But, at the end of the day, the government did not legally recognize land grants issued by the Taliban or the communists before them, just as those regimes had sometimes voided the land papers of the landed tribes. Whether the Taliban or the government was in power, someone was going to lose out. We flagged the need for land reform in our discussions with the provincial reconstruction team and high-level visitors. It was clear that it would demand a huge effort, partly because of the legal intricacies, partly because the Afghan government would resist foreign interference in a domestic matter. This was Afghanistan's toughest problem. There were no easy, ideal solutions. I fear that fact may have deterred the United States from trying harder.

Progress district-wide

Throughout Garmser, tribal leaders and lesser village elders were turning to the government, encouraged by Marine patrolling and the successes of Wakil Manan, Shah Wali Khan, and Ghulam Rassoul. In Darveshan, Taliban activity had lingered into April. Even after the main canal road had been opened in March, IED attacks had persisted to the east. The last pockets of resistance were finally extinguished as more and more posts were set up and Captain Gorman, the Marine commander there, reached out to the elders in Kuchinay Darveshan. Convinced we were not leaving, elders started working with Marines. Their families watched over their villages at night and projects, including the reconstruction of two schools, got underway. A local council formed, just as had occurred in Mian Poshtay, and Gorman started funneling projects through it. Success culminated at the end of April when the Marines detained the local cell leader, Abdul Ahad, who had been running operations throughout Darveshan for over six months. 'There are no Taliban in Darveshan,' reported the Amir Agha police post commander, 'They have nothing. You took Abdul Ahad and they disappeared.'[13] A week later, Roh Khan, the father of Tooriali, the most powerful tribal leader in Kuchinay Darveshan, came back of his own accord.

A week after that, Khodirom returned, the biggest tribal leader in Loya Darveshan and former Noorzai mujahidin commander. The Taliban had imprisoned him in the 1990s. When the Taliban had attacked in 2006, he had fled to Lashkar Gah. Loya Darveshan was a large area with Noorzai living along the canals and poor Taraki near the desert. Its size and absence of tribal leaders made it difficult to control. Many of the mullahs who had called for the January riots against the district center had come from villages there. Village elders had long been telling me that Khodirom needed to return. NDS Chief Mir Hamza encouraged Khodirom to come back. He knew of Abdullah Jan's tribal strategy and wanted Khodirom to be part of it. The improving situation in the district convinced Khodirom. He owned several hundred hectares of land, both in Loya Darveshan and in Kandahar. His power also came from his four wives, eighteen sons, and twelve daughters. He had over twenty grandsons and at least eight sons-in-law. This made for a huge network of people who owed him their loyalty. If needed, he could field a platoon from his direct descendants alone. No clearer explanation can be found as to why Pashtuns value large families. The provincial governor's office endorsed his return, accompanied by a small five-man tribal militia. By the beginning of May, he was back in his home near the desert. He would soon send police to the academy and advocate that the community council expand southward.

Under this pressure, the Taliban all but gave up their role in governing and focused on guerrilla activities. With the Marines on their doorstep in Safar, the Taliban district governors became consumed with tactical matters and defending the new front line in southern Laki. Rotating every few months, Taliban district governors increasingly moved from place to place, trying to hide themselves, which made it difficult to govern or work with local people. A Taliban district governor was now really a commander of several cadres, rather than a government leader with responsibilities in justice and delivery of goods and services. Additionally, Taliban judges largely disappeared. A few still lived in the district, no longer taking cases. The vestiges of open Taliban rule hung on to some extent in poppy taxation. The Taliban sent collectors to gather tax for poppy, which had to be smuggled through their territory to the south. The Taliban movement was far from discredited. It remained an alternative to the government and had appeal. But it is fair to say that, in Garmser, and especially north of Safar, the term 'shadow' accurately depicts their state of affairs.

The situation in Garmser had changed dramatically. Tribal leaders and their tribesmen were now standing up against the Taliban. Tribal leaders from Hazar Joft to Laki were visiting the district center and working with the government. The new tribal front was visible in early May when Ghulam Rassoul, Shah Wali Khan, Wakil Manan, Lieutenant Colonel Hezbollah, Captain Cuomo, and a few others knelt in Wakil Manan's cavernous hall to declare solidarity against the Taliban. The days of digging for police recruits were over. Tribal leaders were volunteering more men for the police than there were open posts in the police force. At least 100 men were asking to join. Most were from south of Hazar Joft, where the situation was the least peaceful. Spaces for the academy were limited, so we could not immediately get the police force to its authorized strength. It would take time. Those willing bodies would help in the summer battles to come.

Abdullah Jan was no longer in the district, but the success was his. At the small cost of about twenty tribal militia and a handful of quick impact projects, he had raised the tribal leaders against the Taliban. He had crafted a good plan based on forming alliances, even with people who had been his political opponents, exploiting the Taliban's own failures in winning over the tribal leaders.

10

THE TALIBAN COUNTER-OFFENSIVE

Pe yeow gul ne pesserlie keegee.
'One flower does not make it springtime.'
Pashto proverb

It was the first week of January 2010 and I was sitting in the district governor's office watching Abdullah Jan argue with Mohammed Nabi— his old soldier, one-time Taliban commander, and now community council member. Mohammed Nabi was furious. Taliban were coming to his village at night. 'They will kill Atlas Khan and me,' he spat. 'You don't know them. You don't know the young Taliban. I do. They will kill us. Give me weapons and I will kill them all. I can defend myself better than ten police!' Abdullah Jan coolly replied, 'Then they will kill you. You work for the government now. You cannot have a militia.' He turned to me, 'You have to help them. The Taliban are always in their villages.' I took his request seriously. Mohammed Nabi was a friend. Atlas Khan was the most honest member of the community council. I directed projects to their villages and encouraged them to buy one AK-47 apiece for self-defense. I did not buy them weapons myself. It seemed wrong. My morals came with a price. On the evening of 5 May 2010, four Taliban entered Atlas Khan's home, shot him in the face, and knee-capped his son. So began the Taliban spring offensive.

The Taliban had not fared well over the previous six months. Darveshan to Lakari to Laki had fallen to the Marines. Key tribal leaders had joined the government. Only Safar was under open Taliban control. Mullah Naim, Taliban governor of Helmand, did not want to give up. He planned to frighten the tribal leaders back into submission. Before, he had been careful about killing tribal leaders working with the government. He had not wanted to offend the local people or create feuds. Now, with the Taliban's position worsening, he eased his restraint.[1] Fighters were sent to Hazar Joft, Majitek, Mian Poshtay, Lakari, and Laki with orders to kill community council members and elders. Those in Hazar Joft and Majitek would deal with the community council. Mullah Ismael—the Taliban cadre leader with the crippled shoulder who had pushed Wakil Manan out of Mian Poshtay in 2006—would take out the southern elders. Naim dispatched Mullah Ismael and twenty men to Lakari and Mian Poshtay with instructions to kill forty elders. They worked out of hard-to-reach villages by the river.[2] Mullah Ismael was uniquely hateful. He sent warnings to the elders and had local laborers beaten. He threatened to kill everyone in Shah Wali Khan's village. I knew of no other Taliban commanders like him. I am not sure even Naim realized how far he would go.

Meanwhile, Mullah Naim reinforced the Taliban front line in southern Laki in order to defend Safar bazaar. As the strategic crossroads between Iran, Pakistan, Kandahar, and the rest of Afghanistan, Safar's bazaar had long been a Taliban supply point and command and control node. It was still their district capital. If Safar fell, the Taliban would be left with Benadar, too dry and sparsely populated to serve as a base for operations. Lines of Taliban filed into southern Laki.

The attack on Atlas Khan was one of several. That same day, roughly a kilometer away in Majitek, insurgents laid an IED that killed eight Afghan soldiers. Three days later, Naim's men kidnapped Ghulam Rassoul's brother, the learned and beloved Mamoor Zahrif Shah, who had been receiving medical care in Pakistan. All Helmand knew Zahrif Shah from his work with NGOs and teaching at the agricultural high school. Naim sent a message to Ghulam Rassoul. To get his brother back, it said, Ghulam Rassoul had to pay 36 hectares of land and 210 kilograms of poppy, secure the release of the two insurgents he had turned over to the police in Lashkar Gah back in late 2009, cease working with the government, and leave Garmser.

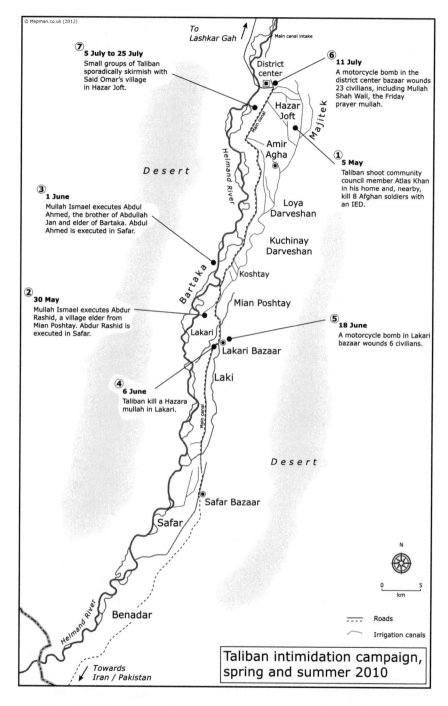

Map 10: Taliban intimidation campaign, spring and summer 2010.

197

Attacks and threats persisted over the coming weeks. Worry spread throughout the tribal leadership and community council. The Taliban posted leaflets in Laki and beat three of Shah Jahan's relatives. Later, twenty-five Taliban tried to infiltrate Shah Wali Khan's village and kill Shah Wali Khan and Ghulam Rassoul. A Marine patrol scared them off.[3] Fortunately, the community council held on and Ghulam Rassoul, while visibly upset, stayed in the fight in spite of his brother's kidnapping. Still, if the Taliban killed elders or forced them to flee, the government's successes of the past few months would be reversed. Support for the government depended on the elders. Without them, no one would dare to accept projects, local shuras would fall apart, information on Taliban activity would dry up. Another hit on the community council could result in mass resignations, crippling Garmser's one political institution capable of representing the people. The death of Wakil Manan, Ghulam Rassoul, or Shah Wali Khan would be equally devastating. Their militias would dissolve and few if any other tribal leaders would dare to come back to Garmser. Taliban would be able to reassert control of Mian Poshtay, Laki, or Lakari, even if Marines prevented them from massing in large numbers. Marine posts would become islands in a sea of unhelpful Pashtuns.

Fighting while adapting to political change

The Taliban offensive coincided with a period of political vulnerability. Abdullah Jan's district governorship petered out on 29 April 2010, when the new district governor, Mohammed Fahim, arrived. The attorney general's investigation into the riots had found Abdullah Jan innocent. Nevertheless, Governor Mangal sacked him a few days later. The Taliban had succeeded: the riots had taken down their toughest opponent in Garmser. We never learned who was actually behind the sacking. There were rumors it was Karzai; and there were rumors it was Mangal. Police chief Ghuli was also removed, sent to Sangin. NDS chief Mir Hamza and Deputy District Governor Ayub Omar survived.

The loss of Abdullah Jan stressed our strategy. We had to adapt to political change and at the same time fend off the Taliban offensive. When Ayub Omar announced Abdullah Jan's removal to a shura of Garmser's tribal leaders and community council members, the response was decidedly hostile. Whittling away at their worry beads, Said Omar,

Mohammed Anwar, and many other tribal leaders demanded Abdullah Jan's return. Without him, they feared that the government would be too weak to stop Taliban attacks. In the tone of a disapproving father, the venerable Said Omar, who rarely attended shuras, warned: 'Haji Abdullah Jan brought security. We need him. What will *you* do when the fighting starts?'[4] With the fighting season upon us, Garmser wallowed in political uncertainty. The Taliban had a real chance to recapture the losses of the past four months.

The whole affair revealed inadequacies in how the Afghan government selected its leaders. President Karzai, the Independent Directorate for Local Governance (which answered to Karzai), and influential governors such as Mangal chose district governors. The Ministry of Interior, with some input by the provincial chief of police, chose district police chiefs. Other than Karzai, none of these officials were elected. In too many cases, appointments became a tool to gain political advantage or wealth (bribes and paying for positions were known to be widespread). The most effective leaders were not always kept in the districts or sent there. Abdullah Jan had lacked the political weight or wealth to keep himself in power. Neither his accomplishments nor the thoughts of the people of Garmser mattered.

Abdullah Jan's replacement was Mohammed Fahim, twenty-two-year-old son of a powerful Kabul family. Pashtuns from the Wardak tribe, his family had moved to Marjah when the canals were being built. Fahim was intelligent—having attended twelve grades of school—and had strong political connections. He had to face the Taliban onslaught at a young age. Deputy District Governor Ayub Omar and the new police chief, Omar Jan, helped him out.

Police chief Omar Jan was a welcome addition. Aged thirty-five with thick, jet-black eyebrows, a short but full pointed beard, and a perpetual scowl, Omar Jan always looked angry. That his tribe was Andar, from the Ghilzai tribal confederation, traditional supporters of the Taliban, added to his angry image. His brother (his parents had died) was an influential elder in Marjah. Omar Jan himself had been in the police for at least ten years, with experience fighting the Taliban throughout Helmand. He came to Garmser from Sangin, where he had given a good accounting of himself as police chief. He led from the front and preferred acting to careful planning, often to the dismay of his advisors. Such boldness was exactly what was needed in the summer of 2010.

Omar Jan faced a difficult challenge when he arrived in Garmser. Besides the Taliban attacks, the number of police was dangerously low. Of Garmser's eighty-five policemen, Ghuli had taken thirty-five with him to Sangin. A younger man, with a smaller personal retinue, Omar Jan had only ten of his own men to replace them. On top of this, Abdullah Jan's forty veterans, the most experienced Afghan force in the district, might soon disappear. After his dismissal, Abdullah Jan had decided to live in Lashkar Gah. In early May, with no more need for them, Abdullah Jan told us he was going to sell off his weapons and dismiss most of his men. I asked him to leave his men, with their weapons. I promised we would pay their salaries. He consented. I then spoke to Omar Jan about putting them under him. Anxious to set up new posts and looking to form ties with tribal leaders, even a discredited district governor, Omar Jan agreed. Ten of Abdullah Jan's men were already trained police. We paid the salaries of the rest. The majority went to Koshtay, between Kuchinay Darveshan and Mian Poshtay, under police sergeant Ahmed Shah, Abdullah Jan's cousin who had been fighting since the jihad. Koshtay was where Abdullah Jan had built his private home, later taken over by Naim and then flattened by the British in 2007. Many of Abdullah Jan's old fighters were from Koshtay and knew how to defend it. When they arrived, looking rather grizzled, the Marine company commander in the area asked an old Noorzai elder his opinion. The elder replied: 'Those men fight the Taliban. They have been fighting them for years. They will not stop. It is good they are here.' On 22 May, an Afghan flag went up over the ruins of Abdullah Jan's home. There, twenty veteran fighters slept outside while the new post was built around them. It was Abdullah Jan's contribution to the security of Garmser; forty fully armed men were nearly impossible to come by.

Omar Jan established good relations with Wakil Manan in Mian Poshtay and Ghulam Rassoul in Laki as well. By doing so, he was able to control their tribal militias, a source of new police recruits. Tribal militia had always been notionally under the police chief. Omar Jan solidified the arrangement. We formalized a system by which he handed out all salaries, vetted all fighters to ensure they were trustworthy, and briefed provincial police chief Hakim Angar on them. Every fighter had a personal interview with Omar Jan before being accepted, including those already in the field. Salaries were set at $160 per month, less than the

$200 per month of a policeman. We handed Omar Jan the money and then observed him distribute it to the militia. Both the tribal leaders and their men were required to obey Omar Jan's instructions when it came to security. He gave the militia blue uniforms so they could be identified as part of his police force. And he started sending more to the academy. Omar Jan was off on a solid footing with the tribal leaders and tribal militia, avoiding what could have been a serious gap in manpower.

Police, together with tribal militia, followed a different way of war from the Marines and Afghan army. Marines and Afghan army operated like soldiers, living in well-fortified outposts, mounting well-organized patrols and clearing operations, well-supplied with computers, food, ammunition, fuel, armored vehicles, and IED-detectors. Police and

Image 12: Police chief Omar Jan on operation.

tribal militia operated like guerrillas—among the people. They worked out of tribal leaders' homes or in old mud compounds secured by a few strands of barbed wire, sleeping out in the open or under crumbling roofs. Over time we built them walls and towers, but it did not start out that way. They lived off the population, purchasing food and fuel at their local bazaar. A post's standard equipment were AK-47 rifles, a blue Ford Ranger pickup, two or three ICOM radios, and, if lucky, a PK machine gun and an RPG with a few spare rounds. No computers. No armored vehicles. Patrols were conducted on the basis of experience rather than formal training. Among the trees and villages, police or militia walked in a nonchalant disjointed file so that no one would get split off. In the open fields, they walked in a rag-tag line abreast, a man with a PK machine gun in the middle and others with AK-47 rifles covering the flanks, so that attackers could not surround them. Marines admitted that it worked. We bought the police motorcycles, so that they could go out in pairs and cover large swathes of ground. Good officers sent their men out in plain clothes to surprise Taliban. The police were wonderfully impatient. When they received information about the Taliban, they did not wait, they did not plan for long, but hastily launched an operation—on foot or in pickup. Early on, Lieutenant Colonel Hezbollah scolded Omar Jan for not enduring a day's worth of proper planning before going off after a lead. Omar Jan could never wait that long. He once boasted proudly: 'My advisor is always ready to go. When I call him, he takes only fifteen minutes to get all his men and tanks [MRAPs] ready. He knows I cannot wait any longer than that.' Indeed, when the Marines were not ready, Omar Jan left without them. He often frightened us with his disregard for IEDs—driving around in an unarmored Ford Ranger pickup—but he had unsurpassed tempo and drive.

After the attack on Atlas Khan, Taliban barraged community council members with night letters and phone threats. Naim rang a few members personally. Abdullah Jan called and berated me for having moved too slowly to protect Atlas Khan. He warned that just one more attack would break the council. The community council members themselves became very worried about their security and demanded to be armed. In accordance with standing guidance from Governor Mangal, we refused to do so and instead offered permits to those who already owned weapons. The community council did not care for this suggestion and accused us of neglecting them. After a series of painful community council meet-

202

ings, Fahim went to Lashkar Gah and spoke with Mangal face to face. A few days later, Mangal finally relented and allowed community council members to have arms or guards. Omar Jan gave each community council member one AK-47 for self-defense and registered a family member who would carry that weapon. That process would not be complete until July. For the time being, the council was still in danger.

Meanwhile, Lieutenant Colonel Benjamin Watson, the new battalion commander, attacked southern Laki in order to put himself in position to seize Safar bazaar. Every six months, Marine battalions turned over. At the end of April, Lieutenant Colonel McDonough and 2nd Battalion, 2nd Marine Regiment had gone home. Lieutenant Colonel Watson and 3rd Battalion, 1st Marine Regiment (3/1) had replaced them. Watson was intent on taking Safar. To get there, he first had to push the insurgents out of southern Laki. The Taliban had laced the road with IEDs, which slowed Marine progress. At the same time, groups of ten to twenty insurgents ambushed the Marines as they drove south. Reports came in that more than 100 insurgents were trying to slow the Marine advance. Over the month, at least twenty Taliban were killed. The Marines suffered seven casualties themselves.

We took no other steps to counter the intimidation. Abdullah Jan's warning against building large numbers of tribal militia, lest we lose control, still rang in my head. When Alizai elders from Lakari asked to form their own militia, Lieutenant Colonel Watson and I decided to wait. It was not clear that tribal militia were needed in Lakari and we wanted to hold down the numbers, as Abdullah Jan had advised. By waiting, we allowed the Taliban to steal a march on us.

The execution of Abdul Ahmed

At the end of May, the Taliban military shura in Safar—made up of Mullah Ismael and the commander in Safar and other leaders—issued a statement that any elders working with the government would be killed.[5] Mamoor Abdur Rashid was an elder of a village in Mian Poshtay. He occasionally spoke with Marine patrols passing through his village. Mullah Ismael, carrying out his intimidation mission in southern Garmser, had been unable to attack anyone directly in Mian Poshtay—there were too many Marines, police, and Afghan soldiers. So he ordered Abdur Rashid to go to Safar to explain himself. Abdur Rashid complied.

In Safar, on 30 May, Mullah Ismael and Zalmay, his deputy, stabbed Abdur Rashid to death and sent his body back to his village. Mian Poshtay and Lakari panicked. Before we could do anything, Mullah Ismael struck again.

Two days later, 1 June, Mullah Ismael kidnapped and executed Abdul Ahmed, Abdullah Jan's eldest and last remaining brother. Abdul Ahmed lived in Bartaka, the collection of villages and farms on the west side of the river, across from Koshtay and Mian Poshtay. Bartaka was the territory of the Barakzai tribe in Garmser and the birthplace of Abdullah Jan. The Barakzai lived between the river and the grey 50-meter high bluffs that marked the beginning of the western desert. On 31 May, Mullah Ismael's crew burned a farmer's tractor south of Bartaka for no apparent reason. Abdul Ahmed chastised those Taliban for doing so. One day later, as he left prayer at the mosque, Mullah Ismael kidnapped him. Mullah Ismael drove him to the sandy dunes overlooking the Helmand across from Safar. There, Zalmay shot him.

Fear gripped Garmser. The lesser elders of Lakari and Mian Poshtay lost their nerve. Every Alizai elder from Lakari and every immigrant village elder from Mian Poshtay fled to Lashkar Gah. Some had even possessed weapons to defend themselves. The execution of Abdul Ahmed, on top of the execution of Abdur Rashid, broke them. 'We have lost all of them,' said Deputy District Governor Ayub Omar.[6] The Taliban had rarely resorted to such ruthlessness. The whole structure of elders and the valuable information they provided was about to fall apart in Mian Poshtay, Lakari, and Laki. The gains of nearly a year of hard work were in jeopardy. Only Ghulam Rassoul, Shah Wali Khan, and Wakil Manan stayed. A far cry from the hesitation of six months before, Wakil Manan strutted through the bazaar like a rooster and gloated: 'Everyone left but me. You can only trust me. I told you that you could not trust them [the village elders].'[7] His determination made up for his poor sportsmanship. Ghulam Rassoul and Shah Wali Khan were in a worse position, all but surrounded in Laki with Ghulam Rassoul's brother imprisoned in Pakistan. Ghulam Rassoul's mother told him to keep fighting. 'Do not worry,' she counseled. 'Let the Taliban do what they will.'[8]

It was clear that we had to stop the fear as soon as possible. On the military front, Lieutenant Colonel Watson encouraged police chief Omar Jan and Lieutenant Colonel Hezbollah to respond as quickly as possible. On the political front, Deputy District Governor Ayub Omar and District Governor Mohammed Fahim worked out a plan to reinforce the tribal leadership and assure the people that the government was in control. The death of Abdul Ahmed created a sense of urgency, a sense we needed to do whatever was necessary to defeat the Taliban offensive.

Police chief Omar Jan moved first. None of his police or tribal militia had deserted. On 4 June, he raced down to Mian Poshtay, conferred with Wakil Manan and Ahmed Shah (who had been gathering intelligence for him from his post in Koshtay), coordinated with Captain Matthew McGirr (the new company commander in Mian Poshtay), and then went after the Taliban. He rounded up six, including two IED cell members whom the Marines had been trying to capture for months. He also detained the brother of Mullah Ismael and the father of Mohibullah (another cell leader known to operate in the area). Tit for tat. If the Taliban were going to go after relatives of Ghulam Rassoul and Abdullah Jan, Omar Jan was going to go after relatives of Taliban (both were released a few weeks later because there was not enough evidence to prosecute them). The war was getting messy. Before the operation was over, he had also confiscated the fuel tanks of boats on the Helmand and shut down the ferries that Mullah Ismael had been using to cross the river. Follow-on operations the next day took two more Taliban, one of whom was a member of Mullah Ismael's cadre. Thereafter, Omar Jan patrolled intensely from Hazar Joft to Mian Poshtay, taking twelve more Taliban the next week. Omar Jan's rapid response had been a case study in how to use tribal leaders and locally recruited police to the utmost advantage.

While Omar Jan blitzkrieged through Mian Poshtay, Ayub Omar, Fahim, and I finalized a political plan. We wanted to reinforce the tribal leaders still standing against the Taliban and bring back those who had fled. Ever since Ghulam Rassoul and Shah Wali Khan had returned to Laki, we had been in communication with Shah Jahan, the other powerful Alizai tribal leader. He had fled with Ghulam Rassoul and Shah Wali Khan to Pakistan in 2008 and returned with them to Lashkar Gah in 2009. He had been anxious to come back but we had held off because I had not been sure if we could control someone so powerful. Now, his return seemed worth the risk. His political skills and stature as a former district governor would reassure the Alizai. He had the influence to bring the Lakari elders who had fled to Lashkar Gah back with him. To

Image 13: Tribal militia, better known as 'arbekai'. (Photo by Patricio Asfura-Heim)

reinforce our position further, we hoped to convince Abdullah Jan to go live on his lands in Koshtay. His presence would form a powerful check on Taliban activity in Koshtay and Bartaka. We arranged a meeting between Abdullah Jan (who was about to return to hold the funeral for his brother), the government, and the other key tribal leaders—Shah Jahan, Ghulam Rassoul, Shah Wali Khan, and Wakil Manan. We wanted these key tribal leaders to declare their intention to fight the Taliban and, on top of that, promise to put aside the rivalries that had wrecked Garmser in the first place. The idea was both to forge an alliance against the Taliban and to foster the tribal unity that would enable lasting peace following a Taliban defeat.

On 7 and 8 June, Fahim, Omar Jan, and Hezbollah met with Abdullah Jan, Ghulam Rassoul, Shah Wali Khan, and Shah Jahan (Wakil Manan agreed to the concepts laid out but could not break free from day-to-day operations in Mian Poshtay). Shah Jahan promised to return to his home in Laki and bring back with him the Lakari elders who had fled to Lashkar Gah. In order to regain control of Lakari, a new twenty-man Alizai tribal militia would be formed. The ten-man Alizai militia in Laki would be expanded to twenty-five in order to keep hold of the situ-

Image 14: NDS chief Mir Hamza (center) speaks with Shah Jahan (right). (Photo by Patricio Asfura-Heim)

ation there. As before, we would pay the salaries and tribal militia would be sent to the police academy as soon as possible. The tribal leaders also pledged not to fight with one another in the future and to remain united. In front of everyone, Shah Jahan gave his word that he would not clash with other tribal leaders, implicitly referring to his old power struggle with Abdullah Jan.

Abdullah Jan, however, did not want to return to Koshtay. We had probably been naïve to try. With his brother gone, he explained, if he too was killed, there would be no one to look out for his own five young sons; and without his overall leadership, the extended family would also be in peril. A lifetime of fighting had taken its toll on the small Barakzai tribe. Abdullah Jan pledged to oppose the Taliban together with the Alizai and Wakil Manan (he had brought them to Garmser, after all), to encourage new elders to fight behind the government, to leave his forty veterans under Omar Jan, and even to come to Garmser from time to time to speak at shuras and rally the people; but he would not live in Garmser. In the end, it was good enough.

Getting tribal leaders back into the field and new tribal militia and police deployed took a few weeks. In the meantime, terror spread. Mullah Ismael's men flowed into the villages around Lakari bazaar, set up checkpoints, and beat people who had worked with the Americans.[9] They executed a Hazara mullah who had spoken openly in favor of the government during the riots. Shop owners started to leave the bazaar. To raise the pressure on the Alizai, Taliban kidnapped Shah Wali Khan's younger brother, who lived in Safar. In retaliation, Shah Wali Khan kidnapped the uncle of Qari Abdullah (one of Naim's most prominent lieutenants) who happened to be wandering through Shah Wali Khan's village at an inopportune moment. In due course, Shah Wali Khan's brother was released, as was Qari Abdullah's uncle.

Mullah Ismael himself took over Bartaka, on the western side of the river. He had murdered Abdullah Jan's brother, Abdul Ahmed; now he took over his village too. Barakzai villagers piled their belongings and families onto their tractors and fled to the eastern side of the river. Mullah Ismael walked straight into Abdul Ahmed's home, where Abdullah Jan had grown up. Abdul Ahmed's wife, daughters, and son locked themselves into the main hall. Mullah Ismael stood outside and explained through the door how he was going to kill them. The son escaped through a window and made it to Abdullah Jan at the district center. Omar Jan and Abdullah Jan drove south and crossed the river. Mullah Ismael must have heard because he was not to be found. He would be back once Omar Jan departed. Abdullah Jan evacuated the family and abandoned his father's home. A few days later, he returned to Lashkar Gah.

Shah Jahan arrived in Laki on 16 June. As promised, he brought the elders from Lakari back with him. He, Ghulam Rassoul, and Shah Wali Khan had met with them in Lashkar Gah and convinced them to return. Captain McGirr, the Marine commander in Mian Poshtay, assigned a lieutenant or sergeant to each elder, with orders to check on their safety daily. The Lakari elders provided men for the tribal militia and introduced them to police chief Omar Jan. They would be led by Abdul Baqi, the nephew of one of the village elders. Akhtar Mohammed, a landowning immigrant and old mujahidin, would help train and supervise the men. In spite of the intimidation, the elders were steadying.

The political front

Over this difficult time, there was a real danger that violence would deter people from interacting with the government at the district center or even cause members of the government themselves to flee. With Fahim being confirmed as district governor in Kabul between late June and September, the weight of governance fell upon Ayub Omar's shoulders as deputy district governor. Well educated by his father, Said Omar, Ayub Omar had gained valuable experience and tutelage under Abdullah Jan. He understood tribal politics, district administration, community council processes, and the technicalities of getting schools and clinics going. He was able to carry on initiatives that had been started during Abdullah Jan's tenure. In Fahim's absence, Ayub Omar kept the district government running and encouraged everyone—elders, mullahs, villagers—to stand up against the Taliban.

In spite of the violence, Ayub Omar carried on the program that he and Abdullah Jan had created in the winter for bringing religious leaders closer to the government. Throughout the spring and summer, he met monthly with them. Thanks to his father's schooling, he knew how to speak to the religious leaders in a way no foreigner could. He never made demands or threatened them. He merely presented his viewpoint and accepted their counter-arguments. The respect for Islam is what mattered. At more than one meeting, I thought Ayub Omar had lost the debate only to discover later that the religious leaders had in fact heeded his request. Patience paid off. Over time, the tenor of the meetings improved. Many mullahs stopped calling for jihad and stopped refusing to work with the government. Rather, they said they wanted the government to accept their advice. At one shura, which the Provincial Director of Hajj (religious affairs) attended, a noted scholar demanded that the government involve the religious leaders in its activities:

'We want all the military forces—ISAF and Afghan—and the Afghan government to respect mullahs. We will demand from the people and the government to accept mullahs. We do not think the government accepts us. So we will not share our problems with the government. The government must follow religion and respect the Koran and hadiths. Mullahs must be allowed to guide the police and the army.'[10]

His demands were in stark contrast to the condemnation of the government heard at religious shuras six months before. They encouraged the government to keep on reaching out.

Although the religious leaders would not agree to a formally appointed religious council, they did agree to meet informally when called upon by the government. Additionally, Ayub Omar convinced the community council to spend some of its resources on the religious leaders. The community council subsidized the activities of the district center mosque and purchased 30 loudspeakers and 150 carpets for mosques elsewhere in the district. The council let the religious leaders decide how the loudspeakers and carpets would be distributed.

Ayub Omar's real coup was Friday prayers, which had been absent from the district center for over four years. In late May, after debating with the religious shura for two hours, Ayub Omar got them to select a mullah—Mullah Shah Wali—to lead the prayers. That Friday, prayers resumed. Soon shopkeepers, villagers, elders, government officials, and mullahs were attending prayers every week. The mullahs were hardly speaking out against the Taliban but they were now openly working alongside the government, something unheard of a year before.

The biggest political challenge was the community council. With new areas south of Hazar Joft outposted, the community council needed to expand. The Independent Directorate for Local Governance (IDLG), which ran the election, the same body that appointed all district governors and provincial governors, set the date for early July. As before, the process involved elders, mullahs, teachers, and other notables coming to the district center to 'elect' a representative for their community. The plan for July was that representatives would be elected for Loya Darveshan, Kuchinay Darveshan, Koshtay, Bartaka, and Mian Poshtay. With intimidation raging, support for the elections demanded a special effort. If people failed to attend the election shura, it would be a propaganda victory for the Taliban and a setback for Garmser's most important political institution. Major portions of the district would be left unrepresented until the Independent Directorate for Local Governance decided to try again, which would be a year in the future, if at all.

Again, Deputy District Governor Ayub Omar led the way. He personally rallied the elders, holding several shuras in the weeks before the event to change the minds of the most reticent. The people of Koshtay, frightened by Taliban activity, were particularly reluctant. They did not want to elect anyone, which would leave a gap in representation in Garmser between Kuchinay Darveshan and Mian Poshtay—not a good formula for good governance. Ayub Omar rushed down to Koshtay, held a shura, and met with the elders face to face. He gave a fine performance. He explained the whole election process to them (they were terribly confused), broke them into working groups, sent them to deliberate, and then debated with them over the proper course of action. In the end, he convinced them. Ayub Omar also made a special effort to get the Baluch represented on the council. The Baluch were anxious to join. In the past, they had been shunned by the government, being largely landless nomads and squatters. Ayub Omar successfully lobbied the Independent Directorate for Local Governance to give them a seat on the council—a step forward in bringing the landless closer to the government.

Elections on 6 July were a success. Roughly 190 elders, mullahs, and other notables attended, including 40 from Koshtay. They elected 9 new representatives, giving a new total of 27 members (8 seats were still empty). Whereas before no tribal leaders had served on the community council, two joined the expanded council: Khodirom (Loya Darveshan) and Wakil Manan (Mian Poshtay). Mohammed Sakhi, the Baluch policeman who had fought with Abdullah Jan at the district center mosque back in 2006 and then protected Wakil Manan in January 2010, was elected to represent the Baluch.

While the community council elections took place, there was another attempt at leadership change in Garmser. The Ministry of Interior in Kabul tried to replace police chief Omar Jan. Sher Mohammed Akhund-zada, former Helmand provincial governor, had lobbied for one of his allies to become the Garmser police chief and the ministry had agreed. Mangal did not have control over police appointments so the decision was made without him knowing. We obviously did not want to lose Omar Jan in the middle of the Taliban offensive. Lieutenant Colonel Watson and I spoke with the Marine headquarters and provincial government. After two weeks of discussions, Governor Mangal and provincial chief of police Angar agreed to challenge the Ministry of Interior. In the end, they won and Omar Jan stayed. It was another example of how absence of hierarchy within the Afghan government caused friction on the ground. If Mangal had been given authority over police chief appointments, this time-consuming political intrigue would not have occurred.

Spiral of violence

Violence did not end with tribal militia recruitment or community council elections. It spiraled up. Looking back, it had escalated step by step. In 2009, the Taliban had held the people under their thumb through night letters and the mullahs. They had not needed to shoot elders. Then we brought back the tribal leaders, who gave the intelligence necessary to capture insurgents. We let them field militia to protect themselves. To circumvent the militia, the Taliban went after unprotected family members, kidnapping and killing them. So, in turn, the police and militia went after Taliban family members. The next step was that the Taliban harmed totally innocent people—people who had nothing to do with us or the government—in their attempts to kill and frighten government officials and tribal leaders. It was becoming a dirty civil war.

Unable to kill District Governor Fahim himself, the Taliban settled for his cousin in Lashkar Gah. Before executing him, they called Fahim's uncle and told him that his son was being killed because of Fahim—a sobering event for the young district governor. He held up well, if with a sadness in his eyes, carrying on with his work until Mangal ordered him to Kabul for his confirmation. That was not the end of the civilian casualties. On 18 June, a motorcycle bomb went off in the Lakari bazaar. The target was Ghulam Rassoul's tribal militia who were then in the bazaar. The bomb missed them but wounded six civilians and damaged Ghulam Rassoul's car. Another went off in the district center bazaar on 11 July, 200 meters from the governor's compound, wounding twenty-three, including Mullah Shah Wali, the new pro-government Friday prayer mullah, who was motorcycling through the bazaar at the time of the attack. He suffered lacerations to his neck and shoulders.

The district center bombing was part of a Taliban effort to destabilize Hazar Joft. In addition to the bombing, they tried to infiltrate into the villages of Hazar Joft's most government-friendly tribal leaders: Mohammed Anwar and Said Omar (Deputy District Governor Ayub Omar's father). In Mohammed Anwar's village near Amir Agha, night watchmen opened fire on two armed insurgents—the first incident in the area in seven months. Less than 2 kilometers south of the district center, Taliban set up checkpoints near Said Omar's village and killed two day laborers who had taken part in a USAID agricultural program. Shortly thereafter, on the night of 11 July, insurgents crossed the river and shot into the village itself. In response, police chief Omar Jan ran nightly patrols, set up a temporary post in Majitek and a new outpost between Hazar Joft and Amir Agha on top of a mound that was once a Ghaznavid fort. Deputy District Governor Ayub Omar organized an unpaid tribal militia within his father's village. He gathered the few weapons in the village and bargained with police chief Omar Jan and NDS chief Mir Hamza for a few more. Then he drew up a rotating schedule for watch duty. All the men in the village, young and old, rich and poor, were assigned days and times to stand watch at night. The village's old muja-hidin showed the inexperienced what to do and set up a village defense plan (which Marines later found surprisingly sound). They skirmished with the Taliban repeatedly over the next two months, keeping them out of the village. It was no surprise that Ayub Omar had come up with such a community-based solution; one that epitomized what a good tribal militia should look like.

As violence rose, I began to worry about what the Taliban would do next and how the government and tribal leaders would retaliate. Would tribal leaders or police chief Omar Jan build their own secret prisons? Would the Alizai wreak vengeance upon Mullah Naim's village in Laki for the detention of Ghulam Rassoul's brother? Would we start finding the relatives of Taliban dead on the side of the road? This was the dark side of counterinsurgency.

Fortunately, by early July, the decisions of early June were starting to be felt. Tribal militia were taking the field. Police were coming out of the academy. A total of 150 academy-trained police and 74 tribal militia were patrolling. Between April and August, the number of police and militia outposts increased from five to thirteen and the total number of militia and police nearly doubled (see Fig. 1). After June, no more elders were killed and no more community council members were attacked. The Marines and Afghan army prevented large attacks—actual assaults or ambushes. Police and tribal militia defended the elders and identified Taliban. It just took a few police, tribal militia, or even brave villagers to stop intimidation by three or four Taliban in the night. If more than that massed, the Marines and Afghan soldiers would get them. As Ayub Omar explained to the new expanded community council: 'Villagers must help defend the government against the small number of Taliban. We cannot place a checkpoint everywhere. We cannot put a checkpoint next to a school because students will then not come to school. Only the villagers can protect the school. The people can stop bombs like the one that went off the other day in the bazaar.'[11]

With these changes visibly underway, the attacks did not shake the government's supporters. Terror was escalating but the tribal leaders and government were holding firm. During the days following the

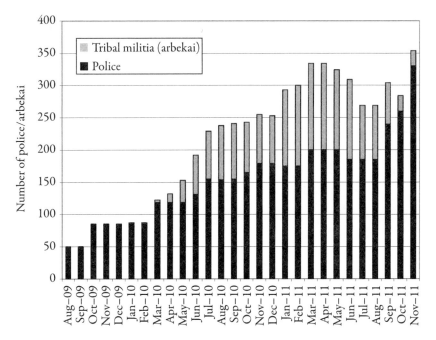

Fig. 1: Police and tribal militia in Garmser, 2009–11.

district center bombing, the bazaar remained lively. The religious leadership rallied and brought in a respected scholar from Koshtay to lead Friday prayers in the wounded Mullah Shah Wali's stead. The following week Mullah Shah Wali himself resumed leading the prayers. All in all it was an unexpected and strong showing on the part of Garmser's religious leaders.

As more and more police and tribal militia took the field, with their knowledge of who was who, the government took Taliban after Taliban. In Hazar Joft, NDS chief Mir Hamza captured the perpetrators of the district center bazaar bombing and the IED that had killed the eight Afghan soldiers back in May. To the south, Ahmed Shah and Abdullah Jan's veterans kept Koshtay locked down. One elder said of Ahmed Shah: 'Ahmed Shah patrols all the time. He caused all the enemy to flee, along with their families. The Taliban fear him. He is honest.'[12] In Lakari bazaar, Ghulam Rassoul took two IED layers and his old nemesis Noor Ali, now a cell leader. Abdul Baqi, the young new Lakari tribal militia commander, picked up two more Taliban (who confessed). Half mad and alarmingly daring, Baqi rode about everywhere on his motorcycle looking for Taliban, sometimes alone and unarmed. Rumor had it that he had once been Taliban himself. Regardless, he was quite good at capturing them. In mid-August, he and his men caught three in the act of laying an IED. In late August, they drove down to Safar in the middle of ongoing Marine operations and rolled up on a Taliban checkpoint. Miles from any support, they opened fire and swept up three of the Taliban. In the words of one Lakari elder, 'The Taliban fear the Alizai because we know who they are. They fear the arbekai [tribal militia]. They fear Shah Wali Khan, Ghulam Rassoul, and Shah Jahan.'[13]

Wakil Manan had the greatest success. He got a bead on Zalmay, Mullah Ismael's lieutenant who had carried out the executions of Abdur Rashid and Abdul Ahmed. Captain McGirr organized a joint operation between the Afghan army and Wakil Manan's tribal militia. On 28 June, the militia identified Zalmay. The army soldiers went to his location and grabbed him, as well as another of Mullah Ismael's men. A huge success, Mullah Ismael's crew went to ground and intimidation in Mian Poshtay abruptly ended. Zalmay was sent to prison in Lashkar Gah. The Afghans never released him.

Meanwhile, since May, Lieutenant Colonel Watson and his Marines and the Afghan army had been fighting hard battles with the Taliban in southern Laki, steadily driving them south. By the end of June, reports came in that the Taliban were retreating. They had suffered too many losses, from the Marine offensive and police and militia raids. Ghulam Rassoul reported: 'The Taliban are finished in Laki.'[14]

In early July, Naim was running Taliban activities in Helmand from Pakistan and sent an inspection team to discover why operations in Garmser were not progressing well. The team found that the tribal leaders and village elders strongly supported the government, in spite of the Taliban offensive. The team advised the relief of Mullah Ismael and the front-line commander in Safar (I do not know his name), who had failed to defend southern Laki. Naim recalled Mullah Ismael personally, angry at his failure and reports of his viciousness. It was rumored that he exiled Ismael to Iran. A cell leader who later surrendered said: 'Mullah Ismael was bad. He killed many people.'[15] After the middle of July, violence dropped off. IED and small arms attacks continued but at a much lower level. Throughout the district, intimidation fell off. We no longer had to worry about how much worse the violence would get. The tribes and the government had weathered the storm.

Capture of Safar and the end of the second Taliban regime

After their defeat in southern Laki, the Taliban retreated to Safar, their last major refuge, where they tried to recover. The battles in southern Laki had been taxing. The Taliban leadership did not want to fight the Marines face to face again. Therefore, they did not plan to defend Safar bazaar. Instead, they laid scores of IEDs, hoping the Marines would blow themselves up clearing them.[16]

Watson gave them scant breathing space. The regiment loaned him two extra infantry platoons in July, which he placed on the western side of the river and temporarily disrupted insurgent operations there. Watson had carefully planned the offensive. Since he would get no permanent reinforcements with which to hold Safar, he had to free up forces. He took them out of Kuchinay Darveshan. This meant that the Marines in Loya Darveshan had to stretch south, thinning themselves out into even smaller posts, a very bold move (see Table 4 and Map 11 to get an idea of how the Marines spread out in more and more posts over time). In early August, Watson led 200 Marines and fifty Afghan soldiers against Safar. Some Marines assaulted by helicopter, others by vehicle via the desert to the east. Any Taliban holding out in northern Safar were completely bypassed. The Taliban in the bazaar itself withdrew to the south and west. By 5 August, Safar bazaar was in Marine hands. The Marines painstakingly removed the IEDs and then set up outposts and patrolled. There were few gunfights with Taliban, who had retreated south and west. The bazaar re-opened a few weeks later.

The capture of Safar bazaar put an end to open Taliban authority in Garmser. They lost their logistics and supply node. They now had to operate in southern Safar and Benadar, which were dry and open, with few places to hide. Small-scale attacks and IEDs still occurred, but the Taliban no longer fielded significant numbers of fighters. In the future, only small teams of two to four men could operate in Garmser, often without weapons. The Taliban's two remaining clinics were also captured. Wounded fighters had to go all the way to Pakistan for medical care. Demoralization set in. According to one Taliban cell leader who later surrendered, 'Fighters thought the loss of Safar was very bad.'[17]

Safar delighted the tribal and government leaders. Elder after elder told us that the Taliban were finished. The fact that this was not really the case underscored the resounding effect that the capture of Safar had on popular opinion. Perception mattered more than reality. Mohammed Nabi said: 'Safar bazaar is very important to the Taliban, as Amir Agha was. The capture of Safar bazaar means the end of the Taliban in Garmser.'[18] When we informed Deputy District Governor Ayub Omar and police chief Omar Jan of Safar's capture, both stood up with glowing faces and outreached hands and thanked us profusely. 'Thank you!' Ayub Omar declared, 'The Taliban have been defeated. They cannot come back. This is a great victory!' When District Governor Fahim returned from Kabul, he went to Safar, along with the police chief, NDS chief, and the Afghan army battalion executive officer, for a 200-person shura to explain how the government of Afghanistan could help the people of Safar. The government had not been there since June 2006.

Table 4: Expansion of Marine posts in Garmser.

Location	October 2009	April 2010	October 2010	April 2011
Hazar Joft	2	1	1	1
Loya Darveshan	6	11	11	7
Kuchinay Darveshan	3	4	3	3
Koshtay	0	2	3	3
Mian Poshtay	4	6	6	6
Lakari	0	4	6	6
Laki	0	4	7	7
Safar	0	0	5	12
Benadar	0	0	0	2
Total for Garmser	15	32	43	48

The 2010 Taliban offensive nearly unhinged tribal support for the government. If that had occurred, the police would have fallen apart and intelligence to go after insurgent leaders would have dried up, leaving the Marines and Afghan army nearly blind. The district government would have ruled in name only. None of this happened. Ironically, Naim believed Mullah Ismael's terror had lost popular support and turned the tribal leaders against the Taliban. In reality, terror had genuinely frightened people. What had defeated the terror was the grim resolve of the government and a handful of tribal leaders. In war: resolution.[19]

Those hard months showed that there were Afghan leaders who could take their country forward. Their leadership traits did not fit the Western ideal. They were not highly educated, uncorrupt, or untainted by the past. No, these leaders were a hard-bitten lot. What is more, their

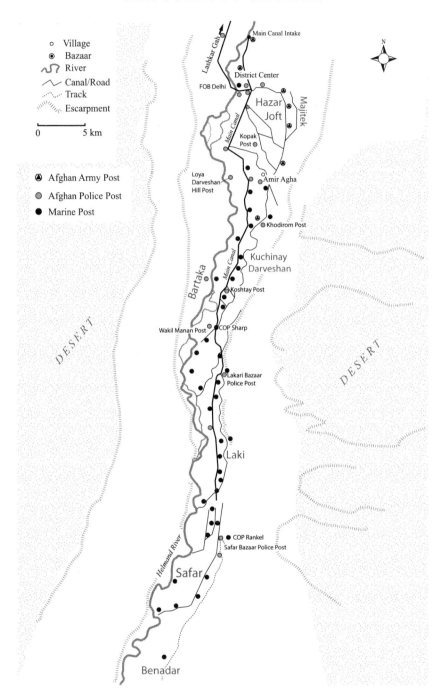

Map 11: Marine, Afghan army, and police posts in Garmser, c. January 2011 (Mike Markowitz).

traits were shared with their Taliban counterparts. The similarities between Abdullah Jan, Omar Jan, Naim, and Abdul Hadi Agha (Taliban district governor 2006–7) are striking. All had years of combat experience, Abdullah Jan and Naim both wounded fighting. All were what the Pashtuns call 'baydara,' a combination of being active, seizing the initiative, and taking risk. Locals often commented on how much Omar Jan was doing or spoke in reverence to Abdullah Jan's old aggressiveness. And all respected Islam and believed in its emphasis on reconciliation and unity. They tried to bring Garmser together. At the same time, these leaders shared faults, faults that would have been unacceptable in the West. They were poorly educated. They were corrupt—if less so than other, worse, leaders. And they were harsh, partly to enforce discipline among their men, partly because they just were. What differentiated them from Afghanistan's worst warlords and Taliban commanders was that they understood that they had a duty to protect the innocent. This could be seen in Abdullah Jan's reaction to Nasim Akhundzada's excesses after the jihad and Naim's disapproval of Mullah Ismael's brutality. But that understanding was often knocked and jarred by Garmser's feuds, land disputes, and violence. Hence Abdullah Jan's intolerance of squatters and Naim's killing of elders. These were neither the kinds of men that Kabul's official governor examination screened for, nor what the real system of bribes and political connections regularly produced. Fortunately, the government had received enough of them to outlast the Taliban in the summer of 2010. Whether it would continue to have them was an entirely different question.

Success, of course, could not have occurred without the Marines. Their patrolling, outposting, and numbers made it impossible for the Taliban to launch large-scale attacks. By the end of the summer, forty-three Marine outposts had been established (see Table 4). By shielding them from major attacks, the Marines had allowed the Afghan government and tribal leaders to organize themselves against Taliban intimidation. On top of that, operations in southern Laki and Safar inflicted irreplaceable losses on the Taliban. The final offensive against Safar spelled the end of Garmser as a major Taliban operating area—at least while the Marines were present. By spreading themselves out as much as possible, the Marines had been able to clear and hold most of the district.

Poor Atlas Khan came home in July. Over two months had passed since the Taliban had entered his home and shot him and his son—the event that had started their counter-offensive. Immediately after the attack, Atlas Khan's family had rushed him to FOB Delhi, the Marine base in Hazar Joft. Captain Donahue, the battalion surgeon, had stopped the bleeding and saved his life. Doctors in Kandahar had then nursed him back to health. His right arm was permanently paralyzed and part of his jaw was missing. Otherwise, he had recovered.

It was another four months before Ghulam Rassoul's kidnapped brother, Zahrif Shah, was free. Through the autumn, long negotiations between the Alizai and Naim's representatives went nowhere. Eventually, the provincial government became aware of Zahrif Shah's plight. Mangal brought in Baluch tribal leaders and had them open negotiations with the kidnappers (who were also Baluch) and Naim. Under the governor's auspices and Baluch shuttle diplomacy, the two sides worked out an agreement. The two Taliban whom Ghulam Rassoul had helped the Lashkar Gah police to detain back in late 2009 were released in return for his brother. On 22 December 2010, Zahrif Shah was driven through the desert and dropped off in Safar. His wrists and ankles lacerated from months in shackles, he made his way back to Laki. It was a welcome relief.

WINNING THE PEACE

Ka Pashtun yeow sil kala woroosta badal wakhlee, no byaa hm wayee chay zhr may wkhst.

'Even if a Pashtun takes revenge after one hundred years, he will still say: "I acted in haste."'

Pashto proverb[1]

At the onset of the autumn of 2010, Garmser was more peaceful than it had been since 2006. Outside southern Safar, the district suffered few attacks. The Taliban fighters further north retreated to the western side of the river and the eastern edge of the canal zone. Parliamentary elections went off on 18 September without incident. Soon Afghans were freely driving back and forth to Safar bazaar. Success was not limited to Garmser. Throughout Helmand the situation was improving. The British had pacified the center mass of Lashkar Gah, Nadi Ali, and Gereshk, plus Musa Qala to the north. Marines had pacified Nawa and Khaneshin, had almost quelled violence in Marjah in the west, and were clearing out Sangin. The Taliban were being driven into the northern and southern reaches of the province, away from the vast majority of the population.

What was left was to make sure the government was strong enough to prevent the Taliban from returning. Back in December 2009, President Obama had announced that American forces would begin to withdraw in late 2011. It was expected that he would announce the scale of the drawdown during the summer of 2011. Lieutenant Colonel Watson (the Marine battalion commander), Gail Long (our USAID development officer), and I assumed that after the announcement the Marine headquarters in Helmand would thin the number of Marines in Garmser, and that by 2014 only advisors would be left. The question in our minds in the autumn of 2010 was whether the government could hold Garmser after the Marines drew down. Violence had subsided before in Garmser: after the jihad, after the civil war, after the fall of the Taliban. Each time, conflict had returned, largely because of political infighting and the absence of a strong government. If history repeated itself, the counterinsurgency effort of the previous two years would be proven pointless.

As the Taliban receded, the Marine and civilian strategy in Garmser stayed roughly the same. The Marines protected the people and advised the Afghan security forces. The district support team loosely followed the course set by the provincial reconstruction team's road map. With an end of sorts in sight, we accelerated efforts to foster a government strong enough and popular enough to keep the Taliban in check. In coordination with the provincial reconstruction team (PRT) and the road map, Lieutenant Colonel Watson, Long, and I put together a rough plan that focused on mentoring the new district governor, reaching out to the religious leaders, addressing land issues in order to help the immigrants, expanding the community council, turning the tribal militia into official police, and facilitating long-term economic growth. The plan was designed to complement, not supersede, existing efforts to protect the population, bring tribal leaders together, clear out the last remaining Taliban pockets, and advise the Afghan army.

Strengthening the government

District Governor Mohammed Fahim had been called away to Kabul for most of the difficult summer of 2010. He returned in September. Fahim was exactly the kind of person Americans and British wanted to see in a new Afghanistan: young, educated, with no connections to the warlords of the past. He was learning English and understood sophisticated ideas more quickly than anyone else in the district. He was amenable and easy to deal with. The elders showed him proper respect, ignoring his young age. Mangal called Fahim daily to check on things, assigning him discreet tasks. Politics fascinated Fahim. I often encouraged him to go to college, but his heart lay elsewhere. In Afghanistan, college lies off the path to political greatness.

Fahim ruled at a time when the district government was expanding rapidly. Since 2008, the goal of the PRT's 'Helmand road map,' in keeping with parts of counterinsurgency doctrine, had been to create a government that could rule effectively. That meant building a government that was well-staffed, could deliver goods and services to the people, and had judges and prosecutors and courts in place to administer just rule of law. The idea was that such actions would cause the people to prefer the government to the Taliban. Steps had already been taken—in the establishment of the community council, for example. From mid-2010 on, progress accelerated.

Between August 2010 and May 2011, Kabul and Lashkar Gah doubled the number of officials in the district center. Fahim received a

Image 15: District Governor Mohammed Fahim stands between Tooriali (son of Roh Khan, the head of Garmser's oldest Pashtun family), on the right, and Mahboob Khan, on the left. They are at Tooriali's home in Kuchinay Darveshan.

financial officer, an administrative officer, and a communications advisor to spread information on the radio and help put together shuras. Besides the governor's personal staff, the number of representatives from line ministries doubled. Goods and services in Afghanistan are provided through line ministries headquartered in Kabul, such as the Ministry of Education or Ministry of Public Health, rather than through budgets held by provincial or district governors. The ministries in Kabul decide what types of programs will be conducted in each province. Money is then sent down from Kabul to the provinces to execute the programs. Most of the important line ministries came to work in the district: education, health, transportation, agriculture. Those line ministries had the budgets to run their respective sectors, though that money was quite modest at this point. Beginning in November 2010, Garmser also had three mayors. The head mayor ran the district center bazaar; the two others were for Lakari and Safar. Their main job was to collect taxes from shop owners and pass the revenues directly to the provincial mayor in Lashkar Gah. The money was to be used for bazaar upkeep. In reality, the money fed the whole government. The mayors, district governor, provincial officials, and police all took a cut.

Of greater impact than the line ministries and mayors was the justice system. Locals had often commented that Taliban rule of law had provided swift, fair, and Islamic decisions. In the middle of 2010, a prosecutor and huqooq (an official in the Afghan legal system who can mediate minor civil disputes) arrived, followed by a judge in January 2011. The judge had authority to punish crimes and resolve nearly every kind of dispute within the district. Garmser was especially fortunate in that the new judge was an Islamic scholar with a master's degree in Shari'a from Saudi Arabia. His presence showed the people that the government truly was Islamic. The Taliban had Islamic judges; the government now had one too. During the first half of 2011, the judge conducted two murder trials, investigated numerous crimes, held seminars for the district leadership and community council on the law, and led nightly prayers in the district center. In November 2011, two more judges and another prosecutor arrived. The presence of judges, prosecutors, and a huqooq made a difference. Over 80 percent of the respondents to a PRT-funded survey in April 2011 expressed confidence in Garmser's judicial system. Only 12 percent preferred to live under Taliban rule of law.[2]

While the number of district officials expanded and the justice system formed, the community council—the only body in the district selected by the people—took on a larger role. Members gradually became less interested in conducting projects in their own villages and more interested in helping the district as a whole. Over the course of the year, the council executed two budgets arranged by the PRT—one of $200,000 for 2010 and one of $100,000 for 2011. The money was spent on a variety of initiatives, including rural quick-impact projects, refurbishment of the police jail, assistance for mullahs, and charity for the poor. In addition, USAID continued to fund small sets of projects identified by the council, which Long had started doing back in 2009. Besides the project work, the community council participated to a greater degree in public shuras and in lobbying Lashkar Gah for goods and services. Several members took part in local village councils run by the Marines in order to hear the concerns of their constituency, which they then brought to the district center. Mohammed Sakhi, the Baluch representative who had fought for Abdullah Jan at the district center in 2006, was particularly impressive. Dismissive of danger, he drove up and down the desert Baluch communities, resolving disputes, hearing complaints, arranging projects, and spending the night in village elders' homes in order to stiffen their resolve against the Taliban.

In order to strengthen the role of the community council further and get goods and services to the districts, Jon Moss (the British governance expert at the PRT who had helped start the community council program in Helmand) worked with the Independent Directorate of Local Governance to implement the district delivery program (DDP). Goods and services in Afghanistan were distributed via the line ministries, such as the Ministry of Education or the Ministry of Agriculture. The people in the districts traditionally had no input. The idea behind the district delivery program was to give people a say by having the community council sit with representatives from the line ministries and work out the plan for the year. The PRT gave the line ministries and the Independent Directorate for Local Governance additional money for the program, which included raises for district officials and a small budget for the district governor. The Garmser community council met with the line ministry representatives in August 2010 and worked out a plan. After lengthy bureaucratic delays in Kabul, money to execute the program arrived in September 2011.

Perhaps the most striking sign of growing government authority was the re-opening of schools throughout the district. In 2009, three schools

225

had been open; in the summer of 2010, two more re-opened; two others were under reconstruction. Lieutenant Colonel Watson realized that a Garmser-based school system might make Afghans less susceptible to Taliban propaganda and keep children out of Pakistani madrasas. Pashtuns valued education, in many cases for girls as well as boys. Even during the war against the Russians, tribal leaders had taken pains to run their own schools in Garmser. The absence of schools in refugee camps during the 1990s is what prompted many Garmser refugees to send their children to Pakistani madrasas, where they were exposed to Taliban teachings. In Garmser itself, the education systems of the Taliban regimes had been a disappointment. The mullahs could not teach reading, writing, and math at the same level as a government teacher. Thus, there was a desire for better education that only the government could fill. Watson understood this.

In the autumn of 2010, Lieutenant Colonel Watson decided to try to open all the schools from Hazar Joft to Safar, a total of twenty-one. There were not enough buildings to house all the students—many had been destroyed since 2006—so Gail Long arranged for tents to be distributed where needed. Meanwhile, the Marine company commanders worked with the tribal leaders to identify teachers and get the villages to send students. Once identified, prospective teachers went to the district center to speak with the director of education who signed up the qualified ones and gave them salaries and school supplies. Over time, the director took charge of the entire process. By November 2010, seventeen schools had been opened, mainly in tents, with roughly 3,000 students in attendance.

Over the next six months, from November 2010 to May 2011, the Marines constructed new schools in Laki, Lakari, and Mian Poshtay. The Mian Poshtay school opened in January 2011 with 400 students rushing the doors. The Laki girls' school followed a month later. It had originally been built in 2004 by USAID but the Taliban had shut it down two years later. The Marines refurbished it and the Alizai tribal leaders Shah Jahan and Shah Wali Khan re-identified teachers and mobilized the Alizai to send 100 of their young girls to class. Girls could attend three other schools near the district center, but this was the only dedicated female one. The crown jewel of the Garmser school system was the old, long-shuttered agricultural high school. It had been built in the district center in the 1960s as part of the canal project, but had remained closed since the jihad (other than as a Taliban madrasa). The object of a million-dollar reconstruction project, it re-opened in autumn 2011. By that time, twenty-three schools were open in Garmser, with over 5,000 students and nearly 130 paid teachers, including one woman, over twice the number that had taught during Abdullah Jan's 2001–4 district governorship.

These developments in delivery of goods and services, the legal system, the community council, and education marked significant progress. Something similar to what the government had envisioned in the PRT's road map had taken form. A well-staffed government was in place. The people had better representation than ever before. New schools gave the people something superior to what the Taliban could offer. The question was whether any of this meant that the root causes of violence in Garmser—the fractured society, infighting, and land issues—would be addressed.

Afghan forces

For years, General Petraeus (Commanding General of coalition forces in Afghanistan) and his predecessors had been emphasizing that success in Afghanistan depended upon the growth of the police and army. Defending the country would be their burden once American and Allied forces drew down. In Garmser, we expected that Taliban out of Pakistan would attack at some point following American withdrawal. The Afghan police and army could not expect to defeat them by sheer numbers alone. The cost of maintaining the Afghan security forces, paid for by the international community, was approximately $7 billion per year, or as much as Pakistan's defense budget. In 2011, the US government refused to authorize further growth in yearly spending. Consequently, the Marines worked hard to ensure that the army and the police had not only the numbers but also the leadership, supplies, and *esprit de corps* to defeat the Taliban attack when it came.

Like the government, the Afghan National Army grew far stronger between September 2010 and May 2011. Lieutenant Colonel Hezbollah's battalion had been in Garmser since August 2008. Whereas at that time there had been only 200 soldiers, there were now 550, veterans of countless firefights. The Taliban could not defeat them, partly because there were always Marines nearby. Watson created a robust thirty-man advisory team to help strengthen and mentor the battalion. Three of the battalion's five companies lived and worked with the Marines in southern Garmser. The two northernmost ran their own battle-space, assisted by twenty Marine advisers. Lieutenant Colonel Hezbollah, the old communist, visited his men in their posts regularly. Several times a week he was down south. He also met with villagers, especially the poor, and listened to their concerns. His side meetings sometimes annoyed the district governor, but his heart was in the right place. I heard few complaints about the army, although they had been known to lose their temper from time to time with villagers suspected of helping insurgents. From my perspective, the population tended to consider them fair and just, if occasionally harsh.

The police also grew stronger. After the summer fighting ended, police chief Omar Jan continued to expand the force and build new posts. The Ministry of Interior raised the authorized number of official police from 150 to 380. This allowed recruitment to accelerate. The force grew from 50 in August 2009, to 150 in August 2010, to 200 by March 2011; 140 tribal militia supplemented the force, for a total of 340 police and militia. There was no shortage of people waiting to join. The only delay was getting recruits through the academy, a process carefully managed by the provincial police headquarters.

As the police grew, more and more posts popped up. In one week in December, Omar Jan set up three new posts: Loya Darveshan, Bartaka, and Safar. It was particularly heartening to see the new post go up in Bartaka, on the west side of the Helmand, where Mullah Ismael had done such damage. Sergeant Abdul Hadi, Abdullah Jan's English-speaking nephew, took command of the post. Safar absorbed the most effort—three months of negotiations with elders. Omar Jan put twenty-five police and tribal militia there, under the command of Ahmed Shah, Abdullah Jan's old lieutenant. Taliban lurking in the bazaar cleared out upon his arrival. A few surrendered to the district governor. One said: 'I surrendered because Ahmed Shah arrived. He knows everyone and would have known I was with the Taliban.'[3] By May 2011, there were twenty-one police posts in Garmser; three were partnered with Marines; the rest were independent, regularly visited by Marine advisors. Omar Jan worked so hard that he gave himself a minor ulcer (which fortunately healed within a month).

As had been the case since 2009, a thirty-man Marine advisory team worked with the police. In late 2010, under Captain Matthew Taylor, they broke up into small detachments in order to partner closely with the various police posts. Police chief Omar Jan appreciated the help we gave him, listened to our advice, and adored Captain Taylor for watching his back (he was glum for days when Taylor's tour ended). At the same time, Omar Jan refused to be beholden to Americans. When the Bartaka post was established, Omar Jan was short on officers. We sat down to discuss the matter with the battalion commander. Captain Taylor and I suggested Sergeant Abdul Hadi because he was sharp and always taking the lead. I added, in Pashto: 'But this is your decision. We are only telling you our thoughts.' He replied, 'That is right. Because *I* am the commandant,' with a look that suggested personnel decisions were his business, not ours. Only later in private did he whisper to me: 'The boy is good.'

Table 5: Growth of Afghan security forces.

	Sept. 2009	Sept. 2010	May 2011	Dec. 2011	May 2012
Army on duty	200	500	550	550	1,200
Police on duty	50	155	200	330	300
Tribal militia	0	86	140	0	0
Afghan local police	0	0	0	105	300
Army posts	4	5	6	8	29
Police posts	5	15	21	22	26
Marine posts	12	43	48	46	2
Marines	1,000	1,000	1,000	1,000	150

Police throughout Afghanistan have a well-deserved reputation for corruption and abuse. Within the Garmser police, there was ongoing taxation and occasional cases of physical abuse. Fortunately, under Omar Jan, it was nowhere near as bad as what Kabeer Khan had done back in 2005 and 2006. The Marines and Omar Jan tried to address problems by removing guilty personnel, jailing them, or sending them to the academy for retraining. The Marines and I also pressured the police leadership to reduce the low-level taxation and protection schemes that we knew they were running, often at the behest of the provincial government itself. The corruption did not seem to cause serious damage to public perceptions. A PRT-funded survey in July 2011 found that 95 percent of respondents had confidence in the police, up

Image 16: Police chief Omar Jan (right) shaking hands with Lieutenant Colonel Ben Watson. NDS chief Mir Hamza stands between them. (Photo by US Marine Corps Combat Camera)

from 62 percent in October 2010 and on a par with the 94 percent confident in the ANA. The same survey found that the percentage of respondents who believed that the police acted in the interest of the people rose from 65 percent to 90 percent between September 2010 and July 2011.[4]

Both the army and the police had two major shortcomings. The first was air and artillery support, without which any armed force, American or Afghan, cannot easily overcome insurgents entrenched in mud-walled villages. The Afghans relied on their advisors to call in US artillery and air strikes. This was a technical issue not easily remedied. Calling in artillery and especially air strikes required specialized training and encrypted equipment not cleared for Afghans. The second shortcoming was that the police and army suffered from delays in receiving reinforcements and ammunition, a problem which, if left unchecked, could turn an otherwise motivated unit ineffective in combat. These shortcomings could be managed as long as advisors stayed with the police and army. They could call in air and artillery strikes and teach Afghans how to ensure timely arrival of supplies and reinforcements from Afghan stock-piles and depots.

At this point, leadership in the army and police was quite strong. Lieutenant Colonel Hezbollah and police chief Omar Jan were active, battle-hardened commanders who instilled discipline. They went out to visit their officers and men at their far-away posts and made sure they were doing their jobs. The officers and men followed their example. Solid leadership made a difference. With it, the Afghan soldiers and policemen went to great lengths to hold back the Taliban. Without it, many could lapse into sitting in their posts and drinking tea—or worse. In 2010, leadership was not a shortcoming. Under different commanders, it might very well be. It all depended on whom the Afghan system selected.

All this time, I had not forgotten Abdullah Jan's warning to restrain the growth of tribal militia lest they abuse the people or turn into the tribal leaders' personal armies. I cannot say that we had done a good job of following his advice. By September 2010, there were 100 tribal militia, recruited in response to the summer intimidation campaign. The problem was that demand did not let up. Without tribal militia, Omar Jan could not set up new posts. The flow of recruits out of the academy was too slow. The new posts in Loya Darveshan, Safar, and Bartaka all depended upon a contingent of militia. The same was true of additional posts occupied by the police over the spring. For that reason, 140 militia were in the field by March 2011. Omar Jan capped the militia at that number. He felt that any more could not be managed responsibly. We had always known that a long-term militia program was a bad idea and therefore re-focused on our plan to make them part of the government by sending them to the police academy. At least twenty had gone to the academy during the summer of 2010, but Omar Jan sent no more until September, after the fighting had calmed down. Nearly every month thereafter, he sent up a new contingent. By the end of the summer of 2011, all but forty of the original Garmser tribal militia had gone to the police academy (see Fig. 1 in Chapter 10).

Besides sending tribal militia to the academy and placing them under Omar Jan, four additional measures were taken to reinforce government control. First, Marines established a week-long academy in the district center to train tribal militia and refresh official police. Second, as had been the case since spring 2010, tribal militia were not to be used for law enforcement, only for defending against the Taliban. Third, Marines

Image 17: One of the older, experienced tribal militia (arbekai). (Photo by Patricio Asfura-Heim)

and Afghan army soldiers continued to keep an eye on the militia. Fourth, as police posts were constructed in Laki and Mian Poshtay, official police and tribal militia were moved out of the homes of Ghulam Rassoul and Wakil Manan (leaving a handful for personal protection) and into the posts. Mangal was keen on this point. He did not want tribal leaders influencing large numbers of armed men. Ghulam Rassoul was gracious, confident of his power in Laki. With Wakil Manan, it was like pulling teeth. He did not want to let them go. Memories of being abused by the mujahidin and then imprisoned by the Taliban haunted him. The shame of having the police he had recruited taken away was no less upsetting. But, after hours of infuriating negotiation, he did the right thing and relinquished authority.

In the end, in spite of these measures, I fear that the United States pushed aside Abdullah Jan's advice. During the autumn of 2011, a new tribal militia program known as the 'Afghan local police' was initiated. Since the beginning of 2010 and Wakil Manan's first tribal militia, the debate in Kabul over the establishment of an official tribal militia program had dragged on. Championed by General Petraeus, a program was finally established in 2010 that allowed 'Afghan local police' to be recruited throughout most of Afghanistan. Under the program, elders would produce volunteers to defend their community. Those volunteers would be approved by the community council, the district governor, and the Ministry of Interior. They would be trained by local coalition forces, placed under the district police chief, and paid and armed by the Ministry of Interior. In October 2011, the Ministry of Interior allotted Garmser 300 slots for local police, a useful supplement to the official police, which were restricted to 380 men. By this time, roughly 300 official police were in the field. The remaining forty tribal militia who had not yet gone to the police academy were transferred into the Afghan local police, meaning that all the old tribal militia were paid by the Afghan government. New Afghan local police were recruited to fill the remaining slots, many by tribal leaders. Wakil Manan was one of them—pleased to have increasing numbers of armed men under his influence once again, six months after he had agreed to relinquish that role. By the end of 2011, 105 local police were in the field. Whether they would bolster the government or become a source of strife, as Abdullah Jan feared, was yet to be seen.

Economic development

Since 2008, Garmser had seen significant reconstruction activity. Between October 2009 and February 2011, $21.5 million in US funds were expended: $5.2 million by Marines using commander's emergency response program (CERP) funds, $7.9 million by USAID's Office of Transition Initiatives, and $8.4 million by USAID's Afghanistan Vouchers for Increased Production in Agriculture (AVIPA Plus) program. Against a district of 150,000, the sum was significant. It was roughly equivalent to the amount of US project spending in Kunar, a province of 420,000, in 2007; or the amount needed to keep 1,000 Afghan soldiers in the field for a year. The main focus was on using quick-impact projects of about $5,000 each—small culverts, wells, foot bridges, and canal clearings—to convince people to work with the government. Scores of small-scale canal clearings were lumped together as cash-for-work under AVIPA. Since parts of the district were violent for most of this period, quick-impact projects made sense. Their purpose was to show people that their lives were improving, provide short-term employment so that young men would be less tempted to work with the

Taliban, and to reward elders for helping the government. A smaller number of longer-term development projects were executed, ranging in cost from $50,000 to $500,000. The entire main canal road was repaired; the Mian Poshtay and Lakari bazaars were paved; Safar bazaar was graveled; the main canal intake was repaired. Roughly $6 million of the total $21.5 million was spent on these larger projects.

The projects seem to have made a difference. Average monthly salary rose from 13,000 to nearly 16,000 Afghani (from about $250 to $300) between September 2010 and June 2011.[5] This was slightly above the average monthly salary in Helmand (15,000 Afghani in June 2011) and much more than the monthly salary of a policeman (10,000 Afghani). In the April 2011 PRT-funded survey of Garmser, 71 percent of respondents said that employment opportunities had improved; only 40 percent had said so in September 2010. In the opinion of many Afghan leaders, quick-impact projects helped reduce violence. Elders and shop owners often told me that young men were getting jobs and therefore, either because of the money or just plain lack of time, were not interested in being Taliban. One of that same survey's most impressive findings was a correlation between economic prosperity and support for the government: 'Of those who stated that the District Govt has improved employment opportunities, 85 percent also agreed GIRoA listened and acted on behalf of the people.'[6] Nevertheless, the same political and economic effect might have been attained for less than $21.5 million. A few hundred thousand dollars of that sum were used to empower the community council, religious leaders, and tribal leaders. It did a lot to compel those groups to work with the government and against the Taliban. This money was conditioned upon recipients doing something for the government. The millions spent in large-scale cash-for-work programs and infrastructure projects were not. Too often, locals were happy to take the projects and do nothing in return. For this reason, I think that the large-scale programs and infrastructure projects made a difference, but that $21.5 million might have been overkill.

As of early 2011, most of the projects had provided a short-term boost rather than long-term economic growth. Garmser's agricultural goods were primarily sold within the district and did not reach larger markets. The only industry was gravel, crushed by little factories across the river from the district center. It would be unsustainable past the boom resulting from the construction of hundreds of gravel-hungry US bases throughout Helmand. Above all, Garmser did not yet have a lucrative alternative for poppy. Without one, poppy cultivation was sure to resume within a few years. Despite years of wheat seed distributions, eradication campaigns and discussions about saffron, pomegranates, cotton, and grapes, no serious attempt had been made by the Afghan government, the United States, or anyone else to put forward an alternative.

After October 2010, Gail Long tried to spur long-term development. With her lengthy experience with USAID, she knew better than anyone else how to transition away from quick-impact projects. Her preference was to nurture agricultural cooperatives. Gary Lewis, the experienced head of USAID's AVIPA program in Garmser, was a strong proponent of them and helped explain how best to take them forward. Earlier in the year, Lewis had organized twenty-three cooperatives. Participants included some of the most powerful landowners in the district. By banding together, they could bear the otherwise prohibitive expenses involved in experimenting with new crops. Long believed that the cooperatives stood a good chance of identifying lucrative crops—whether grapes, pomegranates, or cotton—and getting that produce to the market. Such activity might form a basis for economic growth. The cooperatives were brought into a series of weekly meetings with the director of agriculture, meant to guide them in the benefits of working together. Long left us in November 2011 to oversee USAID projects throughout Helmand. Her successor in Garmser, Deborah Murphy, found a non-governmental organization to train the cooperative members. It eventually based itself in the district and trained cooperative members how best to work together.

In the middle of 2011, AVIPA ended in Garmser. Near the end of the year, a new USAID program, SRAD, came to Garmser to execute a one-year multi-million-dollar agricultural development program. It was dedicated to refurbishing the canal system, which still needed a good deal of repair to get back to its 1970s state of efficiency. Between the cooperatives and SRAD, long-term economic development was receiving attention. Whether it would come to anything was unknown. If the cooperatives did not develop and the SRAD program was not successful, there was a real risk that growing poppy and working with the Taliban could again become attractive for young men of Garmser.

The fractured society

Late 2010 and the first half of 2011 was a time of growth for the Afghan government and a time of defeat for the Taliban. Yet belief in the Taliban could not be extinguished overnight. In September 2010, society was still fractured. On the one hand, the tribal leaders had rallied behind the government and were not fighting among themselves. On the other hand, the religious leaders—though closer to the government than at any time since 2004—and the poor landless immigrants often preferred the Taliban.

Having already declared their opposition to the Taliban and impressed with the strength of the Marines, the tribal leaders worked with the government. Throughout Garmser, tribal leaders tended to keep the Taliban out of their communities and to support the police and Afghan army. The PRT-funded survey in July 2011 found that 88 percent of respondents were satisfied with the role of the tribal leaders in keeping the district secure, just below confidence in the army and police.

Shah Jahan, Alizai political leader from Laki, emerged as the foremost tribal leader in Garmser. As a former district governor, this was not surprising. His political skills continued to stand out. After over two years away from the district, he had returned to Laki in the summer and, as promised, helped keep things in order. By staying close to the government and fighting the Taliban alongside Ghulam Rassoul and Shah Wali Khan, he quickly rebuilt his position. He worked with Fahim to rally tribal leaders together and to bring issues of concern to Lashkar Gah. Shrewd as always, he was careful to pay heed to Fahim's wishes and do nothing to overshadow him.

In the autumn of 2010, only the Noorzai tribal leaders from Safar were not with the government. With its large Noorzai community, wide dusty fields, and thriving bazaar, Safar was an important part of Garmser. Strategically, it was a crossroads between Pakistan, Iran, Kandahar, and Lashkar Gah and the southern entry-point into Garmser and Helmand as a whole—reasons why the Ghaznavids had built great mud forts there centuries before.

Tribal relations in Safar were a mess. It had been over twenty years since the bloodshed of the post-jihad tribal civil war. The two Noorzai clans were hopelessly divided. The clan of Salay Mohammed, the great tribal leader from Safar, traditionally ruled the region. The other, smaller Noorzai clan had long bucked at their dominance. During the tribal civil war that had followed the jihad, when the Noorzai fought the Alizai throughout Garmser, the smaller clan had turned against Salay Mohammed's dominant clan. They helped the Alizai capture Safar. The fighting had been bloody and ugly. Salay Mohammed had been forced to flee to Pakistan. The feud lived on. The two clans would not even pay respects at funerals, a grave insult in Pashtun culture. On top of that, because of the mistreatment he had suffered at the hands of Governor Sher Mohammed Akhundzada in 2005, Salay Mohammed would not work with the government. Governor Sher Mohammed had dissolved Salay Mohammed's border police and undermined his authority in Safar. Upset and angry, Salay Mohammed had gone to Kabul, where he now lived. Governor Mangal tried to convince him to return but he refused, the only one of Garmser's great tribal leaders to do so. None of the remaining, less powerful Safar elders were willing to stand up for the government.

After long negotiations, Governor Mangal convinced Salay Mohammed to send his brother, Sultan Mohammed, back to Safar. Sultan Mohammed had been working with Mullah Naim, Taliban governor of Helmand, for years. In April 2011, he met with Mangal and promised never to help the Taliban again. He returned to Safar but held himself aloof from the district government, looking down upon District Governor Fahim as a young upstart and boycotting the June 2011 community council elections. The smaller Noorzai clan started spreading rumors that he was working with the Taliban. Together with his off-putting attitude, this impeded cooperation and raised suspicions. Although the Taliban were very weak in Safar, the tight government–tribal alliance of elsewhere in Garmser did not form.

Sultan Mohammed notwithstanding, tribal unity had improved. Tribal leaders were both working with the government and cooperating with each other. Old feuds largely lay dormant. The religious leaders and the landless immigrants, on the other hand, were more sympathetic to the Taliban; and, moreover, the government was far more reluctant to work with them.

Before 1978, religious leaders had played an apolitical role in Garmser. They led prayers and taught about Islam but avoided speaking in favor of the government or leading opposition movements. This changed with communist oppression and the Russian invasion. The religious leaders called for jihad and rallied mujahidin for war. They became politicized.

Even so, during the jihad, the tribal leaders, not the religious leaders, remained the rulers of the district. It was the Taliban that lifted Islam and the religious leaders into a new dominant role. For these natural reasons, religious leaders tended to support the Taliban long after the fall of the first Taliban regime in 2001. The fact that police or government officials too often disrespected religious leaders for having associated with the Taliban did not help. The Taliban return in 2006 brought the religious leaders back into positions of influence. When the Marines started pushing the Taliban back in 2008, few religious leaders had much reason to help the government.

It was in this environment that, in 2009, then-District Governor Abdullah Jan and Deputy District Governor Ayub Omar had developed their plan to reach out to the religious leaders. The first meetings had been contentious but relations slowly improved. After Abdullah Jan's removal, Ayub Omar had carried on with the plan. Over the summer of 2010, in cooperation with the community council, he had formed an informal council and started Friday prayers. Now, in the autumn, he expanded the effort to southern Garmser and started meeting with mullahs there too. The main focus was on building religious support for the construction of two madrasas, one of Abdullah Jan's original goals. Ayub Omar wanted to build one government-run madrasa in the district center and another in Lakari. Ayub Omar had long believed that building madrasas would show the religious leaders that the government was serious about supporting Islam. He also believed that it would allow religious students from Garmser to be educated in Afghanistan instead of in Pakistan. After a series of meetings, religious leaders from the north and south endorsed Ayub Omar's plan and promised to identify mullahs and scholars who would make good teachers. At an October meeting of the religious council, Garmser's leading religious scholar said: 'Build a madrasa to show us that you trust us…We do not want to be used for political purposes…[but] we are ready to help the government teach people about Islam. We fear being used as Pakistan and Russia used us.'[7] The same scholar a year earlier had said that the religious leaders should only support the government if the foreigners left. Even scholars who had helped the Taliban supported the plan. With their blessing, construction of the madrasas began.

Other progress occurred as well: two of the district's foremost religious scholars agreed to help reconcile Taliban to the government; a pro-government mullah took over the large symbolic mosque next to the shrine in Amir Agha; and the religious council expressed interest in the provincial government's plan to build a new district center mosque. Unfortunately, in January 2011, Ayub Omar was transferred to Nawa, the district between Garmser and Lashkar Gah. Governor Mangal wanted a better deputy district governor there. With Ayub Omar's departure, progress on the religious front stalled. District Governor Fahim was too busy on other matters and Ayub Omar's replacement lacked the requisite negotiating skills. We ourselves could not take over. Talking with Islamic religious leaders is the hardest of things. We could not go to them directly, lest we taint the whole effort. The last thing we wanted was for religious leaders to believe that the government was a tool of the infidels. We tried to have tribal leaders take the lead, but they proved too interested in their own affairs. Months were spent trying to get the Alizai tribal leaders to convince the Laki and Lakari mullahs to nominate someone to lead Friday prayers in Lakari bazaar. Neither the tribal leaders nor the district governor would pressure the religious leaders sufficiently. Thus, the government never got as far as Abdullah Jan and Ayub Omar had hoped. The madrasas eventually opened but without the religious fanfare or the number of students that would have pleased Abdullah Jan or Ayub Omar.

In the summer of 2011, I sat down and spoke with Maulawi Mohammedullah, the former Taliban judge for Mian Poshtay. He was trying to offer the government advice when and where appropriate. In his eyes, the Taliban had lost some of their luster, although the government was still too oppressive:

"The Taliban oppresses people by killing elders who talk with the government. The government oppresses people by bombing the homes of people who talk with the Taliban. You oppress people by entering their homes. Searching homes is oppression. Before the United States arrived, Taliban did not oppress people. Only the government did."[8]

He felt that the religious leaders needed to be given a larger role: "The government and the elders must start talking to the ulema [religious leadership] more. They are not asking for the advice of the mullahs."[9] His words were a fitting illustration of the changed, more conciliatory attitudes of the religious leaders as well as the fissures that still divided Garmser.

Efforts to reach out to the landless immigrants were more disappointing. Thousands of families still resided on government land without a legal deed—roughly 20 percent of the total population.[10] They had come in waves: first, during the Zahir Shah and Daoud governments in the 1970s, then during the brief communist tenure from 1978 to 1980, next during the first Taliban regime in the 1990s, and finally during the second Taliban regime from 2006 to 2010. The first Taliban regime gave many of these immigrants deed to the land they had been farming. The Karzai government revoked those deeds. The second Taliban regime reinstated them, but, with the return of the government, all these immigrants were again without title and fearful.

According to Afghan law, anyone living on government land without a deed from the Karzai government or a pre-communist government would eventually have to leave. In practice, nothing was enforced. In some respects this was good. No farmer lost his home or farm. In other respects this was bad. Even if unenforced, the standing law made many landless immigrants see the Taliban as the only sure way to keep their homes and farms. For example, in 2011, one group of 3,500 landless immigrants, who were aligned with the Taliban and had fled to Pakistan, wanted to return to Garmser. Their condition was that the government should grant them permission to live on the land that the Taliban had given them, which, of course, was not forthcoming. They stayed in Pakistan, with the Taliban. In Garmser itself, the Taraki tribe on the eastern edge of the canal zone, the largest group of landless farmers, housed and fed the handful of transient surviving Taliban fighters. Mullah Naim's village in Laki did the same. A prominent Taraki religious scholar said that among his people there was 'great nostalgia for the time of the Taliban.'[11] Police chief Omar Jan told us: 'If the government takes back government land, it will create a big problem. A small tax would be better. All problems were created by government land.'[12]

To say that all landless immigrants hated the government would be wrong. Plenty were tired of violence—refugees in Pakistan among them—and believed that life under the government was better than more war. But the land policy prevented the government from fully exploiting this opportunity and solving one of the deepest sources of violence in Garmser.

I advised District Governor Fahim on some options for reaching out to the landless, such as asking the courts in Lashkar Gah to write temporary leases or asking Governor Mangal to grant a temporary period of amnesty. Doing so, I thought, could allay fears that the government was about to seize the land and thereby reduce support for the Taliban. Mangal viewed American advice in this matter as interference in private Afghan business. As a result, nothing ever happened. There was no easy way for us to press the issue. The PRT had already warned us to stay away from land reform. It was a sensitive issue in Lashkar Gah and Kabul. The PRT and the US Embassy did not want to touch it. In the view of Afghan officials, government land was government property, a national resource. They considered American or British advice as tantamount to colonialism. The arrival of the judge at the beginning of January 2011 offered a legal solution to the land issues: he was authorized to sign off on leases and decide who could legally occupy government land; but he too had his own agenda and disliked American interference in what he considered private Afghan affairs.

There was one bright spot on the land front: District Governor Fahim helped solve the land dispute between the Alizai and Mullah Naim's family in Laki. The decades-long feud had been a constant source of tension in the area. Mullah Naim's family, immigrants from the Tarin tribe, lived on government land that had once belonged to the Alizai, as well as some private Alizai land taken during the Taliban regimes. Shah Wali Khan and Ghulam Rassoul argued that Naim had taken their land by force. Naim's family argued that the land had been given to them fairly. Truth and lie coursed through both stories. The two sides clearly hated each other. Ignoring the feud any longer risked open fighting. The Alizai had taken no action through the summer, keeping their promise to let the issue be; but by 2011, with insurgent violence subdued, they wanted resolution. Fahim recognized this and, in June, established a land commission to resolve the dispute. Three of the district's most important Pashtun tribal leaders, two Baluch tribal leaders, a former Taliban judge (Maulawi Mohammedullah), a powerful mullah, and two community council members sat on the thirteen-person commission, overseen by Omar Jan and Fahim himself. After three months of deliberations, the commission came to a decision that was sent to the provincial government in Lashkar Gah for confirmation. The fact that religious leaders, tribal leaders, and Baluch sat on the same shura together arbitrating a dispute between landless immigrants and Garmser's most powerful khans demonstrated that the government, when focused, could bring its people together. The fact that Taliban supporters were willing to accept government-sponsored arbitration demonstrated the movement's weakness at that time. The commission showed what could have been accomplished had we put more effort into reaching out to Garmser's religious leaders and landless immigrants.

Me against my brother

The divisions between the tribes, religious leaders, and immigrants were one type of long-standing fracture in Garmser society. Competition between power-brokers—whether warlords, tribal leaders, or government officials—was another. Abdullah Jan, Ayub Omar, Fahim, and Omar Jan had forged a loose alliance of tribal leaders: Wakil Manan, Shah Wali Khan, Ghulam Rassoul, Shah Jahan, Khodirom, Said Omar, Mohammed Anwar Khan, and Abdullah Jan himself. That loose alliance solidified security in the district, providing police recruits, intelligence, and protection for numerous villages. Cracks in the alliance could result in tribal leaders leaving the district or even re-aligning with the Taliban, as had happened too often before in Garmser's history. The difference between the past and 2011 was the presence of the new government. It had the potential to keep the alliance in place. Strength was key. The government needed a robust police and army and governors, police chiefs, and army commanders who cooperated. Such a government might balance the tribes in the way that Zahir Shah's had done before 1973, putting an end to the days of tribal leaders competing with each other rather than uniting for the common good. Worryingly, as the Taliban threat receded, political feuds between government leaders themselves came into view. This was dangerous.

Competition between governors, police chiefs, and NDS chiefs (NDS was the national intelligence service) was a systemic problem in Afghanistan. The district governor was the senior official in name only. He had no real power over the police chief or NDS chief. Their bosses were the provincial police chief and NDS director. The district police chief and NDS chief were supposed to obey the district governor's wishes; but if they did not, the district governor's only recourse was to complain to the provincial governor, who would then have to pressure the provincial police chief or provincial NDS director to address the problem, something a busy provincial governor rarely had time to do. Like the district governor, the provincial governor could not just issue an order. The provincial police chief or NDS director reported to the Minister of Interior or NDS director in Kabul. This essentially meant that any district had three fairly independent government leaders, a recipe for competition. District governors often also found themselves at odds with provincial police chiefs and NDS directors who could use their authority to intervene in a district regardless of the district governor's wishes. A different political system that gave the district governor control of the police and limited the power of the NDS might have prevented this sort of thing.

The division of tax revenue exacerbated the problem. The district governor, police chief, and NDS chief had no legal right to tax within Afghanistan. Yet beneath the surface taxation went on. Bazaars, project contracts, gravel mines, and poppy were all taxed. We were aware of the taxation and had private conversations with our key leaders to reduce it. Provincial government officials were in on the schemes and received a cut. Afghan officials were smart enough to know that over-taxing the population risked revolt, a reality that made competition over limited tax revenue all the fiercer.

In Garmser, feuds burdened District Governor Fahim. Fahim showed potential, but was young. Police chief Omar Jan, NDS chief Mir Hamza (head of the national intelligence service in Garmser), and certain other leaders overshadowed him. Their influence and accomplishments became a natural bone of contention. Westerners might view this as petty. In Afghan political culture, it was anything but. A good leader is not overshadowed. This was the example of one of Afghanistan's most effective rulers, Emir Abdur Rahman (1880–1901). He succeeded partly by marginalizing anyone who became influential among the people, lest they grow too powerful, challenge him, and throw the country into civil war.[13] Given such historical lessons, the fact that friction broke out between a young district governor and older, more accomplished leaders should hardly be surprising.

Two main feuds broke out. The first was between Fahim and provincial NDS director Nazr Ali Waheedi. Nazr Ali was a Noorzai and former communist from Garmser, who was close with Salay Mohammed from Safar as well as several other Kabul politicians. He was powerful enough that even Governor Mangal had a hard time controlling him. Nazr Ali repeatedly intervened in Garmser political and business affairs. Fahim had to react or he would appear weak. The two were soon trying to remove each other and each other's supporters. On both sides, good pro-government Afghans lost their jobs. The feud also meant that Salay Mohammed and his brother, Sultan Mohammed, would not work with Fahim, which left Safar's continuing problems unattended.

The other feud was between Fahim and police chief Omar Jan. It was probably inevitable that the two would clash. The feud was a symptom of the Afghan governmental system: two leaders in one district, neither clearly in charge. As early as June 2010, Omar Jan did not want to listen to Fahim and Fahim wanted Omar Jan removed. Through his effective campaign against the Taliban and expansion of the police force, Omar Jan had become increasingly powerful. Impressed with Omar Jan, elders and tribal leaders flocked to him to discuss issues. Often his office was packed. Omar Jan hosted well-cooked dinners in his courtyard, bringing in musicians from Lashkar Gah to entertain. The dinners unintentionally insulted Fahim. A district governor usually hosted such affairs. The amount of funds we dedicated to the police versus the district governor's offices did not help. Much of that funding was necessary, the police being a much larger organization. Some was not. In 2008, the US-led military training command in Kabul had contracted a giant new police headquarters, overlooking the river in Hazar Joft. Contractors from Kandahar took three years to build the two-storey modern station, with gas ovens, a sewage system, lights, fans, and two giant diesel generators. The Marines and I disliked this great elephant: the Marines because the Afghans would never be able to keep it running; I because the structure would elevate Omar Jan's stature vis-à-vis Fahim. The government center where Fahim lived was an eminently practical one-storey building with a courtyard in the middle; no sewage system, no fans, no river-side view. In March, the PRT head of mission visited Garmser and toured the newly finished police headquarters. As we walked through the two-storey atrium with Omar Jan and Fahim, Jon Moss, who had come down for the visit, whispered to me: 'Carter, your district governor looks really angry.' I could not blame him.

This level of infighting between commanders, governors, and other officials had never afflicted the Taliban. I heard of plenty of Taliban commanders having disagreements, but they were neither so indeterminable nor so widespread. The two Taliban regimes had structured themselves hierarchically. Everyone in a district was placed under the district governor. He was the top civilian and military authority. The same went for the provincial governor. There were no police commanders or intelligence directors who would freely interfere in the districts. The Taliban's unwavering attention to Islam, with its emphasis on unity, further helped reduce infighting. The Karzai government should have followed the Taliban's example. It should have granted the provincial and district governors greater control over the other government actors in their provinces and districts. If impossible to enact permanently, such a course of action could have been taken temporarily, until the stresses of war had eased. The relationships between governors, police chiefs, line ministries, and NDS directors were not enshrined in the constitution. They could have been changed, forming a much more cohesive political organization.

As it was, in this environment, one of my main duties became managing feuds and protecting strong leaders. Lieutenant Colonel Watson and I did not believe that we could risk losing any police officers, government officials, or pro-government tribal leaders who were active and willing to fight hard for the government. The removal of such leaders from the battlefield would only strengthen the Taliban's hand. We could not be sure that replacements would be competent, or would come at all. The logic of Afghan politics was not meritocratic. Even if good replacements did come down, the cycle of competition would merely start anew, a gift to the Taliban. Since it seemed to me that the primary job of a political officer was to mediate disputes rather than let them run their unfettered course, I tried to advise Fahim and pressure other leaders to compromise with him. Ayub Omar was invaluable, at least until his departure, tirelessly finding ways to ease tensions, especially with police chief Omar Jan. The idea of a united Afghanistan, with the tribes allied behind it, became one of my major talking points at shuras and in one-on-one discussions with Fahim, Omar Jan, Mir Hamza, and tribal leaders. Lieutenant Colonel Hezbollah of the Afghan army was a vociferous critic of tribal leaders and the police and therefore an unlikely ally. He strongly believed in a united Afghanistan. Over and over again, he emphasized the importance of cooperation. On top of this detailed diplomatic work, Lieutenant Colonel Watson (followed by the next battalion commander, Lieutenant Colonel Matt Reid) and I tried to make sure that the government could keep control of the tribes by building up Fahim, the NDS, police, and Afghan army. In the end, we believed they were the structure that could hold Afghanistan together—as long as they themselves got along. Despite the time it absorbed, between Marine presence, the respect people held for the Afghan army, and our project funds, we had enough weight to keep political infighting from getting out of control.

Mopping up

The Taliban position worsened as the months passed by. The number of attacks fell from 74 in August 2010 to 16 in November 2010. There were just thirty or so active fighters in one or two cadres. They operated out of the western side of the river south of Bartaka and settlements near the eastern desert. They had few weapons and usually had to travel unarmed if they wanted to avoid capture. As had been the case since 2009, nearly all the Taliban fighting in Garmser were from Garmser families. Insurgents born to families from outside Garmser were rarely, if ever, detained. It was no longer safe, however, for fighters to live in Garmser all the time. The chance of their whereabouts being passed to the Marines, Afghan soldiers, or Afghan police was too great. The majority now resided in Pakistan and traveled back and forth.

Using a few fighters and a lot of propaganda, the Taliban managed a short-lived bout of intimidation in November and December 2010. In November, reports appeared of a Taliban cadre operating in Loya Darveshan, near the river. Shortly thereafter, two unarmed Taliban beat an elder in the area. The elder was largely unharmed but the event frightened him and two other elders into going to Pakistan and pledging allegiance to Mullah Naim, still governor of the Taliban in Helmand. Having paid attention to the international news, Naim told those elders that the United States would leave Afghanistan in 2011, that the Taliban would then return, and that he would punish anyone who had worked with the government. The same threat was issued via phone and letters to elders in Lakari, Mian Poshtay, and Kuchinay Darveshan. Fortunately, no one fled. Over the following weeks, there was an outbreak of IED attacks and five different schools closed down. The response was quick and effective. Police chief Omar Jan placed a new post by the river in Loya Darveshan. Meanwhile, Ayub Omar and the community council pressured the teachers into re-opening the schools. Reports of insurgent activity in the area disappeared overnight.

In mid-January 2011, Lieutenant Colonel Reid and Lieutenant Colonel Hezbollah cleared southern Safar and Benadar, where steady but

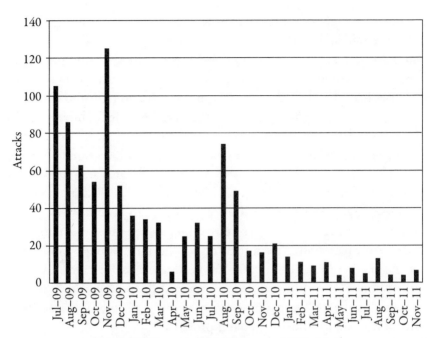

Fig. 2: Taliban attacks in Garmser, 2009–11.[14]

ineffective IED activity had persisted. Two border police detachments helped outpost Benadar, the parched southern end of Garmser. Its leaders, Noorzai relatives of Said Omar and Ayub Omar and friends of Abdullah Jan, immediately came over to the government. By the end of January, a total of forty-eight Marine posts covered Garmser, on top of over twenty police and army posts. To thin the battalion out in this way meant that Reid had to accept a lot of risk—at this point his men were more spread out than McDonough's or Watson's had been. More than one Marine general came through awestruck.

These operations put the entire district officially back under government control. Insurgents were forced to operate in twos and threes at the edges of the district, often unarmed. By spring, the Taliban were struggling to keep fighting in Garmser. Widespread reports came in that Taliban commanders were desperately short of money and supplies. Cell leaders and fighters were refusing to work in the district for fear of being captured. In March, police chief Omar Jan removed an entire eight-man cell, along with four weapons and 210 pounds of bomb material. NDS chief Mir Hamza captured half an IED cell, with their materials, out by the desert. As fewer and fewer men with homes in Garmser wanted to fight, the Taliban had to conscript more and more fighters from refugee communities, largely Ghilzai, inside Pakistan. Those who refused were beaten. According to reports we were receiving, many in those communities had grown tired of fighting and wanted to return to Garmser.

Poppy growth, a major source of Taliban revenue, fell substantially. In 2010, the tribal leaders and community council members from Laki to Hazar Joft had promised not to plant poppy. By and large, in the spring of 2011, that area was poppy free, leaving only Safar and Benadar as major cultivation areas. Taliban tax collectors busily called upon poppy growers in Safar and Benadar, but were unable to do much elsewhere. Even in Safar and Benadar themselves, Taliban revenues were curtailed. The government eradicated a total of 560 hectares of poppy in March and April (there are 31–33,000 total hectares of usable land in Garmser). Without enough tractors to eradicate all the poppy fields, the government also taxed the poppy growers, without telling us or the PRT. The money went to the district and provincial government.

Partly because of all this pressure, Taliban started surrendering in larger numbers: fifteen insurgents reconciled with the government between December 2010 and July 2011. A similar uptick had happened in early 2010. That year, most had been low-level fighters. This time cell leaders and major facilitators turned. Sultan Mohammed (discussed above) was one. Dr Salam, one of the architects of the Taliban's 2006 seizure of Garmser, was another. He was tired of hiding in Pakistan where he was nothing but an unemployed pharmacist. He wanted a life with his family again.[15] 'The people in Pakistan and Baluchistan,' he said, 'did not respect me. They taxed me heavily.'[16] He surrendered to Fahim and Mangal and then went back to live in Lakari. Reconciles gave different reasons for surrendering. A few were convinced that fighting the Marines was pointless. A few, such as Dr Salam, knew that life was better in Afghanistan than Pakistan. One felt that the Taliban cause was hurting his family: 'I want to help Afghanistan now. I do not want to do any more damage to my home…I realized that the government is helping my home. I realized that Pakistan is hurting it. So I left the Taliban.'[17]

At the time these Taliban were turning, the Afghan government and the United States and its Allies introduced a nationwide reintegration plan, known as the Afghan Reintegration Program. The program set up a formal process for Taliban to surrender to the government, involving

248

reintegration committees in the provinces and districts. The US Department of Defense allocated funds for the program that could be used to pay salaries for the reintegration council members and to pay expenses involved in running negotiations with insurgents. In Garmser, Governor Mangal had District Governor Fahim stand up an eight-member reintegration advisory committee. He told Fahim to reach out to prominent Taliban from Garmser.

In spring 2011, Fahim opened a dialogue with Taliban political and religious leaders. He sent envoys back and forth to Pakistan to talk with them. Out of the effort, a Taliban religious leader and a cadre leader returned to Garmser to cooperate with the government. Others expressed interest but were not ready to commit. Fahim's envoys reported that Taliban leaders were demoralized and upset that their people were living in poor conditions in Pakistan. I heard story after story that the death of Osama bin Laden on 2 May 2011—greeted by a surprising degree of bloodthirsty cheer by Garmser tribal leaders—had frightened the Taliban leadership into hiding. We learned that whole villages of refugees, entirely disaffected landless, were anxious to return to Garmser, where they knew that life was better. Poppy income from harvests in Garmser was down. The Pakistani government was mistreating them, taxing them, and not delivering goods and services. Taliban mullahs had to run about convincing families to stay put.

As May approached, reports filtered in about the upcoming spring offensive. Mullah Omar had supposedly planned a major offensive named 'Operation Badr,' which would strike key government locations and try to kill Afghan leaders in Kandahar and Helmand. The offensive came late. The Taliban were not set until late May, two weeks after the end of the poppy harvest. It met disaster.

As the few remaining Taliban cadres in Pakistan tried to infiltrate back into the district, police and NDS sources picked up information on their whereabouts. That information was a function of the degree of tribal support the government now enjoyed and of the aggressiveness of the police and NDS. During the first two weeks of May, border police in Benadar gathered enough intelligence to capture two well-known Taliban, both of whom were on US wanted lists. A week later, on 20 May, the day before the spring offensive hit Lashkar Gah and Marjah, the police, army, and NDS launched a second set of pre-emptive strikes. NDS chief Mir Hamza, working with the army, detained an eight-man cell in Majitek, including a cadre leader, together with hundreds of pounds of bomb-making material and IED components intended to resource the spring offensive. To the south, in Laki, Ghulam Rassoul had been watching the southern outskirts of the district. His kidnapped brother's release had not settled the score for him. He wanted revenge. As Mir Hamza struck into Majitek, Ghulam Rassoul had the Laki police screen the desert. That morning, the Garmser and Nawa shadow governors, Mullah Matiullah and Haji Selani (also a former Garmser shadow governor), drove north to take over operations in their respective districts. They rolled up onto the police screen. After a brief, one-sided gunfight, both were captured. Two other Taliban and a truckload of IED-making materials were taken as well. They were the most important Taliban captured or killed in Garmser since Dadullah Lang, Taliban commander for southern Afghanistan, had been shot in 2008. We knew nothing of the operation until it was finished. It was a huge success, the fruit of a year of effort. A year earlier, Ghulam Rassoul had been surrounded in Shah Wali Khan's village and those police had been militia. Now Ghulam Rassoul was keeping the Taliban leadership out of the entire district and the militia had gone to the academy and become official police.

The Afghan strikes pre-empted the spring offensive. The Taliban no longer had the bench to replace losses quickly. Consequently, the offensive made little ground in Garmser. Naim sent in two or three more cadre leaders, there was minor intimidation over the summer, and IEDs went off from time to time. The Taliban had a hard time doing anything against the defenses and intelligence network that Mir Hamza and Omar Jan had set up. Omar Jan took two more cadre leaders in June and another eight-man cell in July. For most of the summer, the Taliban could not regain the initiative.

The next round of community council elections took place in June 2011. It expanded representation to the remainder of the district, allocating seats to Lakari, Laki, Safar, and Benadar. Altogether 350 elders participated, more than any previous election. Shah Jahan and several other tribal leaders ran and were elected. With their election and that of Khodirom and Wakil Manan the previous year, the community council went from being a body of lesser elders to the forum for the district's tribal leaders to meet. The fact that the tribal leaders—minus Sultan Mohammed in Safar—were meeting under a government-sponsored body demonstrated how the tribes had come together with the government.

Thus, by June 2011, the Taliban appeared thoroughly defeated in Garmser. Attacks were lower than they had been in the winter (the traditional time of respite). Governance and economic development, the meat and bones of long-term stability, were progressing, sometimes more slowly than we had wanted, but apparent over the *longue durée*. According to the April 2011 PRT survey, 87 percent of people believed that the security situation had improved over the previous six months; only 53 percent had thought so in September 2010.[18] Things were not yet perfect: sympathy for the Taliban remained among the religious leaders and immigrants, underlined by the fact that 22 percent of survey respondents still thought it would be a good thing if the Taliban returned to power. Nevertheless, the level of unity was better than at any time since the jihad. Tribal infighting was low. Notable religious leaders were tentatively working with the government.

The day Ghulam Rassoul captured Haji Selani and Mullah Matiullah, I was with Omar Jan in Safar talking with elders (Fahim was in Kabul). When the Laki post radioed the news, we rushed northward. There was a feeling of great achievement as our blue Ford Ranger pickups wound out of Safar's sprawling bazaar, with its wide graveled streets, onto the main canal road. The police had scored a major victory entirely on their own. It filled me with hope that the Afghans could handle a future without Americans or British. At the new concrete police station in Laki, next to the refurbished clinic and brand new school, we picked up the captives from Ghulam Rassoul and twenty beaming policemen. From there we headed into Lakari, making a short stop at the now-paved Lakari bazaar, with its single main street and painted shops, the prettiest of Garmser's bazaars. We sped on past Mian Poshtay, past its huge new police post, gleaming white school, clinic, and Wakil Manan's fortress-like home. At the Koshtay police station, Abdullah Jan's veterans hailed us from the rooftop. Flanked by the pine trees lining the main canal road, we raced through Kuchinay and then Loya Darveshan, passing Roh Khan's sprawling Noorzai village where the first Pashtuns had settled in Garmser. Finally, we entered Hazar Joft and crossed the main canal bridge into its busy working bazaar, paved by Peter Chilvers over two years before when the effort to retake Garmser had just begun.

The looming question

In 2009, President Obama had promised that the Afghan surge would end in 2011. The Marine leadership and civilians in the PRT anticipated that the drawdown would begin after the President's scheduled speech that June. The looming question was: would Helmand last after the Marines had withdrawn? Or had our efforts merely amounted to a momentary lapse in an unfinished civil war, or, worse, permanent Taliban rule? Garmser had progressed under the cover of 1,000 Marines and millions of dollars of assistance. Those Marines had endowed the central government with the authority that it had so sorely lacked since 2001. Whether peace would prevail or violence would return once US forces departed in many ways depended upon whether there was a determined, united government and a strong army and police that could hold the district's factions together. Alas, history has a way of repeating itself.

On 22 June 2011, President Obama announced that 10,000 US troops would depart Afghanistan by the end of 2011, followed by 23,000 in 2012. By 2014, Afghanistan would take the lead in security. That, however, did not mean that all US military forces would leave Afghanistan by then. The timeline for the withdrawal of the remaining 67,000 US troops was not set. President Obama promised to continue supporting the Afghan security forces without specifying how many men that would entail. Following the announcement, the Marine headquarters in Helmand informed us that the number of Marines in Garmser would be reduced before the end of the year, and that by 2014 only advisors and a handful of others would be left.

The announcement caused a bit of a panic within Garmser. It raised fears (and hopes) that the Taliban would soon return. The large number of people now working with the government feared what the future would bring. The smaller number who preferred the Taliban suddenly had reason to hold out for them. The district had been cleared for less than a year. In the minds of most of the people, the government had not been present long enough to prove itself. The Afghans did not catch the announcement's nuances. They did not understand that the bulk of US forces would remain in Afghanistan after 2012. Two village elders, whom I knew to be honest men who cared about their community, came 25 kilometers north from Mian Poshtay, solely to talk to me about the speech. They informed me that villages were holding shuras to decide what to do since the Americans were about to leave and the Taliban were about to return. 'We heard President Obama's speech,' the elders said. 'Without the Marines the situation will go backwards. All the people are worried. The people have great fear…The Taliban will oppress our women. There are thousands of Taliban in Pakistan. They can take Garmser in one month. The national army can do nothing. They have no equipment and no tanks.'[19] Ayub Omar came from Nawa to relay a similar message: 'Everyone is very worried about this. If you leave, the Taliban and the terrorists will think that they have won. Then they will attack America…the Taliban are telling people the Marines are leaving…Because of the announcement, the Taliban's morale has risen, the government's morale has fallen.'[20] District Governor Fahim was worried enough to lobby Governor Mangal and President Karzai to stop any Marines from leaving his district.

The crisis of confidence could be seen in polling. At a time when security, the police, and the army were all rated as stronger than ever before, the percentage of respondents who believed security would continue to improve fell from 68 percent in the April 2011 PRT survey to 42 percent in July 2011, right after Afghans in Garmser became aware of US withdrawal plans. The drop was mirrored throughout Helmand.[21] Additionally, Taliban stopped laying down arms and reconciling with the government. Over the next year, none would come in.[22] There was a danger that the change in perceptions could cause tribal leaders or the police to waver. Deputy police chief Baba, the old grey-beard who had joined the police as a communist way back in 1978, had warned me that 'if the Marines leave, everyone will desert the police. Elders will flee, as when the Russians left. Their strategy was a failure.'[23] A new atmosphere emerged in which many religious leaders, tribal leaders, and village elders reconsidered their alignment with the government. It was clear that, just as in 2006, a few might turn to the Taliban in the future. Ayub Omar observed: 'Elders are waiting. They want to see if the government can control the situation. If it cannot, they will go back to the Taliban.'[24] It was at this time that a strong, united Afghan government was most needed.

Many American officials argued that the impending US drawdown would spur cooperation, rallying Garmser's leaders together against the common Taliban threat. That did not happen. The tendency toward political competition was too strong. At the same time, our strategy changed. We no longer tried to enforce cooperation. We launched an aggressive police anti-corruption campaign that June. The worry was that police taxation and occasional abuse of the population would cause a backlash against the government.[25] I was still present (I left in July) and concurred with the overall effort, believing that corruption could be fought without damaging cooperation. I was wrong.

We publicly aired allegations of corruption (many unsubstantiated) and publicly pressured police chief Omar Jan to reform the force. While such openness was laudable in terms of good governance, public accountability, and our own Western system of justice, it was poison in Afghanistan's highly conspiratorial political atmosphere. Anyone who held a grudge against the police seized the opportunity to criticize. Masses of false reports, put forward by rivals of various police officers as well as the Taliban themselves, accompanied true reports. Under our spotlight, Omar Jan's political position weakened. Fahim recognized his vulnerability. With the old American demands for cooperation gone, Fahim had a green light. Trying to please the Marines, Omar Jan was actually reducing corruption within the police. An inspection team from the headquarters for all Marine forces in Helmand even rated the Garmser police as the best in the province. It was too late. In September, Fahim used his political leverage to convince provincial chief of police Angar to move Omar Jan to Nadi Ali, the district abutting Lashkar Gah. The transfer of a police chief is a natural event that any effective police force must endure; one hopes the decision is made carefully to avoid unnecessary friction. In this case, political competition caused Omar Jan's transfer to come at an inopportune moment with seemingly little consideration of how the loss of a strong leader could damage security. It would be yet another example of how competition weakened the government in its fight against the Taliban.

The feud between Fahim and provincial NDS director Nazr Ali carried on as well. Nazr Ali continued to intervene in Garmser political and business matters that Fahim considered his purview. Each politicked to defend their respective positions. As a result, Sultan Mohammed, the main tribal leader in Safar and Nazr Ali's ally, was never brought into the fold. Fahim was leary of working with a friend of Nazr Ali. And Nazr Ali would not pressure Sultan Mohammed to work with Fahim. Sultan Mohammed himself looked down on Fahim and would not help out on his own. Allegations that he worked for the Taliban swelled, unchecked by any real effort to compel him to work with the government. The Marines detained him in October. A year after its capture, Safar listed, lacking the tribal leadership of Mian Poshtay, Laki, or Kuchinay Darveshan.

Without Omar Jan, the intensity of police operations—the aggressive raids, night-time patrolling, undercover intelligence collection, and intensive personal vetting of patrolmen—fell off. His successor lacked his fighting spirit. The fact that Lieutenant Colonel Hezbollah had been re-assigned to Sangin and replaced with a less aggressive officer unfamiliar with Garmser made things worse. Garmser was now missing two of its battle-hardened leaders. The police and army became less active. Fahim and the tribal leaders found the police and army too willing to stay in their posts rather than patrol.[26] A few army and police officers were scared to stick their necks out because they believed that the United States was abandoning Afghanistan.[27] The community council widely criticized the officer leadership. Shah Jahan noted: 'There are plenty of soldiers and police, but the leadership is faulty.'[28] Skilled police commanders such as Ahmed Shah continued to capture insurgents, but the force's overall effectiveness dropped. Meanwhile, the Marines closed several of their own outposts. The net effect was that Taliban freedom of movement improved. Seeing this and mindful of America's impending withdrawal from Afghanistan, a handful of religious leaders and lesser village elders re-opened relations with the Taliban.

Worst of all, Omar Jan's iron grip over the individual police was gone. The police are at heart tribal Pashtuns and can switch sides, as can tribal and religious leaders. Omar Jan had tirelessly kept an eye on them and prevented those driven by tribal feud, incensed over a personal slight, or out for a fast buck from joining the Taliban. That oversight was sorely missed. One disgruntled policeman started conspiring with what was left of the Taliban.

In this environment, between September and November 2011, the Taliban were able to re-start an intimidation campaign. With decreased police vigilance and the help of the police turncoat, a handful of Taliban infiltrated into the canal zone. The overall number of attacks stayed low throughout the autumn (there were only four in September 2011) but were more lethal. In October, a Taliban hitman shot Sher Mohammed Khan, a friendly, if slightly senile, elder from Kuchinay Darveshan. He had been talking to Marines for years at the post near his village. When the post was closed and no police were put in its stead, the Taliban got to him.

On 6 November, the Taliban struck a much more damaging blow. They blew up an IED on the new police chief and Baba as they patrolled near Amir Agha. Both were killed. Old Baba had been a policeman since 1978 and had done as much as anyone to build a better government and police. The people of Garmser and the government shuddered. Fortunately, the attack did not cause elders to break and run for Lashkar Gah, as had occurred the previous summer. The police did not collapse and the overall number of attacks and Taliban active in the district remained very low. Most of the perpetrators, including the police turncoat, were captured. It was no small thing that Garmser's institutions and organizations could survive such a blow. That said, the attack reinforced the weakness of the government at exactly the time, with US withdrawal looming, when it needed to appear strong. Political infighting had damaged stability once again. Most discouraging, it had done so when large numbers of Marines were still in the district. Their presence, and that of the army and expanding police, doubtless prevented the situation from regressing too far.

In this time of uncertainty, leadership of the district fell more and more on District Governor Fahim's shoulders. Garmser ran through five different police chiefs in the year following Omar Jan's transfer, and Mir Hamza took a new job as deputy provincial director of NDS in Lashkar Gah. Fahim had learned a great deal since he had taken office. He recognized the importance of holding the tribal leaders together as one. He made a point of reaching out to them and preventing the alliance that had been forged from collapsing. They were brought regularly to shuras to encourage the people to work with the government. Fahim also took great care to dampen tribal feuds, and resolved a variety of small disagreements that could have turned into something larger.

Because of his tribal relationships, intelligence started flowing to Fahim. He often put himself in danger by going after insurgents. On one occasion, Abdullah Jan's veterans brought intelligence that a Taliban cell was operating across the river from Safar. Fahim went to the nearby army post with the new police chief and several police and asked the army post commander to go with him across the river. The army post commander refused. He said that doing so was not his job. He also told

Fahim not to go. Fahim then asked the new police chief to go with him. He too refused—another sign of how the standard of leadership within the police and army had dropped with the departure of Omar Jan and Hezbollah. So Fahim picked out Abdul Baqi (the wily Lakari policeman) and Ahmed Shah (commander of Abdullah Jan's veterans). They gladly went along. The small group captured six Taliban fighters, including the former Nadi Ali shadow district governor.[29]

Successes aside, Fahim found himself under political siege. The arrest of Sultan Mohammed of Safar back in October 2011 came to haunt him. Salay Mohammed (Sultan Mohammed's powerful brother) and provincial NDS director Nazr Ali (Fahim's long-standing rival) rallied important Noorzai leaders throughout Afghanistan to call for Sultan Mohammed's release and to criticize Fahim for the detention. The director of the Independent Directorate for Local Governance, who was also Noorzai, placed Fahim under scrutiny, forcing the young man to fight for his district governorship. Infighting threatened Garmser's last capable government leader.

War in Garmser

In May 2012, the last full Marine battalion to work in Garmser, the seventh, departed. The Marines drew down to 150 or so men (one under-strength company plus police and army advisors). They occupied two outposts: FOB Delhi in the district center and Combat Outpost Rankel next to Safar bazaar. Small detachments of advisors lived with the army and police in two or three other posts. The arrival of another Afghan army battalion (roughly 600 soldiers) in January 2012, together with the growth of the local police to 300, helped shore up Garmser's defenses. Over 1,800 Afghan forces, more than ever before, were stationed in the district. The police and local police ran 26 posts of their own; the army 29. Of the 75 total Marine, army, and police posts that had existed in May 2011, 57 were still up, a testament to the growth of the Afghan army and police.

Over the spring and summer, Taliban attacks escalated. The number of Taliban fighters went from 30 or so to as many as 100, armed with PK machine guns and AK-47 rifles. Naim had organized them in Pakistan and sent them to attack the army and especially the local police and official police. Cadres of fighters came to Garmser from Pakistan and set up in the small hard-to-reach villages on the western side of the river or near the eastern desert. Poor immigrant communities in these places were willing to let them in, or at least would not oppose them. The fighters then raided into the canal zone. The Afghans who worked with the government had to protect themselves; the Taliban were targeting them. Another village elder who had been friendly to the Marines was killed in Kuchinay Darveshan. Groups of four to eight fighters harassed police and army posts, especially in Safar and Laki. They usually came at night and shot at the posts with their machine guns and rifles. The police and army did their job, regularly driving off the skirmishers, usually inflicting casualties on them. Local police detachments even assaulted Taliban groups and chased them back across the river.

The insurgents did not regain much ground, at this time at least. The worst Taliban attack was the suicide bombing of the Lakari police post. Four Alizai police were killed and seven were injured. Shah Jahan's son was one of the wounded. The Alizai did not fold. The police carried on. The suicide bomber in this particular attack was a young local policeman planted by the Taliban. Naim and Mullah Omar were attempting a new tactic in which young men were sent to join the police or army and then killed their comrades—or their Marine partners.

Afghan police and soldiers shooting the British and Americans who worked with them had always been a problem in Afghanistan but it had never afflicted Garmser. These shootings had often occurred because of cultural clashes over honor or Islam. Now, Taliban started infiltrating the army and police with that goal in mind. The number of shootings increased in Afghanistan and threatened to undermine trust between the Afghans and the British and Americans. In August 2012, a young man working in the Garmser police headquarters shot four Marine advisers inside the compound and was then captured. Governor Mangal intervened immediately and relieved the police chief (the fourth since Omar Jan's transfer) and sent Ayub Omar back to Garmser (Fahim was fighting for his district governorship in Kabul). Mangal's decisive action helped prevent the tragic event from damaging trust between the Afghans and the Marines. The actions of a few disgruntled Afghans and Taliban operatives did not cause the hundreds of other police and soldiers to hate the Marines.

From what I heard from tribal leaders and others, the Taliban did not yet appear stronger than the government, and their violence upset people. Indeed, when an IED killed several children in Safar in April 2012, locals tracked down the single Taliban who had laid it and handed him over to the police—after hacking off his ears. A final round of community council elections drew a stunning 2,200 voters, nearly six times more than the previous round. Such events hardly suggested that the Taliban were about to win a quick victory. All summer long, throughout the district, the government and the tribal leaders kept fighting. No villages or posts fell.[30]

But what would happen as the Afghans had to survive month after month without the help of a full Marine battalion was unknown. The moral and physical attrition of combat might lead to defeat. And political infighting, the old scourge of Helmand, lived on. If the damage from police chief Omar Jan's removal was temporary, its cause was not. The tide of cooperation continued to ebb and flow; Afghan leaders were too often ready to fight against each other for political power rather than unite against the Taliban. Five hours' drive from Pakistan, Garmser's final test still lay ahead.

By the time the Marines drew down in May 2012, US forces had been in Garmser for four years. Step-by-step counterinsurgency had made substantial progress: attacks had been brought down, Afghan forces had stood up, and a capable district government had formed. A force of just one battalion (over several rotations) had accomplished this, without any real reinforcements—in many ways a model of what the tactical side of counterinsurgency should look like. After pre-empting the Taliban spring offensive, momentum in mid-2011 seemed unstoppable. The next year brought problems into focus: political feuding, the chance that local leaders might turn back to the Taliban, the mixed quality of Afghan leaders. It was unclear whether there would be enough strong government leaders to keep the tribes together or see the district through the years of hard fighting that might follow the American withdrawal. The counterinsurgency effort had not attained the fullest measure of success—the creation of a government that would definitely survive following American and British withdrawal. We had achieved a half-victory. To be sure, the troubles of late 2011 and 2012 did not signal that full-scale war would resume and the government would fall. Rather, those months signaled that the possibility still existed, casting a shadow on the four years of British and Marine counterinsurgency in Garmser.

I left Garmser in July 2011, before the difficulties of that autumn and the following year. Phill Horne, who had replaced Peter Chilvers as the

British stabilization advisor, took over the district support team following my departure. Chilvers had left Garmser in 2010, but returned to Helmand in 2011 to work in Sangin. Gail Long left Helmand for the United States shortly before me, in April 2011. The Marine battalion commanders with whom I had worked—Cabaniss, McDonough, Watson, and Reid—carried on their careers in the United States. It is too early to say who will go back to Afghanistan. In terms of the Afghans, Omar Jan had a very successful tenure in Nadi Ali. His exploits filled Afghan newspapers. Ayub Omar also gained a reputation for success. He became Mangal's fire brigade. After he fixed various problems in Nawa, Mangal sent him to Kajaki to help in the effort to push back the Taliban there, and then to Garmser, as I have mentioned. Back in Garmser, Fahim hung on past the summer of 2012, gaining experience that would serve him well in his future political career. Meanwhile, the tribal leaders watched over their land and villages. Wakil Manan shored up his power in Mian Poshtay. Khodirom and Roh Khan guided the Noorzai of Loya and Kuchinay Darveshan, ever mindful that their tribe had been the first Pashtuns to come to Garmser. Ghulam Rassoul, Shah Wali Khan, and Shah Jahan ran the great Alizai tribe out of Laki. Shah Jahan remained Garmser's foremost tribal leader, careful to stay in Fahim's shadow.

Away from Garmser, in Lashkar Gah, Abdullah Jan lived in exile, occasionally traveling up to Kabul. For a long time, I pressed him to take a new job in the government. Apparently Mangal asked him several times too, offering him the governorship of Sangin or Gereshk. Abdullah Jan steadfastly refused. To some extent, the riot affair had soured him. But more than that, he was not going to put his family at risk for a district other than Garmser. Garmser was his home, where he felt he belonged. Although he never said so, I think he still hoped to return as district governor. Any other job would be a disgrace, not worth his family's blood. I never asked him what he was going to do about Mullah Naim and Mullah Ismael. A Pashtun is patient. Only occasionally did he confide that his eye remained upon them. In February 2011, an IED had killed his beloved nephew, Sergeant Abdul Hadi, the Bartaka police post commander. He had been patrolling dangerous desert rat-lines with the Marines. Sitting at the long Pashtun wake for Abdul Hadi, Abdullah Jan had reassured me that the losses came with the territory: 'If you work for the government for twenty years, you will lose family members.'

The most frustrating thing about leaving Garmser in July 2011 and now watching it from afar is that I cannot be certain that the government will be able to stand on its own. We will not really know until more time has passed. Hopefully 2008 to 2012 set the stage. In spite of tactical setbacks, as of autumn 2012, the vast majority of tribal leaders were still united and willing to side with the government, as long as it appeared strong. Before I left, as I spoke to the Afghans about withdrawal, I saw that they took heart in the growing strength of their police and army. The perspective of veterans such as Abdullah Jan and Ghulam Rassoul was that Garmser could hold and the improvements could stick as long as US air power and artillery backed them up. Ghulam Rassoul's words gave me hope: 'If we have 1,000 Afghan National Army here and 600–700 police [with US artillery and air support], there will be no problem...the Taliban will not fear them and will attack us. [But] In the end, the army and police will be able to defeat the Taliban.'[31]

CONCLUSION

THE END OR THE INTERMISSION?

'When the curse of anarchy and lawlessness is replaced in this region by the blessings of peace and order; then Garmsel will once more become the seat of prosperity and plenty. But when can one hope to see such a revolution effected in this home of robbers and outlaws?'

1872 British expedition to Sistan[1]

By 2012, Garmser had undergone fifty years of upheaval, beginning with the digging of the canal system, continuing on to the jihad and then the Taliban regime, and finally ending with the brutal war years of the British and American intervention. Over the course of these years, Garmser's society, politics, and economy were transformed. Thousands of new immigrants came to the district. The government became communist and then dissolved altogether. Under the Taliban, Islam took on a political role never seen before that is still powerful today, even with the advent of Karzai's democratic government. Cultivation of wheat and cotton gave way to poppy, turning Garmser into a breadbasket of opium. With change came conflict, violence, and loss. The human cost of these years is unknown. A conservative estimate is that 2,500 Afghans were killed, but a figure as high as 20,000 is possible.[2] Thousands more were wounded. It is hard to find an Afghan who has not lost a father, brother, or son. Out of a population of 150,000 (92,000 in 1978), over 67,000 people fled to Pakistan or Iran at one time or another as refugees. At least 5,000 still reside in camps in those countries today.

Great Britain and the United States put forth a tremendous effort to fix Garmser, replete with professional governance programs, over $21 million in reconstruction projects, and over 1,000 new Afghan soldiers and police (costing around $40 million, including operating expenses). Roughly 7,000 different British soldiers and US Marines passed through the district between 2006 and 2012.[3] Their efforts witnessed marked success, as numbers show. Attacks fell from over 100 in July 2009 to fewer than 10 in November 2011. Over that same period, the number of police rose from 50 to 330, the number of civilian government officials from 3 to 17, and the number of students from 0 to over 5,000. These numbers merely illustrate what was obvious to the eye. By 2011, the Taliban were struggling in Garmser. A government official could travel unarmed from Hazar Joft to Benadar, a 70-kilometer distance formerly entirely under Taliban control. With a court, community council, and thriving school system, Garmser had not known such a capable government since the days of King Zahir Shah.

Nevertheless, the American and British effort fell short of total victory. When most of the Americans left in spring 2012, the ability of the government to keep out the Taliban, even with US financial and advisory support, was still in question. Important parts of society remained disaffected and government leaders betrayed a disturbing tendency to compete with one another, regardless of the damage done to efforts to keep out the Taliban. In sum, by driving back the Taliban and building up the government, the British and the Marines had put the government in a better position to survive than it had enjoyed in the past. What they had not done was create a situation in which the government was sure to win future battles against Taliban coming out of Pakistan. It was quite unclear if progress would be enduring or an intermission in a longer war. In that respect, success for the United States and Great Britain was incomplete.

United we stand, divided we fall

This book has tried to explain why conflict lasted so long in Garmser, specifically why conflict with the Taliban lasted so long, with no clear-cut victory for the Karzai government or the United States and Great Britain. The same question is often asked of Afghanistan as a whole. Many answers have been thrown about, such as the poor policies and abusiveness of Karzai's government, endless numbers of Taliban coming out of safe havens in Pakistan, and the recalcitrance of the Afghans themselves. In Garmser, three factors stand out: first, rifts within society and within the government, particularly the reluctance of Afghans opposed to the Taliban to ally together; second, Taliban safe havens in Pakistan; and third, the after-effects of the canal project.

Garmser's society was divided, as was its government. The religious leaders, immigrants, and different tribal leaders each held their own views and often a good deal of power and autonomy. Competition and infighting cursed them. The religious leaders and the immigrants, marginalized by the tribal leaders and later the government, leaned toward the Taliban. The tribal leaders, meanwhile, competed with these groups but also with each other. They were especially given to competition because there was no overarching hierarchy within a tribe, let alone between them, that might have enforced cooperation. They often failed to unite against the Taliban, a movement with which they shared few interests. Ideally, the Karzai government would have been strong enough to hold these disparate factions together. Like society, however, the government was structured in a way that hindered cooperation. It too had no strong centralized hierarchy. Consequently, government leaders tended to try to remove each other—the equivalent of tribal feuding within the government itself.

Much of the violence that followed the jihad can be traced to this competition and infighting. It is the reason why civil war broke out once the jihad ended—formerly united tribal leaders fought over the spoils of victory. It is the reason why the Taliban first captured the district in 1994—well-armed Garmser and Helmand tribal leaders would not organize a united front. It is the reason why the Taliban recaptured Garmser in 2006—tribal feuds dissolved the 700 tribal militia and border police that had been defending the district and allowed 500 Taliban to walk in. And it is one reason why a few Taliban could survive in Garmser as the Marines drew down in 2012—political infighting within the government removed some of the Taliban's toughest opponents. In each case, tribal and government leaders turned on one another. Against the Taliban, tribal and government leaders were like the Great Powers facing Napoleon: unable to form an alliance to defeat the common threat.

By comparison, the Taliban were cohesive. They did not feud among themselves like the tribal leaders or the Karzai government. A centralized hierarchy, all the Taliban working in Garmser answered to their district governor and he to their provincial governor. As a result, the Taliban were able to enforce a degree of order during their two regimes. It was not perfect. Land disputes were a headache for them too; tribal leaders were never really brought on board. Nevertheless, the Taliban were able to reduce internal competition to such a degree that it was not a direct threat to their rule. If not for outside intervention, both of Garmser's Taliban regimes probably would have ruled for many more years. True, as many have pointed out, their success was partly due to infamously harsh punishments, but that harshness never would have worked if they had been fighting with each other in the first place. Disciplined political organization mattered. In that regard, the Taliban regimes were models of how to govern Garmser. There was no reason why the Karzai government could not have emulated the Taliban's better practices and attained greater success itself.

The Taliban safe havens in Pakistan made Garmser's divisions especially lethal. Because of them, the Taliban could always attack Garmser. No matter how great their defeats—and they suffered many—Taliban cadres could return to Pakistan to rest and refit, and have another go during the following fighting season or the next. Without that sanctuary, there would not have been 500 well-armed and well-trained Taliban to attack Garmser in 2006 or a place for their tattered remnants to hide after the Marines and Afghan army captured Safar in August 2010. To face down the recurring threat, the Afghan government and the tribal leaders had to be united. Too often they were not.

The other factor, ironically, that fostered conflict within Garmser was the canal system, that great social and economic modernization project. The United States had funded the canal system to counter Soviet influence and spur economic growth. Instead, by introducing thousands of immigrants and by marking out wide swathes of newly irrigated yet unoccupied government land, the project laid the groundwork for decades of friction between immigrants, especially landless squatters, on one side, and the old landed tribes, and eventually the Karzai government, on the other. The divide became a well-spring of Taliban popular support. The immigrants and the Taliban naturally allied together, forming a bloc that would last through the Taliban's victories and defeats. Thus, the well-meaning US canal project was part of the reason why the Taliban could survive in Garmser. It is hard to find a better example of

CONCLUSION

Samuel Huntington's old thesis that economic modernization can lead to political disorder.[4]

What could have been done differently?

The divisions within society and state, the Pakistan safe havens, and land issues amount to a formidable battery of reasons why the Taliban were not defeated quickly in Garmser and remained a threat at the end of the US time there. Together, they reinforce the image of an ungovernable country and beg whether US intervention was misguided. In academic terms, they imply that conflict may have been 'over-determined,' meaning that so many factors were pushing Garmser toward violence that no other outcome was possible—no matter what the United States tried to do. Careful examination of Garmser's history reveals that this probably was not the case. There were several points when the United States or Great Britain could have changed the course of Garmser's history, points when Garmser's fate was far from determined, when different actions might have prevented further conflict. American and British strategy, therefore, must be one final reason for Garmser's long history of conflict and for American and British success there being incomplete.

The initial years of US involvement in Afghanistan, from 2002 to 2006, were a time of real opportunity in Garmser. Because the Taliban were weak, the United States had a chance to prevent them from regaining power at a lower cost of men and material than the later surge. Sadly, in Garmser, the United States went missing in action. Critics such as Ahmed Rashid have blamed America's inattention to Afghanistan after 2002 on the diversion of forces to Iraq. In Garmser, the opportunity was bigger than that; hundreds of US troops were not required. Three simpler actions could have made a difference. First, a few military and civilian advisors could have been sent to live in the district center and in Lashkar Gah in order to give the Afghan police a military edge and help stop political infighting from getting out of control. Second, the United States could have built an Afghan army larger than 70,000 soldiers. Doing so would have cost money but would have demanded few additional US forces (far more expensive per man than Afghan forces). If a 700-man Afghan army battalion with US advisors had been located in Garmser in 2005, the 2006 Taliban offensive would not have succeeded.

As it was, only 36,000 Afghan soldiers were in the field by the end of 2006, too late and far too few to handle the Taliban. Third, during the 2006 offensive itself, US and Allied leaders could have salvaged the situation, not just in Garmser but throughout southern Afghanistan, through innovative solutions such as drafting soldiers from northern Afghanistan and dispatching them immediately to Helmand and Kandahar or giving Karzai money to recruit Pashtun militias in the south. All these actions, all of which were perfectly feasible, suggest that for want of imagination the United States and its Allies lost Helmand and Kandahar in 2006, perhaps their worst defeat in a decade of war in Iraq and Afghanistan.

From 2008 on, US and Allied strategy in regard to Garmser generally improved. Still more could have been achieved if the strategy had focused on building a government able to bond Afghanistan's disparate groups together and mend their various fractures. Measures to contain rivalries and talk to the religious leaders, landless immigrants, and major tribal leaders were ad hoc. We lacked formal Afghan programs for religious outreach, land reform, or even bringing key tribal power-brokers together. Ayub Omar once commented to me: 'America has spent how much on reconstruction in Garmser? $20 million? How much did you spend on the mullahs? If you had spent a fraction of that sum on mullahs, we could have had a very great impact.'[5] Our attitude toward land reform was worse. We explicitly shunned any attempt at it, ignoring land's central role in the conflict. In spite of all the talk of addressing Afghan grievances, we refused to do anything official or pressure the Afghan government about the deepest one.

Of greater importance, we shied away from larger structural (and admittedly more intrusive) changes that might have reduced infighting within the government. The common refrain was to stay out of internal Afghan politics, for it was their business, not ours. Yet those politics were what really mattered. We should have established a hierarchical chain of command between governors, police chiefs, and other officials. This would not have required time-consuming constitutional change. The chain of command was not enshrined in the constitution. Control of all government activities and security forces in a province or region could have been delegated to a single governor or general, answering to Karzai. If given control over appointments and money, a governor or general could have forced government leaders to cooperate with each other. If resistance in Kabul proved too great, the model could have been applied selectively in just the critical provinces (or even districts) and still made a difference. In places such as Garmser, five hours from the Pakistan border, strong capable Afghan leaders, forced to cooperate with one another, were crucial. We should have been bolder.

Lastly, little was done to ensure that hardened, active, yet conciliatory district governors, NDS chiefs, army commanders, and police chiefs—people who could hold things together—worked in the district. The government system did not naturally select such leaders. Too often such leaders were taken out of Garmser, usually because of some feud. Too often inexperienced, rash, or complacent leaders were sent down. Appointments were not based on willingness to fight. They were based on political connections and bribes, which allowed weak leaders to hold important positions. Solving the problem required that the United States and Great Britain dig deeper into Afghan sovereignty, checking that strong leaders were going to the districts and preventing them from being removed. Too often we assisted whoever was sent down under the argument that we were building the government and had to respect its decisions. We should have linked our support and our projects to a leader's combat performance rather than unconditionally to his office. We should have clearly laid out that we wanted leaders who could fight, placing that above education or absence of corruption. We were often unwilling to do these things. But they were necessary, as American and British efforts to keep Governor Mangal himself in office, against the criticism of Karzai and Sher Mohammed Akhundzada, prove. Similar action on the district level would not have been easy and would have expended political leverage negotiating with Karzai, provincial governors, and ministers. It would have been a better use of resources, though, than efforts to fight corruption, create long-term economic growth, and professionalize government leadership through written examinations: efforts that could have no long-term benefit if the Afghan government lacked the leadership on the ground to survive American withdrawal.

So, prolonged conflict in Garmser should be attributed to deep social and political cleavages, Pakistani safe havens, and the after-effects of a great modernization scheme, but also to shortcomings in America's own strategy. Opportunities were missed, opportunities that existed not only in Garmser but all of Afghanistan. After a decade of war in Iraq and Afghanistan and major innovations in counterinsurgency, the idea that our own strategy still had flaws is hardly comforting. In fairness, quite a lot was achieved—but not all that might have been. Coming from one district, this criticism can only be just a start. It is beyond the scope of this book—and my own experience—to understand fully why mistakes occurred; why the United States acted so late to stop the Taliban resurgence in 2006; why, between 2008 and 2011, our strategy did not adapt better to divisions in Afghan government and society. Future historians, who can access the records of generals, ambassadors, and presidents, will have to answer such questions. From my vantage point, I can only say that opportunities existed on the ground.

What Garmser says about Afghanistan

Garmser is a small place. Its significance lies less in any strategic role it played than in what it tells us about the war in Afghanistan as a whole. For Americans, the debate revolves around whether the country was ungovernable—incurably prone to violence—as its history, or at least a cursory reading of it, suggests; in other words, whether the United States ever had a chance of making a difference there, whether its intervention was bound to be just another chapter in failed foreign adventures, in the footsteps of the British and Russians. By 2011, many Americans had come to see the Afghans as hopeless, unwilling to stand up for themselves and settle their own problems, unwilling to do anything but steal and fight among themselves. US soldiers were deemed too crude and undisciplined to handle the Afghans, especially after the Koran burnings of early 2012.[6] In this view, the whole US enterprise in Afghanistan was a decade-long waste of blood and treasure; a tragic, idealistic, and ultimately foolish attempt at nation-building; a second Vietnam.

Garmser does not fit this story. Challenges existed. Garmser's rifts were hard to understand and even harder to address. Yet Garmser was not incurably prone to violence. Not only did the Taliban themselves enforce a modicum of order but the Karzai government did so too, if of shorter duration and with greater difficulty. The period between 2001 and 2006 showed that peace was possible. The reasons why it did not blossom into something greater have as much to do with lapses in our own strategy as the inherent intractability of Afghans. The period between 2008 and 2012 showed the same thing. Even if Garmser falls in a few years, there is good reason to believe that defeat could have been avoided. The fact of the matter is that the United States and its allies made plenty of mistakes, often glaring strategic ones. The failure to seize upon large opportunities that were far from fleeting makes it impossible to argue that Garmser was doomed to failure. Other paths were open but not taken. The United States could make a meaningful difference, just as it could miss opportunities to set a better course.

Even less evidence backs the idea that the Afghans were recalcitrant and unwilling to stand up for their country. Without the work of Abdullah Jan and Ayub Omar, Fahim and Omar Jan, and many many more, government in Garmser would have been a hollow shell with few people standing behind it. Their sacrifices prove there was hope. That sacrifice can be seen in Mullah Shah Wali, who led Friday prayers week after week, in spite of wounds and intimidation. It can be seen in Ghulam Rassoul, who fought unflinchingly for seven months while his brother was being held in chains in Pakistan. And it can be seen in Abdullah Jan: fighting the Taliban for over fifteen years, he was thrice wounded and lost his last brother, his cousin, and his beloved nephew. The list does not end there. The Taliban could not get to Fahim, so they killed his cousin. Mir Hamza lost two of his brothers to the Taliban, along with several of his men. The Taliban shot community council member Atlas Khan; unfazed, when he returned from hospital, he sent one of his nephews to join the Afghan army and the other to join the police. These are not select cases but a body of evidence that there was an Afghanistan that wanted a better future. In spite of all the violence, they carried on, year after year, working to build some kind of order out of war. Their experience was not one of futility but of fortitude.

Nor were Americans too crude or undisciplined to handle Afghanistan. Misunderstandings were indeed a problem. Marines did not always speak to villagers respectfully. Marines and Afghan soldiers sometimes scuffled. Certain officers had difficulty getting along with Afghan leaders. A few wanted to reorder Afghan society in an American mold, often unaware of the intricacies and dangers of such an action. Special operations forces out of faraway bases launched night raids and upset the people. One poorly executed instance lit off the riots of January 2010. Worst of all, from time to time, Americans killed innocent Afghans by accident. That said, regardless of Taliban propaganda, no Americans or British damaged Korans or purposefully harmed civilians in Garmser. My overwhelming memory is of young officers such as Scott Cuomo tirelessly telling their men to respect the Afghans and

Islam. Mistakes that were made never caused Afghan commanders, officials, tribal leaders, or elders to ask the Marines to leave. When Marines did tragically die in the police headquarters, it was because of Taliban infiltration, not misbehavior or cultural disagreement. Misunderstandings cost us time. But they did not stop progress, and at the end of the day they are not what prevented a fuller victory in Garmser. The choices of policy-makers, generals, ambassadors, and political officers in FOB Delhi did that. The infantryman on the ground should not be the scapegoat for our decisions.

Garmser is not unique in all this. Nawa, Marjah, Nadi Ali, and Musa Qala experienced similar success, as did districts in Kandahar. By their account, Afghanistan's course could be changed, whatever the extent of problems with governance, corruption, and Pakistan. By their account, the United States and its Allies could intervene, establish a new government, and enforce a pause on decades of war. Of course, Garmser and the rest of these districts are just parts of Afghanistan. Other places, such as Kunar and Nuristan, could not shake the Taliban, in spite of great effort. In a few regions, serious differences may have divided America's military from the Afghan people. Above all, the national government in Kabul seemed unable to make good decisions and run the war on its own, failures which, if unaddressed, will inevitably dissolve the successes of Helmand and Kandahar. I do not mean to gloss over these issues. Glances of them were possible from Garmser. I cannot claim that the experience of Garmser disproves that America's intervention in Afghanistan as a whole was doomed to failure. Garmser merely casts doubt on the idea. Rather than deride Afghanistan as ungovernable, America might study its own decisions and mistakes. Intervention in Afghanistan was always going to face stiff odds, partly because of America's difficulties in understanding the country, but poor strategic choices closed off opportunities that existed. The Taliban might have been prevented from returning in 2006 or the government might have been toughened enough to survive with minimal foreign assistance after 2012. A better outcome might have been possible. The value of a few better decisions should not be dismissed.

What might have been impossible was to build an ideal state. The tension between our ideals and the imperfection of reality was quite visible in Garmser. It was apparent in how the democratic political system failed to produce good leaders; how efforts to combat corruption backfired and weakened the police; how poppy eradication marginalized the poorest parts of society; how governance programs and slowly-built Western-style police did not deal with the Taliban as effectively as a warlord tribal leader and a quickly recruited militia. The tension is best exemplified by the philosophical divide between those Americans (and British) who believed that only a good government able to win the hearts of the people could succeed and those who believed that we needed to settle for a hard-bitten government able to win a straight fight against the Taliban. Ideals were crashing into the realities of Afghanistan. Corruption, oppression, and some degree of brutality could not be quickly abolished, because, with Pakistan's tribal zone on its border, Afghanistan needed a government that could fight. Building an ideal government stole precious time from preparing to do so. Unless the United States was willing to leave tens of thousands of troops in Afghanistan for decades, there was never going to be time to create a good, clean government. In that sense, America's frustration with Afghanistan is deserved.

One last question remains: Was America's decade-long effort in Afghanistan worth it? Even though progress was possible, did the gains merit thousands of casualties and over $400 billion in expenses? US forces invaded Afghanistan in 2001 to stop al-Qaeda. They generally succeeded in that aim. Other than the handful of Arabs who fought as Taliban from 2006 to 2008, I found little to suggest that al-Qaeda was active in Garmser, as seemed to be the case throughout Afghanistan. By 2009, US experts widely agreed that few al-Qaeda were operating in the country. The point of the US presence had become to set up a government that could prevent al-Qaeda from ever returning. Many US policymakers looked upon this mission skeptically, especially after the death of Osama bin Laden. In Garmser, just about every Afghan believed that without US forces or strong Afghan army and police, the Taliban would come back; a few claimed that al-Qaeda would come with them. Still, it was an impossible, far-off thing to judge. Such a nebulous threat scarcely seemed commensurate with the investment of 100,000 troops. For those of us on the ground, I think two things probably mattered more. One was a deep distaste for the idea of defeat. To pull out at any time between 2008 and 2011 threatened to throw away everything we had fought so hard to achieve, right as the tide appeared to be turning. The other was that defeat would be the end of most of the Afghans who had fought beside us. I always knew that in hard, practical terms such things could not justify the cost of the war. But the Marines could not succeed on the ground if we were not ruthlessly determined to win. This was war after all; lives were at stake. Nor could we succeed if we did not care about the Afghans—genuinely, not as pawns in some great game. They had to put their lives on the line alongside ours. That is the difference between the soldier or diplomat on the ground and the policy-maker. Thinking objectively about strategy demands a degree of detachment that the individual on the ground must foreswear—at least if he is to do his job. Emotional commitment, with all its biases, is irreplaceable. Grand strategic calculations on costs and benefits are best left to far-off policy-makers.

What I think I can say is that Afghanistan surely will not be the last of America's interventions in messy wars in developing states—our history is too full of them to think otherwise. The same questions about why we are there and whether the conflict is unwinnable will re-emerge. Future conflicts will challenge our ideals in the same way. Democracy will be weak, corruption will be rife, and the host security forces will use tactics we do not always approve of. At home, opinion about the intervention will become contentious. Ambivalence over Afghanistan fits the mold of Vietnam and Iraq—long wars that did not clearly involve America's vital interests so that, when costs rose and victory appeared uncertain, the value of pressing on came into question. Garmser offers no answers as to whether such conflicts are worth it. It merely suggests they are likely to be troublesome, murky, messy, and grey.

LIST OF NAMES

Abdul Ahmed   Barakzai leader in Bartaka and elder brother of
                     Abdullah Jan.

Abdul Baqi   Lakari police and tribal militia commander.

Abdul Ghafar   Helmand provincial governor in 1994 and
Akhundzada   brother of Mohammed Nasim and Mohammed
                     Rassoul Akhundzada.

Abdul Hadi   police sergeant and Abdullah Jan's nephew.

Abdul Hadi Agha   Taliban mullah from Hazar Joft and Taliban
                     district governor of Garmser from 2006 to
                     2007.

Abdul Hakim,   mujahidin commander, religious scholar, and
Maulawi   tribal leader of the Taraki tribe; Taliban deputy
                     district governor of Garmser (1995–7) and
                     Taliban provincial governor of Uruzgan (1997–
                     2001).

Abdul Majan, Mullah mullah from the Taraki tribe, Taliban assistant
                     deputy district governor of Garmser (1995–7),
                     and Taliban deputy provincial governor of
                     Uruzgan (1997–2001).

Abdul Qayum   mujahidin commander and community coun-
                     cil member from 2009 to 2012.

Abdul Razik   Noorzai religious scholar from Loya Darveshan
                     who was the senior Taliban judge in Garmser
                     from 2006 to 2008.

Abdullah Jan	mujahidin commander, Barakzai tribal leader, and Garmser district governor.
Abdullah, Mullah	Taliban cadre leader from Kuchinay Darveshan.
Abdullah, Qari	Taliban cadre leader from Safar.
Abdur Rahman Jan	Noorzai warlord from Marjah.
Ahmed Shah	police sergeant and leader of Abdullah Jan's veteran police; Abdullah Jan's cousin.
Ahmed Shah Durrani	founder of the Afghan state and king from 1747 to 1773.
Ahmed Shah Massoud	famous Tajik mujahidin commander who held off both the Soviets and the Taliban in the Panjshir Valley in northern Afghanistan.
Allah Noor	Barakzai commander of the communist militia in Lashkar Gah.
Angar, Hakim	Helmand provincial chief of police from 2010 to 2012.
Atlas Khan	community council member from the Kharoti tribe from 2009 to 2012.
Aurang Khan	Noorzai mujahidin commander from Safar and uncle of Salay Mohammed.
Ayub Omar	Son of Said Omar and deputy district governor of Garmser from 2009 to 2011.
Azizullah, Mullah	Taliban cadre leader from Safar.
Baba (Mohammed Agha)	policeman since 1978 and Garmser deputy police chief from 2008 to 2011.
Baqi Khan	Noorzai mujahidin commander from Kuchinay Darveshan and brother of Roh Khan.
Baz Mohammed, Maulawi	religious scholar who taught many of Garmser's mullahs before and during the jihad.
Baz Mohammed, Wakil	tribal leader of the Kharoti tribe.
Dadullah Lang, Mullah	commander of Taliban forces in southern Afghanistan from 2006 to 2007.

276

Ghulam Rassoul — Alizai tribal leader from Laki and mujahidin commander.

Ghuli Khan — Garmser district chief of police from 2008 to 2010.

Habibullah, Doctor — Norozai pharmacist from Hazar Joft and chairman of the community council from 2009 to 2012.

Hezbollah, Lieutenant Colonel — commander of the Afghan National Army battalion in Garmser from 2009 to 2011.

Ismael Khan — Tajik mujahidin commander and warlord from Herat.

Ismael, Mullah — Taliban cadre leader who worked in Mian Poshtay.

Kabeer Khan — Garmser district chief of police from 2005 to 2006.

Karmal, Babrak — Communist President of Afghanistan from 1979 to 1986.

Karzai, Hamid — President of Afghanistan from 2001 to 2012 (term expected to end in 2014).

Khodirom — Noorzai tribal leader (khan) of Loya Darveshan.

Lala, Akhundzada — Taliban district governor of Garmser from 1995 to 1997.

Mangal, Ghulab — Helmand provincial governor from 2008 to 2012.

Matiullah, Mullah — Garmser shadow district governor in 2011.

Mir Atem — educated Barakzai and cousin of Abdullah Jan.

Mir Hamza — Garmser chief of NDS (intelligence) from 2006 to 2012.

Mir Hamza, Barakzai — Barakzai tribal leader from Bartaka and father of Abdullah Jan.

Mohammed Anwar Khan — tribal leader (khan) from southern Hazar Joft.

Mohammed Anwar Khan — tribal leader (khan) from Loya Darveshan.

Mohammed Daoud	President of Afghanistan from 1973 to 1978.
Mohammed Daoud, Engineer	Helmand provincial governor from 2005 to 2007.
Mohammed Fahim	Garmser district governor from 2010 to 2012.
Mohammed Hanif, Maulawi	religious scholar from Koshtay and judge for the mujahidin during the jihad.
Mohammed Nabi	one of Abdullah Jan's lieutenants and community council member 2009–12.
Mohammed Nadir	Alizai mujahidin commander from Lakari who competed with Yahya Khan for power in Garmser.
Mohammed Nasim Akhundzada	Alizai warlord from Musa Qala who was the most powerful mujahidin commander in Helmand during the jihad.
Mohammed Rassoul Akhundzada	brother of Mohammed Nasim Akhundzada and Helmand provincial governor from 1993 to 1994.
Mohammed Sakhi	Baluch and one of Abdullah Jan's policemen; he was later elected to the community council.
Mohammed Shah, Maulawi	Taliban judge for all Garmser during their first regime.
Mohammedullah, Maulawi	Taliban judge in Mian Poshtay from 2006 to 2009.
Naim Barech, Mullah	Tarin mullah from Laki, Taliban Minister of Aviation (1995–2001), and Taliban shadow governor of Helmand.
Najibullah, Dr Mohammed	President of Afghanistan from 1986 to 1992.
Nazr Ali Waheedi	Helmand NDS director from 2010 to 2012.
Noor Ali	Taliban enforcer in Lakari.
Obaid Rahman	Taliban district governor of Garmser from 2007 to 2008.
Omar Jan	Garmser district chief of police from 2010 to 2011.

Omar, Mullah Mohammed	leader of the Taliban.
Pakol	Taliban frontline commander in 2008.
Qadrat, Mullah	Taliban frontline commander in 2007.
Rabbani, Burnahideen	leader of *Jamiat Islami* and President of Afghanistan from 1992 to 1996.
Roh Khan	tribal leader of the Noorzai in Kuchinay Darveshan; descendant of the first Pashtun family to settle in Garmser.
Said Omar	mujahidin commander and tribal leader of the Omarzai sub-tribe of the Noorzai in Hazar Joft.
Saifrahman	lieutenant in the Afghan National Army.
Salam, Doctor	Alizai landowner and pharmacist in Lakari who helped the Taliban.
Salay Mohammed	mujahidin commander and tribal leader of the dominant Noorzai clan in Safar.
Selani, Haji	Taliban shadow governor of Garmser in 2009.
Shah Jahan	Alizai tribal leader from Laki and district governor of Khaneshin from 2005 to 2006.
Shah Wali Khan	mujahidin commander and tribal leader (khan) of the Alizai in Laki.
Shah Wali, Mullah	Garmser Friday prayer mullah from 2010 to 2012.
Sher Mohammed Akhundzada	Helmand provincial governor from 2002 to 2005; son of Mohammed Rassoul Akhundzada and nephew of Mohammed Nasim Akhundzada.
Sultan Mohammed	younger brother of Salay Mohammed from Safar.
Taraki, Noor Mohammed	Communist President of Afghanistan from 1978 to 1979.
Tooriali	Noorzai tribal leader from Kuchinay Darveshan and son of Roh Khan.
Wakil Manan	Sayid, communist militia commander, and tribal leader of Mian Poshtay.

Yahya Khan	Noorzai mujahidin commander from Nawa who had influence over most of the Noorzai in Garmser during the jihad.
Zahir Khan	Noorzai tribal leader from Benadar.
Zahir Shah	king of Afghanistan from 1933 to 1973.
Zahrif Shah	brother of Ghulam Rassoul who was imprisoned by the Taliban in 2010.
Zalmay	Mullah Ismael's deputy.

LIST OF TRIBES AND POLITICAL ENTITIES

Alikozai   Pashtun tribe of the Durrani confederation that immigrated in very small numbers to Garmser in the 1970s.

Alizai   large Pashtun tribe in Garmser that is part of the Durrani confederation.

Andar   Pashtun tribe of the Ghilzai tribal confederation that immigrated to Garmser in the 1970s.

Baluch   large non-Pashtun ethnic group that resides in the deserts south of Garmser and in the Pakistani province of Baluchistan and the Sistan region of Iran.

Barakzai   Pashtun tribe of the Durrani confederation whose members dominated the Afghan government and were kings during most of the nineteenth and twentieth centuries.

Durrani   confederation of Pashtun tribes that has traditionally held positions of power in Afghanistan; the Noorzai, Alizai, Barakzai, and Popalzai are all Durrani.

Ghaznavid   empire that ruled Afghanistan from 961 to 1186.

Ghilzai   large Pashtun tribal confederation that includes the Andar, Kharoti, and Taraki tribes. The Ghilzai tribes are traditional rivals of the Durrani tribes. Key communist and Taliban leaders were Ghilzai.

Harakat Inqilab Islami   Islamic political party that was connected to Mohammed Nasim Akhundzada. It was one of the major parties in Helmand during the jihad.

Hazara	Afghan non-Pashtun ethnic group that are descendants of the Mongols and live in central Afghanistan. Several Hazara families were given land near Lakari and immigrated to Garmser in the 1970s.
Hezb Islami	Islamic political party led by Gulbuddin Hekmatyar. Mohammed Nadir and Yahya Khan were its leading representatives in Garmser.
Jamiat Islami	Islamic political party led by Burnahideen Rabbani. Ahmed Shah Massoud was its most famous member. Abdullah Jan was part of the *Jamiat Islami*.
Kakar	a poorer Pashtun tribe from south-eastern Afghanistan near the Pakistani border. Small groups immigrated to Garmser in the 1970s.
Kharoti	a Pashtun tribe from the Ghilzai confederation. Nomads from the Kharoti immigrated to Garmser in the 1970s and were given land by the government.
Noorzai	Pashtun tribe that is the largest in Garmser and is part of the Durrani confederation.
Omarzai	Pashtun sub-tribe of the Noorzai that resides in Hazar Joft (specifically Kharako) and Benadar.
Popalzai	Pashtun tribe of the Durrani confederation. Both Ahmed Shah Durrani and Hamid Karzai were Popalzai.
Sayid	Afghan tribe that claims descent from Arabs who came to Afghanistan in the seventh and eighth centuries. They speak Pashto and are often considered Pashtuns.
Tajik	non-Pashtun ethnic group from northern Afghanistan. Several Tajik families were given land and immigrated to Garmser in the 1970s.
Taraki	Pashtun tribe of the Ghilzai confederation that were nomadic and immigrated to Garmser in the late 1970s. They were a poor tribe that lived on dry government land near the eastern desert.
Tarin	a poorer and nomadic Pashtun tribe from south-east Afghanistan, near the border with Pakistan.
Uzbek	non-Pashtun ethnic group from northern Afghanistan. Several Uzbek families were given land and immigrated to Garmser in the 1970s.

GLOSSARY OF TERMS

akhundzada	a family that comes from a religious background.
arbekai	tribal militia.
Deobandi	a school of Islamic thought taught in India.
dshka	a Russian-made heavy machine gun.
hadith	sayings or deeds of the Prophet Mohammed.
huqooq	an official who could mediate civil disputes.
IDLG	Independent Directorate of Local Governance.
jerib	an Afghan land unit equal to about one-fifth of a hectare.
jirga	a meeting of a group of elders, mullahs, or the general community. It is synonymous with shura.
khan	a landowner and tribal leader with influence over several villages.
Koran	the book of Allah's revelations to the Prophet Mohammed.
madrasa	religious school.
maulawi	a religious scholar with formal training.
mujahidin	holy warrior.
mullah	village religious leader.
naqilen	immigrants who were given land by the government. They were considered separate from immigrants who leased or lived on government land illegally. Most of the naqilen arrived in the 1970s.
Pashtunwali	the Pashtun tribal code.
PRT	provincial reconstruction team.
qazi	judge.

GLOSSARY OF TERMS

sangar	fighting position, makeshift bunker.
shari'a	religious law.
shura	a meeting of a group of elders, mullahs, or the general community. It is synonymous with jirga.
ulema	the community of religious leaders.
USAID	United States Agency for International Development.
wakil	the tribal leader of an immigrant tribe in Garmser or a member of a provincial council or the national parliament.
zerkat	religious alms, usually 10 percent of the harvest.

NOTES

PREFACE: SMALL PLACES

1. William Slim, *Unofficial History* (London: Cassell, 1959), 120.
2. Jeffrey Race, *War Comes to Long An: Revolutionary Conflict in a Vietnamese Province* (Berkeley: University of California Press, 1972).
3. Henry Kissinger, *Diplomacy* (New York: Simon & Schuster, 1995), 22–3.
4. See, for example, see Felix Gilbert, *To the Farewell Address* (Princeton: Princeton University Press, 1961).
5. Sarah Chayes, '"Lower your sights" is the wrong vision for Afghanistan,' *Los Angeles Times*, 27 March 2009.
6. *The US Army/Marine Corps Counterinsurgency Field Manual* (Chicago: University of Chicago, 2007), 37.
7. Ibid., xxxiii, 39.
8. icasualties.org, accessed 18 August 2009.
9. ABC-*Washington Post* poll, 6 June 2011.
10. 'The Unwinnable War,' *Time*, vol. 178, no. 16 (24 October 2011).
11. David Edwards, *Heroes of the Age: Moral Fault Lines on the Afghan Frontier* (Berkeley: University of California Press, 1996), 3.
12. Thomas Barfield, *Afghanistan: A Cultural and Political History* (Princeton: Princeton University Press, 2010), 337.
13. Ahmed Rashid, 'How Obama Lost Karzai,' *Foreign Policy*, no. 185 (March/April 2011). Robert Blackwill, 'Plan B in Afghanistan,' *Foreign Affairs*, vol. 90, no. 1 (January/February 2011).
14. Robert Blackwill, 'Plan B in Afghanistan,' *Foreign Affairs*.
15. Ahmed Rashid, 'The Way Out of Afghanistan,' *New York Review of Books*, 13 January 2011.
16. Lydia Saad, 'Americans Give Record-High Ratings to Several US Allies,' www.gallup.com, 16 February 2012.

17. Bing West, *The Wrong War* (New York: Random House, 2011), 250.

18. For an argument along these lines, see Rajiv Chandrasekaran, *Little America: The War Within the War for Afghanistan* (New York: Knopf, 2012), 329–32.

1. GRAND PLANS

1. Discussion with Mahboob Khan, Laki village elder, Garmser police head-quarters, 4 December 2010.

2. The first Arab raid into southern Afghanistan was against Garmser and, for seventy years, Garmser was the front line between invading Arab armies and pre-Islamic Afghans trying to defend their land against the Arabs. Abdul Hai Habibi, *De Afghanistan Land Tarikh* (Peshawar: Danish Khperndoyah Tolenah, 2003), 99, 105–8.

3. The Omarzai were originally Popalzai. They settled in Hazar Joft and Bena-der between 1820 and 1830 when Dost Mohammed, from the Barakzai tribe, overthrew Ahmed Shah's Popalzai dynasty and became king. In order to hide from any tribal retribution, the Omarzai joined the Noorzai tribe. The original Noorzai clan that settled in Darveshan are the Ghorai. Dis-cussion with Tooriali, tribal leader from Kuchinay Darveshan, Garmser dis-trict center, 4 July 2010. Tooriali is the son of Haji Roh Khan, the leader of the first Noorzai clan to have settled in the district. See also Christine Noelle, *State and Tribe in Nineteenth-Century Afghanistan: The Reign of Amir Dost Mohammed Khan (1826–1863)* (London: Routledge, 1997), 233.

4. Henry Walter Bellew, *Record of the March of the Mission to Seistan under the Command of F. R. Pollock* (Calcutta: Foreign Department Press, 1873), 44.

5. *Historical and Political Gazetteer of Afghanistan: Farah and Southwestern Afghanistan*, vol. 2, ed. Ludwig Adamec (Austria: Akademische Druck-u. Verlagsanstalt Graz, 1973), 85. Thomas Barfield, *Afghanistan: A Cultural and Political History* (Princeton: Princeton University Press, 2010), 98.

6. For the sake of simplicity, land will be referred to in hectares henceforth.

7. Cynthia Clapp-Wincek, 'The Helmand Valley Project in Afghanistan,' AID Evaluation Special Study no. 18, US Agency for International Develop-ment, December 1983, 17.

8. Nick Cullather, 'Damming Afghanistan: Modernization in a Buffer State,' *Journal of American History*, vol. 89, no. 2 (September 2002), 1, 10.

9. Richard Scott, 'Tribal and Ethnic Groups in the Helmand Valley,' Occa-sional Paper no. 21 (New York: Asia Society, 1980), 24.

10. *Historical and Political Gazetteer of Afghanistan: Farah and Southwestern Afghanistan*, vol. 2, ed. Ludwig Adamec (Austria: Akademische Druck-u. Verlagsanstalt Graz, 1973), 107.

11. Discussion with Tooriali, COP Koshtay, 10 January 2010. Discussion with Qari Dad Mohammed, religious scholar, Amir Agha shrine, 14 October 2009.

12. Abdul Hai Habibi, *De Afghanistan Land Tarikh*, 163–4, 168.

13. Cynthia Clapp-Wincek, 'The Helmand Valley Project in Afghanistan,' AID Evaluation Special Study no. 18, US Agency for International Development, December 1983, 11.

14. Discussion with Mohammed Anwar Khan, Garmser district center, 13 January 2011. Haji Mohammed Anwar Khan was a 65-year-old Noorzai tribal leader from Loya Darveshan.

15. Abdul Latif Talibi, *Pashtunee Qabilay* (Quetta: Mazhbi Kitabkhana, 2004), 132.

16. Discussion with Abdul Qayum, police headquarters, 6 March 2011. Abdul Qayum was an elder from Hazar Joft who had been a mujahidin commander.

17. Olivier Roy, *Islam and Resistance in Afghanistan* (Cambridge: Cambridge University Press, 1990), 12.

18. Discussion with Tooriali, Haji Roh Khan Kalay, 4 May 2011.

19. The governor of Helmand was also director of the Helmand Valley River Project. He decided where all work would occur.

20. There were also malangs, who watched the shrines; and pirs, who taught Sufism. For the sake of simplicity, I do not deal with their roles.

21. Abdur Rahman Zamani, *De Ghazi Mir Zaman Khan Wndah* (Kabul: Haji Zaman Zamani, 2010), 63–5.

22. Discussion with Mohammed Anwar Khan, FOB Delhi, 5 January 2011.

23. Richard Scott, 'Tribal and Ethnic Groups in the Helmand Valley,' 24.

24. Ibid., 24.

25. 'MSF Exploratory Mission in Helmand,' Médecins Sans Frontières Report, February 1989, 9–11 (http://scottshelmandvalleyarchives.org/docs/hea-89–01.pdf, accessed 9 March 2011). This report has Landay and all of Bagat within Garmser. I excluded these figures because they are not considered part of Garmser today. See also Abdul Latif Talibi, *Pashtunee Qabilay* (Quetta: Mazhbi Kitabkhana, 2004), 78.

2. THE JIHAD

1. Olivier Roy, *Islam and Resistance in Afghanistan* (Cambridge: Cambridge University Press, 2001), 84.

2. Discussion with Mohammed Agha, Garmser district center, 1 November 2010.

3. Discussion with Wakil Manan, Garmser district center, 27 January 2011.

4. Discussion with Sakhi Jan, servant, Garmser district center, 1 February 2011.

5. Discussion with Mohammed Agha, Garmser police station, 1 November 2010.

6. The first new district governor was Abdul Hakim. He was followed by Sultan Mohammed, the brother of Khano, who would later become one of the three most powerful communist leaders in Helmand. He and his brother were Noorzai. There is a popular story that Sultan Mohammed resolved disputes by throwing a stone and basing his decision on whether it landed on the right or left side of the room.

7. In Garmser, the immigrants that came after the fall of Daoud were not known as naqilen. The term was reserved for the original immigrants. The old landed elite respected their right to live in Garmser. New immigrants that came later were not so respected. For the sake of simplicity, I will refer to them all as immigrants.

8. Discussion with Mohammed Anwar Khan, FOB Delhi, 5 January 2011.

9. Said Omar was jailed for fourteen months and released under Amin, Taraki's successor.

10. Discussion with Ayub Omar, son of Said Omar, Mian Poshtay, 28 December 2010.

11. Interview with Abdul Qayum, a mujahidin commander from Hazar Joft, Garmser district center, 22 November 2010.

12. Discussion with Shah Wali Khan, Garmser district center, 16 January 2011. Discussion with Haji Mullah Ismael, FOB Delhi, 14 February 2011.

13. Discussion with Shah Wali Khan, Garmser district center, 16 January 2011.

14. Under Stor Jan, a communist from Darveshan.

15. Discussion with Haji Khodirom, mujahidin cadre leader from Loya Darveshan, Garmser district center, 31 October 2010.

16. Discussion with Khudai Nazar, Said Omar's logistics officer, Garmser district center, 17 November 2010.

17. Discussion with Mohammed Agha, police headquarters, 19 April 2011.

18. Discussion with Shah Wali Khan, Garmser district center, 16 January 2011.

19. Discussion with Khodirom, Loya Darveshan tribal leader and former mujahidin commander, Garmser district center, 31 October 2010.

20. Discussion with Shah Wali Khan, Garmser district center, 6 January 2011. 'MSF Exploratory Mission in Helmand,' Médecins Sans Frontières Report, February 1989, 21 (http://scottshelmandvalleyarchives.org/docs/hea-89–01.pdf, accessed 9 March 2011).

21. Interview with Abdul Qayum, Garmser district center, 22 November 2010.

22. Discussion with Shah Wali Khan, Garmser district center, 6 January 2011.

23. Two main routes—the Choto and Karwanra roads—were used. Discussion

with Khudai Nazar, Said Omar's logistics officer, Garmser district center, 17 November 2010.

24. 'MSF Exploratory Mission in Helmand,' 21.

25. Antonio Giustozzi, *Empires of Mud: War and Warlords in Afghanistan* (New York: Columbia University Press, 2009), 51.

26. Discussion with Tooriali, COP Koshtay, 10 January 2010.

27. Discussion with Abdul Qayum, Garmser district center, 1 February 2011.

28. UNHCR Garmser District Profile, 2002.

29. Discussion with Abdullah Jan, Garmser district center, 8 October 2009.

30. Interview with Abdul Qayum, Garmser district center, 22 November 2010.

31. 'MSF Exploratory Mission in Helmand,' 15.

32. Discussion with Mohammed Zahir, Lakari village elder and former mujahidin fighter, FOB Delhi, 1 November 2010. For a discussion of Soviet sweeping tactics see *The Bear Went Over the Mountain: Soviet Combat Tactics in Afghanistan*, ed. Lester Grau (Washington, DC: National Defense University Press, 1996), 24–6.

33. Discussion with Mohammed Agha, police headquarters, 19 April 2011.

34. Garmser Proper Orientation, 24th Marine Expeditionary Unit paper, 10 July 2008.

35. 'MSF Exploratory Mission in Helmand,' 9–11.

36. Ibid.

37. Ibid., 36.

38. 'Agriculture in the Middle Helmand River Valley,' Mercy Corps International, August 1991, 15. Richard Scott, 'Tribal and Ethnic Groups in the Helmand Valley,' Occasional Paper no. 21 (New York: Asia Society, 1980), 24.

39. Garmser did not have the Kabul-educated Islamic intellectuals (to be differentiated from the traditional madrasa-trained scholars) of Jalalabad, Panjshir, Kunar, and many other places in Afghanistan.

40. Maulawi Mohammed Agha, the religious scholar from Darveshan, for example, fled to Pakistan and eventually died there.

41. Discussion with Mohammed Anwar Khan, FOB Delhi, 5 January 2011.

42. Discussion with Maulawi Abdullah Jan, district center, 17 January 2011.

43. Discussion with Haji Mullah Ismael, Koshtay tribal leader (not the Taliban cadre leader), FOB Delhi, 14 February 2011.

44. Discussion with Mohammed Emir, brother of Mohammed Nadir, Garmser district center, 23 February 2011.

45. Christine Noelle, *State and Tribe in Nineteenth-Century Afghanistan: The Reign of Amir Dost Mohammed Khan (1826—1863)* (London: Routledge, 1997), 11, 235, 243. Henry Walter Bellew, *From the Indus to the Tigris: A*

Narrative of a Journey through the Countries of Balochistan, Afghanistan, Khorassan and Iran, in 1872 (London: Trubner & Co, 1874), 171–2.

46. A year after the Soviets recaptured the district center, the mujahidin conducted a major operation—at least by their standards—to its north. The mujahidin target was a canal crossing north of the district center. Its capture would give them room to maneuver against the district center. As many as fifty of their best men went. Unfortunately, their secrecy left something to be desired. The police found out about the operation and ambushed the mujahidin as they formed up on the eastern side of the main canal. In the large gunbattle that ensued, the mujahidin did not fare well. Among the dead were three important leaders: the two sons of Mir Hamza, the Barakzai khan of Bartaka (Abdullah Samed and Obaidullah), and the uncle of Mohammed Nadir, the Alizai khan of Lakari.

47. Discussion with Ahmed Shah, Abdullah Jan's cousin, Safar, 31 December 2010. Discussion with Abdul Qayum, FOB Delhi, 3 January 2011.

48. Discussion with Mohammed Nabi, one of Abdullah Jan's fighters, Garmser district center, 22 January 2011.

49. Discussion with Haji Mullah Ismael, village elder from Koshtay, FOB Delhi, 14 February 2011.

50. Discussion with Abdul Ghafour, one of Abdullah Jan's fighters, Garmser district center, 10 March 2011.

51. Henry Walter Bellew, *From The Indus to the Tigris*, 24, 102.

52. Mike Martin, *A Brief History of Helmand* (Warminster, UK: Afghan COIN Center, August 2011), 38.

53. Discussion with Mahboob Khan, COP Koshtay, 23 April 2011.

54. Discussion with Mohammed Zahir, FOB Delhi, 1 November 2010. Discussion with Mohammed Nadir, COP Sharp, 5 May 2010.

55. A spetznaz battalion held onto Kajaki and its dam until October 1988.

56. Discussion with Ahmed Shah, Garmser district center 31 January 2011.

57. Discussion with Abdul Qayum, Garmser district center, 1 February 2011. Discussion with Shah Wali Khan and Ghulam Rassoul, Garmser district center, 29 February 2011.

3. CIVIL WAR

1. Randall Olson, *Speaking Afghan Pashto* (Peshawar: Interlit Foundation, 2007), 208.

2. Discussion with Mohammed Nabi, Garmser district center, 22 January 2011.

3. Discussion with Khodirom, Garmser district center, 31 October 2010.

4. Discussion with Abdul Qayum, Garmser district center, 1 February 2011.

5. Sher Zeman, who commanded Yahya's frontline forces, operated out of a large castle-like home on the frontline.

6. Discussion with Mohammed Nabi, Garmser district center, 22 January 2011.

7. Discussion with Abdul Qayum, FOB Delhi, 3 January 2011.

8. The dominant clan was the Khanozai, led by Salay Mohammed. The family feared the aspirations of Nasim Akhundzada, and therefore had sided with Yahya Khan. The other clan was the Ahmed Khanozai, led by Mohammed Ikhlas. They had fought alongside Aurang Khan and Salay Mohammed in the jihad. Discussion with Obaidullah Khan, Lashkar Gah PRT, 6 October 2010.

9. 'MSF Exploratory Mission in Helmand,' Médecins Sans Frontières Report, February 1989, 16 (http://scottshelmandvalleyarchives.org/docs/hea-89–01.pdf, accessed 9 March 2011).

10. Discussion with Ahmed Shah, Safar, 31 December 2010. Discussion with Khodirom, Garmser district center, 31 October 2010.

11. Maulawi Khan Mohammed, an Alizai from Kajaki and one of Mohammed Nasim's supporters, briefly became district governor but before long was sent to Musa Qala.

12. Discussion with Abdul Qayum, FOB Delhi, 3 January 2011.

13. Silt had accumulated in the canals and sluice gates had ceased working. Soviet bombing had damaged many of them. The sluice gates at the main canal intake were inoperable, which meant that water in Garmser's main canal could no longer be regulated. The river had washed out the Hazar Joft bridge, the only bridge between the populated portion of Garmser, as well as the district center, and the western side of the river, where the rest of central Helmand's population lies. Fortunately for the communists, the bridge had washed out after their retreat to Lashkar Gah. 'Agriculture in the Middle Helmand River Valley,' Mercy Corps International, August 1991, 8–10. 'MSF Exploratory Mission in Helmand,' 32.

14. His brother Khan Noor shared command with him.

15. Discussion with Abdul Qayum, FOB Delhi, 3 January 2011. Antonio Giustozzi, *Empires of Mud: War and Warlords in Afghanistan* (New York: Columbia University Press, 2009), 51.

16. Discussion with Abdullah Jan, Lashkar Gah PRT, 3 February 2011.

17. In 1992, Rassoul tried to dislodge Allah Noor from Lashkar Gah. At first, Allah Noor (with the 20 men from Abdullah Jan) held Nasim off. Then, in 1993, Ismael Khan forged an alliance with Rassoul, defeated Allah Noor, and captured Lashkar Gah. Discussion with Abdullah Jan, Lashkar Gah PRT, 3 February 2011.

18. '1995 Comparative Survey, Helmand Province, Afghanistan,' Afghanistan Drug Control and Rehabilitation Programme, November 1995 (http://scottshelmandvalleyarchives.org/docs/sas-95–04.pdf, accessed 9 March 2011), 9.

19. 'Agriculture in the Middle Helmand River Valley,' 15. Richard Scott, 'Tribal and Ethnic Groups in the Helmand Valley,' Occasional Paper no. 21 (New York: Asia Society, 1980), 24.

4. THE TALIBAN REGIME

1. Jens Enevoldsen, *Sound the bells, O moon, arise and shine! A collection of Pashto proverbs and tappas* (Peshawar: InterLit Foundation, 2000), 17.
2. Abdul Salam Zaeef, *My Life with the Taliban*, eds Alex Strick van Linschoten and Felix Kuehn (New York: Columbia University Press, 2010), 65.
3. The Durrani tribal confederation included the Barakzai, Popalzai, Alizai, and Noorzai tribes. The Ghilzai tribal confederation included the Taraki, Andar, and Kharoti.
4. Ahmed Rashid, *Taliban: Militant Islam, Oil and Fundamentalism in Central Asia* (New Haven: Yale University Press, 2001), 22–30.
5. Discussion with Abdullah Jan, Lashkar Gah PRT, 3 February 2011.
6. Discussion with Abdul Qayum, police headquarters, 6 March 2011.
7. Discussion with Abdullah Jan, Lashkar Gah PRT, 3 February 2011. Discussion with Abdul Qayum, police headquarters, 6 March 2011.
8. Discussion with Abdullah Jan, Lashkar Gah PRT, 3 February 2011.
9. Discussion with Abdullah Jan, Lashkar Gah PRT, 6 May 2012.
10. Discussion with Mohammed Nabi, Garmser district center, 22 January 2011.
11. Richard Scott, 'Final Report, Helmand Irrigation Rehabilitation, 1 December 1998–31 March 1999,' 1999 (http://scottshelmandvalleyarchives.org/docs/fpr-98-01.pdf).
12. Mullah Ibrahim, a Safi naqilen immigrant from Garmser, was actually the first Taliban district governor. He only lasted a few months. Akhundzada Lala was followed by Mohammed Lal, who ruled for eighteen months, and then Qari Mohammed Nabi, who ruled for two years. The latter treated the elders very badly.
13. Discussion with Mohammed Nabi, FOB Delhi, 1 March 2011.
14. Abdul Latif Talibi, *Pashtunee Qabilay* (Quetta: Mazhbi Kitabkhana, 2004), 42–51.
15. Discussion with Shah Jahan, Laki, 22 October 2010.
16. Discussion with Hazrat Ali, Garmser district center, 12 July 2011.
17. Discussion with Ayub Omar, son of Said Omar, Washington, DC, 9 April 2012.
18. Interview by Patricio Asfura-Heim with Maulawi Mohuddin Baluch, Kabul, 30 April 2012.
19. Discussion with Shah Jahan, Lashkar Gah PRT, 5 May 2012.

20. Ibid.

21. Discussion with Khodirom, Garmser district center, 25 September 2010.

22. Discussion with Ayub Omar, Garmser district center, 2 November 2010.

23. Discussion with Mamoor Mohammed Abdullah, Kuchinay Darveshan, 12 April 2010.

24. Discussion with Kharoti Elders, FOB Delhi, 27 November 2009.

25. Discussion with Shah Jahan, Laki, 22 October 2010.

26. Discussion with Dr Salam, Garmser district center, 27 December 2010.

27. The Taliban made an attempt to ban it in Helmand in 1995 but quickly reversed their decision. Alex van Linschoten and Felix Kuehn, *An Enemy We Created* (London: Hurst, 2011), 117.

28. Discussion with Khodirom, Garmser district center, 31 October 2010.

29. Discussion with Shah Wali Khan, Garmser district center, 29 January 2011.

30. Discussion with Maulawi Salam, Garmser district center, 20 January 2011.

31. Discussion with Professor Sayid, religious professor at Kabul University, ISAF headquarters, 1 May 2012.

32. Discussion with Shah Jahan, PRT Lashkar Gah, 5 May 2012. Discussion with Ayub Omar, PRT Lashkar Gah, 6 May 2012.

33. Discussion with Haji Ismael (not the Taliban commander), FOB Delhi, 14 February 2011.

34. Discussion with Abdul Qayum, Police headquarters, 6 March 2011.

35. Discussion with Haji Ismael, FOB Delhi, 14 February 2011.

36. Discussion with Maulawi Abdullah Jan, 18 January 2011.

37. Discussion with Haji Abdul Rashid, Mian Poshtay, 22 January 2010.

38. Discussion with Ali Shah Khan, Noorzai village elder, Garmser district center, 3 March 2011.

39. Discussion with Abdul Rashid, Mian Poshtay, 22 January 2010.

40. Discussion with Mohammed Agha, police headquarters, 19 April 2011.

41. Ibid.

42. Discussion with Richard Scott, telephone, 14 October 2011.

43. Discussion with Tooriali, Kuchinay Darveshan, 22 January 2011.

44. Discussion with Abdul Qayum, police headquarters, 6 March 2011. Discussion with Mohammed Agha, police headquarters, 19 April 2011.

5. VICTORY INTO DEFEAT

1. A Marine battalion did establish a base at the Saudi-constructed airfield on the border with Kandahar in the desert. There were a few skirmishes but nothing that affected the people of Garmser. Those Marines were focused upon Kandahar.

2. Discussion with Ayub Omar, Mian Poshtay, 28 December 2010.

3. His mentor, Maulawi Abdul Hakim, with Abdullah Jan's acquiescence, fled to Pakistan from elsewhere in Afghanistan. Abdul Hakim later became a member of the Quetta shura, which governed all Taliban affairs.

4. Conversation with Abdullah Jan, Lashkar Gah PRT, 6 May 2012.

5. Discussion with Ayub Omar, road from Lakari to Hazar Joft, January 2011.

6. Discussion with Lieutenant Soor Gul, Garmser deputy police chief, Nawa, 11 February 2011.

7. The Taliban had taxed more than Abdullah Jan in his first term. Abdullah Jan in his second term, in turn, outstripped the Taliban. Reactions differ to this taxation. Some, like immigrant and Taliban-sympathizer Mohammed Wali, say the tax was just; after all, Abdullah Jan received little help from the government and he had to pay for the tribal militia and the operating expenses of a robust district government. Others, such as Tooriali, son of the great tribal leader, Roh Khan, say it was unjust and draconian. Discussion with Mohammed Wali, Laki, 25 October 2010.

8. Discussion with Abdullah Jan, Garmser district center, 8 October 2009.

9. Discussion with Lieutenant Soor Gul, Nawa, 11 February 2011.

10. Discussion with Khodirom, Khojibad, 9 November 2010.

11. The religious scholar was Maulawi Ajab Noor. Under Afghan law, religious scholars with graduate degrees in Shari'a could be official judges.

12. Ajab Noor left a few years later. Wali Sahab, from Bost, replaced him. He spent six months in Garmser. Discussion with Ali Shah Khan, Garmser district center, 3 March 2011.

13. Discussion with Doctor Salam, Garmser Police Headquarters, 18 April 2011.

14. Besides a small number of wells and concrete ditches, the National Solidarity Program (NSP) mainly constructed electrical power systems in over twenty villages between the district center and Koshtay. Those villages used their grant to purchase a generator, build a room to house it, and set up power lines to distribute the electricity. Each community planned to pay for the fuel and maintenance costs. Unfortunately, the diesel expenses were too great for most of the villages. By 2006, nearly all the generators had stopped running and been sold off, leaving only empty rooms and derelict power lines. Discussion with Ministry of Rural Rehabilitation and Development (MRRD) officials, Garmser, 7 September 2009. Discussion with PRT Helmand, Lashkar Gah, 5 September 2009. Discussion with Deputy District Governor Ayub Omar, FOB Delhi, 26 December 2010.

15. Garmser had four health clinics, in Hazar Joft, Mian Poshtay, Laki, and Safar.

16. Discussion with Deputy Director of Education, FOB Delhi, 31 January 2011.

17. Discussion with Maulawi Mohammedullah, FOB Delhi, 30 June 2011.
18. Discussion with Maulawi Abdullah Jan, Garmser district center, 18 January 2011.
19. Discussion with Mohammed Wali, Laki, 25 October 2010.
20. Discussion with Mamoor Mohammed Abdullah, Kuchinay Darveshan, 12 April 2010.
21. Discussion with Haji Ismael, FOB Delhi, 14 February 2011.
22. Discussion with Alizai elders, FOB Delhi, November 2010.
23. Ahmed Rashid, *Descent into Chaos* (New York: Viking, 2008), 322, 326–7.
24. Discussion with Shah Jahan, Garmser district center, 13 July 2011.
25. Elizabeth Rubin, 'In the Land of the Taliban,' *New York Times Magazine*, 25 October 2006.
26. Abdul Salam Zaeef, *My Life with the Taliban*, eds Alex Strick van Linschoten and Felix Kuehn (New York: Columbia University Press, 2010), 87.
27. Discussion with Mohammed Nabi, Garmser district center, 10 March 2011.
28. Ibid.
29. The first was Shadi Khan; the second was Nabi Khan.
30. Discussion with Kharoti elders (Baz Mohammed and Saifullah Khan), FOB Delhi, 27 November 2009.
31. Ira Lapidus, *A History of Islamic Societies* (Cambridge: Cambridge University Press, 1988), 73.
32. Discussion with Shah Wali Khan and Ghulam Rassoul, Garmser district center, 29 January 2011. Discussion with Lieutenant Soor Gul, Nawa, 11 February 2011. Discussion with Haji Ismael, FOB Delhi, 14 February 2011.
33. Discussion with Obaidullah, Ahmed Shah, and Hikmatullah, Safar elders, FOB Delhi, 27 August 2010.
34. Discussion with Noor Allah, Kharoti elders, Garmser district center, 31 January 2011.
35. 'Taliban beats people for listening to music,' *Pajhwok Afghan News*, 5 December 2005.
36. Discussion with Haji Ismael (not the same person as Mullah Ismael), FOB Delhi, 14 February 2011.
37. I met with Dr Salam in 2010 when he returned to Garmser from Pakistan. I asked him why he turned against the government but he would not say.
38. Discussion with Ghulam Rassoul, FOB Delhi, 11 March 2011.
39. Discussion with Lieutenant Soor Gul, Nawa, 11 February 2011.
40. Discussion with Mahboob Khan, Roh Khan Kalay, Kuchinay Darveshan, 22 January 2011.
41. Mahboob Khan and his sixty men fought for Choto, the border town west of Baram Chah, for over six months, once even losing it before retaking it in a counter-attack. By the end of that time his forces had dwindled to six-

teen men. Sher Mohammed refused to give them any ammunition or any reinforcements. He had no choice but to retreat. Discussion with Mahboob Khan, COP Koshtay, 23 April 2011.

42. Discussion with Mohammed Hanif, Garmser district center, 12 March 2011.
43. Discussion with Mahboob Khan, Rohullah Khan Kalay, 22 January 2011.
44. Discussion with Ghulam Rassoul, FOB Delhi, 11 March 2011.
45. Michael Clarke, ed., *The Afghan Papers: Committing Britain to War in Helmand, 2005–06* (London: RUSI, 2011), 15–20.
46. Discussion with Ghulam Rassoul and Shah Wali Khan, Garmser district center, 29 January 2011.
47. Discussion with Mohammed Nabi, Garmser district center, 10 March 2011.
48. Ibid.
49. Discussion with Abdullah Jan, Garmser district center, 1 February 2010.
50. Discussion with Obaidullah, Ahmed Shah, and Hikmatullah, FOB Delhi, 27 August 2010.
51. Discussion with Alizai leaders, FOB Delhi, 1 November 2010.
52. Sher Mohammed Akhundzada admitted to the *Daily Telegraph* in 2009 that he had given permission for his followers to work with the Taliban, since he himself could no longer support them. Damien McElroy, 'Afghan governor turned 3,000 men over to Taliban,' *Daily Telegraph*, 20 November 2009.
53. Discussion with Abdullah Jan, Garmser district center, 1 February 2010.
54. Discussion with Ghulam Rassoul, Camp Delhi, 11 March 2011.
55. Discussion with Obaidullah, Ahmed Shah, and Hikmatullah, Camp Delhi, 27 August 2010.
56. Discussion with Fazl Nabi, Garmser bazaar, 12 January 2011. Fazl Nabi was a policeman who fought against the Taliban in both Khaneshin and Garmser. He had been a soldier in the Afghan National Army for four years before joining the police.
57. Discussion with Ghulam Rassoul, FOB Delhi, 11 March 2011.
58. Discussion with Mohammed Nabi, Garmser district center, 10 March 2011.
59. Discussion with Ahmed Shah, Safar, 14 December 2010.
60. Discussion with Abdullah Jan, Lashkar Gah PRT, 3 February 2011.
61. Discussion with Ahmed Shah, Safar, 1 January 2010.
62. Doug Beattie, *An Ordinary Soldier* (London: Pocket Books, 2008), 89. Discussion with Fazl Nabi, Garmser bazaar, 12 January 2011.
63. Discussion with Abdullah Jan, Lashkar Gah PRT, 3 February 2011.
64. Ahmed Rashid, *Descent into Chaos*, 132–4.
65. A US soldier or Marine costs roughly $1 million per year to be deployed in Afghanistan. An Afghan soldier costs roughly $20,000 per year (based

on dividing the total number of Afghan security forces in 2011 by their cost that year of \$6 billion).

6. THE SECOND TALIBAN REGIME

1. Jens Enevoldsen, *Sound the bells, O moon, arise and shine! A collection of Pashto proverbs and tappas* (Peshawar: InterLit Foundation, 2000), 25.
2. Tom Coghlan, 'Outnumbered and short of food, British troops win six-day battle with Taliban,' *Daily Telegraph*, 22 September 2006. Doug Beattie, *An Ordinary Soldier* (London: Pocket Books, 2008), 83–104.
3. Discussion with Hazrat Ali, Garmser district center, 12 July 2011.
4. Discussion with Taliban cadre leader, Garmser district center.
5. Discussion with Ahmed Shah, Safar, 31 December 2010.
6. Discussion with Mohammed Nabi, Garmser district center, 22 January 2011.
7. Discussion with Haji Raess Mangal, Mian Poshtay elder and businessman, COP Sharp, 23 April 2011.
8. Tom Coghlan, 'The Taliban in Helmand: An Oral History,' *Decoding the New Taliban*, ed. Antonio Giustozzi (New York: Columbia University Press, 2009), 133.
9. Discussion with Taliban fighter, Garmser district center.
10. Discussion with Mohammed Emir, Garmser district center, 9 December 2010.
11. Visit to Bartaka school, Bartaka, 5 January 2011.
12. Discussion with Wakil Manan, Garmser district center, 6 January 2011.
13. Discussion with Dr Salam, Garmser district center, 27 December 2010.
14. The ubiquitous building block of American and British fortifications in Afghanistan, a HESCO barrier is a chain-linked basket with fabric lining that is filled with dirt. Baskets are stacked together to construct walls, towers, and bunkers. They absorb the blast of an RPG, 107 mm rocket, or car bomb remarkably well.
15. Discussion with Ahmed Shah, Safar, 31 December 2010.
16. Discussion with British officers, Joint Service Command Staff College, Shrivenham, 20 October 2008. 'Afghanistan—Decision Point 2008,' Senlis Council Report, February 2008, 108.
17. Sean Rayment, *Into the Killing Zone: The Real Story from the Frontline in Afghanistan* (London: Constable, 2008), 134–7.
18. Discussion with Taliban fighter, Garmser district center.
19. Ed Macy, *Apache* (New York: Atlantic Monthly Press, 2008), 194–200, 210–60.
20. Discussion with Taliban cadre leader, Garmser district center.

21. Ann Scott Tyson, 'In Helmand province, a tug of war,' *Washington Post*, 2008.

22. Later district governors were Obaid Rahman (Noorzai from Kandahar), Mullah Misher (Alizai from Loya Darveshan), and Sayid Wali (Noorzai from Amir Agha).

23. Discussion with Shah Jahan, Lashkar Gah PRT, 5 May 2012.

24. 'Man publicly executed in Helmand,' *Pajhwok Afghan News*, 2 September 2006.

25. Discussion with Taliban fighter, Garmser district center.

26. Discussion with Maulawi Mohammedullah, FOB Delhi, 30 June 2011.

27. Ibid.

28. Discussion with Ghulam Rassoul, FOB Delhi, 11 March 2011. Abdul Ahad, an Alizai scholar, was the judge in Mian Poshtay. He was also well respected. Other judges included Maulawi Agha (a Sayid who worked in Mian Poshtay) and Ahmed Jan Akhundzada (a Baluch who worked in Laki). I do not have details on the remaining judges. Discussion with Mohammed Emir, Garmser district center, 9 December 2010.

29. Tom Coghlan, 'The Taliban in Helmand: An Oral History,' 149.

30. Discussion with Abdullah Jan, Garmser district center, 2 December 2009. Garmser Proper Orientation, 24th Marine Expeditionary Unit paper, 10 July 2008.

31. Discussion with Shah Jahan, Lashkar Gah PRT, 5 May 2012.

32. Discussion with Taliban fighter, Garmser district center.

33. Kate Clark, 'The Layha, Appendix 1: Taliban Codes of Conduct,' Afghan Analysts' Network (aan-afghanistan.com, accessed 7 July 2012), June 2011, 26.

34. Discussion with Shah Jahan, Laki, 22 October 2010.

35. Discussion with Ali Shah Khan, Garmser district center, 4 July 2010.

36. Jerry Meyerle, Megan Katt, and Carter Malkasian, 'The War in Southern Afghanistan,' CNA research Memorandum (Alexandria: Center for Naval Analyses, 2009), 38–40.

37. Discussion at Joint Services Command and Staff College, Shrivenham, UK, 20 October 2008.

38. Discussion with 1st Battalion, 6th Marine Regiment intelligence officer, Marine Corps Quantico, 8 August 2011.

39. Discussions at 24 MEU headquarters, Kandahar Air Force Base, 30 April 2008.

40. Discussion with 1st Battalion, 6th Marine Regiment intelligence officer, Marine Corps Quantico, 8 August 2011.

41. Discussion with Taliban cadre leader, Garmser district center.

42. After Action Review (AAR) and Lessons Learned from Operation Endur-

ing Freedom Phase III, 1st Battalion, 6th Marine Regiment, 25 September 2008, 60.

43. Discussion with 1st Battalion, 6th Marine Regiment intelligence officer, Marine Corps Quantico, 8 August 2011.

44. After Action Review (AAR) and Lessons Learned from Operation Enduring Freedom Phase III, 1st Battalion, 6th Marine Regiment, 25 September 2008, 28–9.

45. Ibid., 53.

46. Ibid., 53.

47. Discussion with Taliban fighter, Garmser district center.

48. Discussion with Mohammed Nabi, Garmser district center, 22 January 2011.

49. Discussion with Maulawi Mohammedullah, Garmser district center, 29 June 2011.

50. Discussion with Taliban, Garmser district center.

51. Discussion with Mohammed Emir, Garmser district center, 9 December 2010.

52. Discussion with 1st Battalion, 6th Marine Regiment intelligence officer, Marine Corps Quantico, 8 August 2011.

53. After Action Review (AAR) and Lessons Learned from Operation Enduring Freedom Phase III, 1st Battalion, 6th Marine Regiment, 25 September 2008, 27.

54. Tom Coghlan, 'Taleban stage audacious 'Tet-style' attack on British HQ city,' *The Times*, 13 October 2008.

7. PUSHING FARTHER SOUTH

1. Randall Olson, *Speaking Afghan Pashto* (Peshawar: Interlit Foundation, 2007), 384.

2. Discussion with Mohammed Arif, Lashkar Gah PRT, 6 May 2012.

3. Jerry Meyerle and Carter Malkasian, 'Provincial Reconstruction Teams: How do we know they work?' Strategic Studies Institute Monograph (Carlisle: Strategic Studies Institute, 2009).

4. The Afghan army battalion had arrived in August. The battalion was supposed to have 900 men, but until 2010 only 200 were active in Garmser at any time.

5. Census numbers were always very rough in Garmser. These numbers are what the provincial government went by.

6. His predecessor, Abdul Rahim, had been detained in Pakistan in June 2008.

7. Discussion with immigrant family, Loya Darveshan, 25 December 2009.

8. Taliban jails were located in Marjah and Safar. Discussion with Kakar tribesman, Kuchinay Darveshan, 17 September 2009.

9. Sam Kiley, *Desperate Glory* (London: Bloomsbury, 2009), 21.

10. Discussion with Abdullah Jan, Garmser district center, 7 October 2009.

11. The border police worked for Allah Noor, the old communist militia commander of Lashkar Gah. He had risen to a high position within the border police.

12. This was part of the Ministry of Interior's 'focused district development' program.

13. Discussion with Police Mentoring Cell, Lashkar Gah, 5 September 2009.

14. Elders, religious leaders, teachers, and other notables would come to the district center on the day of the 'election' to select a representative for their region. If fewer than ten notables registered to vote from a region, that region could not participate. So registration and voter turnout mattered if Garmser was to have a truly representative council.

15. Discussion with Abdul Gafar, Garmser district center, 11 November 2009.

16. The rest of the surge would not be seen for eight months, when the Marines cleared Marjah.

17. Discussion with Maulawi Mohammedullah, 29 June 2011. Mohammedullah was present in Mian Poshtay during these events. Discussion with Taliban cell leader, Garmser district center.

18. Discussion with Captain Eric Meador, Echo Company Commander, COP Sharp, 3 November 2009. The events are also featured in the documentary, *To Hell and Back Again*.

19. Discussion with Maulawi Mohammedullah, 29 June 2011.

20. Discussion with Taliban fighter, Garmser district center.

21. Discussion with Mullah Mohammed Lal, Kuchinay Darveshan, 19 September 2009.

22. Discussion with Mohammed Yunis, Kuchinay Darveshan, 19 September 2009.

23. Discussion with Abdullah Jan, Garmser district center, 7 October 2009.

24. Patrol in Dezakriya, southern Hazar Joft, 26 September 2009.

25. Garmser ulema shura, Garmser district center, 6 January 2010.

26. Ibid.

27. The *kalima* is a recitation about Allah and the Prophet Mohammed, one of the five pillars of Islam believers must follow. Garmser ulema shura, Garmser district center, 6 January 2010.

28. Discussion with mullahs, Garmser district center, 1 February 2010.

29. Discussion with community council member, FOB Delhi, 1 December 2009.

30. Discussion with Ayub Omar, Garmser district center, 7 October 2009.

31. Discussion with Mohammed Nabi, Garmser district center, 7 October 2009.

32. Kate Clark, 'The Layha, Appendix 1: Taliban Codes of Conduct,' Afghan Analysts' Network (aan-afghanistan.com, accessed 7 July 2012), June 2011, 20–3.

33. Mohammed Anwar fielded his own tribal militia (arbekai), partly armed by Abdullah Jan. At night, about twenty unpaid tribesmen with AK-47s patrolled Mohammed Anwar's villages just north of Amir Agha. In August 2009, he was one of the few tribal leaders to vote in the presidential elections. Afterwards, he returned home and went to his mosque. Five Taliban followed, intent on punishing him. They opened fire and tried to grab him. The villagers called out and, enraged, his fighters rushed from their homes, surrounded the Taliban, and arrested them—an impressive show of community solidarity. The captives were later turned over to the Afghan army.

34. Discussion with Atlas Khan, FOB Delhi, 25 December 2009.

35. Discussion with Abdullah Jan, Garmser district center, 15 November 2009.

36. Discussion with Abdullah Jan, Garmser district center, 8 October 2009.

37. Discussion with Dr Habibullah, Garmser district center, 30 September 2009.

38. Discussion with community council, Garmser district center, 21 November 2009.

39. Discussion with Ayub Omar, Garmser district center, 23 September 2009.

8. WAKIL MANAN, MIAN POSHTAY, AND THE RIOTS

1. Randall Olson, *Speaking Afghan Pashto* (Peshawar: Interlit Foundation, 2007), 169.

2. Discussion with Maulawi Mohammedullah, 29 June 2011.

3. Discussion with Mamoor Abdur Rashid, Potai, Mian Poshtay, 27 January 2010.

4. Discussion with Abdullah Jan, Garmser district center, 15 November 2009.

5. Discussion with Abdullah Jan, Garmser district center, 1 December 2009.

6. Ibid.

7. Discussion with Abdullah Jan, Garmser district center, 9 December 2009.

8. Discussion with police chief Ghuli Khan, Garmser police headquarters, 3 January 2010.

9. Discussion with Abdullah Jan, Garmser district center, 3 January 2010.

10. Discussion with police, Garmser district center, 31 January 2010.

11. Discussion with Mullah Ibrahim, Mian Poshtay, 14 January 2010.

12. Koran shura with Koshtay and Mian Poshtay residents, Afghan army post, Mian Poshtay, 13 January 2010.

13. On 13 January, the police and border police held off 300 protesters at the bridges that control movement into the district center.

14. Discussion with Wakil Manan, Mian Poshtay, 28 January 2011.

15. This incident occurred in spring 2010, after the events of this chapter. The original civil affairs leader in Mian Poshtay was Captain Nichols.

16. Discussion with Wakil Manan, Mian Poshtay, 17 January 2010.

17. Discussion with Wakil Manan, Afghan army post, Mian Poshtay, 13 January 2010.

18. Discussion with Abdul Qayum, Garmser district center, 1 February 2011.

19. Discussion with Maulawi Mohammedullah, Mian Poshtay, 29 June 2011.

20. Discussion with former Taliban, Mian Poshtay.

21. Discussion with Taliban who surrendered, Garmser district center.

9. THE ALIZAI RETURN

1. Discussion with Ghulam Rassoul, Garmser district center, 27 July 2010.

2. Discussion with Ghulam Rassoul, Garmser district center, 21 January 2011.

3. Discussion with Abdullah Jan, Lashkar Gah PRT, 6 October 2010. Discussion with Mohammed Wali, Laki, 25 October 2010. Discussion with Shah Jahan, Laki, 25 October 2010. Discussion with Abdul Ali, Mullah Naim's uncle, Garmser district center, 2 March 2011.

4. Discussion with Ghulam Rassoul and Shah Wali Khan, Garmser district center, 29 January 2011.

5. Discussion with Abdullah Jan, Lashkar Gah PRT, 3 February 2011.

6. Discussion with Abdullah Jan, Garmser district center, 1 February 2010.

7. Discussion with Haji Raess, village elder, Garmser district center, 30 April 2010.

8. In that engagement, the Marines had been patrolling a few kilometers south of their base. As they pushed south, insurgents observed them from rooftops. Then, twenty men ambushed them while others maneuvered in vehicles around their flanks. The gunfire was very heavy. The helicopters sent to evacuate the wounded were shot up. No one was killed but it was a very tough fight.

9. Discussion with Shah Wali Khan and Ghulam Rassoul, Garmser district center, 24 April 2010.

10. Discussion with Shah Wali Khan and Ghulam Rassoul, Laki, 18 May 2010.

11. Meeting with Lieutenant Colonel Hezbollah and Alizai leaders, Laki, 13 June 2010.

12. Discussion with Mahboob Khan, brother of Shah Wali Khan, Laki, 26 October 2010.

13. Discussion with Shah Nazr, Garmser police headquarters, 29 April 2010.

10. THE TALIBAN COUNTER-OFFENSIVE

1. Under the Taliban code of conduct of May 2010 issued by Mullah Omar, Naim as Helmand provincial governor had authority to issue orders to kill people. Kate Clark, 'The Layha,' Afghan Analysts' Network aan-afghanistan.com (accessed 7 July 2012), June 2011.
2. Insurgent confession to police, Garmser police headquarters, 4 June 2010.
3. Discussion with Ghulam Rassoul and Shah Wali Khan, Laki, 18 May 2010.
4. District center shura, Garmser district center, 18 April 2010.
5. Garmser community council meeting, Garmser district center, 8 June 2010.
6. Discussion with Ayub Omar, Garmser district center, 4 June 2010.
7. Discussion with Wakil Manan, Garmser district center, 4 June 2010.
8. Discussion with Shah Wali Khan and Ghulam Rassoul, Garmser district center, 6 June 2010.
9. Tribal shura, Garmser district center, 6 June 2010.
10. Shura with Director of Hajj Said Mukhtar, Garmser district center, 8 April 2010.
11. Garmser community council meeting, Garmser district center, 13 July 2010.
12. Discussion with Haji Yousef, Mian Poshtay village elder, Garmser district center, 11 June 2010.
13. Discussion with Lakari elders, Garmser district center, 9 July 2011.
14. Discussion with Ghulam Rassoul, Garmser district center, 1 July 2010.
15. Discussion with Taliban cell leader, Garmser district center.
16. Ibid.
17. Ibid.
18. Discussion with Mohammed Nabi, FOB Delhi, 6 August 2011.
19. Winston Churchill, *History of the Second World War: The Hinge of Fate* (London: Cassell, 1950).

11. WINNING THE PEACE

1. Randall Olson, *Speaking Afghan Pashto* (Peshawar: Interlit Foundation, 2007), 405.
2. HMEP 2011 Q1 District Report—Garmser, June 2011. This survey was conducted every quarter in Garmser after September 2010. The results were based on a sample of roughly 400 people from throughout Garmser. All respondents were interviewed by Afghans. Although any survey in Afghanistan faces difficulties in randomization and coverage of contested areas, this survey was by far the most comprehensive and methodologically sound source of public opinion in Garmser.

3. Discussion with re-integree, Garmser district center.

4. Numerous surveys have found that Afghans tend to give positive answers about the government out of respect. In this case, the high percentages of support for the police are less interesting than the increase in support over time and the fact that their approval levels were roughly the same as those for the army. HMEP 2011 Q2 District Report, Garmser, September 2011.

5. HMEP 2011 Q2 District Report, Garmser, September 2011.

6. HMEP Annual Review, 31 July 2011, 103, 104.

7. Meeting with Garmser religious leaders, Garmser district center, 19 October 2010.

8. Discussion with Maulawi Mohammedullah, FOB Delhi, 1 July 2011.

9. Ibid.

10. The one act the government took was to order that anyone who constructed a new building on government land would be sent to prison.

11. Discussion with government madrasa headmaster, Garmser district center, 20 October 2010.

12. Security shura, FOB Delhi, 27 September 2010.

13. David Edwards, *Heroes of the Age: Moral Fault Lines on the Afghan Frontier* (Berkeley: University of California Press, 1996), 159.

14. Garmser significant activity (sigact) data, ISAF, cleared for public release by ISAF foreign disclosure office on 2 May 2012.

15. Discussion with Shah Jahan, Garmser district center, 27 December 2010.

16. Discussion with Dr Salam, Garmser district center, 27 December 2010.

17. Discussion with Taliban cell leader, Garmser district center.

18. Satisfaction with the Taliban had fallen from 24 percent to 5 percent. HMEP 2011 Q1 District Report, Garmser, June 2011.

19. Discussion with Mian Poshtay elders, FOB Delhi, 7 July 2011.

20. Discussion with Ayub Omar, FOB Delhi, 8 July 2011.

21. HMEP 2011 Q2 District Report, Garmser, September 2011.

22. Discussion with Mohammed Fahim, Kabul, 29 April 2012.

23. Discussion with Mohammed Agha, police headquarters, 19 April 2011.

24. Telephone discussion with Ayub Omar, 30 November 2011.

25. In *Little America*, Rajiv Chandrasekaran mentions a possible case of paedophilia, citing two teenage insurgents being detained in women's clothes (they were trying to hide and were part of a larger insurgent crew) and then kept imprisoned in those clothes. I was present with Omar Jan when he took hold of these prisoners and for most of the time surrounding their detention and processing. Additionally, Marines slept on the second floor of the police headquarters, above the jail. They regularly checked the jail. Neither the Marines nor I witnessed anything untoward going on. It is well known that homosexuality is prevalent in Pashtun society. Throughout

Garmser, the Marines and I took an active stance against any forms of pae-dophilia that we encountered. I never saw Omar Jan mistreat a child or teenager or heard any such accusation. In this particular case, Chandrasek-aran notes that there was no evidence. Rajiv Chandrasekaran, *Little America: The War Within the War for Afghanistan* (New York: Knopf, 2012), 318.

26. Discussion with Mohammed Fahim, ISAF headquarters, Kabul, 27 April 2012.
27. Discussion with Ayub Omar, Washington, DC, 7 April 2012.
28. Phone conversation with Shah Jahan, 30 April 2012.
29. Discussion with Ahmed Shah, telephone, 19 April 2012.
30. Discussion with Mohammed Fahim, telephone, 19 April 2012.
31. Discussion with Ghulam Rassoul, police headquarters, 9 July 2011.

CONCLUSION: THE END OR THE INTERMISSION?

1. Henry Walter Bellew, *From the Indus to the Tigris: A Narrative of a Journey through the Countries of Balochistan, Afghanistan, Khorassan and Iran, in 1872* (London: Trubner & Co., 1874), 205–6.
2. A rough breakdown is that 1,000 died in the jihad, 150 died in the civil war, 300 died fighting for the Taliban in the north from 1995 to 2001, 500 died fighting the British and the government from 2006 to 2008, 498 died fight-ing the 24th Marine Expeditionary Unit, and at least 200 died from 2009 to the present.
3. The cost for those forces totals between $6 and $7.5 billion.
4. Samuel Huntington, *Political Order in Changing Societies* (New Haven: Yale University Press, 2006), 3–5.
5. Discussion with Ayub Omar, Washington, DC, 7 April 2012.
6. In late February 2012, a set of Korans were burned in a trash pit at Bagram Air Base. Widespread riots broke out in Kabul, Herat, around Bagram, and elsewhere. The riots culminated in the murder of two US advisors in the Ministry of Interior, allegedly in retaliation for the burnings. The riots and murders shook US domestic confidence in the war effort. They passed in Garmser with a single peaceful demonstration.

BIBLIOGRAPHY

'1995 Comparative Survey, Helmand Province, Afghanistan,' Afghanistan Drug Control and Rehabilitation Programme, November 1995 (http://scottshelmandvalleyarchives.org/docs/sas-95–04.pdf, accessed 9 March 2011).

Abdul Hai Habibi, *De Afghanistan Land Tarikh* (Peshawar: Danish Khperndoyah Tolenah, 2003).

Abdul Latif Talibi, *Pashtunee Qabilay* (Quetta: Mazhbi Kitabkhana, 2004).

Abdur Rahman Zamani, *De Ghazi Mir Zaman Khan Wndah* (Kabul: Haji Zaman Zamani, 2010).

Abdul Salam Zaeef, *My Life with the Taliban*, eds Alex Strick van Linschoten and Felix Kuehn (New York: Columbia University Press, 2010).

Adamec, Ludwig, ed., *Historical and Political Gazetteer of Afghanistan: Farah and Southwestern Afghanistan*, vol. 2 (Austria: Akademische Druck-u.Verlagsanstalt Graz, 1973).

'Afghanistan-Decision Point 2008,' Senlis Council Report, February 2008.

'Agriculture in the Middle Helmand River Valley,' Mercy Corps International, August 1991.

Barfield, Thomas, *Afghanistan: A Cultural and Political History* (Princeton: Princeton University Press, 2010).

Beattie, Doug, *An Ordinary Soldier* (London: Pocket Books, 2008).

Bellew, Henry Walter, *From the Indus to the Tigris: A Narrative of a Journey through the Countries of Balochistan, Afghanistan, Khorassan and Iran, in 1872* (London: Trubner & Co., 1874).

Bellew, Henry Walter, *Record of the March of the Mission to Seistan under the Command of F. R. Pollock* (Calcutta: Foreign Department Press, 1873).

Blackwill, Robert, 'Plan B in Afghanistan,' *Foreign Affairs*, vol. 90, no. 1 (January/February 2011).

BIBLIOGRAPHY

Chandrasekaran, Rajiv, *Little America: The War Within the War for Afghanistan* (New York: Knopf, 2012).

Chayes, Sarah, '"Lower your sights" is the wrong vision for Afghanistan,' *Los Angeles Times*, 27 March 2009.

Chayes, Sarah, *The Punishment of Virtue: Inside Afghanistan after the Taliban* (New York: Penguin Books, 2006).

Clapp-Wincek, Cynthia, 'The Helmand Valley Project in Afghanistan,' AID Evaluation Special Study no. 18, US Agency for International Development, December 1983.

Clark, Kate, 'The Layha, Appendix 1: Taliban Codes of Conduct,' Afghan Analysts' Network (aan-afghanistan.com, accessed 7 July 2012), June 2011.

Clarke, Michael, ed., *The Afghan Papers: Committing Britain to War in Helmand*, 2005–06 (London: RUSI, 2011).

Coghlan, Tom, 'Outnumbered and short of food, British troops win six-day battle with Taliban,' *Daily Telegraph*, 22 September 2006.

———— 'The Taliban in Helmand: An Oral History,' in *Decoding the New Taliban*, ed. Antonio Giustozzi (New York: Columbia University Press, 2009).

———— 'Taleban stage audacious 'Tet-style' attack on British HQ city,' *The Times*, 13 October 2008.

Cullather, Nick, 'Damming Afghanistan: Modernization in a Buffer State,' *Journal of American History*, vol. 89, no. 2 (September 2002).

Edwards, David, *Before Taliban: Genealogies of the Afghan Jihad* (Berkeley: University of California Press, 2002)

———— *Heroes of the Age: Moral Fault Lines on the Afghan Frontier* (Berkeley: University of California Press, 1996).

Enevoldsen, Jen, *Sound the bells, O moon, arise and shine! A collection of Pashto proverbs and tappas* (Peshawar: InterLit Foundation, 2000), 25.

Garmser Proper Orientation, 24th Marine Expeditionary Unit paper, 10 July 2008.

Gilbert, Felix, *To the Farewell Address* (Princeton: Princeton University Press, 1961).

Giustozzi, Antonio, *Empires of Mud: War and Warlords in Afghanistan* (New York: Columbia University Press, 2009).

———— *Koran, Kalashnikov, and Laptop: The Neo-Taliban Insurgency in Afghanistan* (London: Hurst, 2007).

Grau, Lester, ed., *The Bear Went Over the Mountain: Soviet Combat Tactics in Afghanistan*, (Washington, DC: National Defense University Press, 1996).

Huntington, Samuel, *Political Order in Changing Societies* (New Haven: Yale University Press, 2006).

Gul, Imtiaz, *The Most Dangerous Place: Pakistan's Lawless Frontier* (New York: Penguin, 2011).

BIBLIOGRAPHY

Kalyvas, Stathis, *The Logic of Violence in Civil War* (Cambridge: Cambridge University Press, 2006).

Kennedy, Hugh, *The Great Arab Conquests: How the Spread of Islam Changed the World We Live In* (New York: Da Capo Press, 2008).

Kilcullen, David, *The Accidental Guerrilla* (New York: Oxford University Press, 2009).

Kiley, Sam, *Desperate Glory* (London: Bloomsbury, 2009).

Kissinger, Henry, *Diplomacy* (New York: Simon & Schuster, 1995).

Lapidus, Ira, *A History of Islamic Societies* (Cambridge: Cambridge University Press, 1988).

Macy, Ed, *Apache* (New York: Atlantic Monthly Press, 2008).

'Man publicly executed in Helmand,' Pajhwok Afghan News, 2 September 2006.

Martin, Mike, *A Brief History of Helmand* (Warminster, UK: Afghan COIN Center, August 2011).

McElroy, Damien, 'Afghan governor turned 3,000 men over to Taliban,' *Daily Telegraph*, 20 November 2009.

Meyerle, Jerry, Katt, Megan, et al., 'The War in Southern Afghanistan,' CNA Research Memorandum (Alexandria: Center for Naval Analyses, 2009).

———— and Malkasian, Carter, 'Provincial Reconstruction Teams: How do we know they work?' Strategic Studies Institute Monograph (Carlisle: Strategic Studies Institute, 2009).

'MSF Exploratory Mission in Helmand,' Médecins Sans Frontières Report, February 1989 (http://scottshelmandvalleyarchives.org/docs/hea-89–01.pdf, accessed 9 March 2011).

Nagl, John, *Learning to Eat Soup with a Knife* (Chicago: Chicago University Press, 2007).

Noelle, Christine, *State and Tribe in Nineteenth-Century Afghanistan: The Reign of Amir Dost Mohammed Khan (1826–1863)* (London: Routledge, 1997).

Ponzio, Richard, *Democratic Peacebuilding: Aiding Afghanistan and other Fragile States* (Oxford: Oxford University Press, 2011).

Race, Jeffrey, *War Comes to Long An: Revolutionary Conflict in a Vietnamese Province* (Berkeley: University of California Press, 1972).

Rashid, Ahmed, *Descent into Chaos* (New York: Viking, 2007).

———— 'How Obama Lost Karzai,' *Foreign Policy*, no. 185 (March/April 2011).

———— *Taliban: Militant Islam, Oil and Fundamentalism in Central Asia* (New Haven: Yale University Press, 2001).

———— 'The Way Out of Afghanistan,' *New York Review of Books*, 13 January 2011.

Rayment, Sean, *Into the Killing Zone: The Real Story from the Frontline in Afghanistan* (London: Constable, 2008).

BIBLIOGRAPHY

Roy, Olivier, *Islam and Resistance in Afghanistan* (Cambridge: Cambridge University Press, 1990).

Rubin, Barnett, *The Fragmentation of Afghanistan* (New Haven: Yale University Press, 1995).

Rubin, Elizabeth, 'In the Land of the Taliban,' *New York Times Magazine*, 25 October 2006.

Saad, Lydia, 'Americans Give Record-High Ratings to Several US Allies,' www.gallup.com, 16 February 2012.

Scott, Richard, 'Final Report, Helmand Irrigation Rehabilitation, 1 December 1998–31 March 1999,' 1999 (http://scottshelmandvalleyarchives.org/docs/fpr-98–01.pdf).

———— 'Tribal and Ethnic Groups in the Helmand Valley,' Occasional Paper no. 21 (New York: Asia Society, 1980).

Slim, William, *Unofficial History* (London: Cassell, 1959).

'Taliban beats people for listening to music,' Pajhwok Afghan News, 5 December 2005.

Tyson, Ann Scott, 'In Helmand province, a tug of war,' *Washington Post*, 2008.

'The Unwinnable War,' Time, vol. 178, no. 16 (24 October 2011).

The US Army/Marine Corps Counterinsurgency Field Manual (Chicago: University of Chicago, 2007).

van Linschoten, Alex, and Kuehn, Felix, *An Enemy We Created* (London: Hurst, 2011).

West, Bing, *The Wrong War* (New York: Random House, 2011).

INDEX

provincial reconstruction team (PRT):
128–9, 136, 141, 178–9, 225, 241,
248; funding provided by, 139–40;
personnel of, 132, 225, 244; 'road
map', 156, 222–3, 227; surveys
funded by, 224, 229, 234, 236,
251, 253

Qadrat, Mullah: death of (2007), 110;
headquarters of, 109

Rabbani, Burnahideen: 64; leader of
Jamiat Islami, 49
Rahman, Obaid: Taliban district governor of Garmser, 117, 120, 123,
125, 130, 145
Rassoul Akhundzada, Mohammed:
49, 65; death of, 54; defeat of Allah
Noor, 50; family of, 46, 54; rise to
power (1993), 51
Reid, LtCol Matt: 245–6, 247, 260
Roh Khan, Haji: 8, 67–8, 73, 251;
family of, 54, 80, 148, 193; land
holdings of, 13; territory controlled
by, 48

Safar: 2–3, 5, 9, 15, 28, 42, 44–5,
48, 73, 77, 93, 95–6, 108, 112,
114–15, 131, 149, 161, 171, 193,
196, 203, 208, 215–17, 219, 221,
224, 228, 231, 236–7, 246, 248,
250–1, 254, 256–8, 266
Safavid Empire: territory of, 2
Said Omar: 8, 24, 44, 46, 60, 72–4,
83, 140, 198–9, 242; escape to
Pakistan, 63; family of, 139, 150,
209, 212, 247; imprisonment
of, 20; influence of, 24, 73; land
holdings of, 13; return to Garmser
(2008), 139; shuras led by, 73; territory controlled by, 48
Saifrahman, Lt.: 170–2
Sakhi, Mohammed: 165, 174; Baluch

representative on community council, 211, 225
Salam, Dr Abdul: 88, 89, 96, 108,
110, 248; background of, 88
Salay Mohammed: 45, 46, 73, 77,
89–90, 93, 236; escape to Pakistan,
45, 55, 63, 237; family of, 44–5,
95, 237, 244; territory controlled
by, 48
Samad, Abdul: 32–3
Sangin: 54, 92, 104, 136, 198–200,
260
Sardar Mohammed: 165, 174
Saudi Arabia: 224; support for mujahidin, 23
Selani, Haji: 120, 145; capture of
(2011), 250–1; Taliban governor of
Nawa, 250
Shah Jahan: 44–45, 60, 72–3, 93,
95–6, 114, 117, 185, 206, 215;
236, 255, 260; background of,
44–5; escape to Pakistan, 118, 184,
188, 205; family of, 198; former
district governor of Khaneshin, 90,
93, 186; leader of Garmser Alizai
community, 82, 112, 118; territory
controlled by, 48
Shah Wali, Mullah: role in leading
of Friday prayers, 210, 214, 271;
wounds sustained by, 212
Shah Wali Khan: 20–1, 25, 33,
36, 38, 42, 54, 72, 81, 88–9,
93, 95–6, 116–17, 156–7, 181,
183–7, 191–2, 194, 196, 198,
204, 206, 215, 241–2, 250, 260;
attempted assassination of (2009),
185; background of, 20–1; escape
to Pakistan, 55, 118, 184, 188,
205; family of, 20–1, 44, 47, 73,
94, 182, 208; land claims of, 81,
182–3; leader of Garmser Alizai
community, 82; leader of Alizai

Alizai

Abdul Baqi, of Lakari, militia commander.

Doctor Salam, of Lakari, Alizai Taliban facilitator.

Ghulam Rassoul, of Laki, frontline commander.

Mohammed Nadir, mujahedin commander of Lakari.

Shah Jahan, of Laki, political mind of the Alizai.

Shah Wali Khan, of Laki, patriarch of the Alizai, mujahedin leader.

Noorzai

Baqi Khan, mujahedin commander, brother of Roh Khan from Kuchinay Darveshan.

Khodirom, tribal leader from Loya Darveshan.

Mohammed Anwar Khan, tribal leader from Hazar Joft.

Said Omar, Omarzai tribal leader from Hazar Joft.

Salay Mohammed, great tribal leader of Safar.

Sultan Mohammed, brother of Salay Mohammed.

Tooriali, son of Roh Khan from Kuchinay Darveshan, leader of Garmser's oldest family.

Yahya Khan, mujahedin warlord from Nawa.